applerouth
tutoring services llc

READY SAT GO!

THE FABULOUS GUIDE TO THE SAT
2nd Edition

Illustrations & Explanations Ideal for Visual Learners

Proven Strategies to Master the SAT Content & Testing Process

Hundreds of Practice Problems with Solutions

MORE FUN than you would ever imagine from an SAT Prep Manual!

Applerouth Tutoring Services, LLC
P.O. Box 49348
Atlanta, GA 30359
E-mail: info@applerouth.com

Author: Jed Applerouth
Chief Editor and Layout Design: Linda Dreilinger
Contributing Editors: Steve Hulett, Brandon Pitman, Randy Schultz, Jr.
Contributing Writers: Linda Dreilinger, Steve Hulett, Randy Schultz, Jr.
Cover Art: Jessica Chriss
Interior Page Design: Justine Rubin
Interior Illustrations: Jeffrey Poole, Alexander Rubin, Brandon Sadler
Interior Graphics: Callie Scott
Production Contributors: Cory German, Reeve Maddox

January 2011

Manufactured in the United States of America.

ISBN 978-0-9823330-2-0

Special Thanks

We'd like to thank all of the contributors who have made this book possible.

Michael Goodman, Julie Johnson and Brandon Pitman who helped us get Critical Reading off the ground.

Kyle Glenn, Corey Orton and Eric Scott who provided inspiration for the early version of our math guide.

Peter Vulgaris for his technical expertise.

Texas Instruments® and New Scientist Magazine (newscientist.com) for generously allowing us to use their materials for this book.

Many thanks to Natalie Henderson who helped compile and create the original Fabulous Guide to the SAT.

And a BIG thank you to all of our tutors, past and present, who have provided inspiration and support for this book.

Table of Contents

Introduction to the SAT

Letter from Jed

Every year over a million students partake in the time-honored ritual of taking the SAT. If you are reading this book, then your time has come to join the ranks and see just how high you can raise your score.

The SAT, like any other test, can be studied and mastered. Succeeding on the SAT does not require the waving of a magic wand. It requires a combination of effort and the proper tools. We've worked for years, literally, to create the ultimate SAT preparation tool. And now it's in your hands.

We kept several principles in mind when we designed this book:

    1) Keep things simple and clear.

    2) Break things into smaller steps and build on them.

    3) Keep things visually interesting.

    4) Use humor whenever possible: it's okay to laugh while
       you are learning.

This book is comprehensive. We've analyzed every aspect of the SAT to bring you the strategies included in this book. And most importantly: this book works. We've been using preliminary versions of this book with our students for several years and have watched them achieve impressive gains. On average, our private students pick up more than 180 points on the SAT. Some of our students have achieved score increases of more than 600 points. We've helped some students hit the golden 2400, and we've helped other students bring section scores in the 300s up into the 600s. Our approach has worked for students at every score level.

We hope you enjoy the book, use it well and hit the scores you need to get into the schools of your dreams. If you are looking for additional information or resources to help you along the way, please check us out online at www.applerouth.com.

Thanks again and good luck!

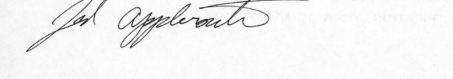

 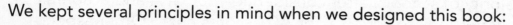

SAT FAQs

What is the SAT?

The SAT is the mother of all standardized tests. It has undergone numerous changes since it first came on the scene in the 1920s when it was created to identify students who would thrive in a university setting. The most recent change in March 2005 introduced the Writing section to the SAT, beefed up the reading comprehension in the Critical Reading section and introduced Algebra II to the Math section.

How important is the SAT?

The SAT and ACT tests are profoundly important to the college admissions process. For the vast majority of schools, after considering your GPA and academic schedule strength, colleges look to your SAT or ACT scores next. Other aspects of your application—recommendations, admissions essays and activities—are subordinate to SAT and ACT scores. Strong scores open the doors to better colleges and universities and create the chance to win valuable scholarships.

Why do colleges put so much weight on the SAT?

Colleges want to ensure that the students they pick for their incoming classes will be able to succeed academically. To make better picks, admissions officers first look to high school GPA: the single best predictor of success in college. But a 3.2 cumulative GPA at one school means something completely different from a 3.2 at another school, even one right down the street. Colleges need another measure that is standardized, the same for all students; that's where the SAT fits in.

Despite all the critiques of the SAT, it turns out the SAT is a decent predictor of collegiate academic performance. Students with stronger SAT scores tend to achieve stronger grades in college. Additionally, the SAT allows admissions officers to quickly and efficiently compare students. Schools use GPA and SAT scores to narrow down the pile of applications, making the task of selecting an incoming class more manageable.

For these reasons, it is unlikely that the SAT will be going away any time soon. A few schools can afford to go SAT-optional and do "deeper reads" of each application, but most schools will continue to rely upon objective measures like the SAT to process all of the applications coming their way.

What does the SAT test?

The SAT tests one thing: **your ability to take the SAT**. It is not an intelligence test, and it certainly does not test any innate aptitude. Given enough time, energy and dedication to the process of preparing for this test, a student can see a dramatic increase in his or her test score.

What do the scores actually mean?

The section scores have to do with statistics. You achieve a raw score based on the number of questions you get right minus a fraction of those that you get wrong. This raw score is placed on a bell curve, the famous normal distribution that you may have come across in your math classes. The curve ranges from the lowest score of 200 to the highest score of 800, with a score of approximately 500 as the median score. If you score a 200 on a section, you are at the base of the curve. If you score a 300, you have out-scored roughly 2% of students. If you score a 400, you've out-scored 16% of students. A section score around 500 indicates that you are at the 50th percentile. A score around 600 puts you at the 84th percentile, 700 at the 98th percentile and 800 at the 100th percentile.

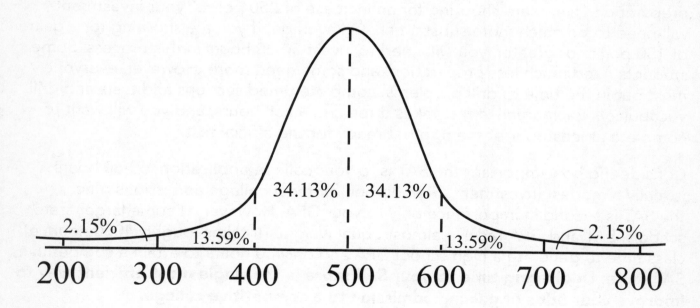

What score do I need to get into a particular college?

More competitive schools require more competitive scores. To find out the average scores at a particular school, visit its web site or contact the admissions office of any school. The College Board's website, www.collegeboard.com, has a great tool, the College Search, which allows you to enter the name of a school, go to the

SAT/ACT tab and see the range of scores for the middle 50% of applicants. We always encourage our students to aim for the top 25% of SAT scores for a given school to be sure they are submitting more competitive applications.

How much can I improve my SAT score?

Most students have the potential to dramatically improve their SAT scores. Our average students pick up over 180 points, and some achieve much greater gains, attaining increases over 600 points. What differentiates the most successful students from those who are less successful is their level of dedication, motivation and the amount of time they invest in the process. If you invest 100 hours toward achieving a higher score, your chance of picking up 300 points is much greater than if you invest 20 hours. The more time students invest, the more homework they complete and the more practice tests they complete under timed conditions, the better they do on the SAT.

How much time do I need to spend on this process?

That completely depends on your introductory score and your ultimate goal. If you need to pick up a mere 30 points, you may only need a handful of hours of preparation. If you are shooting for an increase of 250 points, your investment will need to be much more substantial. On average, if you are shooting for a gain of 150 points or greater, you will need to invest 50-60 hours in this process. Some students need much less preparation, and some need more. However, everyone must put in the time to drill problems, complete timed sections and tests and drill vocabulary. Each practice test takes three and a half hours, and you will want to complete at least four of them to get ready for the official test.

Considering how important the SAT is to your college application, 50-60 hours is really a modest investment. Remember, for most college admissions offices, the SAT is second in importance only to your GPA. However, at some larger state schools, SAT and GPA receive almost equal weight. It takes roughly 4000 hours of class time to generate a high school GPA and only 60 hours to attain a competitive SAT score. **Dedicating time to your SAT score is the single most efficient way to improve your odds of gaining admission to a competitive college.**

How often should I take the SAT?

Generally three to four times should be adequate to achieve your optimal score, but there is no penalty for taking the SAT as many times as you need to achieve the score you seek. Most schools will "superscore" your tests and create a composite SAT score, combining the highest section scores from different administrations to create your "Super" score.

Because SATs vary in difficulty from one administration to the next, it's in your best interest to take this test multiple times until you reach your target score. Just as there are easier and harder tests, students have good and bad days. Even when you are fully prepared, certain factors beyond your control can influence your score: did you study vocabulary that was on this particular test? Were the passages easy or hard for you? How effectively did you guess? Did you make careless errors? There is some luck involved, and the more frequently you take the SAT, the more you minimize the "luck" component.

Beyond solving for the variability of the tests and individual performance, the more you take this test, the more comfortable and confident you become. You eventually move into a zone where you know what to expect and achieve a level of mastery of the testing process. As students move from their first to their second SAT, they tend to achieve their biggest score increases. Students generally see smaller, but consistent, gains through their fourth SAT.

Should I set goals for each test I take?

Absolutely! Always keep your ultimate goal in mind, and view each test as a stepping stone towards this goal. Set distinct section goals for each test you plan to take. For example, if your introductory score is a 620 CR, 600 M and 550 WR and you want to pick up 270 points, set short term goals for each test you plan to take. Write your goals down. "In October my goal is 650 CR, 630 M, 580 WR. In December my goal is 680 CR, 650 M, 610 WR, and my goal for June is 710 CR, 680 M and 650 WR." Setting and attaining short term goals has a positive impact on your sense of confidence and your level of motivation. Use these short term goals to help you attain your ultimate goal.

When should I take the SAT?

Fall and winter of junior year are ideal times to take the first SAT. Most students will be taking the PSAT in October of their junior year. For students who have prepared for the October PSAT (those seeking the National Merit scholarship), the November SAT is a natural first test. Otherwise, December and January are great times to take a first test. For students who are enrolled in Algebra II as juniors, we generally recommend January as the first official SAT; this gives them a semester to hone their Algebra II skills. The majority of our students, having finished Algebra II as sophomores, are ready to jump in at the beginning of junior year.

An important determining factor of when to take this test is the amount of time you have to adequately prepare. If you have a major time commitment in the fall, wait until the winter to start your prep. Or, if your commitments start in the winter and continue into the spring, focus more on the fall assessments.

It is quite common to prep intensely and take two SATs back to back while everything is fresh. We frequently see the November-December combo or a December-January combo. And once you've knocked out a test or two, it's fine to take breaks. If you've completed the December-January tests, step away from the SAT for a while, and come back for the June test.

Many of our students see their greatest gains on the June SAT. This has to do with our students' growing familiarity and comfort with the test as well as their freedom from academic and extracurricular obligations. Once school is out, students can really focus for the June SAT.

Ideally students will take the SAT two to three times junior year. They can save the fall SATs of their senior year for if they need them. The October, November and December tests of your senior year will all count for regular admissions. October is generally the last SAT students can use when applying Early Decision.

Do I need to be concerned about SAT subject tests?

Only if you are applying to a highly selective college or university. College websites will post their individual requirements, and www.collegeboard.com is a great resource for determining which schools require the SAT subject tests.

How do I register for the SAT?

Log in to www.collegeboard.com. Select the tab for "Students." Find the **SAT Quick Link**: Register for the SAT. Follow the instructions. Make sure to sign up early to secure a spot at a preferred location. The good locations can fill up quickly.

What do I need to take to the SAT?
- A few No. 2 pencils (no mechanical pencils)
- Your registration information, printed from the computer
- Your driver's license or other form of photo ID
- A digital watch or one with a second hand
- Your graphing calculator, and extra batteries
- Snacks and water
- Layers of clothing, in the event you are in a cold room

When can I expect my scores to be available?

The College Board has been consistently posting the scores online 17 calendar days after an official SAT. Two-and-a-half weeks after your SAT, your scores should be available to view at www.collegeboard.com. You will need to wait a few additional weeks for your essay and full score report.

How do I report my SAT scores to schools?

You can select up to four schools to receive your SAT scores free of charge with each SAT administration. You can send your scores to additional schools for $10 per school. Log in to www.collegeboard.com. Find the **Quick Link: Get and Send Scores**. Follow directions.

What is Score Choice™ and how will it impact me?

For decades, colleges have received all of your SAT scores at once, and the majority have cherry-picked your top scores to form your best composite score. The College Board now allows you to send particular scores and withhold others. Knowing that most schools will still superscore, it is in your best interest to send all tests which contain your highest section scores. Some colleges require that you continue to send all of your scores, and this should not be an issue. Colleges have historically been able to see all of your scores. Score Choice™ should have a minimal impact on the college admissions process.

What is extended time? Do I need it? Can I get it?

Some students with diagnosed disabilities are allowed to take the SAT with accommodations such as extended time. Only a licensed psychologist can make the diagnosis of whether a student needs extended time to compensate for an attentional or learning disability. Before the College Board will consider granting extended time or any other accommodation, your high school must acknowledge your disability and grant you accommodation for it.

Do I need additional SAT prep materials to supplement this book?

Most of our students buy the College Board's Official SAT Study Guide™ in addition to this book. The 10 practice tests are perfect for mock tests, and the timed sections will allow you to work on your pacing and time-management skills. Most of our students also purchase the supplemental flash cards we have created to help reinforce the vocabulary and key math and writing concepts tested on the SAT. You can find these online at www.applerouth.com/materials.

The Structure of the SAT

The SAT consists of 10 timed Sections: 3 Critical Reading, 3 Math, 3 Writing and an experimental section. The College Board uses the experimental section to develop new questions and determine the difficulty levels of certain question types. Even though this section will look and feel just like one of the scored Critical Reading, Math or Writing sections, it will not impact your score.

Below is an example SAT test structure:

Critical Reading Sections

CR1	CR 2	CR 3	Total
8 Sentence Completions + 16 Reading Comprehension	5 SCs + 19 RCs	6 SCs + 13 RCs	**19 SCs + 48 RCs**
24 Questions	24 Questions	19 Questions	**67 Questions**

Math Sections

Math 1	Math 2	Math 3	Total
20 Multiple Choice	8 Multiple Choice + 10 Grid-ins	16 Multiple Choice	**44 Multiple Choice + 10 Grid-ins**
20 Questions	18 Questions	16 Questions	**54 Questions**

Writing Sections

Writing 1	Writing 2	Writing 3	Total
Essay	11 Improving Sentences 18 Identifying Errors +6 Improving Paragraphs	14 Improving Sentences	**25 Improving Sentences 18 Identifying Errors +6 Improving Pargraphs**
	35 Questions	14 Questions	**49 Questions + Essay**

The SAT will always open with the essay and close with the 3 shorter sections of Critical Reading, Math and Writing. The middle sections will vary. The experimental section can appear anywhere on the SAT and has taken every position, except for the first.

When you sit for the SAT, you will need to open strong with a well-written essay. Then you must work through the body of the test, knocking out one 25-minute section after another. By the time you arrive at section 8, the sections get shorter, and before you know it, you will arrive at the final 10-minute Writing section.

Here is one potential structure of an SAT:

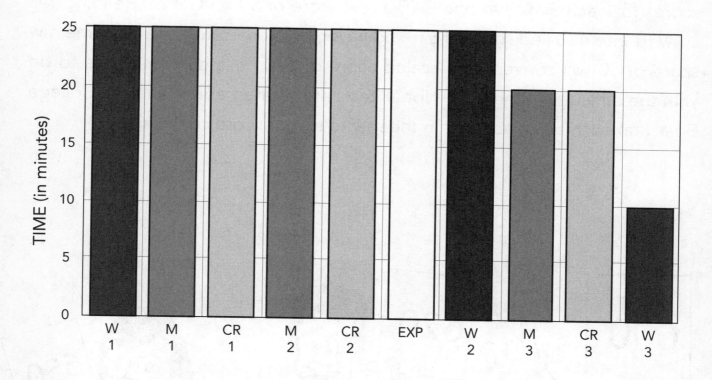

Notice that the experimental section is currently the sixth section on this particular SAT. Also, the last three sections are shorter than the previous seven sections.

With practice, you will become very familiar with all of the sections and possible structures of the test. You will learn to anticipate what sections are around the corner when you sit for an official SAT. This will help you manage your expectations and regulate your energy and concentration on test day.

Scoring the SAT

For each section of the SAT, the College Board will convert your raw score (the number you answered correctly minus a fraction of the number you missed) into a scaled score ranging from 200 to 800. Placing everyone on the same scale allows colleges to more easily compare admissions candidates to one another. The test-makers calibrate the conversion tables from raw to scaled scores for each SAT. On one SAT, a raw score of 50 on Critical Reading will convert into a scaled score of 610; however, on a different test that same raw score of 50 will convert to a scaled score of 640. This difference has to do with the difficulty of the test. Not all tests are created equal, and the College Board takes this into account in the raw to scaled score conversion.

Here is an example of a typical Raw to Scaled conversion table.

Scaled Score	Raw Score		
	Math	Critical Reading	Writing (assuming an essay score of 9)
	54 Possible	67 Possible	49 Possible
500	27	30	20
520	29	33	23
540	31	36	26
560	33	40	29
580	36	43	31
600	39	46	34
620	40	49	36
640	42	52	39
660	45	55	41
680	46	58	42
700	48	60	43
720	50	61	44
740	51	62	46
760	52	64	47
780	53	65	48
800	54	67	49

Notice that for each section of the test, you will need to get a different raw score to achieve the same scaled score. To achieve a score of 600 on Critical Reading, you will need 46 raw points. To achieve a 600 on Math, you will need 39 raw points. To achieve a 600 on Writing, assuming you score a 9 on the essay (more about that later), you will need to score 34 raw points. Every SAT has its own conversion table, and you will need to become familiar with these tables to understand how many questions you will need to get right to achieve a certain score.

The Impact of Wrong Answers

For multiple choice questions, when you correctly answer a question, 1 point will be added to your raw score. When you miss a multiple choice question, ¼ of a point will be deducted from your raw score. For the 10 student-response or "grid-in" math questions, 1 point will be added for each correct response, but no points will be deducted for wrong answers. What does all this information tell you? **ANSWER EVERY GRID-IN**, even if you are guessing randomly.

Let's examine how wrong answers impact your score in the context of the Math sections.

Math 1	Math 2	Math 3	**Total**
20 Multiple Choice	8 Multiple Choice + 10 Grid-ins	16 Multiple Choice	**44 Multiple Choice + 10 Grid-ins**
20 Questions	18 Questions	16 Questions	**54 Questions**

The Math portion of each SAT consists of 44 multiple choice and 10 grid-in questions. Let's say you omit 9 multiple choice questions and answer 35. Of the 35 questions you answer, you miss 10 and answer 25 correctly. For the grid-ins, you answer all 10 questions, 6 of them correctly.

How do we calculate your score?

The formula is

$$\text{\# correct} - \frac{\text{\# incorrect}}{4}$$

In this case we add our 25 multiple choice to our 6 grid-ins to give us our base of 31 raw points. Now we must deduct the missed multiple choice questions, not worrying about the missed Grid-ins, which never count against you.

$$31 - \frac{10}{4} = 31 - 2.5 = \boxed{28.5}$$

28.5 will round up to a scaled score of 29. Let's check back to our Conversion Table on the previous page. We can see that our 29 raw score becomes a 520 scaled score.

The Art of Guessing

In general, the SAT **rewards strategic guessing** and penalizes random guessing. The penalty for guessing is fairly modest, only ¼ of a point, and the benefit of a correct answer is much greater, a gain of 1 point. So, you will need to guess incorrectly four times to cancel out one correct answer.

Knowing when to omit and when to guess is a balancing act. When students **never omit** any questions, they are generally hurting their score because they will lose ¼ of a point for every question they miss. These quarter point deductions can add up quickly. For example, on the Critical Reading section of the SAT, when students miss 30 questions and omit zero (common for untrained SAT students), they are sacrificing 30/4 = 7.5 raw points! That is significant. A drop of 7.5 raw points can translate to a scaled score drop of 50 points!

On the other hand, when students always omit questions in the face of any uncertainty, they are limiting their potential to maximize their scores. Clearly these "never-guessers" will avoid the ¼ penalty for wrong answers but miss the opportunity to gain full points from successful guesses.

Students with a very high omit to wrong ratio are likely leaving points on the table and should consider pushing some of those omits toward strategic guesses.

To help students make educated guesses, there are a few simple rules.

Guessing Rules

1 If you can eliminate NO ANSWER CHOICES, OMIT.

If you cannot eliminate a single answer choice, then you are guessing randomly. The SAT does NOT reward random guessing. For example, if you guess randomly on 5 multiple choice questions, the odds are you will answer 1 question correctly and 4 incorrectly. You will gain 1 point for the correct answer and you will be penalized 0.25 points for each wrong answer $(4 \times -0.25 = -1)$. The guessing penalty will wipe out the gains from the correct answer. Because random guessing will not help your cause on the SAT, skip the problems where you cannot eliminate any answer choices.

2 If you can eliminate 1 ANSWER CHOICE, OMIT.

In terms of straight probability, randomly guessing after eliminating one answer choice should have a slightly positive outcome. If you guess randomly on 4 multiple choice questions, after having eliminated one of the answer choices, the odds are you will answer one question correctly and 3 incorrectly. You will gain 1 point for the correct answer and you will be penalized 0.25 points for each wrong answer $(3 \times -0.25 = -0.75)$. In this case, you'd be up 0.25 points. However, the SAT is sneaky, filled with traps and seductive wrong answers. When students are guessing "randomly" frequently, they are making a beeline for a trap. Because of the inherent trickiness of the SAT, we advocate that you OMIT THESE QUESTIONS where you can only eliminate a single answer choice.

3 For EASY AND MEDIUM problems, if you can ELIMINATE 2 ANSWER CHOICES, GUESS.

If you can knock off 2 answer choices and only have 3 remaining, you are in the money! If you guess on 3 problems, having eliminated 2 wrong answers in each problem, the odds are that you will answer one question correctly (+1) and two incorrectly $(-2 \times 0.25 = -0.50)$. You just picked up 0.5 points which will round to a full point! GUESSING HERE IS A GOOD MOVE!

4 For the HARDEST problems, if you can ELIMINATE 3 ANSWER CHOICES, GUESS.

Why do we need a different rule for the hardest problems? Simply because the most difficult problems have the best and most seductive wrong answers. Many students will fall right into an assumption trap when they guess on the hardest problems. The hardest problems for Math, Writing and sentence completions come at the end of each section. The last 2 sentence completions, the last 3-4 math problems and the last 2-3 writing problems of each section are generally designed for students shooting for scores in the high 600s and 700s. For these problems, you should guess if and only if you can eliminate 3 answer choices. If you knock off 3 answer choices, you will have 2 remaining and a 50/50 chance of picking up a point. With these odds, despite the tricky nature of the hardest questions, guessing makes a lot of sense.

5 For MATH GRID-INS, ALWAYS GUESS.

There is no 0.25 point deduction for wrong answers. You won't lose any points if you guess. But, if you don't guess, you may be selling yourself short. Always guess on the Math grid-in problems.

Getting the Score You Want

By now you realize that answering, guessing and omitting are all part of the strategy for achieving an optimal score. It is very important to have a goal for each section of the SAT and to know how many raw points you will need to achieve your goal.

For example, if your goal is to get a 560 on Math, you will need to receive roughly 33 raw points. If you answer 42 questions, 35 correctly and 7 incorrectly, you will be on track for your goal. Your total raw score is the number attempted minus the number wrong minus the penalty for wrong answers (¼ × the number wrong).

42 (attempted) – 7 (missed) – 7/4 (penalty) = 33.25 = 33

To achieve your 560, you do not need to even attempt 12 problems! That's good news.

We've analyzed several thousand tests to determine how our students achieve specific scores on the SAT. We've created three tables to illustrate the balance of right, wrong and omitted problems needed to achieve a particular SAT score. You will notice there is a balance of omits and guesses, an indication that students are guessing strategically and omitting problems when appropriate.

Achieving Critical Reading Goals

Scaled Score	MULTIPLE CHOICE				RAW Score
	Attempt	Omit	Wrong	Correct	
500	54	13	19	35	**30**
520	55	12	18	37	**33**
540	56	11	16	40	**36**
560	57	10	14	43	**40**
580	59	8	13	46	**43**
600	60	7	11	49	**46**
620	61	6	10	51	**49**
640	62	5	8	54	**52**
660	62	5	6	56	**55**
680	64	3	5	59	**58**
700	65	2	4	61	**60**
720	65	2	3	62	**61**
740	66	1	3	63	**62**
760	66	1	2	64	**64**
780	67	0	2	65	**65**
800	67	0	0	67	**67**

To score a 500, you only need to answer 35 of 67 questions correctly. To score a 600, you only need to answer 49 of 67 questions correctly. Once you are shooting for a score in the 700+ range, the margin of error gets smaller, and you end up needing to answer almost every question.

Achieving Math Goals

Scaled Score	MULTIPLE CHOICE			Grid-ins		Total		RAW Score
	Attempt	Omit	Wrong	Attempt	Wrong	Attempt	Correct	
500	37	7	11	10	6	47	30	27
520	37	7	10	10	6	47	31	29
540	38	6	10	10	5	48	33	31
560	38	6	8	10	5	48	35	33
580	39	5	7	10	4	49	38	36
600	39	5	5	10	4	49	40	39
620	40	4	5	10	4	50	41	40
640	40	4	4	10	3	50	43	42
660	41	3	3	10	2	51	46	45
680	41	3	2	10	2	51	47	46
700	41	3	2	10	1	51	48	48
720	42	2	1	10	1	52	50	50
740	43	1	1	10	1	53	51	51
760	44	0	1	10	1	54	52	52
780	44	0	1	10	0	54	53	53
800	44	0	0	10	0	54	54	54

Notice that students answer every grid-in. To achieve a 500, our students generally answer 47 out of 54 questions. To achieve a 600, our students generally answer 49 out of 54 questions, and to achieve a 700, our students generally answer 51 of 54 questions.

Achieving Writing Goals

Scaled Score	MULTIPLE CHOICE				ESSAY Score	RAW Score
	Attempt	Omit	Wrong	Correct		
500	44	5	12	32	7	29
520	45	4	11	34	8	31
540	45	4	10	35	8	33
560	45	4	9	36	8	34
580	46	3	8	38	8	36
600	46	3	9	37	9	35
620	46	3	7	39	9	37
640	46	3	6	40	9	39
660	47	2	5	42	9	41
680	47	2	5	42	10	41
700	47	2	3	44	10	43
720	48	1	3	45	10	44
740	48	1	2	46	10	46
760	49	0	2	47	10	47
780	49	0	2	47	11	47
800	49	0	1	48	11	48

Your score on the Writing section is based on a combination of your essay score and your multiple choice raw score. For each scaled score, we found the average essay score students receive on actual SATs graded by the College Board. For example, the average student who receives a scaled score of 600 receives an essay score of 9. If you score higher on the essay than the average listed, the number of multiple choice questions you should attempt will drop. If your essay score is lower than the average, you will need a higher multiple choice raw score to achieve the same scaled score. The tables at the back of each SAT will reveal the full scoring matrix combining the essay score and the multiple choice raw score.

One thing that is remarkable is the lower number of omits on the Writing section. Students are very comfortable omitting on Critical Reading when they have no clue about particular vocabulary words, and they are comfortable omitting on Math when they are totally stuck. But Writing is more subtle. Students are less likely to recognize when they have missed a grammar error, and, therefore, they omit fewer questions. Now that you know this, you should be wary of the last few problems at the end of each Writing section. Remember to omit when you can't make an educated guess.

Difficulty Levels

Level of Difficulty

SAT questions vary greatly in their level of difficulty. Although each question counts for just one raw point, certain questions will be almost effortless for most students, and other questions will require a great deal of time and effort to solve. The questions are scaled from 1 to 5, depending on how many students answer them correctly in experimental sections of previously administered SATs.

Level 1 questions are very easy. A vast majority of students will ace the level 1s in a very short amount of time. Likewise, a vast majority of students will miss the level 5s and waste a lot of time in the process.

We have analyzed over a thousand actual SAT tests graded by the College Board, and for each difficulty level 1-5, we found the percentage of questions students answer correctly.

> **Level 5: 32% correct responses**
> **Level 4: 47% correct responses**
> **Level 3: 68% correct responses**
> **Level 2: 83% correct responses**
> **Level 1: 92% correct responses**

Our data is skewed toward higher performing students, the ones working with us, but these figures will give you a general sense of how difficulty levels are assigned.

Working through a test using the Order of Difficulty

Difficulty levels on most sections are predictable. For Math, multiple choice questions increase in order of difficulty as do grid-ins. For Critical Reading, sentence completions increase in order of difficulty, but reading comprehension questions do not. For Writing, improving sentences and identifying errors questions increase in order of difficulty, but improving paragraph questions do not.

As we move through a section, we start with the level 1s and progress to the level 5s. The last 2-3 sentence completions, math and writing questions are generally level 5s. Most students waste lots of precious time on these level 5s, time that could have been better spent on easy and mid-level questions.

Here's a look at the 20-question Math section:

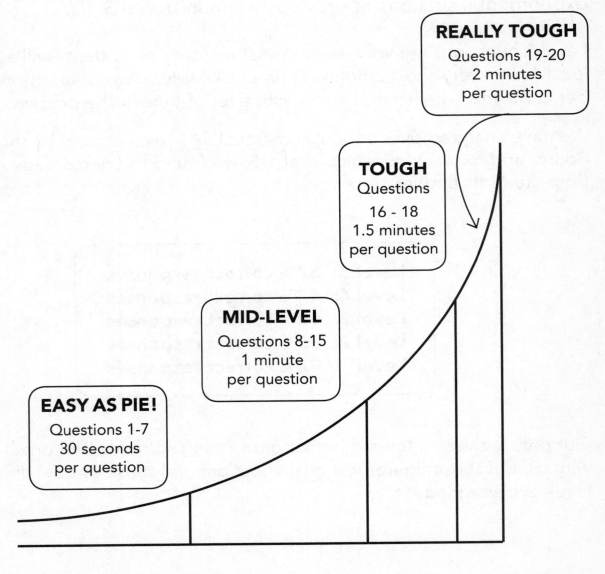

REALLY TOUGH
Questions 19-20
2 minutes
per question

TOUGH
Questions
16 - 18
1.5 minutes
per question

MID-LEVEL
Questions 8-15
1 minute
per question

EASY AS PIE!
Questions 1-7
30 seconds
per question

The section starts with the level 1 and 2 questions that are relatively quick and painless. As we work through the section, we find the mid-level questions, primarily with difficulty levels of 2 and 3. We continue to move on to the tough level 4s, and finally we arrive at the really difficult and time-intensive 5s.

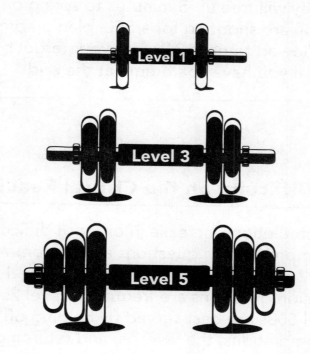

Developing a good strategy for Order of Difficulty

Untrained students, nervous about completing all the questions in the time allotted, frequently rush through the level 1 and 2 questions, making careless errors along the way. They eventually arrive at the level 4s and 5s, where they will spend much more time and rarely receive the payoff of a right answer. They burn easy points and then fail to achieve the hard points. **This is not a good strategy!**

Smart students pace themselves. They move carefully through the early problems, being sure not to make any costly careless errors. They know that an early raw point on a level 1 question is worth just as much as the 1-point prize of a level 5 question. They spend most of their time on the mid-level problems and selectively answer and omit the hardest problems.

Using Order of Difficulty on the Math section

Students shooting for a 550 on Math generally have no business worrying about the last 3-4 problems of each section. If they omit the last 4 problems of a section, they will free up 5 minutes to spend on easy and mid-level problems. If you are shooting for a 550, plan on omitting the hardest problems (you are allowed to omit 21 to hit your target score) or approach these problems only if you have spare time at the end.

Using Order of Difficulty on the Critical Reading section

Though sentence completions increase in order of difficulty, the difficulty levels of reading comprehension questions are random. You can be fairly certain that the last 2 sentence completions will be level 5s, but the last 2 reading comprehension questions are frequently level 2s or 3s. Students shooting for the mid 500s are best served by holding off on attempting the hardest sentence completions, the level 5s, and returning to them at the end of the section if there's time.

Using Order of Difficulty on the Writing section

As you make your way through the writing questions, they will become more challenging and the errors more subtle. The later problems do not necessarily take longer, but they are certainly trickier and test more nuanced rules. Keep in mind that the improving paragraphs questions do not follow the same pattern of easy to difficult. Instead, these questions are like the reading comprehension questions and follow the order of the passage.

Pacing and Practice

You must learn to effectively manage time, your most precious resource, on the SAT. You must learn your relative speeds for different problem types. Some students are Critical Reading wizards, but struggle with time management on Math. Others are speedy on the Math but run out of time on the Essay. Students seem to struggle most with time management on reading comprehension and least on the grammar portion of the Writing test.

You must learn your relative speed for each section and for each question type. Then you must learn to monitor and regulate your pacing.

Timing Drills

If you find that you are struggling with time management, you will need to practice timing drills. Timing drills will help you become more comfortable with the appropriate time intervals for specific types of SAT questions. Each question type has its own timing interval.

Identifying errors problems take less time (roughly 20 seconds) than improving paragraph questions (roughly 1 minute); sentence completions take less time (roughly 45 seconds) than reading comprehension questions (60-75 seconds, including reading time).

A simplistic approach to time management involves taking the number of minutes allotted to a section and dividing by the number of questions on that section. So for a 20-question, 25-minute math section, you would allocate 1 ¼ minutes per question. But because of difficulty order, the first five problems will take less than 75 seconds each, and the last few problems will take longer.

A more sophisticated approach to timing is allocating specific time intervals to certain question types. You will need to experiment and find out the speed that is appropriate for you. You might try allocating 40 seconds per question on the first five math questions, then 1 minute per question for the next 10 math questions and then 1 ½ minutes per question for the last five math questions. If you run over this interval on a particular question, you must force yourself to guess or omit.

And don't forget, if you plan on omitting the last four problems, you can reallocate that time to the earlier questions. This will give you longer time intervals on the easy and medium questions.

Time-interval training: getting faster with practice

To begin, you will need to determine your natural pacing. You should complete a full section, while timing yourself, to determine your natural speed. Let's say you do a timed Math section and it takes you 30 minutes, rather than 25, to answer all the questions. So you are five minutes over the limit. Now what? Ask yourself: Where is that time going? How can I go faster?

Try another Math section, but this time work with the clock and record how long it takes you to do each problem. Then analyze the results. Where are you spending your time? Are you spinning your wheels and spending 2-3 minutes on certain problems? Are you getting these time-intensive problems right? Where can you save time?

At this point, you will need to establish time intervals for each question, after which point you will force yourself to guess or omit. You can begin with longer intervals and gradually decrease them. If you are working on sentence completions, start by giving yourself 70 seconds per question. Then gradually move down to 65 seconds, 60 seconds, 55 seconds, 50 seconds and so on. It may be helpful to have someone, your "timing coach," call out these time intervals and push you to guess or move on.

Importance of Practice Tests

No SAT prep program would be complete without timed, practice tests. Timed tests allow you to practice your time management skills, your guessing and omitting strategies and your self-regulation and motivation strategies. They also help you build mental endurance and concentration. The College Board's Official Guide to the SAT™ contains 10 practice tests. These are fabulous tools to help you prepare for the actual SAT. Timed practice sections and whole timed tests will help you hone your test-taking skills and prepare for your optimal performance on test day.

How To Use This Book

We have divided the book into the key sections of the SAT: Critical Reading, Vocabulary, Writing and Math. Each section contains strategies, explanations and practice sections.

As you make your way through the book you will notice little call-outs in the margins, pictures of our tutors in various situations: these are our Tutor Tips. Tutor Tips highlight material that you want to be sure to remember and provide you with additional strategies and tricks. It's a good idea to flip through a chapter that you've already read and review the Tutor Tips.

The Short List

The sections of this book that focus mainly on teaching you actual content rather than strategy will be followed by what we call a Short List. This list summarizes the most important information from the preceding section. It would be wise to review these Short Lists before you take your exam. A Short List will follow the grammar section, the arithmetic section, the algebra section and the geometry section.

Mantras

At the end of the Critical Reading, Writing and Math portions of this study guide, you will find a series of Mantras. Mantras are helpful, easy-to-remember statements that remind you of your strategies. Repeat these to yourself when you are stuck in traffic, on your way to study hall or in the shower. Know them; love them; use them.

The Practice Problems

This book has over 600 different practice problems—not including examples and vocabulary practice—that are modeled off of real SAT problems created by the test-makers themselves. After completing each set of practice problems, be sure to check your answers. Next to each correct answer in the answer keys, you will see another letter or letter and number in parentheses. This indicates the level of difficulty of each problem.

(E) means it is an easy problem.

(M) means it is a mid-level problem.

(H) means it is a hard problem.

(H5) means it is a Level 5 problem, the hardest of all.

You can practice problems of varying difficulty levels to determine whether you should attempt the hardest questions (*H* and *H5*), or whether it would be better for you to focus your energy on the easy (*E*) and medium (*M*) problems.

Ways To Study

The Comprehensive Review

Each week complete a series of lessons and practice problems from each of the four sections: Math, Writing, Critical Reading and Vocabulary. In week 1, you may tackle Properties of Numbers in Math, Sentence Completions in Critical Reading, The Essay in Writing, and Week 1 Vocabulary. This balanced approach will keep you moving forward on all fronts as you prepare to take on all the sections of the SAT.

Isolate and Focus

Take a practice test. Determine your individual areas of weakness. Use the book to focus on the areas where you are weakest. If your Critical Reading score is low, put your energy there. If you are grappling with Geometry, go there first. You can use your mock tests as feedback to guide your preparation.

No matter which approach you take, **start your vocabulary review as soon as you open the book**. Learning vocabulary takes time. We recommend that you start the vocabulary review a minimum of seven weeks before taking your actual SAT.

Regardless of which approach you take, keep in mind two basic principles to get the most from your studying:

Don't cram: spread out your SAT review over time

Memory researchers have found that cramming, massing all of your review into long sessions, is not nearly as effective as spacing your study over multiple shorter sessions. Each time you review a concept, you are strengthening or "reinforcing" it, etching the material deeper and deeper into your brain, so it will be there when you need it on test day.

Review new concepts within 24 hours of first exposure

As soon as you learn a new concept in this book, review it within 24 hours to help lock it into your memory. Researchers have found that if you review a concept within 24 hours and make yourself recall the definition or concept from memory (AKA forced retrieval practice), it will dramatically impact long-term retention of this material. So whenever you are exposed to a new SAT concept or vocabulary word you want to memorize, be sure to review it within 24 hours.

The following pages outline different courses of study depending on how long you have to prepare for your test. These are only suggestions; focus on finding the schedule that works best for you.

SAT Study Schedules

It goes without saying that this study guide is very long and full of a lot of useful information. Don't be discouraged. We don't expect you to read this whole book cover to cover. If creating your own study schedule is daunting to you, don't worry! We've taken care of that. The following pages contain suggested guided practice based on your intended length of study. Feel free to mix and match and find the perfect study guide for you!

One Day

If you pick up this book, look at a calendar and realize that the SAT you have registered for is tomorrow, don't freak out. Relax. Deep breath. Good. It may or may not be too late to ace this test, but you can always register for the next time the SAT will be given. This will give you anywhere from 1 to 4 months to prepare. In the meantime, perhaps a little crash course is needed to bump up your confidence and your chances. Don't try to study everything; focus on the following sections to get the most bang out of your limited study time.

One Week

Though you are not quite the king or queen of procrastination, you do an excellent impression of one. One week may be enough time to review if you already have a strong foundation. However, if you plan for *this* to be your foundation, you might consider registering for the next SAT offered. If you seriously only have one week to devote to SAT studying, we suggest you spend two hours a day focusing on these topics.

One Month

If you have carved out one month to study for your SAT, you should plan on studying 6 to 7 hours a week—not in one sitting. You'll remember more if you break your study time up into two- or three-hour sessions.

Week 1
1 Math Section in *The Official
Study Guide to the SAT*
1 Reading Section in *The Official
Study Guide to the SAT*

One Month

Week 2

Week 3

Mock Test

When the schedule says *Mock Test*, take a full-length, timed test in your copy of the *The Official Study Guide to the SAT*.

Week 4

1 Math Section in *The Official Study Guide to the SAT*
1 Reading Section in *The Official Study Guide to the SAT*

Three Months

Three months is ample time to prepare for the SAT. You will be able to cover the majority of the material in this book. Starting three months out will make it seem like you have forever to study. The key is to study regularly on a weekly basis. This will help you build momentum up until your exam. Plan on studying 4 to 6 hours a week.

Week 1

1 Timed Math Section in *The Official Study Guide to the SAT*
1 Timed Reading Section in *The Official Study Guide to the SAT*

Week 2

1 Timed Math Section in *The Official Study Guide to the SAT*
1 Timed Reading Section in *The Official Study Guide to the SAT*

When the schedule says *Mock Test*, take a full-length, timed test in your copy of the *The Official Study Guide to the SAT*.

Week 3

Week 4

Week 5

Week 6

1 Timed Math Section in *The Official
  Study Guide to the SAT*
2 Timed Reading Sections in *The Official
  Study Guide to the SAT*

Week 7

1 Timed Math Section in *The Official
  Study Guide to the SAT*
1 Timed Reading Section in *The Official
  Study Guide to the SAT*
1 Timed Writing Section in *The Official
  Study Guide to the SAT*

Week 8

Mock Test
Review Answers

When the schedule says *Mock Test*, take a full-length, timed test in your copy of the *The Official Study Guide to the SAT*.

Week 9

1 Timed Math Section in *The Official
   Study Guide to the SAT*
1 Timed Reading Section in *The Official
   Study Guide to the SAT*
1 Timed Writing Section in *The Official
   Study Guide to the SAT*

Week 10

Review Vocabulary

2 Timed Math Sections in *The Official
   Study Guide to the SAT*
2 Timed Reading Sections in *The Official
   Study Guide to the SAT*
2 Timed Writing Sections in *The Official
   Study Guide to the SAT*

Week 11

Mock Test
Review Answers

When the schedule says *Mock Test*, take a full-length, timed test in your copy of the *The Official Study Guide to the SAT*.

Week 12
Review Vocabulary

2 Timed Math Sections in *The Official
Study Guide to the SAT*

2 Timed Reading Sections in *The Official
Study Guide to the SAT*

2 Timed Writing Sections in *The Official
Study Guide to the SAT*

These last two math topics are very advanced and rarely appear on the SAT. If you are aiming for a perfect score, take the time to learn these new concepts so you are prepared if they show up on your test. If math is not your strongest subject, spend this study time reviewing other math topics that have given you trouble in the past.

CRITICAL READING

Critical Reading

The Critical Reading portion of the SAT has three sections with a total of 67 questions.

Section A	Section B	Section C	Total
8 SC* + 16 RC** <hr> 24 Questions 25 minutes	5 SC + 19 RC <hr> 24 Questions 25 minutes	6 SC + 13 RC <hr> 19 Questions 20 minutes	19 SC + 48 RC <hr> 67 Questions 70 minutes

*SC: Sentence Completions
**RC: Reading Comprehension

Sentence Completions (page 52)

There are 19 Sentence Completions on each SAT. Sentence Completions primarily test your vocabulary knowledge but also assess how effectively you can interpret the logical clues of a sentence.

Reading Comprehension (page 72)

There are 48 Reading Comprehension questions on each SAT. Nearly 70% of your Critical Reading score will be determined by your performance on Reading Comprehension, so you would be wise to invest most of your energy mastering this portion of the test.

Vocabulary

The quickest way to pick up points on the Critical Reading section of the SAT is to ramp up your vocabulary. You will need to flex your vocabulary muscles on the 19 Sentence Completions and 5 Vocabulary in Context questions in the Reading Comprehension section. At least 36% of CR questions test your vocabulary. Whenever you come across a word on the SAT that you do not know, make a flash card and be sure to review these cards frequently.

Sentence Completions

There are 19 Sentence Completions on each SAT. In every Critical Reading section, Sentence Completions increase in order of difficulty as the level of vocabulary becomes progressively more challenging.

There are 5 types of Sentence Completions.

Antonyms

Antonym questions make up about 30% of all Sentence Completion questions. This is a contrasting format; look for words like **although**, **but**, **however** or **yet**, which signal a change in direction.

E Rather than claiming to prefer any one style, such as contemporary, art deco or shabby chic, above the others, the decorator maintained that his tastes were -----.

(A) classical
(B) eclectic
(C) dubious
(D) unorthodox
(E) simplistic

S Rather than claiming to prefer any one style, such as contemporary, art deco or shabby chic, above the others, the decorator maintained that his tastes were **eclectic**.

*The words **Rather than** tell you that you are looking for the opposite of preferring **any one style**. Eclectic means "coming from a variety of sources and influences"—literally the opposite of just one thing.*

E Fans were distraught when Emmanuel's usually ----- apple pies tasted ----- at last year's annual Pie-a-thon.

(A) sublime . . mediocre
(B) capricious . . ludicrous
(C) decadent . . remarkable
(D) nondescript . . inferior
(E) ordinary . . exceptional

S Fans were distraught when Emmanuel's usually **sublime** apple pies tasted **mediocre** at last year's annual Pie-a-thon.

*The word **distraught** tells us that there was something wrong with Emmanuel's pies last year. Now we know that the second blank must be a negative word. The word **usually** earlier in the sentence implies that what happened at last year's pie contest was definitely not the norm. So, the first blank must be a word that is the opposite of the second blank. Since we know that the second blank must be negative and that Emmanuel has fans, we can guess that the first blank must be a positive word. Choice **(A)** is the only choice that has a positive word followed by a negative word.*

Definitions

Definition questions also make up about 30% of all Sentence Completion questions. These sentences give you a blank and then directly define the word that goes in the blank. Often a blank followed by a *comma*, *colon* or *semi-colon* indicates that you are working with a Definition.

E The decrepit old pirate ship was ----- : after years of abuse and decades of neglect, it was literally falling to pieces.

(A) desiccated
(B) foreboding
(C) audacious
(D) indomitable
(E) dilapidated

You don't have to come up with the perfect word to put in the blank all by yourself. Feel free to use words you already see in the sentence.

S The decrepit old pirate ship was **dilapidated**: after years of abuse and decades of neglect, it was literally falling to pieces.

*That colon (:) gives it all away! We know the definition of the missing word is following close behind. Choice **(E)** is the only word that means **falling to pieces**. How convenient.*

E The charity organizers were thrilled with Mrs. Vanderbilt's ----- ; they had never seen such boundless generosity.

(A) perseverance
(B) introspection
(C) munificence
(D) spontaneity
(E) meddling

S The charity organizers were thrilled with Mrs. Vanderbilt's **munificence**; they had never seen such boundless generosity.

*That semi-colon (;) is a big help! We know we need a word that means **boundless generosity**. Choice **(C)** means exactly that.*

Cause and Effect

Cause and Effect questions make up about 27% of all Sentence Completion questions. This kind of Sentence Completion is an exercise in logic. The first part of the sentence logically informs the second part of the sentence: because of X, therefore Y.

E After hiring ----- movers from Movers-R-Us in the past, Gary was ----- to work with them again.

(A) inept . . reluctant
(B) inexperienced . . thrilled
(C) sedulous . . hesitant
(D) jaded . . eager
(E) sullen . . keen

S After hiring **inept** movers from Movers-R-Us in the past, Gary was **reluctant** to work with them again.

This type of question is very tricky. There are few word clues in the sentence that tell us what words should go in the blanks. The movers are either good or bad, and, because of the structure of the sentence, that first missing word will tell us if Gary wants to work with them again or not. So, we have to go to our answer choices and see which word pair works together. If the movers were inexperienced, would Gary be thrilled? Probably not. If they were inexperienced, he probably won't want to work with them again. Following this logic, we see that (A) is the best answer.

E Because of the ----- nature of teenagers, Norma could never quite tell what her 16-year-old daughter was thinking.

(A) enigmatic
(B) cerebral
(C) trivial
(D) rational
(E) morose

S Because of the **enigmatic** nature of teenagers, Norma could never quite tell what her 16-year-old daughter was thinking.

The word **because** *is the big clue. The sentence tells us that Norma* **could never quite tell what her 16-year-old daughter was thinking** *and we can assume the first part of the sentence will tell us why this is so. What kind of nature is difficult to understand? Perhaps a mysterious one? Well, choice* **(A)** *is a synonym for mysterious.*

Synonyms

Synonym questions make up about 9% of all Sentence Completion questions. These sentences present you with two similar words, often joined by the word *and*.

E The sophisticated columnist had an urbane and ----- view of the world around him.

(A) prosaic
(B) ascetic
(C) ineffable
(D) cosmopolitan
(E) narcissistic

S The sophisticated columnist had an urbane and **cosmopolitan** view of the world around him.

What a powerful little three-letter word: **and** *tells us we want a word that means the same thing as* **urbane**. *Choice* **(D)** *is definitely a synonym.*

E Jungian psychologists argue that certain symbols make up our "collective unconscious" and are understood ----- by human beings.

(A) sagaciously
(B) insatiably
(C) viably
(D) divisively
(E) innately

S Jungian psychologists argue that certain symbols make up our "collective unconscious" and are understood **innately** by human beings.

Here, **and** *joins both parts of the sentence together. We need a word that mirrors* **collective unconscious***; a word that means "understanding unconsciously." Choice* **(E)** *is the best synonym.*

Greater or Lesser Degree

This sentence type is rare, only about 4% of all questions. Here you have a vocabulary progression from a moderate to a more extreme kind of word. From happy to jubilant, from sad to despondent, from vivid to garish. These are examples of a change in degree.

E Monte's reaction to the tiny scratch on his Porsche 911 was beyond melodramatic, verging on -----.

(A) histrionic
(B) amicable
(C) jubilant
(D) insolent
(E) treacly

S Monte's reaction to the tiny scratch on his Porsche 911 was beyond melodramatic, verging on **histrionic**.

*The word **beyond** tells us that Monte's reaction was even greater than **melodramatic**. While choice (C), jubilant, is an extreme word, it does not mean melodramatic. Choice **(A)** is the exact answer we are looking for.*

E Janet became irritated, even -----, when telemarketers continually interrupted her family's dinner.

(A) pragmatic
(B) optimistic
(C) contentious
(D) morose
(E) resolute

S Janet became irritated, even **contentious**, when telemarketers continually interrupted her family's dinner.

Even *raises the ante. We know that Janet was **even** more than **irritated**. Choice **(C)** is the correct answer.*

Sentence Completion Strategy

Below are step-by-step instructions for answering one-blank Sentence Completions and two-blank Sentence Completions.

1 Cover the answer choices

This is imperative. The College Board sets you up with numerous traps in the answer choices that will pull your attention away from what really matters. Don't even look at the answer choices until you've read the sentence.

2 Read the sentence critically

You are not just skimming over the sentence; you are reading it analytically and critically, looking for the clues that inform the blank.

3 Circle the logic clues

Every sentence has its own **logic**. Words like 'but,' 'however,' and 'although' tell you that the direction of the sentence will switch; words like 'and' and 'therefore,' as well as commas and colons, tell you that the direction will remain the same. **Circle the words or punctuation clues that reveal the logic of the sentence**.

4 Underline the key content clues that inform the blank

One or two words will directly inform the blank. These words will often be synonyms of the answer; at the very least, they will have the same charge as the answer. It is a good practice to draw a plus "+" or a minus "−" sign to indicate the positive or negative charge of the key content clues.

5 Draw an arrow from the key content clue to the blank

It is very common for the answer to be directly embedded in the sentence. Drawing an arrow from the word to the blank simply points this out and makes your prediction more clear.

6 Make your own prediction

Predict the word that will go in the blank and write it in or directly above the blank. If you cannot choose a single word, several words or a short phrase will do. If you've already drawn an arrow from a word in the sentence to the blank, this will serve as your prediction.

7 Compare your word with the answer choices

As you go down the answer choices, eliminate answers that don't match your predicted word. If you do not know a word, you CANNOT eliminate it; instead make a squiggle "~" next to that answer choice.

8 Analyze the vocabulary of the remaining choices

If you cannot eliminate all of the answer choices, break down the remaining words into roots and look for associations you have with them. If you can, eliminate additional answer choices through this process.

9 Plug the remaining choices into the sentence

Re-read the sentences, plugging in the remaining answer choices one at a time. With context, your ear will be able to discriminate more clearly between the answer choices and will be more likely to discern the right answer.

10 Choose an answer

As long as you have eliminated two answer choices (or three answer choices for the hardest two completions, generally the level 5 problems), you should guess.

If you cannot eliminate two answer choices (or three answer choices for a level 5 problem), you should skip the problem.

Single-blank Questions

We will work through the following single-blank example together, using all the rules we've just learned above.

E Having been reproached by the institutional review board for unethical conduct and unlawful behavior, the researchers were disgraced and their research findings were -----.

(A) embellished
(B) discredited
(C) fabricated
(D) substantiated
(E) corroborated

S ## Step 1   COVER the answers

Having been reproached by the institutional review board for unethical conduct and unlawful behavior, the researchers were disgraced and their research findings were -----.

(A)
(B)
(C)
(D)
(E)

Step 2   Read the sentence CRITICALLY

Step 3   Circle the LOGIC clues

Having been reproached by the institutional review board for unethical conduct and unlawful behavior, the researchers were disgraced (and) their research findings were -----.

*The logic word **and** is a "joiner" and tells us the blank will be connected to what precedes it.*

Step 4   Underline the KEY CONTENT clues that inform the blank

(–)   (–)
Having been <u>reproached</u> by the institutional review board for <u>unethical</u>
(–)   (–)
conduct and <u>unlawful</u> behavior, the researchers were <u>disgraced</u> (and)

their research findings were -----.

*Here we have a lot of negative words. If you don't know the meaning of the word **reproached**, don't worry. You won't need to know it to solve this one. The other negatives, **unethical**, **unlawful** and **disgraced,** let us know that we are in negative territory.*

S **Step 5** Draw an arrow from the KEY CONTENT clue to the blank

Having been <u>reproached</u> by the institutional review board for <u>unethical</u> conduct and <u>unlawful</u> behavior, the researchers were <u>disgraced</u> (and) their research findings were -----.

*The word **and** is our best clue here. The blank is tied to the fact that the researchers were **disgraced**.*

Step 6   Make your own PREDICTION

Having been <u>reproached</u> by the institutional review board for <u>unethical</u> conduct and <u>unlawful</u> behavior, the researchers were <u>disgraced</u> (and) their research findings were -----. *Rejected, dismissed, looked badly upon*

Step 7   COMPARE your word with the answer choices

~~(A)~~ embellished — *Does not look like a negative word – I'll cross this one off.*
(B) discredited — *It's negative – keep it.*
~ (C) fabricated — *Maybe– I'll squiggle it.*
~~(D)~~ substantiated — *Hmm... doesn't look negative – cross it off.*
~ (E) corroborated — *Not sure of this one – I'll squiggle it.*

Step 8   ANALYZE the vocabulary of the remaining choices

(B) discredited — *"dis" = not; "credit" has to do with believe. Keep this for now.*
~ (C) fabricated — *has to do with create or make– not sure about this one*
~~(E)~~ corroborated — *"co" = with. Hmm... We are looking for a negative word to go with **disgrace**, I don't think corroborate would work. I'm crossing this one off.*

If you don't know what a word means, you can't just toss it aside. Put a squiggle mark by it to remind yourself it is still in the running.

It's often a good idea to shorten the sentence to the principal elements when plugging the answer choice back into the sentence; this helps save time.

S **Step 9** PLUG the remaining choices into the sentence

(B) Having been reproached ..., the researchers were disgraced and their research findings were **_discredited_**.

(C) Having been reproached ..., the researchers were disgraced and their research findings were **_fabricated_**.

Step 10 CHOOSE an answer

Reading it in context, (B) still sounds good. **Disgraced** *is a good match for* **discredited**, *but* **fabricated** *makes less sense. It would make sense if their research was fabricated and that led to the researcher's disgrace, but the causality is switched here. Because they were disgraced, that would not lead to their results being fabricated.* **I'm crossing this off and going with (B), which is the correct answer.**

Double-blank Questions

The procedure is essentially the same. You choose a blank to work with, whichever seems easier to you, and you follow the same process of elimination. Going one blank at a time really simplifies the process.

E Although some believe bears to be innately -----, most bear species are actually ----- creatures; they are extremely cautious, easily startled, and avoid conflict whenever possible.

(A) aggressive . . timorous
(B) sympathetic . . enigmatic
(C) gregarious . . serene
(D) timid . . shy
(E) antagonistic . . belligerent

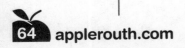

S Step 1 COVER the answers

Although some believe bears to be innately -----, most bear species are actually ----- creatures; they are extremely cautious, easily startled, and avoid conflict whenever possible.

(A)
(B)
(C)
(D)
(E)

Step 2 Read the sentence CRITICALLY

Step 3 Circle the LOGIC clues

(Although) some believe bears to be innately -----, most bear species

are (actually) ----- creatures (;) they are extremely cautious, easily

startled, and avoid conflict whenever possible.

Words like **although** *and* **actually** *provide insight into the logic and structure of this sentence. The pair "Although ..., actually..." tells us that the sentence is going to switch directions (although this, actually that). Additionally, the* **semi-colon** *preceded by a blank tells us that we are working with a Definition for our 2nd blank: the content after the semi-colon informs the blank.*

Step 4 Underline the KEY CONTENT clues that inform the blank

(Although) some believe bears to be innately -----, most bear species

are (actually) ----- creatures (;) they are <u>extremely cautious</u>, <u>easily</u>

<u>startled</u>, and <u>avoid conflict</u> whenever possible.

Step 5 Draw an arrow from the KEY CONTENT clues to the blank

S

Although some believe bears to be innately -----,

most bear species are actually ----- creatures ; they are

extremely cautious, easily startled, and avoid conflict whenever

possible.

Step 6   Make your own PREDICTION

We underlined: **cautious**, **easily startled** *and* **avoid conflict**.
A good guess would be **scared** *or* **shy**.

Step 7   Compare your word with the answer choices, looking only at the blank in question

Let's go through the answer choices and eliminate wrong answers.

~ (A) . . timorous — *Looks like* **timid** – *keep it for now.*
~ (B) . . enigmatic — *Hmm... this does not mean* **scared** *or* **shy**—*cross it off.*
~ (C) . . serene — *This could work– leave it for now.*
~ (D) . . shy — *Definitely keep this one.*
~ (E) . . belligerent — *I'm not sure what this means – squiggle.*

Step 8   Repeat the process with the remaining blank

Although some believe bears to be innately -----, most bear species

are actually ----- creatures ; they are extremely cautious, easily

startled, and avoid conflict whenever possible.

The **although/actually** *combo tells us that we are working with an antonym, a flip. So the opposite of* **scared** *or* **shy** *would be something like* **bold**. *Let's see how that works.*

S

~ (A) aggressive . . — *This goes with **bold**.*
~ (C) gregarious . . — *I don't know this one; squiggle it.*
(D̸) timid . . — *This does not go with **bold**. Cross it off.*
~ (E) antagonistic . . — *This could go with **bold**.*

Let's see what we have left.

<u>bold</u>   <u>scared or shy</u>

~ (A) aggressive . . timorous
~ (C) gregarious . . serene
~ (E) antagonistic . . belligerent

Step 9   PLUG the remaining choices into the sentence

(A) Although some believe bears to be **<u>aggressive</u>**, … [they] are actually **<u>timorous</u>**

(B) Although some believe bears to be **<u>gregarious</u>**, … [they] are actually **<u>serene</u>**

(C) Although some believe bears to be **<u>antagonistic</u>**, … [they] are actually **<u>belligerent</u>**

Now you need to listen to your inner voice: which sounds right? If something sounds wrong to your ear, cross it off. Or, if you can eliminate a choice using word associations or vocabulary roots, that is perfect, too.

*For now we are confident about both words in (A) and the sentence makes sense, but we are uncertain about **gregarious** in (B) and **belligerent** in (C).*

Whenever you find an answer that works, go with that answer. Let's guess (A).

Step 10   CHOOSE an answer

(A) *is our answer.* **Timorous**, *just as it sounds, means fearful.* **Gregarious**, *it turns out, does not mean bold; it means social.* **Belligerent**, *rather than meaning* **shy**, *has it's roots in bellum, war.* **Belligerent** *means inclined toward aggression and war.*

Some people with less confidence in their vocabulary second-guess themselves and assume that the correct answer is more likely to contain a word they do **NOT** know. This is not the case! Never throw away an answer choice that works in favor of an answer choice that has words you don't know.

Easier questions tend to have easier answers; harder questions tend to have harder answers.

Difficulty Level of Vocabulary on Sentence Completions

In general, the more advanced sentence completions, which appear later in the section, tend to have harder vocabulary. Therefore it is important to be aware of where you are in the section. If you are working on the first problem of a SC section, the answer will generally be an easier word. Likewise, if you are working on the final problem of a SC section, the answer will generally be a harder word.

The only exception occurs on some higher level SCs where the sentence itself is so confusing and filled with difficult vocabulary that the answer choices are at a lower vocabulary level.

How to Solve Sentence Completions

Step 1	COVER the answer choices
Step 2	Read the sentence CRITICALLY
Step 3	Circle the LOGIC clues
Step 4	Underline the KEY CONTENT clues that inform the blank
Step 5	Draw an arrow from the KEY CONTENT clues to the blank
Step 6	Make your own PREDICTION
Step 7	COMPARE your word with the answer choices
Step 8	ANALYZE the vocabulary of the remaining choices
Step 9	PLUG the remaining choices into the sentence
Step 10	CHOOSE an answer

Sentence Completions Practice Problems

Choose the answer that best completes the sentence.

1. Despite the great leaps in technology over the past 100 years, the ----- methods of scientific experimentation have largely remained -----.

   (A) fundamental . . constant
   (B) elemental . . ambiguous
   (C) innovative . . unchanged
   (D) worldly . . consistent
   (E) traditional . . mutable

2. Norman Rockwell's sentimental illustrations of simpler times often evoke feelings of ----- in viewers.

   (A) despair   (B) mirth   (C) nostalgia
      (D) reproach   (E) sympathy

3. Omar's indifferent and wearied attitude toward the world led people to believe he was -----.

   (A) empathetic   (B) resolute   (C) objective
      (D) distraught   (E) jaded

4. The opera's ----- plot made it difficult not only to follow the story line but also to ----- the heroine's fate.

   (A) inconsequential . . predict
   (B) convoluted . . anticipate
   (C) unpredictable . . defend
   (D) romantic . . justify
   (E) inspiring . . accept

5. Dr. Maria Montessori challenged traditional educational practices with ----- approach to teaching, which differed greatly from more ----- methods.

   (A) an avant-garde . . circuitous
   (B) a passive . . sanctioned
   (C) a novel . . orthodox
   (D) an informal . . conventional
   (E) an anecdotal . . tedious

6. Many of Blanca's professors described her as -----, for she often offered insightful and perceptive observations during class.

   (A) placid   (B) cantankerous   (C) elitist
      (D) bombastic   (E) astute

7. Uncharacteristically ----- in his last article, the editorialist's writing is usually much more benign.

   (A) timorous   (B) caustic   (C) prudent
      (D) stoic   (E) banal

8. Although many people fear that Marco is ----- because of his tall, muscular frame and numerous tattoos, he is actually very polite and a little timid.

   (A) insidious   (B) apathetic   (C) amicable
      (D) belligerent   (E) incorrigible

9. Often thought of as having extravagant and ----- tastes, Hazel surprised her family with her ----- furnished apartment.

   (A) grandiose . . meagerly
   (B) gaudy . . regally
   (C) pedestrian . . minimally
   (D) prosaic . . selectively
   (E) eccentric . . sparsely

10. Many reports of extra-terrestrial contact are ----- when witnesses' accounts cannot be ----- with hard, empirical evidence.

   (A) disparaged . . insinuated
   (B) debunked . . substantiated
   (C) vindicated . . corroborated
   (D) impugned . . lampooned
   (E) understated . . erradicated

11. South African novelist Mary Faulkner is considered by the *Guinness Book of World Records* to be the world's most ----- author, having written more than 900 books in her lifetime.

   (A) prolific   (B) frivolous   (C) mundane
     (D) vivid   (E) subversive

12. Saxophonist Paul Winter was awarded the Courage of Conscience Award for his works ----- instrumental music with the sounds of wild animals, creating pieces that celebrate the harmony of nature.

   (A) undermining   (B) marring   (C) diffusing
     (D) synthesizing   (E) trivializing

13. Although he is now celebrated as one of the most ----- artists of the early 20th century, Norwegian painter Edvard Munch suffered frequent deep crises of self-doubt during his lifetime.

   (A) illustrious   (B) loquacious   (C) foppish
     (D) capricious   (E) innocuous

14. The senator's ----- campaign strategy proved particularly astute when he was elected by a landslide.

   (A) puerile   (B) shrewd   (C) callous
     (D) divisive   (E) felicitous

15. A particular dietary supplement that ----- its success as an energy enhancer has actually caused feelings of ----- in many users.

   (A) advertises . . vivacity
   (B) insinuates . . narcissism
   (C) belies . . indolence
   (D) touts . . lethargy
   (E) mandates . . torpor

16. As one would imagine, the flamboyant pop-star loved ----- fashions and ornate jewelry.

   (A) tawdry   (B) haughty   (C) ostentatious
     (D) meticulous   (E) gratuitous

17. Once admired for its ----- treatment of a controversial subject, James Frey's book, *A Million Little Pieces*, has now been discredited as nothing more than a ----- tale masquerading as a memoir.

(A) forthright . . cerebral
(B) frank . . guileless
(C) auspicious . . specious
(D) inept . . fallacious
(E) candid . . spurious

18. Goethe's contemplative poetry, shrouded in mystery, attempts to describe the ----- nature of existence, which escapes description.

(A) sullen　(B) ineffable　(C) obtuse
　(D) visceral　(E) tedious

19. Because it is so ----- and ------, many people overlook the nutritive value and cultural significance of bread, a food staple that is virtually indispensable to everyday meals.

(A) pervasive . . pretentious
(B) ubiquitous . . mundane
(C) lauded . . pedestrian
(D) elusive . . enervating
(E) commonplace . . obsequious

20. Considered rudimentary by some, the comprehensive book compensates for its ----- of deep analysis with its ----- details.

(A) abundance . . extensive
(B) dearth . . compendious
(C) surfeit . . compelling
(D) lack . . biased
(E) integration . . technical

Answers on page 199.

Reading Comprehension

The SAT puts more emphasis on reading comprehension than on any other skill. 48 of 67 Critical Reading questions are reading comprehension questions. Reading comprehension will determine nearly 70% of your CR score. In order to raise your SAT score, you must invest significant time and energy into sharpening your SAT reading skills.

To begin, you will need to develop a new approach to reading for the SAT. Most of you have read books for summer reading assignments, books for your English classes and passages on English or History tests. These activities will help you develop general reading skills, but none of these activities will adequately prepare you for success on the SAT. When you are ready to tackle the SAT reading comprehension passages, you must discard many of the techniques that work for you in your classes. The SAT requires a different approach, a different level of focus and concentration.

Frequently students who are good readers, good thinkers and successful students need to undergo a process of "unlearning" the strategies that work for them in high school, especially if those students are creative thinkers. Reading comprehension on the SAT does not reward creativity; it penalizes it. The SAT rewards incredible focus: the ability to zero in on particular words, find synonyms for those words and suppress your instinct to come up with creative answers. In general, the less you think, the fewer connections you create and the more you are able to hone in on particular words, the better you will do on the SAT.

The Structure

The Critical Reading Section has five types of passages: short, short comparison, medium, medium comparison and long. Here is a breakdown:

Passage Type	# of lines	# of questions
Short*	9 – 14	2 (each)
Short Comparison	25 – 30	4
Medium*	45 – 70	5 – 9
Medium Comparison	65 – 100	12 – 13 (for the pair)
Long	65 – 90	12 – 13

* always come in pairs

The Format

The format of the Critical Reading Section is relatively consistent. The SAT will mix and match formats but will always contain two 25-minute sections containing 24 questions each and one 20-minute section with 19 questions.

Example Test Format 1

First Section: 25 minutes	Sentence Completions: 8	Short Comparison: 4	Long: 12	Total: 24 questions
Second Section: 25 minutes	Sentence Completions: 5	2 Short Passages: 4	2 Medium Passages: 15	Total: 24 questions
Third Section: 20 minutes	Sentence Completions: 6	Medium Comparison: 13		Total: 19 questions
Total Time: 1 hr 10 minutes	**Sentence Completions: 19**	**Reading Comprehension: 48**		**Total: 67 questions**

Example Test Format 2

First Section: 25 minutes	Sentence Completions: 5	2 Short Passages: 4	2 Medium Passages: 15	Total: 24 questions
Second Section: 25 minutes	Sentence Completions: 8	Short Comparison: 4	Medium Comparison: 12	Total: 24 questions
Third Section: 20 minutes	Sentence Completions: 6	Long: 13		Total: 19 questions
Total Time: 1 hr 10 minutes	**Sentence Completions: 19**	**Reading Comprehension: 48**		**Total: 67 questions**

Active Reading

Reading for the Reading Comprehension section of the SAT is unlike any other kind of reading you will do in your life. Reading for the SAT requires a unique strategy.

The Hunt

Reading on the SAT is not a passive activity. It requires a much deeper level of concentration and focus than do other forms of reading. To master the SAT Reading Comprehension passages, you must become a hunter. You will need to:

- Become alert for subtle shifts or transitions in the text.
- Narrow your focus to the words on the page, forgetting everything else.
- Track the author and try to understand her every move. What is she trying to achieve? What's her point? How is she building her argument?
- Actively translate the author's words into your own words and constantly check your understanding as you go.

Reading with Your Pencil

As you make your way through a passage, your pencil should be marking up and dissecting the passage. You will eventually need to refer back to the passage when answering specific questions, and it will be so much easier if you have already underlined the important information. When you finish actively reading an SAT passage, your tracks will be everywhere: words will be circled, starred, and underlined; arrows will be drawn showing connections between sections.

The Cure for Boredom

If you are approaching a passage actively, like a hunter, it is next to impossible to become bored or lose your focus. More likely you will break into a sweat from all the concentration, or your hand may cramp from so much underlining and circling!

The Art of Active Reading

Most students do not naturally read like this, and they must learn the art of Active Reading.

1 Underline Key Ideas

If you are actively reading on the SAT, your hand is moving. You are searching for key words and concepts to underline as you seek out the underlying meaning of the passage. Underlining is a process of discrimination; it is analysis in action. Most information in a passage plays only a supporting role, and some is simply there to distract you. You only need to underline content that conveys the main points and key ideas of the author. In general, you will underline roughly 20-30% of the words in a passage.

Don't fall into the trap of underlining everything. If you do that, you will have made no progress distinguishing truly important information from distracting information.

2 Circle Logic Words

Many authors will signal their main point is coming by using a logic word. Words like **but**, **however**, **although**, **despite** let you know that an author is about to tell you what he or she really thinks. Many passages completely shift direction and turn on a **however** or a **but**. When you see logic words like these, circle them, for they reveal that the passage is pivoting and a main point is imminent.

3 Star Main Ideas

When the author lays out the essence of the argument, put a star (★) next to it. When you read back over the passage, this ★ will be your guide and will let you know the point the author is trying to convey.

4 Use Notations to Summarize Main Ideas

When you come across the main point of a passage, translate it into your own words and write a brief summary statement of 10 words or less in the margin. Main idea notations can help you quickly answer author's intent and primary purpose questions.

Now that you are familiar with the art of Active Reading, let's see it in action.

E **Passage 1**

It is highly doubtful that the Allied forces would have won World War II without the help of Polish mathematician Marian Rejewski. At age fourteen, Rejewski enrolled in a secret cryptology* course for German speakers. Soon his full-time occupation was decoding the German *Enigma* machine. Combining his usage of pure mathematics with information provided by French intelligence, Rejewski succeeded in decoding the *Enigma,* and consequently, the Allied forces were able to intercept German intelligence transmissions for six years. Historian David Kahn says that Rejewski's stunning achievement "elevates him to the pantheon of the greatest cryptanalysts of all time." On the 100th anniversary of his birthday, a sculpted memorial was presented to his hometown of Bydgoszcz, Poland.

The study of secret writing, codes and cipher systems.

S **Passage 1**

★ It is highly <u>doubtful</u> that the <u>Allied forces</u> would have <u>won World War II without</u> the help of Polish <u>mathematician Marian Rejewski</u>. At age <u>fourteen,</u> <u>Rejewski</u> enrolled in a <u>secret cryptology* course</u> for <u>German speakers</u>. Soon his full-time occupation was <u>decoding</u> the <u>German *Enigma* machine</u>. Combining his usage of pure <u>mathematics</u> with information provided by <u>French</u> <u>intelligence,</u> Rejewski succeeded in <u>decoding the *Enigma,*</u> and consequently, the <u>Allied forces</u> were able to <u>intercept German intelligence</u> transmissions for six years. Historian David Kahn says that <u>Rejewski's stunning achievement</u>

★ "elevates him to the pantheon of the <u>greatest cryptanalysts</u> of all time." On the 100th anniversary of his birthday, a sculpted <u>memorial</u> was presented to his hometown of Bydgoszcz, Poland.

Polish kid greatest cryptologist— helped win war, memorial

Let's see what we underlined:
38 words out of 116 words: **roughly 32% of the original passage.**
If we strip away all the supporting text, we are left with:

doubtful —Allied forces —won World War II without—mathematician Marian Rejewski—fourteen—secret cryptology course—German speakers— decoding—German *Enigma* machine—mathematics—French intelligence— decoding the *Enigma*—Allied forces—intercept German intelligence— Rejewski's stunning achievement—greatest cryptanalysts—memorial

That pretty much sums it up. The remaining 78 words primarily provide support, but the content we underlined provides the essence of the argument/narrative. Notice that we starred two phrases that conveyed the author's main ideas—in the passage's beginning and end, popular places for main points:

> **It is highly doubtful that the Allied forces would have won World War II without the help of Polish mathematician Marian Rejewski.**
>
> **Historian David Kahn says that Rejewski's stunning achievement "elevates him to the pantheon of the greatest cryptanalysts of all time."**

These two sentences summarize the point of the passage; all the other sentences support the points made in these sentences.

Did you notice our notation:

> *Polish kid greatest cryptologist—helped win war, memorial*

These 8 words help summarize the main point of the passage in our words. If we are asked for the main point of the passage, we have already found it and can quickly search for an answer similar to this among the answer choices.

We did not have any key logic words to circle in this passage.

Does this seem helpful? Do you have a better sense of what the author is trying to do when you are actively working with the material, trying to order it, organize it, prioritize the information and understand it? Most students find this process helpful, especially when they go to tackle the questions.

Now it's your turn to flex your newly-found Active Reading muscles.

E **Passage 2**

Coleman Hawkins, one of the first great saxophonists of the Harlem Renaissance, was a consistently modern improviser who possessed an encyclopedic knowledge of music. Hawkins was a giant of the jazz scene for over 40 years. His musical odyssey began in front of the keys of a piano at the age of five; he moved on to the cello before settling on the tenor saxophone. In the 1920s and 30s, the saxophone was primarily considered a novelty instrument used in marching bands. However, Hawkins saw a greater potential for this instrument. His lyrical tones and innovative style helped usher in a new age of avant-garde jazz known as Bebop and placed the saxophone at the center of the new jazz aesthetic. Succeeding generations of saxophonists, whose members included Sonny Rollins, Lester Young and John Coltrane, acknowledged the profound influence that "Hawk" had on their musical styles.

S **Passage 2**

Coleman Hawkins, one of the first great saxophonists of the Harlem Renaissance, was a consistently modern improviser who possessed an encyclopedic knowledge of music. Hawkins was a giant of the jazz scene for over 40 years. His musical odyssey began in front of the keys of a piano at the age of five; he moved on to the cello before settling on the tenor saxophone. In the 1920s and 30s, the saxophone was primarily considered a novelty instrument used in marching bands. (However,) Hawkins saw a greater potential for this instrument. His lyrical tones and innovative style helped usher in a new age of avant-garde jazz known as Bebop and placed the saxophone at the center of the new jazz ★ aesthetic. Succeeding generations of saxophonists, whose members included Sonny Rollins, Lester Young and John Coltrane, acknowledged the profound influence that "Hawk" had on their musical styles.

Hawkins Jazz great, Saxophone innovator, influential

How did you do? Did you catch the transition signaled by the word *However*? Most main ideas follow those logic word lead-ins.

Below is another passage for you to practice on.

E **Passage 3**

Walter Alvarez, the fourth in a line of eminent and successful scientists, was practically destined for distinction in the world of science. Even with his prominent pedigree, no one could have predicted the magnitude of his contributions to the study of dinosaurs. Alvarez ventured into the field of geology and discovered a significant amount of iridium in the layer of the Earth's crust containing the last fossil remains of many dinosaur species. Because iridium commonly appears in asteroids, Alvarez concluded that an asteroid must have driven the dinosaurs to extinction. His theory is now the most widely-believed answer to the most widespread of questions: what killed the dinosaurs?

The Importance of Practice

This process will naturally slow you down in the beginning. But the more you practice, the faster you will eventually become. Even if you slow down some while you are reading the passages, you will be able to eventually move through the questions at a much quicker pace. When you read actively for deeper comprehension, you won't need to go back and forth so frequently between the questions and the passage.

Attacking Questions

When forming any type of attack, it is necessary to form your strategy from a strong foundation. Below is a short, but valuable, list of general principles to keep in mind when approaching SAT Reading Comprehension questions.

1 Forget what you already know

When you read for the SAT, you have to become a blank slate. You must forget everything that you know about a given subject. Any outside knowledge you bring to the test has the potential to hurt you and lower your score. Outside knowledge may lead you to make conclusions that cannot be directly supported by the text provided. And all that matters is the provided text. Focus your attention exclusively on the words provided.

2 Turn off your brain

Many of our brightest students, the 4.0 GPA, 5's on AP exams students, struggle with their over-active brains. On SAT Reading Comprehension, the more you think, the lower you will score. This may seem counter-intuitive, but it's the over-thinkers who start creating connections and using logic to come up with conclusions not directly supported by the passage. When students use any of the following words to justify an answer choice, they are in trouble:

May
Might
Could
Potentially
It's possible that
I see how that could work
Hmm, that kind of makes sense

These words and phrases indicate that our students are on the slippery slope of independent thought and are moving rapidly toward an SAT trap and a wrong answer.

3 Use notations to summarize main ideas

The College Board writers will set up numerous traps for you in the answer choices. The only way to avoid the well-laid College Board traps is to take the time to think for yourself and answer the question BEFORE you look at the answer choices. Covering the answer choices, craft a reasoned answer to the question, in your own words.

If you create your own answer first, you will be much less tempted by the assumption/familiarity traps, and you will be more likely to rely on your own logic and judgment to arrive at the correct answer.

These traps are designed to lure you toward assumptions that may sound rational but are unsupported by the passage. Other well-laid traps may include familiar words directly taken from the passage but used in such a way as to distort the meaning of the passage. If you are in a hurry, you may be so drawn to the familiar language ("Oh, I think I saw that word/phrase!") that you will ignore the distorting information. The writers are counting on this: they know that if you are moving too quickly and are trying to make a fast decision, the familiar information will be enough to pull you toward a wrong answer.

Identifying Wrong Answers

Now that you know how to read actively, we are going to let you in on a little secret. Don't try too hard to figure out which answer choice is RIGHT. Instead, focus on which answer choices are WRONG. As backward as it may sound, this is the key to a high Critical Reading score. If you can eliminate the wrong answers, you will be left with the correct answer.

Throw-aways

Pay attention: This is the most important concept in the CR section of this book. The writers at the College Board are masters at fabricating well-crafted wrong answers that will ensnare many hurried students. The essence of a wrong answer lies in a tiny word or series of words that cannot be supported by evidence from the passage. These words or phrases that have nothing to do with the passage are called throw-aways.

On the SAT, wrong answers look suspiciously like right answers except for at least one small throw-away, which is often overlooked. In EVERY wrong answer choice, expect a string of good sounding words—many taken directly from the passage—and one critical little word or phrase that invalidates the entire answer choice. SAT writers will expect you to be mesmerized by all of the correct sounding words in an answer choice: "Wow, this sounds perfect!" While your guard is down, ever so gently, the writers will sneak in a throw-away. To avoid these well-laid traps, you must be on high alert and actively scanning, like a hunter, for the tiny throw-away. Narrowing down your focus to a single word will allow you to zero in on right and wrong answers.

Reading for throw-aways will save you time

Reading this way will eventually save you a lot of time on the SAT. The instant you see a completely foreign or unsupported word in an answer choice, you can eliminate that answer choice without reading any further.

Learning to think like the SAT writers

After a little practice, you will begin to understand how the SAT writers craft wrong answers. Eventually you may even be able to anticipate the kind of wrong answers to expect. Once you can anticipate the types of assumptions students naturally make, you will be one step ahead of the writers and on your way to a much higher CR score.

In the following examples we will dissect all the answer choices and point out the throw-aways.

 **Passage 1**

It is highly doubtful that the Allied forces would have won World War II without the help of Polish mathematician Marian Rejewski. At age fourteen, Rejewski enrolled in a secret cryptology course for German speakers. Soon his full-time occupation was decoding the German *Enigma* machine. Combining his usage of
5 pure mathematics with information provided by French intelligence, Rejewski succeeded in decoding the *Enigma,* and consequently, the Allied forces were able to intercept German intelligence transmissions for six years. Historian David Kahn says that Rejewski's stunning achievement "elevates him to the pantheon of the greatest cryptanalysts of all time." On the 100th anniversary of his birth-
10 day, a sculpted memorial was presented to his hometown of Bydgoszcz, Poland.

1. The author most likely mentions historian David Kahn (lines 7–8) in order to

   (A) introduce a lighthearted digression
   (B) offer evidence to support a prior claim
   (C) offer an anecdote revealing the flaw in a popular misconception
   (D) suggest the value perceived in a historical event
   (E) suggest the origins of a branch of mathematics

2. The primary purpose of the passage is to

   (A) explain how the *Enigma* machine was decoded
   (B) emphasize Poland's role in the Allied forces' victory
   (C) illustrate the principles of cryptology
   (D) highlight the contribution of a noted mathematician to the war effort
   (E) provide insight into the motivations of a renowned cryptanalyst

S   1.   The author most likely mentions historian David Kahn (lines 7–8) in order to

(A) introduce a lighthearted digression

Lighthearted? Are you laughing? Are we digressing? Have we changed topics, or is this essential to our passage? Both of these are throw-aways.

(B) offer evidence to support a prior claim

Evidence? What evidence is Kahn bringing to the table? He's simply saying the event was important; this is not new evidence. That's our primary throw-away.

(C) offer an anecdote revealing the flaw in a popular misconception

What part of this answer is not wrong? Anecdote? Flaw? Misconception? All of these are clear throw-aways. But it sure is confusing when you see all these words together. Remember; take it one word at a time.

(D) suggest the value perceived in a historical event

Nothing outlandish here.

(E) suggest the origins of a branch of mathematics

Does this passage suggest that decoding was the original invention of Rejewski? The passage never mentions that decoding the Enigma was the origin of a branch of mathematics. This is our throw-away.

(D)

2.   The primary purpose of the passage is to

(A) explain how the *Enigma* machine was decoded

Is the primary purpose really about explaining how Rejewski decoded the machine? Do you see an explanation? The word "how" is the throw-away.

(B) emphasize Poland's role in the Allied forces' victory

Does this passage have anything to do with Poland's contribution to the war effort? Or is it just about a mathematician from Poland? Poland is the throw-away.

(C) illustrate the principles of cryptology

Does this paragraph give us any clue about the guiding principles of cryptology? Nope. This is just a fancy-sounding throw-away.

(D) highlight the contribution of a noted mathematician to the war effort

Nothing glaringly wrong with this answer; let's move on.

(E) provide insight into the motivations of a renowned cryptanalyst

Do we have any notion of the motivations of Rejewski? We know what he did but not why he did it. So motivations is our throw-away.

(D)

E **Passage 2**

Coleman Hawkins, one of the first great saxophonists of the Harlem Renaissance, was a consistently modern improviser who possessed an encyclopedic knowledge of music. Hawkins was a giant of the jazz scene for over 40 years. His musical odyssey began in front of the keys of a piano at the age of five; he moved on to the cello before settling on the tenor saxo-
5   phone. In the 1920s and 30s, the saxophone was primarily considered a novelty instrument used in marching bands. However, Hawkins saw a greater potential for this instrument. His lyrical tones and innovative style helped usher in a new age of avant-garde jazz known as Bebop and placed the saxophone at the center of the new jazz aesthetic. Succeeding gen-erations of saxophonists, whose members included Sonny Rollins, Lester Young and John
10 Coltrane, acknowledged the profound influence that "Hawk" had on their musical styles.

3. The passage supports which of the following statements about Hawkins?

(A) He broke new ground for saxophonists everywhere.
(B) His innovative lyrics helped usher in a new musical era.
(C) His music earned him international acclaim for many decades.
(D) His modernist style alienated more traditional musicians.
(E) His eccentric instrumentalism defined the Harlem Renaissance.

4. The author references Hawkins' "odyssey" (line 3) in order to

(A) enumerate the steps he took toward becoming an influential jazz artist
(B) suggest the many challenges he faced in his musical training
(C) convey an appreciation for an artist's journey toward self-expression
(D) illustrate the depth and duration of his musical training
(E) reveal that Hawkins was not initially drawn to the saxophone

S 3. The passage supports which of the following statements about Hawkins?

(A) He broke new ground for saxophonists everywhere.
Nothing sticking out here.

(B) His innovative ⎡lyrics⎤ helped usher in a new musical era.
Innovative, you betcha. New musical era. Right on. Lyrics! He played the saxophone. Singing while playing the sax is a feat achieved by few musicians. Lyrics is a clear throw-away in an otherwise perfect answer.

(C) His music earned him ⎡international⎤ acclaim for many decades.
Famous, yes. International? We don't know. It's not mentioned in the passage. Watch your assumptions!

(D) His modernist style ⎡alienated⎤ more traditional musicians.
The passage never mentions the reaction of traditional musicians. For all we know they were huge fans!

(E) His ⎡eccentric⎤ instrumentalism ⎡defined⎤ the Harlem Renaissance.
Yes, he was a great musician during the Harlem Renaissance. Did the passage suggest that he had anything to do with defining that era? And eccentric? Did you read that? Two strong throw-aways.

(A)

4. The author references Hawkins' "odyssey" (line 3) in order to

(A) enumerate the steps he took toward becoming an influential jazz artist

Are we counting steps and numbering them? We never saw that.

(B) suggest the many challenges he faced in his musical training

Challenges? Really? Didn't see anything about a challenge. He seemed like a natural.

(C) convey an appreciation for an artist's journey toward self-expression

Haha! Love that one. Self-expression? Appreciation of the journey? Assumption anyone?

(D) illustrate the depth and duration of his musical training

Remind me, how long did it take him to learn to play the saxophone? Hmmm.... The passage doesn't tell us. We'll have to fill this in with our imaginations.

(E) reveal that Hawkins was not initially drawn to the saxophone

They did say that—piano then cello. Nothing wrong here.

(E)

 Passage 3

Walter Alvarez, the fourth in a line of eminent and successful scientists, was practically destined for distinction in the world of science. Even with his pedigree, no one could have predicted the magnitude of his contributions to the study of dinosaurs. Alvarez ventured into the field of geology and discovered a significant amount of iridium in
5 the layer of the Earth's crust containing the last fossilized remains of many dinosaur species. Because iridium commonly appears in asteroids, Alvarez concluded that an asteroid must have driven the dinosaurs to extinction. His theory is now the most widely-believed answer to the most widespread of questions: what killed the dinosaurs?

5. The author primarily references Alvarez's "pedigree" (line 2) in order to

(A) illustrate the level of fame attained by prominent scientists
(B) explain his early interest in the study of dinosaurs
(C) suggest his tendency toward progressive ideas
(D) show that he was entrenched in the scientific theories of the day
(E) imply that Alvarez was almost certain to achieve scientific renown

6. The statement in lines 7–8 ("His... dinosaurs?") serves primarily to underscore the

(A) scientific foundation of a hypothesis
(B) popular appeal of a theory
(C) impressionability of the public
(D) the general public's fascination with dinosaurs
(E) the level of celebrity achieved by scientists

S 5. The author primarily references Alvarez's "pedigree" (line 2) in order to

(A) illustrate the level of fame attained by prominent scientists

(B) explain his early interest in the study of dinosaurs

(C) suggest his tendency toward progressive ideas

(D) show that he was entrenched in the scientific theories of the day

(E) imply that Alvarez was almost certain to achieve scientific renown

(E)

6. The statement in lines 7-8 ("His...dinosaurs?") serves primarily to underscore the

(A) scientific foundation of a hypothesis

(B) popular appeal of a theory

(C) impressionability of the public

(D) the general public's fascination with dinosaurs

(E) the level of celebrity achieved by scientists

(B)

E Passage 4

Whether as an African-American child in the segregated South or as a young single mother, Maya Angelou never failed to transcend her surroundings. A gifted artist, Angelou has achieved worldwide recognition as an author, poet, playwright, professional stage and screen producer, director, performer and singer. Sidonie Ann Smith of
5 *Southern Humanities Review* attributes Angelou's acclaim to "her ability to recapture the texture of the way of life in the texture of its idioms, its idiosyncratic vocabulary and especially its process of image-making." The same indomitable spirit that helped her overcome early challenges allowed Angelou to succeed in the literary world, becoming the second poet ever invited to speak at a Presidential inauguration.

7. The author most likely refers to events in Angelou's early life (lines 1–2) in order to

(A) indicate the specific hardships African Americans faced in the South

(B) provide insight into the source of Angelou's artistic brilliance

(C) highlight some of the struggles Angelou has had to overcome

(D) account for her international literary appeal

(E) give historical background for the content of Angelou's art

8. The primary purpose of the quotation in lines (5–7) is to

(A) explain the appeal of Angelou's early work

(B) critically evaluate Angelou's work

(C) evoke sympathy for Angelou's hardships

(D) illustrate how Angelou's early life influenced her writing

(E) reinforce Angelou's impact on African-American literature

S 7. The author most likely refers to events in Angelou's early life (lines 1–2) in order to

(A) indicate the specific hardships African Americans faced in the South

(B) provide insight into the source of Angelou's artistic brilliance

(C) highlight some of the struggles Angelou has had to overcome

(D) account for her international literary appeal

(E) give historical background for the content of Angelou's art

(C)

8. The primary purpose of the quotation in lines (5–7) is to

(A) explain the appeal of Angelou's early work

(B) critically evaluate Angelou's work

(C) evoke sympathy for Angelou's hardships

(D) illustrate how Angelou's early life influenced her writing

(E) reinforce Angelou's impact on African-American literature

(B)

The Usual Suspects:

Identifying wrong answer types

Now that you know how to identify and eliminate throw-aways in answer choices, we are going to introduce you to some common answer types that are usually wrong: the Brain, the General and the Money Grubber. They may seem friendly and tempting to choose, but be wary. These common culprits try to distract you from your throw-away hunt and lead you down the wrong path.

THE BRAIN

THE GENERAL

MONEY GRUBBER

The Brain

The Brain is an answer choice that sounds smart, looks smart and can seem intimidating. The Brain wants you to second guess your own reasoning and trust something which looks smart on the surface, but is misleading and generally wrong. The Brain has two primary ways to confuse you:

1 Over-the-Top Vocabulary

2 Generally confusing language (AKA dropping a "Logic Bomb")

Let's examine these more carefully.

1 Over-the-Top Vocabulary

The Brain is a smart-sounding answer filled with smart-sounding words designed to confuse you. Many students will second guess themselves when they come across unfamiliar vocabulary. But it's important that you stick to your guns. Even when you come across a word you do not know, you still have other words in the context of the question and/or passage that will help you work out the general meaning of an answer choice.

Suppose you see the phrase "unmitigated greed" in an answer choice. What if you don't know what the word *unmitigated* means? Skip that word and focus on the word you do know. Does greed make sense in context? If greed doesn't fit, the answer choice is wrong, regardless of what *unmitigated* means. Remember to use all the clues at your disposal and work around the phrases or words that are confusing.

2 The Logic Bomb

Sometimes the Brain answer choice is utterly confusing; it is so perplexing that you have no idea how to read it, much less make meaning of it. This is called a Logic Bomb. If you finish reading an answer choice and are left scratching your head and asking, "What?", more than likely you've been hit with one of these precision instruments of confusion.

Logic Bomb examples

- Depict the ambiguous nature of truth conveyed through dubious third-person narrative

- An attempt to reconcile collective consciousness with individual perceptions

- Prescribe a course of action designed to insulate the members of a cohesive group

If you come across answer choices this confusing, more likely than not, the Brain is trying to lure you to select a wrong answer.

The General

The General loves to make far reaching statements that are way too broad and too general. The implied "All" or "Always" is the trademark of the General. You can recognize the General at work when you see extreme statements such as these:

- Epidemiologists have not made progress in addressing the primary threats to human health.
*Really? They have made **NO** progress? Not one iota of progress? A less extreme answer would be "these people have made little progress", or "few epidemiologists have made progress."*

- Filmmakers, like biographers, attempt to portray events realistically.
***EVERY** single filmmaker on the planet? Isn't this too broad?*

- address the inherent limitations of academic inquiry
*Is **ALL** academic inquiry inherently limited? Not a single exception?*

- The global ecosystem remains baffling to scientists
*Baffling to **ALL** scientists? Every last one of them? Unlikely. Too broad.*

• Scholarly criticism is irrelevant in a society obsessed with celebrity.
IRRELEVANT is an awfully strong word. "Less relevant"—certainly; has "decreased relevance"—that could be argued. But a blanket statement, an absolute statement such as this, is rarely correct.

• investigate the public's long-standing obsession with celebrity
Too broad and too extreme. Obsession is way strong, and is the ENTIRE PUBLIC obsessed? Be wary of Joe Public, he will lead you toward the path of a faulty generalization.

One final trademark of the General is making disparaging comments about large groups of people. The General will lump a bunch of people together and attack them in mass. This kind of judgment is rarely tolerated on the SAT. Here are a few negative comments directed at groups.

• Criticize the absence of analytical thinking among the general public

• Address the naiveté of the public in its selection of leaders

• A derisive commentary on the public's tendency toward believing spurious gossip

• Discuss the arrogant posture that many academics assume

All of these criticisms are directed at the public at large or at specific groups of people. This kind of broad criticism is the mark of the General.

The Money Grubber

A minor character, but one worth mentioning, the Money Grubber answer choice fixates on finance. Most SAT answers that revolve around money or financial motivations are wrong. Our society focuses a lot of energy and attention upon money, but the SAT rarely follows suit. So if the answer choice tries to pin a financial motive on a character, this should raise a red flag. Be wary of the Money Grubber!

Read the following passages and look for our Usual Suspects in the answer choices.

E **Passage 1**

In a species with a reputation for cunningly manipulating others to maximize personal gain, blushing is pretty difficult to explain. Why would humans evolve a response that puts us at a social disadvantage by forcing us to reveal that we have cheated or lied? It is a question that Charles Darwin struggled
5 with. He pointed out that while all people of all races blush, animals—other primates included—do not. When it came to explaining the evolution of "the most peculiar and the most human of all the expressions," he was at a loss. One suggestion is that blushing started out as a simple appeasement ritual: a way to show dominant members of the group that we submit to their authority.
10 Perhaps later, as our social interactions became increasingly complex, it became associated with higher, self-conscious emotions such as guilt, shame and embarrassment. This would seem to put individuals at a disadvantage, but blushing might actually make a person more attractive or socially desirable.

1. In line 7 the phrase "most human of all expressions" most directly suggests

   (A) humans are the only animals that cannot entirely conceal their emotions
   (B) blushing is considered to be an exclusively human trait
   (C) non-human species lack a developed sense of self-awareness
   (D) biologists have failed to find an evolutionary basis for blushing
   (E) scientists have been unable to determine why non-human animals
       do not blush

2. The final sentence in the passage primarily serves to

   (A) provide evidence to support a controversial theory
   (B) present a scholarly interpretation of an emotionally revealing behavior
   (C) suggest a potential benefit of a seemingly disadvantageous behavior
   (D) propose a novel hypothesis for the origin of self-conscious emotions
   (E) downplay an unpopular opinion held by evolutionary biologists

S 1. In line 7 the phrase "most human of all expressions" most directly suggests

(A) humans are the only animals that cannot [entirely] conceal their [emotions]

We have several clues that we are dealing with an overly General answer. The passage limited its scope to self-conscious emotions leading to blushing. It does not discuss all emotions such as fear, sadness, or joy. Additionally, the word entirely is too all-encompassing, another indication of the General.

(B) blushing is considered to be an exclusively human trait

This is a simple, inoffensive answer, drawn directly from the passage.

(C) non-human species lack a developed sense of [self-awareness]

What? You've just been hit by a LOGIC BOMB. What is a developed sense of self-awareness and where was this mentioned anywhere in our passage?

(D) biologists have failed to find an [evolutionary basis] for blushing

This sounds smart, especially the evolutionary basis. Additionally, this has nothing to do with our question! We are looking for why blushing is the most human. We are off topic.

(E) scientists have been unable to determine why [non-human animals do not blush]

This is a tricky answer; it reverses our logic. We are interested in why humans do blush, not why animals do not blush. This takes us away from our topic.

(B)

2. The final sentence in the passage primarily serves to

(A) provide [evidence] to support a [controversial] theory

Several things are wrong. Is the theory controversial? Do we know that? Worse than this is the word evidence. Now that's a throw-away! Does the last sentence really provide us with evidence? Nope. It is simply stating the hypothesis.

(B) present a scholarly [interpretation] of an emotionally revealing [behavior]

Sounds brilliant. They even mention a scholar. Very SAT-like. But it's wrong. The last sentence offers an interpretation of how people respond to blushing, but it certainly does not offer an interpretation of the behavior itself.

(C) suggest a potential benefit of a seemingly disadvantageous behavior

Nothing blatantly offensive here.

(D) propose a novel [hypothesis] for [the origin of self-conscious emotions]

A whole bag of wrong. Origin of self-conscious emotions? Sounds extremely smart and broad. This is the Brainy General. A double whammy.

(E) downplay an [unpopular opinion] held by [evolutionary biologists]

First, this is not an opinion, regardless of its level of popularity- which was not even mentioned. And is it really held by all evolutionary biologists? Is there agreement in the field or was this theory simply proposed? Major assumption and clearly incorrect.

(C)

E **Passage 2**

Like all minority communities, the Jews of Cairo faced a dilemma: how to affirm their ethnic identity in the context of their environment. They soon discovered the power of language as a vehicle for cultural expression. The Jews of Cairo voiced their identity with a distinct dialect of Arabic which came to be
5 known as Judeo-Arabic. Judeo-Arabic mirrored Cairo's dominant variety of Arabic, but incorporated words, expressions and syntax carried over from Hebrew. The result was a synthesis of languages—contemporary Arabic, biblical Hebrew, and a bit of the old Jewish vernacular, Aramaic—that reflected the community's synthesis of identities. Though the community has faded into the pages
10 of history, its voice endures. Scholars around the world devote their careers to meticulously combing through ancient Judeo-Arabic texts, exploring the legacy of this people and their language.

3. The phrase "language as a vehicle" (line 3) primarily suggests

   (A) all minority cultures find a means of self expression
   (B) dominant languages influence the expression of minority cultures
   (C) the importance of the vernacular in identity formation
   (D) the power of the spoken word over the written word to express cultural identity
   (E) culture can be effectively conveyed through linguistic means

4. The phrase "its voice endures" (line 10) primarily emphasizes the

   (A) continuing scholarly interest in cataloguing archaic languages
   (B) importance of oral history among minority groups
   (C) power of language to express a cultural identity long after that culture is gone
   (D) synthetic nature of linguistic evolution among ancient peoples
   (E) ability to transcend cultural barriers through shared languages

S 3. The phrase "language as a vehicle" (line 3) primarily suggests

(A) all minority cultures find a means of self expression

(B) dominant languages influence the expression of minority cultures

(C) the importance of the vernacular in identity formation

(D) the power of the spoken word over the written word to express cultural identity

(E) culture can be effectively conveyed through linguistic means

(E)

4. The phrase "its voice endures" (line 10) primarily emphasizes the

(A) continuing scholarly interest in cataloguing archaic languages

(B) importance of oral history among minority groups

(C) power of language to express a cultural identity long after that culture is gone

(D) synthetic nature of linguistic evolution among ancient peoples

(E) ability to transcend cultural barriers through shared languages

(C)

Identifying Correct Answers

Content in answer choices can generally be divided into 3 categories:

1 Throw-aways

2 Synonyms or verbatim words from the passage

3 Filler: supporting, helping words

To determine a correct answer, focus on **throw-aways** and **synonyms**. Don't worry so much about the filler.

All CORRECT ANSWERS

Lack throw-aways

This is essential. Using the process of elimination, you will be able to knock off every answer choice with a throw-away and narrow down your options.

Contain evidence

Evidence for an answer choice comes in 2 forms:
- words taken directly from the passage (verbatim words)
- synonyms of words taken directly from the passage

The most important thing of all is the throw-away. In general, most wrong answers will contain evidence (synonyms and verbatim words) taken directly from the passage. That's part of their appeal. Students who do not fully understand what they have read will choose something that looks familiar and ignore information that is unfamiliar.

The Great Synonym Hunt

In the event you have eliminated several answer choices and are left with more than one throw-away-free answer choice, you must look more closely and analytically at the remaining choices to determine which is best supported by the passage. You will need to do some hunting in the passage to see if you can make direct linear connections between content in the passage and content in the answer choice.

Show me the Evidence!

Reading Comprehension on the SAT is not primarily concerned with comprehension. Whether or not you fully comprehend the passage is not essential. What RC really tests is how adept you are at playing the game of Word Match or Synonym Hunt. Can you find the word or words in the passage that support the words in an answer choice?

Before you select an answer choice, you must ask yourself these questions:

Did I read that in the passage?

Can I prove this, or is it an assumption?

Can I find direct supporting evidence in the passage?

Can I locate the exact word or words that inform this answer choice?

If you cannot answer a resounding "Yes!" to these questions, there is a good chance the answer choice you are scrutinizing is incorrect. You should literally be able to draw a line connecting the content in the answer choice with the corresponding content in the passage.

The *LEAST* Wrong Answer

What if there is no clearly right answer?

Sometimes the College Board leaves you without a definitive right answer. If you find yourself in a situation where you have crossed off (A), (B), (C) and (D), be very careful not to force (E). Just because (A) through (D) are wrong does not mean that (E) is correct by default. (E) may be the worst answer choice of the five available to you. You must apply the same level of scrutiny to (E) that you applied to each answer before it.

Single cross

(A) Completely ridiculous answer
(B) Doesn't look right
(C) No, don't think so
(D) I don't like it
(E) Not a chance this could be the answer

If you have eliminated (A) through (E), it's time to go back through the choices again and do the **double cross**. On the second pass through the answer choices, put a second slash mark through answer choices that are clearly ridiculous:

Double cross

(A) Completely ridiculous answer
(B) Mostly wrong, don't love it
(C) Utterly, offensively wrong
~ (D) I don't like it, but maybe
(E) Not a chance this could be the answer

Once you go through this process, you will often be left with one or two unpleasant answer choices that are not great but are also not totally ridiculous. Of the remaining answers, you must choose the *LEAST Wrong* answer. Pick it. Then move on to the next question. It's important that you keep moving and don't get hung up on one little question. Remember, each question is only worth one 'raw score' point.

Practice drawing synonym chains in the following examples.

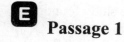 **Passage 1**

Although it is in our nature to be superstitious, cultural and environmental factors clearly influence how superstitious an individual actually
is. For example, when we feel we are losing control over our lives, we
tend to become more superstitious. One study found that people living
5 in high-risk areas of the Middle East, such as Tel Aviv, are much more
likely to carry a lucky charm than other people. Nobody is immune.
"We can all shift our supernatural inclination depending on the circumstances," says Bruce Hood, cognitive psychologist from the University of
Bristol.

1. The author supports his argument by

(A) quoting an authority with whom he or she disagrees
(B) presenting a personal anecdote
(C) exploring a controversial scientific theory
(D) presenting the findings of a study
(E) disproving an alternate hypothesis

2. The actions of the people in Tel-Aviv (lines 4-6) primarily suggest that

(A) certain groups of people are inherently superstitious
(B) environmental factors impact our level of superstitious behavior
(C) the collective power of superstition is reinforced by heightened
      anxiety
(D) people who feel disempowered rely more heavily on supernatural
      interventions
(E) individual superstitious behavior must be interpreted in relation to
      a larger group

Although it is in our nature to be superstitious, cultural and environmental factors clearly influence how superstitious an individual actually is. For example, when we feel we are losing control over our lives, we tend to become more superstitious. One study found that people living in high-risk areas of the Middle East, such as Tel Aviv, are much more likely to carry a lucky charm than other people. Nobody is immune. "We can all shift our supernatural inclination depending on the circumstances," says Bruce Hood, cognitive psychologist from the University of Bristol.

S 1. The author supports his argument by *synonym chain*

(A) quoting an authority with whom he or she disagrees
Quoting is directly supported, but there is no evidence for disagreement or agreement.

(B) presenting a personal anecdote
nothing personal, and there is no story or anecdote

(C) exploring a controversial scientific theory
no direct evidence for controversy or science

(D) presenting the findings of a study *synonym chain*
There is only evidence and no throw-aways. This must be our answer.

(E) disproving an alternate hypothesis
The author does not bring up any alternative explanation or hypothesis.

(D)

Passage 1

synonym chain

Although it is in our nature to be superstitious, cultural and environmental factors clearly influence how superstitious an individual actually is. For example, when we feel we are losing control over our lives, we tend to become more superstitious. One study found that people living in high-risk areas of the Middle East, such as Tel Aviv, are much more likely to carry a lucky charm than other people. Nobody is immune. "We can all shift our supernatural inclination depending on the circumstances," says Bruce Hood, cognitive psychologist from the University of Bristol.

synonym chain

synonym chain

 2. The actions of the people in Tel-Aviv (lines 4-6) primarily suggest that

(A) certain groups of people are inherently superstitious

The author writes that we are all superstitious by nature, not just certain groups.

(B) environmental factors impact our level of superstitious behavior

This is drawn directly from the passage.

(C) the collective power of superstition is reinforced by heightened anxiety

Several throw-aways here. No evidence of collective power, and we cannot assume that the people have a higher degree of anxiety.

(D) people who feel disempowered rely more heavily on supernatural interventions

There are several major unsupported assumptions. We do know that people wear more charms, but we do not know that 1) they feel disempowered or 2) they are relying on these interventions.

(E) individual superstitious behavior must be interpreted in relation to a larger group

We have a group, people in the Middle East, but there is no mention of an individual.

(B)

E **Passage 2**

At a time when natural resources such as oil, coal and natural gas are being depleted at an alarming rate, "alternative energy" seem to be the magic words at the tip of everyone's tongue. One of the most exciting proposals for generating renewable energy comes from an old idea: the solar updraft tower.
5 Conceived in 1903, the solar tower, designed like a giant chimney, draws heated air into openings at its base. Once inside the hollow tower, the heated air rises, accelerating to speeds of 35 mph. As the air rushes upward, dozens of wind turbines turn, generating electricity. A solar updraft tower as high as 1000 meters with a diameter as large as 7 kilometers could eventually power
10 as many as 200,000 typical households.

3. The phrase "magic words"(line 2) most directly emphasizes the

   (A) unsubstantiated belief in a proposed solution
   (B) inevitability of an ecological crisis
   (C) ability of language to capture the public's attention
   (D) the power of collective imagination
   (E) perceived appeal of a solution

4. The last sentence of the passage (lines 8-10) serves to

   (A) convey the importance of a problem
   (B) highlight the potential benefits of an invention
   (C) speculate about the likelihood of an outcome
   (D) defend a widely accepted practice
   (E) offer evidence in support of a prior claim

Passage 2

At a time when natural resources such as oil, coal and natural gas are being depleted at an alarming rate, "alternative energy" seem to be the magic words at the tip of everyone's tongue. One of the most exciting (proposals) for generating renewable energy comes from an old idea: the solar updraft tower. Conceived in 1903, the solar tower, designed like a giant chimney, draws heated air into openings at its base. Once inside the hollow tower, the heated air rises, accelerating to speeds of 35 mph. As the air rushes upward, dozens of wind turbines turn, generating electricity. A solar updraft tower as high as 1000 meters with a diameter as large as 7 kilometers could eventually power as many as 200,000 typical households.

S 3. The phrase "magic words" (line 2) most directly emphasizes the

(A) unsubstantiated belief in a (proposed) solution

The passage does not say whether the proposal is substantiated or not.

(B) inevitability of an ecological crisis

No evidence that there is a crisis afoot, even if you believe that's the case. Watch your assumptions.

(C) ability of language to capture the public's attention

Though the public is talking, we have no evidence that alternative energy is responsible for capturing its attention.

(D) the power of collective imagination

That's not supported by the passage.

(E) perceived appeal of a solution

This is the least wrong answer. Nothing brazenly wrong. It's the best of our options.

(E)

Passage 2

At a time when natural resources such as oil, coal and natural gas are being depleted at an alarming rate, "alternative energy" seem to be the magic words at the tip of everyone's tongue. One of the most exciting proposals for generating renewable energy comes from an old idea: the solar updraft tower. Conceived in 1903, the solar tower, designed like a giant chimney, draws heated air into openings at its base. Once inside the hollow tower, the heated air rises, accelerating to speeds of 35 mph. As the air rushes upward, dozens of wind turbines turn, generating electricity. A solar updraft tower as high as 1000 meters with a diameter as large as 7 kilometers could eventually power as many as 200,000 typical households.

synonym chain

S 4. The last sentence of the passage (lines 8–10) serves to

(A) convey the importance of a problem
This is not about the problem but about a proposed solution.

(B) highlight the potential benefits of an invention
Bingo– this is perfect. Exactly what the passage says.

(C) speculate about the likelihood of an outcome
We are not speculating about the probability of this taking place, just what might happen.

(D) defend a widely accepted practice
We are not defending anything, nor is the practice widely accepted.

(E) offer evidence in support of a prior claim
This final sentence does not offer a shred of evidence. It lays out potential benefits.

(B)

The Sparrow Answer

Many students mistakenly assume that SAT answers are going to be complicated or complex, but this is rarely the case. More often than not, correct answers are surprisingly simple; so simple in fact, that people tend to overlook them in their search for scholarly-sounding answers. One of the most frequently correct answer types is the unassuming, unpretentious, profoundly simple Sparrow. The Sparrow does not call attention to itself. Quite the opposite. It blends in. It avoids the media. It is far from flashy. It states a simple truth in a humble way.

The key to the Sparrow is that by saying so little, it doesn't make any bold statements that can be attacked. It makes no great claims in which throw-aways are embedded. There is nothing glaringly wrong with the Sparrow. It is a pleasant, simple, inoffensive answer.

Here are examples of Sparrow answers.

1 *The primary purpose of the passage is to*

challenge the findings of a particular group of people

How perfect! ***A particular group of people***. It's hard to argue with that. It would be easy to poke holes in an answer such as "challenge the outrageous findings of overqualified scientists." All of those adjectives can be sources of potential weakness. We could easily take on **outrageous** or **overqualified**. But "a particular group of people" is a very hard phrase to attack.

Watch out for adjective-heavy answers!

2 *The author mentions x in line y in order to*

explore possible explanations for a phenomenon

Again, flawless. *Explore possible explanations for a phenomenon.* There are no grand claims here. We are dwelling in possibility, which is fertile ground for the Sparrow.

3 *The author describes x most likely to*

defend a position that might be challenged

This answer screams Sparrow!!! This is very far from an absolute position. It might, could, possibly, may be challenged. This is a nice qualified position. Easy to defend. Hard to attack.

4 *Lines x–y serve primarily to*

suggest the origins of a field of research

When you see *suggest*, you are dealing with a gentle Sparrow answer. Sparrow answers are never extreme and are often qualified so as not to offend.

Now it is your turn to practice spotting sparrows!

E **Passage 3**

Popular tastes in art, music and politics are often as changeable as the wind. But nothing is as capricious as the fashion industry. Witty Victorian writer Oscar Wilde once said, "Fashion is a form of ugliness so intolerable that we have to alter it every six months." Whimsical as it is, fashion is
5   more than a superficial craze. From pencil skirts to bell-bottoms, over-sized sweaters to ruffled dress shirts, clothing signals everything from socioeconomic class to stage in life. For many, fashion is a form of self-expression, and individual personalities have been conveyed through fabric for centuries.

5. This passage indicates that fashion has been

   (A) championed as a superficial symbol of individuality
   (B) the primary means of expressing one's individual identity
   (C) a means of self-expression throughout history
   (D) frequently disparaged by those who do not understand it
   (E) influenced by changes in art, music and politics

6. The list in lines 5–6 ("From...shirts") primarily serves to

   (A) provide specific examples to illustrate a point
   (B) exaggerate the changeable nature of fashion
   (C) celebrate the diverse ways to express one's self through fashion
   (D) reveal how quickly fashion trends become outdated
   (E) support the Victorian perspective on fashion

S 5. This passage indicates that fashion has been

    (A) boxed:championed as a boxed:superficial symbol of individuality

    (B) the boxed:primary means of expressing one's individual identity

    (C) a means of self-expression throughout history

Short and uncomplicated: "fashion is a form of self-expression" straight from lines (7-8). "Throughout history" lines up with "have been conveyed through fabric for centuries" Perfect answer!

    (D) frequently boxed:disparaged by those who do not understand it

    (E) boxed:influenced by changes in art, music and politics

(C)

6. The list in lines 5–6 ("From ...shirts") primarily serves to

    (A) provide specific examples to illustrate a point

This is the perfect Sparrow answer. Doesn't offend or stand out, or try to show off. A harmless little statement- it gives examples to make a point. How could this be wrong?

    (B) boxed:exaggerate the changeable nature of fashion

    (C) boxed:celebrate the diverse ways to express one's self through fashion

    (D) reveal how quickly fashion trends become boxed:outdated

    (E) support the boxed:Victorian perspective on fashion

(A)

E **Passage 4**

As wind instruments go, folded vegetation seems a little on the primitive side.
Orangutans have been found to blow through leaves to modulate the sound of
their alarm calls, making them the only animal apart from humans known to
use tools to manipulate sound. The orangutan's music, if you can call it that,

5   is actually an alarm call known as a "kiss squeak." "When you're walking the
forest and you meet an orangutan that is not habituated to humans, they'll start
giving kiss squeaks and breaking branches," says Madeleine Hardus, a primatologist
at the University of Utrecht in the Netherlands, who documented the practice
among wild apes in Indonesian Borneo. She contends that orangutans use leaves

10   to make kiss squeaks to deceive predators, such as leopards, snakes and tigers,
as to their actual size – a deeper call indicating a larger animal.

7. The author references "wind instruments" (line 1) and "music"
    (line 4) primarily in order to

    (A) emphasize the relationship between humans and orangutans
    (B) offer a possible explanation for the orangutan's complex behavior
    (C) question the aesthetic validity of the orangutan's sound manipulations
    (D) indicate that orangutans are more sophisticated than originally
         thought
    (E) place the orangutan's kiss squeaks in a larger context

8. The last sentence primarily serves to

    (A) highlight an extraordinary phenomenon
    (B) place a natural behavior in its original context
    (C) propose an explanation for a behavior
    (D) defend the use of deception as a means of survival
    (E) underscore the origins of an evolutionary adaptation

7. The author references "wind instruments" (line 1) and "music" line (4) primarily in order

    (A) emphasize the relationship between humans and orangutans
    (B) offer a possible explanation for the orangutan's complex behavior
    (C) question the aesthetic validity of the orangutan's sound manipulations
    (D) indicate that orangutans are more sophisticated than originally thought
    (E) place the orangutan's kiss squeaks in a larger context

(E)

8. The last sentence primarily serves to

    (A) highlight an extraordinary phenomenon
    (B) place a natural behavior in its original context
    (C) propose an explanation for a behavior
    (D) defend the use of deception as a means of survival
    (E) underscore the origins of an evolutionary adaptation

(C)

E **Passage 5**

The year-long Montgomery Bus Boycott, the response to Rosa Parks' arrest for refusing to comply with Alabama's racial segregation laws in 1955, is probably the most famous social protest campaign in U.S. history. Popularized during the American Civil Rights move-ment, boycotting—refusing to cooperate as a means of protesting unjust political, social or
5 economic conditions—originated well before the 1950s. Almost 70 years earlier in a small town in Ireland, a similar movement was launched. Objecting to worker exploitation, a unified group of laborers refused to harvest the estate of a local earl. When a former mili-tary officer attempted to undermine the protest, the Irish Land League launched a campaign of isolation against him. Shops refused to serve him, neighbors openly ignored him and
10 the postman even refused to deliver his mail. The former army captain's name was Charles Boycott.

9. The passage indicates that boycotting is

    (A) a unified social movement that tran-scends class boundaries
    (B) a popular way to promote minority interests
    (C) a method of protest against unjust conditions
    (D) a means of effecting change only fully appreciated in modern times
    (E) an effective tool for transforming society

10. The author mentions Charles Boycott in order to

    (A) compare modern social protest with that of the past
    (B) emphasize the popularity of a social movement throughout history
    (C) reveal the historical origins of a term
    (D) illustrate the international appeal of organized social protest
    (E) offer an example of effective social protest

S 9. The passage indicates that boycotting is

    (A) a ⟨unified social⟩ movement that transcends ⟨class boundaries⟩

    (B) a popular way to promote ⟨minority⟩ interests

    (C) a method of protest against unjust conditions

    (D) a means of effecting change ⟨only⟩ fully ⟨appreciated in modern times⟩

    (E) an ⟨effective⟩ tool for transforming society

(C)

10. The author mentions Charles Boycott in order to

    (A) ⟨compare⟩ modern social protest with that of the past

    (B) emphasize the ⟨popularity⟩ of a social movement throughout history

    (C) reveal the historical origins of a term

    (D) illustrate the ⟨international appeal⟩ of organized social protest

    (E) offer an example of ⟨effective⟩ social protest

(C)

Working Memory

To master Reading Comprehension you must learn to use your memory effectively. It doesn't matter if you can remember the color of your Aunt Ida's hair, but you do need to learn how to hold things for a time in your short-term, or "working," memory. If you want to succeed on the SAT, you need to get your working memory working for you.

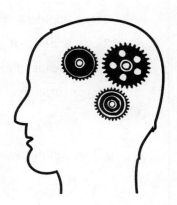

For students who do not know how to use their working memory, Reading Comprehension can be a time-intensive and frustrating process. Here are the steps a student who isn't skilled at using his working memory may take when solving a Reading Comprehension question.

Step 1   Quickly read the question

Step 2   Jump to the passage to look for the answer

Step 3   Pause, wait...
"What exactly did the question ask?"

Step 4   Go back to re-read the question
"Oh, that's what they wanted!"

Step 5   Return to the passage and give it a 2nd pass

Step 6   Go to the answer choices

Step 7   Read answer choice A and refer back to the passage to check if this matches

Steps 8-11   Move on to choice B-E, continually referring back to the passage

Step 12   Finally decide on an answer

Time elapsed: 2.5 minutes.
Time allotted by the College Board: 1 minute

This is a recipe for running out of time and leaving serious points on the table. It also will make you feel rushed because it is inherently inefficient.

Here are the steps a student who knows how to use his working memory may take when solving a Reading Comprehension question.

This is key! Lock it into your working memory banks.

Step 1	**Carefully** read the question for full comprehension, reread if necessary	
Step 2	Paraphrase the question into your own words	
Step 3	Go to the passage to look for the answer to this question that you are actively holding in working memory	
Step 4	**Carefully** read the passage until you find the answer	
Step 5	Write down the answer, or at least put the answer in your own words, again locking it into working memory	
Step 6	Go to the answer choices and find the match for your answer that you locked into working memory	

This process involves more intention and focus than the other. And it's much more efficient. If you follow this method, you will spend more time in 2 areas:

1 Reading and paraphrasing the question before you look for the answer in the passage

2 Carefully reading the passage, finding the answer before you consider looking at the answer choices

All the time you are investing in careful reading and paraphrasing will pay off in a HUGE way when you finally move to the answer choices. With your paraphrased answer locked into memory, you will be able to race through choices A–E to find the perfect match for your answer, easily spotting throw-aways and unrelated information.

Nuts and Bolts

The essence of this strategy is learning how to hold information in your mind, while you look over and process other information. This takes a bit of mental multi-tasking. You need to give out tasks to different parts of your brain. Your **working memory** has a simple, but important job. It needs to hold on to certain information and make it easily accessible to you until you give the word that it is OK to let it go.

Sticky Phrases

You can make the job of working memory much easier when you learn to simplify and personalize any information you put into working memory.

<u>Hard phrase to remember</u>
The collective efforts of the anguished artists yielded few enduring results.

<u>Easier phrase to remember</u>
The artists achieved nothing.

Phrases in YOUR own words are 'stickier' and easier to remember than fancy-sounding SAT sentences.

The second phrase is stickier for your mind because it is **simpler** and **in your language**, rather than the test-writer's language. The simplicity piece is key because the mind can generally hold 5 to 9 pieces of information at a time, (7 on average). When you can simplify and reduce, you make things easier for your mind. Having things in your own language, personalizing things is also essential. Your mind works better when it's dealing with familiar content.

Movie in your mind

Once we have a sticky sentence or phrase, we need to take a moment and lock that sentence into working memory. This requires your full attention. Imagine that your working memory is like a screen upon which you can project information. In this case, we are projecting a paraphrased sentence onto our screen.

Once we have locked that phrase into working memory, it should be there for us as long as we need to refer back to it. And once we no longer need this phrase, we can replace it with a brand new phrase. For most SAT questions, you will need to hold information in your working memory 2 distinct times.

1 What is the question asking?

2 What answer did I find in the passage?

Let's see this process in action.

E 1. Her "reply" in lines 33–36 suggests primarily that Björk believes which of the following to be true?

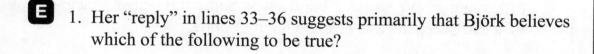

S **Step 1** **Carefully** read the question for full comprehension, reread if necessary

1. Her "reply" in lines 33–36 suggests primarily that Björk believes which of the following to be true?

Step 2 Paraphrase the question into your own words

So we are looking for this information:
"What does Björk believe?"

Let's pop it onto our memory screen and lock it in for a moment:

"What does Björk believe?"

Step 3 Go to the passage to look for the answer to this question that you are actively holding in working memory

In an interview during her European tour, renowned pop singer Björk was asked about her identity as an Icelandic artist living in
35 England. Her reply—"When I was a teenager in Iceland people would throw rocks and shout abuse at me because they thought I was weird. I never got that in London no matter what I wore"— evoked laughter and applause from the crowd of British fans and
40 journalists. Though Björk is forever associated with her Icelandic homeland, and her music is infused with the sounds and rhythms of her native soil, she has found a new home and a greater degree of social acceptance in cosmopolitan London.

S Step 4 **Carefully** read the passage until you find the answer

Step 5 Write down the answer, or at least put the answer in your own words, again locking it into working memory

We were looking for: **"What does Björk believe?"**
From the passage, it seems that she believes she's been accepted by the people of London.
So, our guess would be: **Björk believes she's accepted by Londoners**
Let's lock that into our memory.

Björk believes she's accepted by Londoners

Step 6 Go to the answer choices and find the match for your answer that you locked into working memory

(A) her fashion sense is fundamental to her artistic identity
(B) she needed to leave Iceland to discover her true inspiration
(C) artists should never expect to be socially accepted
(D) humor is one of the keys to social acceptance
(E) she could express her individuality more freely in London

(E)

We can look at each choice one at a time, comparing them to the guess locked into our mental screen and knocking off the throw-aways. We quickly arrive at E, the only answer that matches and has no throw-away.

Remember to lock things into your memory so you never need to go back and forth more than 1 time between the question and the passage.

Common Question Types

At a basic level, all questions on the Reading Comprehension section of the SAT fall into one of two broad categories: specific questions and general questions. You will need to learn strategies for both of these question types as well as strategies for sub-types of questions within these broad categories. Below is a chart detailing the question types you will see on the SAT and how frequently they occur on an average test.

The percentages below indicate there are more specific questions than general questions. Nearly seventy percent of the time, we will be zoning in on a specific detail in the passage, hunting for an answer.

Question Type	% of questions	Avg # of questions
SPECIFIC QUESTIONS	**69.3%**	**33.3**
Inference	**31.7%**	**15.2**
Suggests or implies	16.7%	8.0
Primarily serves to/in order to	15.0%	7.2
Specific Detail	**23.9%**	**11.5**
Vocabulary in Context	**10.2%**	**4.9**
Literary Device used by the author	**3.5%**	**1.7**

Question Type	% of questions	Avg # of questions
GENERAL QUESTIONS	**30.7%**	**14.7**
High Level Understanding of Passage	**7.6%**	**3.6**
Purpose of a paragraph	3.3%	1.6
Primary purpose/ Description of passage	4.3%	2.0
Tone	**5.4%**	**2.6**
Author's tone/attitude	2.9%	1.4
Character's tone/attitude	2.5%	1.2
Abstract Analysis	**2.7%**	**1.3**
What if true	0.8%	0.4
Relationship/Analogy	1.9%	0.9
Dual Passage Comparison	**15.0%**	**7.2**
Relationship between 2 passages	1.7%	0.8
How 2 passages are different	2.5%	1.2
Both authors agree	4.8%	2.3
One author would most likely respond to the other	6.0%	2.9
TOTAL	**100%**	**48**

Specific Questions

Specific questions have a narrowly defined focus, frequently involving an isolated detail in the passage.

Here are a few examples of specific questions.

- *What does the imagery in lines 18 – 22 suggest?*

- *Lines 56 – 58 ("when she...boardwalk") imply that Jenny*

- *In lines 27 – 13 ("You could...horse"), the author distinguishes between*

- *In the final paragraph, the Weimaraners can be best described as*

The majority of the time you will be directed to specific lines within a passage, but other times you will need to locate the detail in the passage without the benefit of a line reference. There are a few principles that govern all specific questions.

Reading in Context

If you are given a line reference, you will generally need to read 5 lines above and 5 lines below the specified lines in order to acquire the context necessary to answer the question. If you are directed to lines 19-21, read lines 14-26. On occasion, you may need to read another line or two beyond this range to find the answer. But do not deviate too far. The writers pointed you to lines 19-21 because the answer is nearby.

Scanning for Specific Words

If you are pointed to a specific detail but are not given a line reference, you must do a quick visual scan of the passage to find the word or words in question. Once you isolate the detail mentioned in the question, read in context, 5 up and 5 down, to acquire enough information to answer the question.

Bracketing

A good strategy to keep your attention focused on material relevant to a particular question is bracketing relevant information. In the margins of the passage, draw brackets around the 5 lines above and below the specified lines. Brackets tell you: "Look in this range." Also underline the word or lines specified by the question.

 1. In line 17, the phrase "dancing...time" suggests

Occasionally you will need to read a few additional lines beyond the brackets, but in general, the brackets will focus your attention on the meaningful content.

The snaggletoothed dancing man was wild-eyed and crazed from hours and hours of impromptu dancing, flailing about like a willow tree caught in the middle of a class 5 hurricane. He imagined himself caught up in the storm, the great storm, the mindless, soul-drenching storm. He felt himself <u>dancing his way through time</u>, around time, over and through and between time. He danced the dance of his forefathers, his forbearers, his pallbearers and ring bearers and grudge bearers. His was a dance that knew neither time nor place. A dance conceived before culture gave birth to the very idea of dancing. As the hours passed and his dancing grew more frenzied, more urgent, he felt himself merging with the elements, with the universe, as physical boundaries melted away.

17

If you limit your reading to the material within the brackets, you will save time and avoid reading content that is never tested. This is very helpful for students struggling with time management.

Types of Specific Questions

Inference

The most popular specific sub-type question is the **inference** question. Roughly 15 of the 48 questions on an average SAT, 32% of all RC questions, will fall into this category. There are 2 main kinds of **inference** questions.

1 *Suggests/Implies*

- The description in lines 14-17 ("It was...Sinbad") suggests that the author found the book to be

- Fernando's comments in lines 20-23 ("Please...way") imply that

- In line 28, the author implies that being American involves

2 *Primarily serves to/In order to*

- The question in lines (44-55) ("who did...chimpanzee?") chiefly serves to

- The statement in lines 6-9 ("Welcome to...jungle") functions primarily to

- The reference to the "flaming snack-pack" (line 8) primarily serves to

Inference questions are fairly straightforward. Use your standard rules of evidence, looking for synonyms and watching out for throw-aways. And always read in context.

Multi-part Inference Questions

These questions require a degree of mental gymnastics; you must first understand something in the passage, such as a viewpoint, a prediction, a remark—then you must understand what that information (the viewpoint or prediction or remark) **suggests** or **implies** or **how it is characterized**.

- The author of Passage 2 would most likely claim that the view presented in lines 20-26, Passage 1 ("Every...complaints") is

- In context, the researcher would probably characterize the narrator's remark in line 34 as

- Why are the reasons discussed in lines 35-41 characterized by the author as "disconcerting?"

- The author of Passage 1 would likely respond to the actions attributed to "the elect" in lines 51-53 in Passage 2 ('the elect... synthetic") by asserting that

- The phrase "without consequence" (line 45) emphasizes the politician's view that the story of the Bridge to Nowhere should NOT

- In lines 60-62 ("he...outsiders"), the author characterizes the commentator's argument as

To solve these multi-part questions, you must slow down and be absolutely sure you know what you should be looking for in the passage. Just as you have to follow the Order of Operations for math, you have to follow one for multi-part questions, too. Before we try to understand the interpretation or characterization of something in the passage, we must get a very clear picture of what that 'thing' is.

Order of Operations for Multi-part Questions

Step 1 Identify WHAT is being evaluated

Step 2 Identify WHO is *evaluating*, *interpreting* or *characterizing*

Step 3 Identify HOW that 'who' would respond, given his or her values as we see them in the passage

It is fundamental that you break these problems into discrete steps, and identify the answers to the parts of the question. If you try to tackle them all at once, without separating out the parts, things get tricky.

Think of answering these problems as a serious balancing act. You have to keep several different plates spinning: you have to balance your understanding of the information in the passage, who the evaluator is and what is his or her interpretation.

E In context, the biographer would probably characterize the actor's remark in lines 33-34 as

(A) deliberate self-regard
(B) witty repartee
(C) servile flattery
(D) self-conscious distortion
(E) exaggerated hyperbole

1 Identify WHAT is being evaluated

In context, the biographer would probably characterize the actor's remark in lines 33-34 as

The question is asking about the **actor's remark**. Let's go to the passage and see what that **remark** is.

> The actor coyly responded, "<u>People say I acted</u>
> <u>with Katharine Hepburn. The truth is I acted near</u>
> 35 <u>Katharine Hepburn.</u>" This was another example of
> an actor speaking tongue-in-cheek about a fellow...

The remark we need to remember is: "People say I acted with Katharine Hepburn. The truth is I acted near Katharine Hepburn."

2 Identify WHO is evaluating

In this case, it is the biographer who is evaluating the remark we underlined in the passage. And, what do we know about him? We know that he said the actor was "speaking tongue-in-cheek."

3 Identify HOW he/she would respond

We said above that the biographer described the remark as "tongue-in-cheek." That is a humorous characterization. Only answer (B) matches that characterization.

(A) deliberate self-regard
(B) witty repartee
(C) servile flattery
(D) self-conscious distortion
(E) exaggerated hyperbole

Let's look at a few more multi-part questions and focus on the discrete steps we need to follow to arrive at the correct answer.

E The author of Passage 1 would likely respond to the actions attributed to "the elect" in lines 51-53 in Passage 2 ("the elect…synthetic") by asserting that

Order of Operations for Multi-part Questions

Step 1   Identify WHAT is being evaluated
*What are the specific actions attributed to **the elect**?*

Step 2   Identify WHO is *evaluating, interpreting* or *characterizing*
*What is the opinion of **the author of Passage 1** toward the elect?*

Step 3   Identify HOW that 'who' would respond, given his or her values as we see them in the passage
*How would the author of Passage 1 **respond to the actions of the elect**?*

Remember, it's like a math problem with PEMDAS. Always start from the inside and move to the outside. For these kinds of multi-part questions we should always start by identifying the item in question, **then** move on to the interpretation.

In math, PEMDAS, Please Excuse My Dear Aunt Sally, is the order of operations you follow when solving a problem: **P**arentheses **E**xponents **M**ultiplication/ **D**ivision **A**ddition/ **S**ubtraction

E The phrase "without consequence" (line 45) emphasizes the politician's view that the story of the Bridge to Nowhere should NOT

Order of Operations for Multi-part Questions

Step 1   Identify WHAT is being evaluated
*What is the **view of the politician** towards the Bridge to Nowhere?*

Step 2   Identify WHO is *evaluating, interpreting* or *characterizing*

What does the phrase "without consequence" emphasize about the politician's view?

Step 3   Identify HOW that 'who' would respond, given his or her values as we see them in the passage

What does the politician believe we should do with the story?

Step 4   Now we need to solve for the NOT

What does the politician believe we should NOT do with the story?

Specific Detail

Roughly 12 of the 48 questions, 24% of questions, will fall into this category. **Specific Detail** questions direct you to a word or small phrase. Find your evidence and always read in context.

- The statement "we snorkled...night" (lines 46 – 49) refers to the tendency to

- In lines 35 – 38 ("They should...bonfire"), the author distinguishes between

- In line 45, "Detroit" serves as an example of a place that is

Vocabulary in Context (VIC)

Roughly 5 of the 48 questions, 10% of questions, will fall into this category.

- In line 45, "question" most nearly means

- In line 65, "disturbed" most nearly means

- In line 22, "exploring" most nearly means

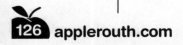

You will notice that the words themselves is not too challenging. The SAT uses simple words as the roots of **VIC** questions, words such as:

primitive, open, compensation, drawn, suffered,
drive, claims, summons, searching, sense, fair,
finished, poor, history, bleak, order, compromised,
regular, crash, sign, death, true, given, false, adapted, ran

None of these words are particularly challenging. But don't be fooled! The SAT will use these easy words in a novel or unusual way. Even if you know the most common definition of a word, it will most likely be the wrong answer. You need to read in context to determine how the SAT is using these words.

Strategy for VIC questions

Step 1	READ the question.
Step 2	Find the line specified in the passage containing the vocabulary word. Read in context, 5 LINES UP AND DOWN. If you come to the end of a paragraph while reading 5 up or down, you do not need to read further for a VIC question.
Step 3	Make your own PREDICTION.
Step 4	ELIMINATE any choices that don't match your guess.
Step 5	PLUG the remaining choices into the sentence in the passage, one at a time, to see which ones make sense in context.
Step 6	Using the process of elimination, CHOOSE an answer.

E In line 26, "peculiar" most nearly means

(A) abnormal
(B) characteristic
(C) uncustomary
(D) outrageous
(E) fantastic

1 Read the question

In line 26, "peculiar" most nearly means

(A) abnormal
(B) characteristic
(C) uncustomary
(D) outrageous
(E) fantastic

2 Read in context

Read 5 lines up and 5 lines down (lines 21-31)

Traveling opens up doors and expands horizons. It is a means of enriching one's knowledge and expanding one's conception of the world. Additionally, travel can greatly expand one's understanding of the many ways in which cultures interpret language. For many travelers, unaccustomed to the cultural milieu of a particular destination, they will need clarification of
26 the terminology peculiar to a particular region and its history. For the meaning of a phrase may be isolated to a particular region. Travel 30 miles outside of one locale, and the same phrase may have a completely different connotation.
All meaning is locally defined.

3 Make your own guess

The terminology peculiar to a particular region.
The meaning of "peculiar" has to do with the word particular.
Terminology "that is linked" to a particular region. My guess is
"*linked to.*"

4 Compare your answer with the choices

Now we need to go and see which words might work.

(A) abnormal   *Does not mean "linked to." Nix it.*
~ (B) characteristic   *Sounds similar to "linked to," so we keep it.*
(C) uncustomary   *Does not mean "linked to." Nix it.*
(D) outrageous   *Does not mean "linked to." Nix it.*
~ (E) fantastic   *hmm... sounds funny, but not as wrong as the others; keep it for a moment.*

5 Plug in the answer choices

Next we plug the remaining answer choices back into our original
sentence, replacing the word "peculiar" with the words from the answer
choice:

(B) characteristic   "terminology *characteristic* to a particular region"
(E) fantastic   "terminology *fantastic* to a particular region"

6 Choose your answer

After reading the 2 options in context, "*characteristic*" seems to be
a better match.

The answer in this case is **(B) characteristic**.

Author's Device
Roughly 2 of the 48 questions, 4% of questions, will fall into this category.

- In line 45, quotation marks are used to
- The author's use of italics in line 18 serves primarily to
- The rhetorical device primarily featured in this passage is

Here are a few things to look for when faced with author's device questions:

Personal voice
Watch out for the use of "I", indicating first-person, personal voice.

Rhetorical question
Look out for the "?"

Metaphorical Language
Metaphors, similes and imagery are very common in SAT passages.

Anecdote
That simply means a narrative or story.

Italics
Italics are often used to add emphasis.

Paradox
A paradox is a statement or proposition that seems self-contradictory or absurd but in reality may express a possible truth.

Irony
Irony is when an author uses words to convey a meaning that is the opposite of what they really mean. And, in literature, irony is when an author uses a character or a plot development to indicate an intention or attitude opposite of what is really happening.

Quotation marks
These are frequently used to question the use of a phrase. For example, when the author writes, "the classroom was the only "proper" place for a child," imagine the author raising up her hands and making the bunny ears around the word "proper," with a hint of sarcasm. She is calling attention to and questioning how appropriate that phrase is. Is the classroom really the "proper" place for a child? The author doesn't think so.

General Questions

Not all CR questions direct you to a specific line or detail in a passage. Many questions involve multiple parts of a passage, overarching themes in a passage or an analysis of the passage as a whole.

Here are a few examples of general questions:

- *The primary purpose of this passage is to*

- *The author of Passage 1 would most likely criticize the author of Passage 2 for*

- *The author's attitude toward the Calypso natives is best described as*

- *Which best describes the relationship between Passage 1 and Passage 2 ?*

When you are dealing with general questions, you must integrate information from various parts of the passage. It is best to answer these questions after you have answered all of the specific questions for a given passage.

Types of General Questions

High Level Understanding of a Passage

Roughly 4 of the 48 questions, 8% of questions, will fall into this category. There are 2 types of **high level understanding** questions.

1 *What is the primary purpose of this paragraph?*

- The primary purpose of the fourth paragraph (lines 65 – 74) is to

To answer this question, you need to understand how the paragraph functions in the context of the passage. What job is it doing? Clarifying a point? Adding evidence? Offering a contrast? You will need to read the 5 lines preceding and following the paragraph in addition to reading the paragraph itself. Be on the lookout for transitions and directional shifts. Circle words or phrases like "although," "however," or "in spite of," which indicate such transitions.

2 *Primary purpose/ high level description of a passage:*

- The passage as a whole is best characterized as
- The primary purpose of Passage 2 is to

Frequently the answer to these high level questions lies in the italicized introduction to the passage. Remember that we are looking for the overarching significance of the passage. Do not get stuck in the weeds, in the details or in the content of one isolated paragraph. The primary purpose must be the dominant theme of the entire passage.

Bookending

A good strategy to determine the primary purpose of a passage is bookending. You skim the first and last

sentence, the "bookends," of each paragraph. You are not reading for detail but merely to get a general sense of each paragraph. You can bookend a passage quickly to get its "gist" and solve these questions.

Tone/Attitude Questions

Roughly 3 of the 48 questions, 5% of questions, will fall into this category. There are 2 main kinds of **tone/attitude** questions.

1 AUTHOR'S tone or attitude

When we are exploring an SAT AUTHOR'S attitude or tone, we must remember the identities of the authors of SAT passages. Generally SAT passages are written by historians, scientists, sociologists: level-headed, precise and highly opinionated people. SAT authors are **NEVER:**

A quick mnemonic to help: When dealing with SAT Authors, there is NO ICE:

Indifference
Confusion
Emotional
 Extremes

Indifferent, apathetic or aloof
They always care and have an opinion.

Confused, perplexed or puzzled
They write from a place of authority.

Emotionally extreme
They are level-headed and scientific.

However, SAT Authors can be:

• *Sarcastic*, and quite often they are. Authors can exhibit *mockery*, *scorn* or *disapproval*, even *condescension*, *mild contempt* or *disdain*, but **never resentment**.

• *Ambivalent*, weighing the pros and the cons. They actually love to hedge their opinions and show *qualified appreciation* or *mild disapproval*.

• *Analytical*, *detached* or *objective*.

• *Skeptical* or *doubtful* about claims made by others.

Let's practice our new strategy on an AUTHOR'S attitude question without even reading a passage. How many answer choices do you think we'll be able to cross off immediately?

E The author's attitude toward _____ can best be described as

(A) ironic
(B) objective
(C) hopeless
(D) doubtful
(E) offended

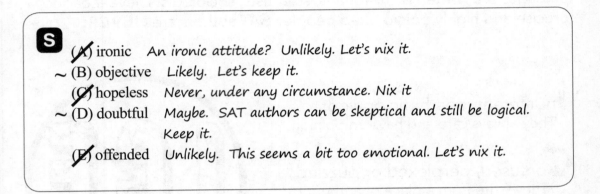

S

~~(A)~~ ironic   *An ironic attitude? Unlikely. Let's nix it.*

~ (B) objective   *Likely. Let's keep it.*

~~(C)~~ hopeless   *Never, under any circumstance. Nix it*

~ (D) doubtful   *Maybe. SAT authors can be skeptical and still be logical. Keep it.*

~~(E)~~ offended   *Unlikely. This seems a bit too emotional. Let's nix it.*

We have just eliminated three answer choices without even seeing the passage. Excellent! It will now be that much easier to go back, reference the passage and determine the final answer.

2 CHARACTER'S tone or attitude

When we are dealing with fictional, rather than analytical, passages, characters can be much more emotionally extreme. With character's tone questions, **ICE** does NOT apply.

Abstract Analysis

Some of the most challenging questions on the SAT, these questions occur rarely, generally once per test; 3% of questions fall in this category. There are 2 main kinds of **abstract analysis** questions.

1 How might the author respond

With these questions, you need to get into the head of the author and figure out how he/she might respond if presented with new information beyond the scope of the passage.

- Which of the following, if available, would best support the author's assertions about the inevitability of finding alien life?

- Which of the following, if true, would most directly disprove what "doctors hold as sacred"?

Strategy for Abstract Analysis questions

Step 1   Identify the AUTHOR'S POSITION on an issue, as indicated in the passage.

Step 2   Determine WHAT EVIDENCE WOULD SUPPORT that position. WHAT EVIDENCE WOULD ATTACK that position?

Step 3   Go down the list of answer choices and determine which choices would ATTACK, SUPPORT or have NO IMPACT on the author's position.

2 The Analogy

The analogy section of the SAT is gone, but analogies have moved into the CR section. Reading Comprehension analogy questions are not concerned with surface level content; they are interested in deeper relationships. If the content of an answer choice matches the content found in the passage, this answer choice is most likely a trap. Go deeper, beneath the surface, beyond external similarities, to solve analogies.

- A "horse on a treadmill" (line 34) is most analogous to a

- Which of the following most resembles the relationship between "The Beatles" and "The Jonas Brothers" (lines 23-25) as described in the passage?

- Which is most analogous to the situation described in lines 12-15 ("He . . . carpet")?

Dual Passage Comparison Questions

Roughly 7 of the 48 questions, 15% of questions, will fall into this category. These questions require you to be very clear on the positions of the 2 authors. It is essential to notate the main positions of each author and refer to them when solving these questions.

- The author of Passage 2 and the "scholars" mentioned in line 34, Passage 1, would probably disagree regarding which of the following about *War and Peace*?

- Which best describes the relationship between the two passages?

Important principles for dual passage comparison questions

1 Circle the PASSAGE the question focuses on

When you are answering a dual comparison question about one author's view, you can count on the SAT to provide you with an answer choice reflecting the views of the other author. Very sneaky! You need to be absolutely clear which author you are focusing on. To achieve this, always circle the author in question.

- The author of (Passage 2) and the "scholars" mentioned in line 34, Passage 1, would probably disagree regarding which of the following about *War and Peace*?
- Unlike the author of Passage 2, the author of (Passage 1)

This simple step will help you avoid making the common mistake of answering for the wrong author.

2 Authors tend to agree on basic ideas

SAT authors rarely approach a topic from similar viewpoints, and often their views are diametrically opposed. But the SAT will ask for points of agreement. More often than not, the 2 authors will agree on the most basic, general idea. Ex: "Both authors agree that science has some value." Who could argue that science has *some* value? The perfect Sparrow. Simple answers such as this are frequently the right answers for dual comparison agreement.

3 The relationship between the two authors

Frequently, the SAT sets you up with a contrast, as this leads to more interesting questions. You have to imagine: what would happen if these two authors met on the street and started talking? Would they agree? Would one reject the claims made by the other? You can generally anticipate a question regarding how the 2 authors would respond to each other. Here are some likely options:

- The authors would disagree.

- One author would question the approach/assumptions/findings of the other.

- One author would be surprised to learn what the other has discovered.

- The authors are making the same essential point but from a different frame of reference.

If you can anticipate these common relationships, you will be one step ahead of the game.

Reading Strategy

There is a strategy for everything on the SAT, even reading. For most students reading ALL the passages straight through is a daunting prospect. So, we have created unique approaches to reading the different passages that will save you time.

Short Passages

Since short passages are only 10-12 lines long, we approach them directly. In short—read them.

1 **Read the *entire* passage actively**
- Underline key content
- Circle Logic Words
- Star the Main Idea
- Notate

2 **Briefly summarize the passage**

In a few short words paraphrase the meaning of the passage.

3 **Answer the questions**
- Make your own guess
- Watch out for throw-aways
- Look for evidence

E Passage 1

Do you ever get the impression that civilization has degenerated into an
unedifying free-for-all? Like pigs gobbling at their troughs, we all seem to
be out to get as much as possible of whatever is on offer. Everyone is at it,
from loggers felling the Amazonian rainforest and fishers fighting over the
5 last few cod to SUV drivers running the oil wells dry and politicians on their
gravy trains. Science even has a name for the phenomenon—one that seems
eerily prescient following the recent revelation about the Parliament Members' expense claims in the United Kingdom. It is called the Tragedy of the
Commons. Four decades ago, ecologist Garrett Hardin published a ground-
10 breaking paper on this phenomenon, arguing that when personal and communal interests are at odds, overexploitation of resources is inevitable.

1. The author uses which of the following?

  (A) rhetorical question
  (B) technical jargon
  (C) direct quotation
  (D) hypothetical scenarios
  (E) scholarly analysis

2. Which of the following, if available, would most directly refute
Garrett Hardin's argument (lines 10–11)?

  (A) reports that big game hunters have driven endangered species
     to the brink of extinction
  (B) proof that manufacturers continue to pollute the air despite
     concerns regarding global warming
  (C) studies revealing that homeowners are much more likely to
     voluntarily conserve water during a drought
  (D) confirmation that large companies dump their waste into local
     rivers to avoid high waste removal costs
  (E) evidence that individual car owners continue to use the freeway
     to get to work in spite of the increasing prevalence of major
     traffic jams

Metaphorical language

S Step 1 Read the passage ACTIVELY

Do you ever get the impression that <u>civilization</u> has <u>degenerated</u> into an unedifying free-for-all? Like <u>pigs</u> gobbling at their troughs, we all seem to be out to <u>get as much as possible</u> of whatever is on offer. <u>Everyone</u> is at it, from <u>loggers felling the Amazonian rainforest</u> and fishers fighting over the last few cod to <u>SUV drivers</u> running the oil wells dry and politicians on their gravy trains. <u>Science even has a name</u> for the phenomenon—one that seems eerily prescient following the recent revelation about the Parliament Members' expense claims in the United Kingdom. It is called the <u>Tragedy of the Commons</u>. Four decades ago, <u>ecologist Garrett Hardin</u> published a <u>ground-breaking paper</u> on this phenomenon, arguing that <u>when personal and communal</u> ★ <u>interests are at odds, overexploitation of resources is inevitable</u>.

Step 2 Briefly SUMMARIZE the passage

When personal and communal interests clash, humans act selfishly.

Step 3 Answer the questions

1. The author uses which of the following?

  (A) rhetorical question
  Aha- we have a question mark in line 2.

  (B) [technical] jargon
  There is nothing overly technical about this language.

  (C) direct [quotation]
  Do you see any quotation marks? Nope.

  (D) hypothetical scenarios
  The author only mentions events that have actually transpired.

  (E) scholarly [analysis]
  All we have is Hardin's argument; we do not have any analysis or further exploration of his claim.

(A)

2. Which of the following, if available, would most directly refute Garrett Hardin's argument (lines 10–11)?

Aha! This is a two-stepper. We need to first find out what Garrett Hardin is arguing. He claims "when personal and communal interests are at odds, overexploitation of resources is inevitable." Second, we need to find an example of a situation where personal and communal interests are at odds, but exploitation does NOT occur.

   (A) reports that big game hunters have driven endangered species to the brink of extinction

Is this an example where exploitation does not occur? Nope. Animals are being driven to their extinction, supporting Hardin's point.

   (B) proof that manufacturers continue to pollute the air despite concerns regarding global warming

Again, this seems to only support Hardin's point. Manufacturers continue to pollute even though it is harming the shared resource of our atmosphere.

   (C) studies revealing that homeowners are much more likely to voluntarily conserve water during a drought

This looks pretty good. Homeowners are voluntarily conserving water when supplies are low. Hardin would expect the homeowners to continue to use water for their personal needs regardless of the impact on the community. This challenges Hardin's theory.

   (D) confirmation that large companies dump their waste into local rivers to avoid high waste removal costs

Again, this seems to only support Hardin's point. Companies are dumping, hurting the shared resource of the river, to protect their personal interests.

   (E) evidence that individual car owners continue to use the freeway to get to work in spite of the increasing prevalence of major traffic jams

This also supports Hardin's point. Commuters continue to contribute to the congestion in order to serve their personal needs.

(C)

Sometimes, you can't answer the question yourself before looking at the SAT's answers. Both of these questions were too vague for us to make a guess. BUT, this rarely happens. Be sure to make a guess when you can!

Short Passage Strategy

Step 1   Read the ENTIRE passage actively

Step 2   Briefly SUMMARIZE the passage

Step 3   ANSWER the questions

Short Comparison Passages

When you are asked to compare one passage to another, it is best to approach each passage individually before you compare them to each other.

You want to tackle the first passage and its questions before you look at the second passage and any comparison questions.

1 Read PASSAGE 1 actively

- Underline key content
- Circle Logic Words
- Star the Main Idea
- Notate

2 Briefly summarize PASSAGE 1

In a few short words paraphrase the meaning of the passage.

3 Answer questions that refer only to PASSAGE 1

- Make your own guess
- Watch out for throw-aways
- Look for evidence

4 Read PASSAGE 2 actively

- Underline key content
- Circle Logic Words
- Star the Main Idea
- Notate

5 Briefly summarize PASSAGE 2

In a few short words paraphrase the meaning of the passage.

6 Find the relationship between the 2 passages

If the two authors met in a coffee shop, what would they say to each other? "Great idea!" or "That's completely wrong!" or "I never knew that!"

7 Answer questions that refer only to PASSAGE 2

- Make your own guess
- Watch out for throw-aways
- Look for evidence

8 Answer questions that compare or contrast BOTH passages

- Make your own guess
- Watch out for throw-aways
- Look for evidence

Passage 1

If you believe there is no such thing as altruism, you are in good company. In *The Selfish Gene*, Richard Dawkins writes that we must "try to teach generosity and altruism, because we are born selfish." Even if we are nice to members of our family, that doesn't count because there is a pay-off, at least in biological terms: they share some of our genes,

5 so by helping them we indirectly further our own genetic immortality. Meanwhile, other acts of seeming altruism are often just reciprocity. If you scratch my back, then I scratch yours—no matter how much later - that's not selfless either. This all makes good evolutionary sense, since spending time and energy helping someone without any return puts you at a distinct disadvantage in the survival stakes.

Passage 2

10 In every society, humans make personal sacrifices for others with no expectation that it will be reciprocated. For example, we donate to charity, or care for the sick and disabled. This trait is extremely rare in the natural world, unless there is a family relationship or later reciprocation. One theory to explain how human altruism evolved involves the way we interacted as groups early in our evolution. Toward the end of the Pleistocene period—

15 about 12,000 years ago—humans foraged for food as hunter-gatherers. These groups competed against each other for survival. Under these conditions, altruism toward other group-members would improve the overall fitness of the group. If an individual defended the group but was killed, any genes that the individual shared with the overall group would still be passed on.

1. The author of Passage 1 would most likely argue that the behaviors listed in line 11 ("we...disabled")

   (A) contribute to our collective sense of humanity
   (B) are clear examples of the prevalence of reciprocity
   (C) evolved from our experience as hunters and gatherers
   (D) make little sense in today's social climate
   (E) do not make good evolutionary sense

2. Both authors agree on which of the following points

   (A) one motivation for altruistic behavior is to pass on genetic material
   (B) human altruism evolved during the Pleistocene period
   (C) our need for reciprocity negates the existence of true altruism
   (D) altruism always promotes the survival of one's social group
   (E) altruism is necessary to ensure the longevity of the family relationship

3. The quotation in lines 2-3 ("try...selfish") expresses in part a belief that

   (A) altruism is not an innate human trait
   (B) altruism can overcome our selfish instincts
   (C) biological imperatives require a certain degree of selfishness
   (D) human survival is dependent upon altruism
   (E) it is necessary for humans to learn to act altruistically to carry on genes

4. In line 17, "fitness" most nearly means

   (A) exercise
   (B) condition
   (C) prosperity
   (D) flexibility
   (E) comfort

S Step 1 Read PASSAGE 1 actively

If you believe there is <u>no such thing as altruism</u>, you are in good company. In *The Selfish Gene*, Richard Dawkins writes that we must "<u>try to teach generosity and altruism, because we are born selfish.</u>" Even if we are <u>nice to members</u> of our family, that doesn't

★ count because <u>there is a pay-off</u>, at least in biological terms: they <u>share some of our</u>
5 <u>genes</u>, so by helping them we indirectly <u>further our own genetic immortality</u>. Meanwhile, other acts of <u>seeming altruism</u> are often just <u>reciprocity</u>. If <u>you scratch my back, then I scratch yours</u>—no matter how much later —<u>that's not selfless</u> either. This <u>all makes good evolutionary sense</u>, since spending time and energy <u>helping someone without any return</u> puts you at <u>a distinct disadvantage</u> in the survival stakes.

synonym chain

Step 2 Briefly summarize PASSAGE 1

We are naturally selfish, and it makes good evolutionary sense.

Step 3 Answer questions exclusively for Passage 1

3. The quotation in lines 2–3 ("try...selfish") expresses in part a belief that

Our guess: Humans are naturally selfish.

(A) altruism is not an innate human trait
We are born selfish- drawn directly from the passage.

(B) altruism can overcome our selfish instincts
Do we have evidence about overcoming our instincts? Nope.

(C) biological imperatives require a certain degree of selfishness
This is clearly a brain answer choice.

(D) human survival is dependent upon altruism
Again—zero evidence of this—and the passage says the opposite—it's a disadvantage to survival.

(E) it is necessary for humans to learn to act altruistically to carry on genes
Total assumption.

(A)

S ## Step 4   Read PASSAGE 2 actively

10   In every society, humans make <u>personal sacrifices</u> for others with <u>no expectation</u> that it will be <u>reciprocated</u>. For example, we donate to <u>charity</u>, or care for the sick and disabled. This trait is <u>extremely rare in the natural world</u>, unless there is a <u>family relationship or later reciprocation</u>. One <u>theory</u> to explain how human altruism evolved involves the way we interacted as groups early in our evolution. Toward

15   the end of the <u>Pleistocene period</u> —about 12,000 years ago—humans <u>foraged for food</u> as hunter-gatherers. These groups <u>competed against each</u> other for survival. Under these conditions, <u>altruism toward other group-members would improve the overall fitness of the group</u>. If an <u>individual defended the group</u> but was killed, <u>any genes that the individual shared with the overall group would still be passed on</u>.

Step 5   Briefly summarize PASSAGE 2

Altruism in humans comes from our group foraging past.

Step 6   Find the RELATIONSHIP between the 2 passages

1 says altruism doesn't exist—it's all reciprocity. 2 says it does exist but is based on helping one's group, which helps carry on one's genes.

Step 7   Answer questions exclusively for Passage 2

(4.) In line 17, "fitness" most nearly means

This is a **vocabulary in context** *question. Remember our strategy. We need to find the sentence from the passage:*

"altruism toward other group-members would improve the overall **fitness** of the group"

Next, our guess: how about **health**

S *Let's compare that word to our list:*

   (A) exercise   *No, not really. Exercise leads to health, but it's not health.*

~ (B) condition   *Health is a condition—perhaps we leave this for now.*

   (C) prosperity   *That has to do with money—not the right answer.*

   (D) flexibility   *Nope—we aren't talking about yoga.*

   (E) comfort   *No—that's not the same as health. Seems like an assumption.*

Let's plug our answer choice back in, to be sure it flows.

"altruism …would improve the overall **condition** of the group"

(B)   *OK—this sounds reasonable. (B) is our answer.*

Step 8   Answer questions that compare or contrast BOTH passages

1. The author of (Passage 1) would most likely argue that the behaviors listed in line 11 ("we donate...disabled")

Our guess: The author of Passage 1 believes that altruism is not natural to our species and does not help our survival.

   (A) contribute to our | collective sense of humanity |

The author of Passage 1 does not even mention a shared sense of humanity.

   (B) are clear examples of the prevalence of | reciprocity |

This is the opposite! These actions are not reciprocal. That's the point.

   (C) evolved from our | experience as hunters and gatherers |

This is Passage 2 talking!

   (D) make little sense in | today's social climate |

Absolute throw-away.

   (E) do not make good evolutionary sense

Voila! That's exactly what author 1 said.

(E)

S 2. Both authors agree on which of the following points

Our guess: Both authors talk about passing on genes.

(A) one motivation for altruistic behavior is to pass on genetic material

P1 mentions genetic immortality and P2 mentions passing on genes. We have a match.

(B) human altruism evolved during the [Pleistocene period]

Only Passage 2 mentions that.

(C) our need for reciprocity [negates the existence] of true altruism

Passage 2 thinks altruism exists.

(D) altruism [always] promotes the survival of one's social group

Beware the General, and Passage 2 cites some altruistic acts that clearly do not benefit one's social group.

(E) [altruism is necessary] to ensure the longevity of the family relationship

"Altruism is necessary": Passage 1 would never agree.

(A)

Short Comparison Passage Strategy

Step 1	Read PASSAGE 1 actively
Step 2	Briefly summarize PASSAGE 1
Step 3	Answer questions that refer ONLY to Passage 1
Step 4	Read PASSAGE 2 actively
Step 5	Briefly summarize PASSAGE 2
Step 6	Find the RELATIONSHIP between the two passages
Step 7	Answer questions that refer ONLY to Passage 2
Step 8	Answer the questions that compare or contrast BOTH passages

Medium/Long Passages

Medium and long passages require a different approach than the short and short comparison passages. Many students will attempt to read straight through a medium or long passage and then attempt to tackle the questions. Quite frequently students forget many specific details when they move on to the questions. These students then must go back and read the passage again as they move through the questions. This can be very inefficient and eat up a lot of precious time.

We have a different approach. Rather than reading the passage all the way through, you will break it up into parts. You will only read relevant selections of the passage as you move through the questions. By using the questions as your guide, you will end up reading most of the passage but in a way that will save you a lot of time.

1 Read the *ITALICS* actively

The *italics* intro gives you clues about how to approach the passage— who is writing and with what purpose?

2 Read the INTRODUCTION actively

This is roughly the first 15 lines.
- Underline key content
- Circle Logic Words
- Star the Main Idea
- Notate

3 Briefly SUMMARIZE the introduction

In a few short words summarize the main points of the introduction.

4 Answer all of the SPECIFIC questions in order

- Paraphrase the question
- Go to the line(s) referenced in the question
- Remember to read in context 5 lines up and 5 down
- Make your own guess
- Watch out for throw-aways
- Look for evidence

When you come to a general question, circle the number and skip it. We will save those 'til the end.

5 Read the CLOSING actively

Read the last 10-15 lines if you have not already done so while answering the specific questions.

6 Paraphrase the MAIN IDEA of the passage

In a few short words paraphrase the meaning of the passage.

7 Answer all of the GENERAL questions

- Bookend if you need to refresh your memory
- Make your own guess
- Watch out for throw-aways
- Look for evidence

The following is from a nineteenth century novel told from the point of view of a dog remembering his mother's playful love of words.

My father was a St. Bernard, my mother was a Collie, but I am a transcendentalist. This is what my mother told me, I do not know these nice distinctions myself. To me they are only fine large words meaning nothing. My mother had a fondness for such words; she liked to say them, and see other
5 dogs look surprised and envious, wondering how she got so much education. But, indeed, it was not real education; it was only show: she got the words by listening in the dining-room and drawing-room when there was company, and by going with the children to Sunday-school and listening there.

When she told the meaning of a big word the other dogs were so
10 taken up with admiration that it never occurred to any dog to doubt if it was the right one; and that was natural, because, for one thing, she answered up so promptly that it seemed like a dictionary speaking, and for another thing, where could they find out whether it was right or not? For she was the only cultivated dog there was.

15 By and by, when I was older, she brought home the word Unintellec-tual, one time, and worked it pretty hard all the week at different gatherings, making much unhappiness and despondency; and it was at this time that I noticed that during that week she was asked for the meaning at eight differ-ent assemblages, and flashed out a fresh definition every time, which showed
20 me that she had more presence of mind than culture, though I said nothing, of course.

She had one word which she always kept on hand, and ready, like a life-preserver, a kind of emergency word to strap on when she was likely to get washed overboard in a sudden way—that was the word Synonymous.
25 She would say, as calm as a summer's day, "It's synonymous with super-erogation," or some godless long reptile of a word like that. If there was a stranger there of course it knocked him groggy for a couple of minutes, then he would come to, and by that time she would be away down wind on an-other tack, leaving that stranger looking profane and embarrassed.

30 And it was the same with phrases. She would drag home a whole phrase, if it had a grand sound, and play it six nights and two matinees, and explain it a new way every time—which she had to, for all she cared for was the phrase; she wasn't interested in what it meant, and knew those dogs hadn't wit enough to catch her, anyway. She got so she wasn't afraid of any-
35 thing, she had such confidence in the ignorance of those creatures. Yes, she was a daisy!

1. The rhetorical device primarily featured in this passage is

(A) appeal to emotion
(B) paradox
(C) literary allusion
(D) metaphorical language
(E) technical jargon

2. The passage as a whole is best characterized as

(A) a reflection on canine social hierarchy
(B) an examination of a mother's efforts to educate her son
(C) a defense of a mother's fondness for language
(D) a description of a dog's education
(E) a memoir of a mother's artful use of words

3. Which most resembles the "education" mentioned in line 5?

(A) A football player takes dance lessons to improve his flexibility and balance.
(B) A piano player learns to play a concerto by listening to other musicians instead of by learning to read the sheet music.
(C) An artist practices forging master paintings to develop his skill.
(D) A culinary student watches cooking shows to develop new recipes.
(E) A chemistry student memorizes the periodic table to impress his teachers without understanding its purpose.

4. In line 14 "cultivated" most nearly means

(A) elitist
(B) nurtured
(C) educated
(D) pretentious
(E) courteous

5. The phrase "had more presence of mind than culture" (lines 20–21) suggests which of the following about the narrator's mother?

(A) She is a quick thinker but is plagued by a poor memory.
(B) She compensates for her lack of knowledge with quick thinking.
(C) Her personal charm is diminished by her lack of sophistication.
(D) She knows the meanings of many words but not how to use them appropriately.
(E) Her imposing intellect prevents her from participating in canine culture.

6. The phrase "play … matinees" (line 31) suggests

(A) the mother took full advantage of her newfound phrases
(B) the mother derived profound satisfaction from finding new phrases
(C) the mother was more cultured than her audience
(D) the mother enjoys the challenge of creating new definitions for her phrases
(E) the mother presented her new phrases in a highly dramatic fashion

7. The narrator's attitude toward his mother in line 36 ("Yes ... daisy") is primarily one of

(A) incredulity
(B) appreciation
(C) ambivalence
(D) disappointment
(E) criticism

S Step 1 Read the *ITALICS* actively

The following is from a nineteenth century novel told from the point of view of a dog remembering his mother's playful love of words.

Step 2 Read the INTRODUCTION actively

My father was a St. Bernard, my mother was a Collie, but I am a transcendentalist. This is what my mother told me, I do not know these nice distinctions myself. To me they are only fine large words meaning nothing. My mother had a fondness for such words; she liked to say them, and see other dogs look surprised and envious, wondering how she got so much education. But, indeed, it was not real education; it was only show: she got the words by listening in the dining-room and drawing-room when there was company, and by going with the children to Sunday-school and listening there.

When she told the meaning of a big word the other dogs were so taken up with admiration that it never occurred to any dog to doubt if it was the right one; and that was natural, because, for one thing, she answered up so promptly that it seemed like a dictionary speaking, and for another thing, where could they find out whether it was right or not? For she was the only cultivated dog there was.

Step 3 Briefly SUMMARIZE the introduction

It seems the main point is that his mom liked to use big words that surprised and confused others.

Step 4 Answer the SPECIFIC questions first

3. Which most resembles the "education" mentioned in line 5?

First, we should paraphrase the question: **What is similar to the "education?"**

Let's read in context: Normally we would read 5 lines up and 5 lines down. In this case, we have already read the first 15 lines, so we can read fewer lines of context.

S My <u>mother had a fondness for such words</u>; she liked to say them, and see <u>other dogs look surprised and envious,</u> wondering how she got so much **education.** But, indeed, <u>it was not real **education**</u>; it was only show: she got the words by <u>listening in the dining-room and drawing-room</u> when there was company, and by <u>going with the children to Sunday-school</u> and <u>listening there.</u>

*Now, we make our guess: Okay, so this education was not a "real education"- it was "only a show." We need to find an example of another education that is **not a real education, but is only a show.***

    (A) a football player takes dance lessons to improve his flexibility and balance

This seems like a genuine attempt to develop a skill, rather than just for show.

    (B) a piano player learns to play a concerto by listening to other musicians instead of by learning to read the sheet music

This also seems to be a real education, in which a student is acquiring real skills.

    (C) an artist practices forging master paintings to develop his skill

Another example of a student developing or acquiring a skill

    (D) a culinary student watches cooking shows to develop new recipes

And a 4th example of a student attempting to develop a skill

    (E) a chemistry student memorizes the periodic table to impress his teachers without understanding its purpose

So we have a surface level of understanding and learning for show. This is the right answer.

(E)

4. In line 14 "cultivated" most nearly means

*This is a **vocabulary in context** question. Remember our strategy. We need to find the sentence from the passage and the surrounding sentences to get context:*

…<u>admiration</u> that it <u>never occurred</u> to any dog <u>to doubt</u> if it was the <u>right</u> one; and that was natural, because, for one thing, <u>she answered up so promptly</u> that it seemed like a <u>dictionary speaking,</u> and for another thing, where could they find out whether it was right or not? For she was the <u>only **cultivated** dog there was.</u>

S *In context, we can see that she seemed like a "dictionary speaking," implying some appearance of knowledge.*
Our guess: A good synonym of cultivated could have something to do with "smart."

Let's compare that word to our list:

~ (A) elitist   *Does that mean smart? Maybe, let's keep it for now.*
(B̶) nurtured   *Does that mean smart? Nope. Nix it.*
~ (C) educated *That looks pretty good.*
~ (D) pretentious   *Does that mean smart? Not sure, let's keep it for now.*
(E̶) courteous   *Does that mean smart? Nope. Nix it.*

In our final step, we plug the remaining words back into the sentence to see which makes the most sense to our ear.

(A) "she was the only **elitist** dog there was"
(C) "she was the only **educated** dog there was"
(D) "she was the only **pretentious** dog there was"

Our guess was "smart". After reading the sentence filling in our 3 options, (C) sounds okay and still makes the most sense with our original guess.

(C)

5. The phrase "had more presence of mind than culture" (lines 20–21) suggests which of the following about the narrator's mother?

   (A) she is a quick thinker but is plagued by a poor memory
   (B) she compensates for her lack of knowledge with quick thinking
   (C) her personal charm is diminished by her lack of sophistication
   (D) she knows the meanings of many words but not how to use them appropriately
   (E) her imposing intellect prevents her from participating in canine culture

This is an inference question. The mom "had more presence of mind than culture." What does this mean? We need to look to the passage to find the proper context. Let's read in context.

S   By and by, when I was older, she brought home the word Unintellectual, one time, and <u>worked it pretty hard</u> all the week at different gatherings, <u>making much unhappiness</u> and despondency; and it was at this time that I noticed that during that week she was <u>asked for the meaning at eight different assemblages</u>, and (flashed) <u>out a fresh definition every time</u>, which

20   showed me that **she had more presence of mind than culture**, though <u>I said nothing, of course</u>.

    She had one word which she always kept on hand, and ready, like a life-preserver, a kind of <u>emergency word</u> to strap on when she was likely to get washed overboard in a sudden way—that was the word Synonymous. She would say, as calm as a summer's day...

So she keeps changing the definition at every social gathering. She doesn't really seem to know what the word means, but she seems to impress the other dogs.

Our guess: She has more presence of mind than culture. Perhaps this means she is lacking actual knowledge, but knows how to impress others.

Let's look at our options.

    (A) she is a quick thinker but is plagued by a poor | memory |
Memory is an instant throw-away.

    (B) she compensates for her lack of knowledge with (quick thinking)
This is very close to our guess.

    (C) her personal | charm | is diminished by her | lack of sophistication |
Charm is an assumption, as is "lack of sophistication."

    (D) she | knows the meanings | of many words but not how to use them appropriately
This is completely wrong; she does NOT know the meanings of the words.

(E) her imposing intellect | prevents her from participating | in canine culture
She is an active participant with the other dogs, so this is false.

synonym chain

(B)

S 6. The phrase "play … matinees" (line 31) suggests

Let's read in context.

She would say, as calm as a summer's day, "It's synonymous with supererogation," or some godless long reptile of a word like that. If there was a stranger there of course it knocked him groggy for a couple of minutes, then he would come to, and by that time she would be away down wind on another tack, leaving that stranger looking profane and embarrassed.

30   And it was the same with phrases. She would drag home a whole phrase, if it had a grand sound, and **play it six nights and two matinees**, and explain it a new way every time—which she had to, for all she cared for was the phrase; she wasn't interested in what it meant, and knew those dogs hadn't wit enough to catch her, anyway. She got so she wasn't afraid of anything, she had such confidence in the ignorance of those creatures. Yes, she was a daisy!

So she's not so interested in the meaning; she simply likes to use the phrase, explaining it a new way each time.

Our guess: "Playing it" has something to do with **showing off** *her new phrase.*

(A) the mother took full advantage of her newfound phrases
This seems fairly harmless, nothing grossly wrong here. She did like to use her phrases.

(B) the mother derived profound satisfaction from finding new phrases
Profound is a bit extreme, but finding is the kicker. She did not love to find them—she loved to show them off.

(C) the mother was more cultured than her audience
We have no evidence that she was in fact cultured. Nor do we know anything about the cultural level of her audience.

(D) the mother enjoys the challenge of creating new definitions for her phrases
Though she did continually redefine the phrase, there is no evidence that there was any challenge involved.

(E) the mother presented her new phrases in a highly dramatic fashion
Although we have theater language from words such as "play" and "matinee," we have no evidence that the style of her presentation was in any way dramatic. This is an assumption and a throw-away.

(A)

S 7. The narrator's attitude toward his mother in line 36 ("Yes....daisy") is primarily one of

This is a character's tone or attitude question. If this were an author's attitude or tone question, we know to eliminate ICE—but anything goes with fictional characters who can be as extreme as they want to be. Let's look to the passage for evidence concerning the narrator's attitude toward his mom.

"She got so <u>she wasn't afraid of anything</u>, she had <u>such confidence</u> in the ignorance of those creatures. **Yes, she was a daisy!**"

*Our guess: The narrator seems to be impressed with his mom's antics. More than likely, the answer will be **positive** to some extent.*

~ (A) incredulity   *not sure what this is*
~ (B) appreciation   *seems positive*
~ (C) ambivalence   *hmmm—not sure*
~~(D)~~ disappointment   *clearly wrong*
~~(E)~~ criticism   *clearly wrong*

Let's look more closely at the words we don't know right off the bat.

Incredulity
If you can see **cred** or **incred** you may remember that it is one of our roots and means **belief.**
         In-cred = not believing.
Does that seem positive? Not likely. Cross this one off.

Ambivalence
Ambi as in **ambi**dextrous, means **two.** **Valence** comes from the Latin, meaning **strength**, like strong feelings. Does the author seem to have **two** different **strong** feelings about his mom? We don't have strong evidence here. Let's cross this off, too.

(B)

Step 5   Read the CLOSING actively

Now that we have worked through the Specific Detail questions, we need to make sure we read the closing 15 lines. We've already read these, so we are covered here.

S **Step 6** Paraphrase the MAIN IDEA of the passage

Dog Narrative: Mom loved to play with big words without understanding their meaning

Step 7 Answer all the GENERAL questions

1. The rhetorical device primarily featured in this passage is

Another author's device—we simply need to look and find what tools the author is using in the passage.

(A) appeal to emotion
Do we see any appeal to our emotions? Is the author stimulating our emotions? The author may be funny and satirical but does not seem to be making an emotional appeal to the reader.

(B) paradox
Hmmm…. Nothing seems like a paradox, a statement that seems self-contradictory or absurd but in reality expresses a possible truth. Don't be tricked by hard vocabulary.

(C) literary allusion
Seems brainy. Do we see the author reference a work of literature? Nope.

(D) metaphorical language
A popular SAT answer- do we have metaphorical language—metaphors, similes, and such.
  • *seemed like a dictionary speaking (line 13)*
  • *like a life-preserver, a kind of emergency word to strap on (line 24)*
  • *godless long reptile of a word (line 27)*
  • *drag home a whole phrase (lines 32- 33)*
Yep, lots of metaphorical language. Looks good.

(E) technical jargon
Nothing overly technical here—this is wrong.

(D)

S 2. The passage as a whole is best characterized as

*Let's step back for a minute. If you have a good sense of the passage— go on to the question. If you need to take a moment to refresh yourself about the whole passage, you can "**bookend**" the passage and scan the first and last sentence of each paragraph, highlighting the important parts.*

My father was a St. Bernard, my mother was a Collie...she got the words by listening in the dining-room and drawing-room when there was company...

When she told the meaning of a big word the other dogs were so taken up with admiration...For she was the only cultivated dog there was.

By and by, when I was older, she brought home the word Unintellectual...she had more presence of mind than culture...

She had one word which she always kept on hand, and ready, like a life-preserver...leaving that stranger looking profane and embarrassed.

And it was the same with phrases...she had such confidence in the ignorance of those creatures. Yes, she was a daisy!

You can actually get the gist of a passage by bookending in this fashion, and when you are stuck and facing a general question, this is a quick way to refresh your memory.

Our guess: In this case, our passage is a narrative about a mother who loves to use big words incorrectly.

(A) a reflection on canine social hierarchy
That's just plain ridiculous.

(B) an examination of a mother's efforts to educate her son
Not so much about the education of the son—more about the mom.

(C) a defense of a mother's fondness for language
Nothing to be defensive about— fondness I like— but this is a story, not a defense.

(D) a description of a dog's education
Again—this passage is not primarily concerned with a dog's education.

(E) a memoir of a mother's artful use of words
This looks good. It's about the mom's use of words. Perfect.

(E)

Medium/Long Passage Strategy

Step 1   Read the *ITALICS* actively

Step 2   Read the INTRODUCTION actively

Step 3   Briefly SUMMARIZE the introduction

Step 4   Answer all the SPECIFIC questions in order

Step 5   Read the CLOSING actively

Step 6   Paraphrase the MAIN IDEA of the passage

Step 7   Answer all the GENERAL questions

Medium Comparison Passages

When we are asked to compare one medium passage to another, we approach each passage individually before we compare them to each other.

You want to tackle the first passage and its questions before you look at the second passage and any comparison questions.

1 Read the *ITALICS* actively

The *italics* intro gives you clues about how to approach the passage—who is writing and with what purpose? In this case, the *ITALICS* refer to both passages.

2 Read PASSAGE 1 like you'd read a medium passage

- Read the Introduction actively
- Answer the specific questions dealing only with Passage 1
- Read the Closing actively
- Summarize the passage
- Answer the General questions dealing only with Passage 1

3 Read PASSAGE 2 like you'd read a medium passage

- Read the Introduction actively
- Answer the specific questions dealing only with Passage 2
- Read the Closing actively
- Summarize the passage
- Answer the General questions dealing only with Passage 2

4 Find the RELATIONSHIP between the passages

If the two authors met in a coffee shop, what would they say to each other? "Great idea!" or "That's completely wrong!" or "I never knew that!"

5 Answer questions that compare or contrast BOTH passages

- Make your own guess
- Watch out for throw-aways
- Look for evidence

Passage 1 was adapted from a 1914 book by a British art critic known for defending abstract art. Passage 2 was adapted from a series of essays by an 18th century portrait painter who became the first president of the Royal Academy of Art in England.

Passage 1

The one good thing society can do for the artist is to leave him alone. Give him liberty. The more completely the artist is freed from the pressure of public taste and opinion, from the hope of rewards and the menace of morals, from the fear of absolute starvation or punishment, and from the prospect of wealth or
5　popular consideration, the better for him and the better for art, and therefore the better for everyone. Liberate the artist: here is something that those powerful and important people who are always assuring us that they would do anything for art can do.

They might begin the work of encouragement by disestablishing and dis-
10　endowing art; by withdrawing funding from art schools, and confiscating the moneys misused by the Royal Academy. The case of the schools is urgent. Art schools do nothing but harm, because they must do something. Art is not to be learned; at any rate it is not to be taught. All that the drawing-master can teach is the craft of imitation. In schools there must be a criterion of excellence and that
15　criterion cannot be an artistic one; the drawing-master sets up the only criterion he is capable of using—fidelity to the model.

No master can make a student into an artist; but all can, and most do, turn the unfortunate boys and girls who had been made artists by nature into impostors, maniacs, criminals, or just cretins. It is not the master's fault and he ought not
20　to be blamed. He is there to bring all his pupils to a certain standard of efficiency appreciable by inspectors and by the general public, and the only quality of which such can judge is accuracy of representation. The only respects in which one work can be seen to differ from another by an ordinarily insensitive person (e.g. a Board of Education inspector) are choice of subject and fidelity to
25　common vision. So, even if a drawing-master could recognize artistic talent, he would not be permitted to encourage it. It is not that drawing-masters are wicked, but that the system is vicious. Art schools must go.

Passage 2

The principal advantage of an academy is that, besides supplying able men to direct students, it will be a repository for the great examples of art. These bright
30　instructors and masterpieces will inspire future genius; without them, even the strongest intellect may be fruitlessly employed. By studying these authentic models, that idea of excellence which is the result of the accumulated experience

of past ages may be at once acquired. Even the slow and obstructed progress of our predecessors may teach us a shorter and easier way to accomplish our
35 artistic goals. The student receives at one glance the principles which many artists have spent their whole lives divining; and, satisfied with their effect, the student is spared the painful investigation by which these principles come to be known. How many artistic geniuses have been lost to the world for lack of guidance and inspiration? How many men of great natural abilities have
40 gone undiscovered for want of these advantages? They never had an opportunity to see those masterly efforts of genius which at once kindle the whole soul, and force it into sudden and irresistible admiration.

Every seminary of learning is permeated with an atmosphere of floating knowledge. In this environment, every young mind will be drawn to ideas
45 and insights that are particularly well suited to its nature. Knowledge obtained in such a manner is more useful than that which is forced upon the mind by solitary meditation.

I would chiefly recommend that an implicit obedience to the rules of art, as established by the great masters, should be exacted from the *young* students.
50 Those models, which have passed through the scrutiny of the ages, should be considered by them as perfect and infallible guides, subjects for their imitation, not their criticism.

I am confident that this is the only efficacious method of making a progress in the arts; and he who sets out with doubting will find life finished before
55 he achieves mastery over the most basic principles of art. For it may be laid down as a maxim that he who refuses the wisdom of the masters has ended his studies as soon as he has commenced them. Every opportunity, therefore, should be taken to discount that false and vulgar opinion that rules are the fetters of genius. Rules are fetters only to men of no genius; just as armor,
60 which upon the strong becomes an ornament and a defense, upon the weak and misshapen turns into a load, crippling the body it was made to protect.

1. Both authors would agree on which of the following points?

(A) Art schools provide examples of master works of art.
(B) Certain individuals have natural artistic abilities.
(C) Artistic instincts can never be objectively taught.
(D) Beginning students must master the rudimentary rules of art.
(E) Art schools can lead only to imitation, not to original insight.

2. According to the first paragraph of Passage 1, all of the following can restrict artistic expression EXCEPT the

(A) desire for financial reward
(B) hope for fame and popular recognition
(C) fear of upsetting the public's ethical standards
(D) pragmatic concerns of everyday life
(E) longing for praise from art critics

3. The statement in line 13 ("at… taught") serves primarily to

   (A) qualify the initial position of the author
   (B) indirectly advance a personal agenda
   (C) defend an earlier assumption
   (D) subtly downplay the importance of a claim
   (E) put divergent interpretations of art into perspective

4. The author argues that "no master can make a student into an artist" (line 17) because

   (A) artists are created by nature, rather than made by teachers
   (B) art schools lack the necessary funding to achieve their desired goals
   (C) standards of artistic excellence cannot be rigorously enforced
   (D) it is impossible to define the nature of a true artist
   (E) the current system of art schools is excessively restrictive

5. The "accumulated experience of past ages" mentioned in lines 32–33 most likely refers to the

   (A) wisdom of the masters
   (B) technical advances in art
   (C) history of art
   (D) common artistic goals
   (E) archived masterpieces

6. In line 41, the word "efforts" most nearly means

   (A) feats
   (B) attempts
   (C) struggles
   (D) proofs
   (E) imitations

7. The author of Passage 1 would most likely respond to the statements made in paragraph 3 of Passage 2 by arguing that

   (A) it is unwise to consider even the greatest work of art to be perfect
   (B) imitating the masters will only stifle an artist's creativity
   (C) imitation of masterpieces does not develop genuine artistic ability
   (D) experienced painters have no need for academic exercises
   (E) previous works of art can never inspire future works of genius

8. The author's use of italics in line 49 serves primarily to

   (A) underscore the advantages of learning art from a young age
   (B) highlight the importance of using age-appropriate instructional techniques
   (C) emphasize the suggestibility of younger students
   (D) suggest that older students may not require strict adherence to the rules of art
   (E) imply that younger artists are naturally less talented than older artists

9. Unlike Passage 1, Passage 2 makes use of

   (A) sociological analysis
   (B) metaphorical language
   (C) personal anecdote
   (D) historical facts
   (E) hypothetical assumptions

10. Which of the following can be found in both passages?

    I. The effect of art schools on artists
    II. The role of instructors in art schools
    III. The value of accurate representation in art

    (A) I only
    (B) II only
    (C) I and II only
    (D) I and III only
    (E) I, II, and III

11. Compared to the tone of Passage 2, that of Passage 1 is more

    (A) pessimistic
    (B) critical
    (C) dismissive
    (D) resentful
    (E) sympathetic

12. A major point of difference between the two passages is that Passage 1

    (A) argues that art schools are inherently dangerous, whereas Passage 2 argues that they are only useful when properly structured

    (B) argues that artists should be judged by their natural talent, whereas Passage 2 argues that talent must be shaped using established artistic principles

    (C) presents the risks of attending art school, whereas Passage 2 views art schools as entirely beneficial to all students

    (D) emphasizes the need for artistic freedom of expression, whereas Passage 2 rejects that approach as overly simplistic

    (E) argues that formal training can hinder artistic development, whereas Passage 2 advises students to learn from the wisdom of the masters

S **Step 1**   Read the *ITALICS* actively

Passage 1 was adapted from a <u>1914</u> book by a <u>British art critic</u> known for <u>defending abstract art</u>. Passage 2 was adapted from a series of essays by an <u>18th century portrait painter</u> who became the <u>first president</u> of the Royal <u>Academy of Art</u> in England.

Step 2   Read PASSAGE 1 as you would read a Medium Passage

<u>Read the Introduction actively</u>

The one good thing society can do for the <u>artist</u> is to <u>leave him alone</u>. <u>Give</u> him <u>liberty</u>. The more completely the artist is <u>freed from the pressure of public taste and opinion</u>, from the hope of <u>rewards</u> and the <u>menace of morals</u>, from the <u>fear of</u> absolute <u>starvation</u> or punishment, and from the <u>prospect of wealth</u> or popular consideration, the better for him and the better for art, and therefore the <u>better for everyone</u>. <u>Liberate the artist</u>: here is something that those powerful and important people who are always assuring us that they would do anything for art can do.

They might begin the work of encouragement by disestablishing and disendowing art; by <u>withdrawing funding from art schools</u>, and confiscating the moneys misused by the Royal Academy. The case of the <u>schools</u> is <u>urgent</u>. <u>Art schools do nothing but harm</u>, because they must do something. <u>Art is not to be learned; at any rate it is not to be taught</u>. All that the drawing-master can teach is the craft of <u>imitation</u>.

<u>Answer the specific questions dealing only with Passage 1</u>

3. The statement in line 13 ("at…taught") serves primarily to

Read lines 8–18.

Let's look at the exact sentence:

> "Art is not to be learned; at any rate it is not to be taught."

Our guess: "At any rate" indicates that the author is **rethinking** *his initial statement.*

S *Let's see if we can find that in the answer choices.*

(A) qualify the initial position of the author

Qualify means to "modify or limit in some way; make less strong or positive." This certainly seems to fit.

(B) indirectly advance a personal agenda

We have no evidence of any personal agenda.

(C) defend an earlier assumption

Nope. We are introducing a new idea—rather than defending an older one.

(D) subtly downplay the importance of a claim

This is one giant throw-away.

(E) put divergent interpretations of art into perspective

Sounds like the Brain, and it's totally wrong.

(A)

4. The author argues that "no master can make a student into an artist" (line 17) because

Read lines 12-22.

Our guess: The author references that some boys and girls "had been made artists by nature." Let's find that:

(A) artists are created by nature, rather than made by teachers

*Bingo. That's straight from the passage—line 18 "**been made artists by nature.**"*

(B) art schools lack the necessary funding to achieve their desired goals

Nope- beware the Money Grubber.

(C) standards of artistic excellence cannot be rigorously enforced

This may be true, but it has nothing to do with "making a student into an artist." We are not answering the question.

(D) it is impossible to define the nature of a true artist

The author never mentions defining the nature of a true artist. The author says artists are made by nature. Slippery word play. A tricky wrong answer.

(E) the current system of art schools is excessively restrictive

This may be true, but it does not answer our question. We are interested in why teachers cannot make artists. This is another wrong answer.

(A)

S <u>Read the CLOSING actively</u>

It is <u>not the master's fault</u> and he ought not to be blamed. He is there to <u>bring all his pupils to a certain standard of efficiency</u> appreciable by inspectors and by the <u>general public</u>, and the only quality of which such can <u>judge is accuracy of representation</u>. The only respects in which one work can be seen to differ from another by an ordinarily insensitive person (e.g. a Board of Education inspector) are choice of subject and <u>fidelity to common vision</u>. So, even if a drawing-master could recognize artistic talent, he would not be permitted to encourage it. It is <u>not</u> that <u>drawing-masters are wicked</u>, but that the <u>system is vicious</u>. <u>Art schools must go</u>. ★

Summarize the passage

Art schools do more harm than good.

Answer the General questions dealing only with Passage 1

2. According to the first paragraph of Passage 1, all of the following can restrict artistic expression EXCEPT the

This question requires us to scan back and forth between the question and the passage. The word **EXCEPT** *is the key. We need to find which one of the following is not mentioned.*

   (A) desire for financial reward
"The prospect of wealth" is mentioned in line 4.

   (B) hope for fame and popular recognition
"Popular consideration" line 5; this looks like a decent synonym.

   (C) fear of upsetting the public's ethical standards
"Public taste...and the menace of morals" lines 2-3 ; this is a good synonym.

   (D) pragmatic concerns of everyday life
Fear of "absolute starvation" line 4: hmmm, this one is close...

   (E) longing for praise from ⬚art critics⬚
Finally a good throw-away. Art critics are not mentioned anywhere.

(E)

S Step 3 Read PASSAGE 2 as you would read a Medium Passage

Read the Introduction actively

The principal advantage of an academy is that, besides supplying able men to direct students, it will be a repository for the great examples of art. These bright instructors and masterpieces will inspire future genius; without them, even the strongest intellect may be fruitlessly employed. By studying these authentic models, that idea of excellence which is the result of the accumulated experience of past ages may be at once acquired. Even the slow and obstructed progress of our predecessors may teach us a shorter and easier way to accomplish our artistic goals.

Answer the specific questions dealing only with Passage 2

5. The "accumulated experience of past ages" mentioned in line 32–33 most likely refers to the

Read lines 27–38.

When we read in context, we find that the paragraph focuses on the great masterworks of the older artists.

Our guess: Something to do with master painters or paintings.

(A) wisdom of the masters
That is very close.

(B) technical advances in art
Throw-away: nothing about technical advances.

(C) history of art
This is too broad and general.

(D) common artistic goals
The passage never discusses goals.

(E) archived masterpieces
Masterpieces is correct—but archived is our throw-away.

(A)

S 6. In line 41, the word "efforts" most nearly means

Another VIC! We know the drill.
> "…an opportunity to see those masterly **efforts** of genius…"

*Our guess: How about those masterly **works** of genius?*

~ (A) feats *Feats is like an accomplishment—maybe.*
  (B) attempts *No they actually achieved, not just attempted.*
  (C) struggles *Struggle is going too far—we don't know how difficult it was.*
  (D) proofs *Huh? That's just strange.*
  (E) imitations *No. The author addresses imitation in the passage—but not in this particular sentence.*

Let's plug it in to be sure:
> "…an opportunity to see those masterly **feats** of genius…"

This works.

(A)

8. The author's use of italics in line 49 serves primarily to

Read lines 44-54.

This is a device question. Italics often call attention to a point.

*Our guess: In the context of the passage, the author **emphasizes** that **younger students need the obedience.***

(A) underscore the advantages of learning art from a young age
It never mentions the advantages of starting early.

(B) highlight the importance of using age-appropriate instructional techniques
This is never mentioned.

(C) emphasize the suggestibility of younger students
Nope!

(D) suggest that older students may not require strict adherence to the rules of art
This is essentially saying the same thing—in the opposite way. Leave this for now.

(E) imply that younger artists are naturally less talented than older artists
No evidence of differences in levels of talent.

(D)

S ### Read the Closing actively

I am <u>confident</u> that this is the <u>only efficacious method of making a progress</u> in the arts; and he who <u>sets out with doubting will find life finished before he achieves mastery</u> over the most basic principles of art. For it may be laid down as a <u>maxim</u> that he who <u>refuses the wisdom of the masters has ended his studies as soon as he has commenced them.</u> Every opportunity, therefore, should be taken to <u>discount</u> that <u>false and vulgar opinion that rules are the fetters of genius.</u> <u>Rules are fetters only to men of no genius;</u> just us armor, which upon the strong becomes an ornament and a defense, upon the weak and misshapen turns into a load, crippling the body it was made to protect.

Summarize the passage

Art schools develop the genius of young artists.

Answer questions only dealing with Passage 2

There are none.

Step 4 Find the relationship between the passages

They seem to be polar opposites: The author of Passage 1 would likely spill hot coffee on the author of Passage 2. There is no love between these authors.

Step 5 Answer questions that compare or contrast both of the passages

1. Both authors would agree on which of the following points?
Remember to look for very simple and basic points of agreement.

(A) Art schools provide examples of master works of art.
That's only the author of Passage 2.

(B) Certain individuals have natural artistic abilities.
Wow. Can we get more basic? It's hard to argue with this.

S

    (C) Artistic instincts can never be objectively taught.
That's the author of Passage 1.

    (D) Beginning students must master the rudimentary rules of art.
That's the author of Passage 2.

    (E) Art schools can lead only to imitation, not to original insight.
That's the author of Passage 1.

(B)

7. The author of (Passage 1) would most likely respond to the statements made in paragraph 3 of Passage 2 by arguing that

This is a 2-part question. First, what is the main point of the 3rd paragraph of Passage 2: students should obey the rules, learn from the masters, and imitate them.

Next, how would author 1 respond? He would completely reject the idea that students should imitate. Author 1 is all about artistic liberty.

    (A) it is unwise to consider even the greatest work of art to be perfect
Author 1 does not discuss perfection. Throw-away.

~ (B) imitating the masters will only stifle an artist's creativity
Hmmm... This looks close.

~ (C) imitation of masterpieces does not develop genuine artistic ability
This one looks good too. We'll come back to this.

    (D) experienced painters have no need for academic exercises
Author 1 does not discuss the needs of experienced painters.

    (E) previous works of art can never inspire future works of genius
Beware the General! Never say never.

*So we need to decide between (B) and (C). Will imitation of masterworks **always** stifle creativity, or is it simply not a way to develop true artistic ability? According to all the talk of nature-made artists, it seems that (C) is the stronger answer.*

(C)

S 9. Unlike Passage 1, (Passage 2) makes use of

Another author's device question. We simply need to scan both passages to find these devices. The device cannot be in 1, but must be in 2.

   (A) sociological analysis

Hmmm. Sociology. Don't think we saw that one in Passage 2.

   (B) metaphorical language

Passage 1 has no metaphors, and Passage 2, in its final paragraph, presents the following metaphorical language: "rules are the fetters of genius...upon the weak and misshapen turns into a load, crippling the body it was made to protect." This looks good.

   (C) personal anecdote

Author 2 does not tell a personal story. This is incorrect.

   (D) historical facts

Author 2 does not present facts from history.

   (E) hypothetical assumptions

Author 2 does not present any hypothetical situations or assumptions.

(B)

10. Which of the following can be found in both passages?
   I. The effect of art schools on artists
   II. The role of instructors in art schools
   III. The value of accurate representation in art

   (A) I only
   (B) II only
   (C) I and II only
   (D) I and III only
   (E) I, II, and III

We need to go through this systematically. We need to look for I. *If we find it—then we cross off all answers without it. If we cannot find* I., *we cross off all answers that contain* I. *And then we move on to* II. *and* III.

S

      I. *Do both passages mention the effect of art school on artists?*
        Absolutely!

Cross off (B).

      II. *Do both passages mention the role of instructors?*
        Absolutely!

Cross off (A) and (D).

      III. *Do both passages mention the value of accurate representation in art?*

Author 1 mentions this verbatim, but Author 2 never directly refers to the value of accuracy or accurate representation.

So we toss out III., *and we only have one answer choice left.*

(C)

11. Compared to the tone of Passage 2, that of (Passage 1) is more

First—be careful about which author we are looking at: Passage 1.
*And when it comes to author's tone—remember, no ICE. No **I**ndifference,*
***C**onfusion or **E**motional extremes.*

Our guess: The author of Passage 1 attacks art schools in a very direct fashion.

    (A) pessimistic
No. Author 1 is not a pessimist.

    (B) critical
The author of 1 is giving a strong critique of art schools. This could be it.

    (C) dismissive
No. Author 1 does not dismiss art schools, he attacks them.

    (D) resentful
Never, ever!! Remember **ICE**. Resentment is an **emotional extreme**. Nix it.

    (E) sympathetic
This is the opposite. The author of Passage 1 is on the attack. Perhaps he's sympathetic with artists- but his overall tone is more critical.

(B)

S 12. A major point of difference between the two passages is that (Passage 1)

For this kind of question, we need to dive into the answers directly:

(A) argues that art schools are inherently dangerous, whereas Passage 2 argues that they are only useful when |properly structured|

The author of Passage 1's stance is correct, but the argument for the author of Passage 2 is incorrect.

(B) argues that artists should be |judged| by their natural talent, whereas Passage 2 argues that talent must be shaped using established artistic principles

The author of Passage 1 never argues that artists should be judged. Throwaway.

(C) presents the risks of attending art school, whereas Passage 2 views art schools as |entirely| beneficial to |all| students

*Beware the General! Too global. Not **all** students.*

(D) emphasizes the need for artistic freedom of expression, whereas Passage 2 rejects that approach as |overly simplistic|

Author 1 certainly argues for artistic liberty, but Author 2 does not say liberty is too simplistic, rather it is ineffective for releasing genius. Simplistic is the throw-away.

(E) argues that formal training can hinder artistic development, whereas Passage 2 advises students to learn from the wisdom of the masters

This is almost verbatim from the passage. This is the perfect answer.

(E)

Medium Comparison Passage Strategy

Step 1   Read the *ITALICS* actively

Step 2   Read Passage 1 like a Medium Passage

Step 3   Read Passage 2 like a Medium Passage

Step 4   Find the relationship between the passages

Step 5   Answer questions that compare or contrast the both passages

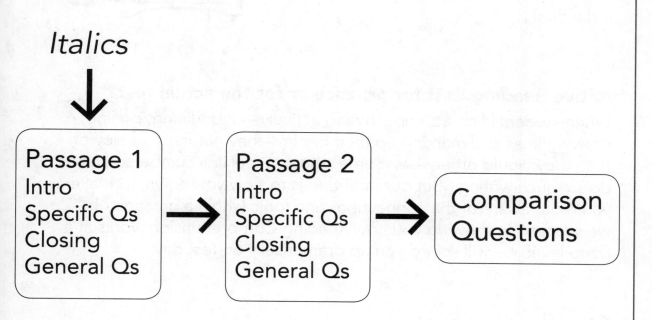

Italics

Passage 1
Intro
Specific Qs
Closing
General Qs

→

Passage 2
Intro
Specific Qs
Closing
General Qs

→

Comparison
Questions

Critical Reading
Time Management

All students must find their own optimal approach to Reading Comprehension.

There is no **perfect strategy** for tackling the passage or the questions. But there is a perfect strategy for each individual.

Active Reading: Is it for practice or for the actual test?

When students first attempt to read actively—underlining, circling, drawing lines and marking up their paper—they naturally go slower than they would otherwise. Some students feel it is cumbersome to do so much writing. But our intention is to slow you down, to make you more aware of the connections and logic within a passage. If we succeed in showing you how Reading Comprehension works at a deep level, we will speed you up dramatically on test day.

Our goal is simple:

We want to **slow you down**, in order to eventually **speed you up on the test!**

Most people who have timing issues tend to race through the passage, missing most of the important details. They may have to go back to the same part of the passage three or four times before they really understand what's happening. A better strategy is to read it with more focus and intention the first time. Then you won't need to go back at all.

If you become more skilled at deeply reading the passage, you will be able to quickly and effectively move through the questions, becoming a much more efficient test-taker.

PRACTICE, PRACTICE, PRACTICE

You will get a sense of your own speed by doing timing drills. Every week you should practice timed drills using complete SAT sections from the College Board's *Official Guide to the SAT*™.

Before you ever try a new SAT strategy on an official SAT, you must first try that strategy on a mock SAT under timed conditions. You may need to adjust or adapt how much you underline, or how much you notate. This will be informed by your mock tests. If you are still running out of time after several rounds of mock test practice, you may need to underline less and skip notating altogether.

People do read at different speeds, and you need to work at a speed that is comfortable to you and fine tune the strategies so that they best serve you.

Different Critical Reading Approaches

TYPICAL Medium/Long Passage Strategy

Step 1   Read the *ITALICS* actively

Step 2   Read the INTRODUCTION actively

Step 3   Briefly summarize the INTRODUCTION

Step 4   Answer all the SPECIFIC Questions

Step 5   Read the CLOSING actively

Step 6   Paraphrase the MAIN IDEA of the passage

Step 7   Answer all the GENERAL questions

Using this method, a student may only read 60-80% of the content in the passage, omitting material in the passage between specific questions.

This method helps many of our students score higher on Critical Reading, but it is not for everyone. Some students do not feel comfortable skipping any content in the passage. If they are fast enough readers, they do not need to skip a word. They can use a modified strategy.

MODIFIED Passage Strategy (for faster readers)

Step 1   Read the *ITALICS* actively

Step 2   Read the INTRODUCTION actively

Step 3   Continue reading until you reach material covered
           by the first specific question

Step 4   Answer the first specific question, reading
           5 LINES UP AND DOWN from the assigned line(s)

Step 5   Read any material in the passage between the lines
           referenced by the first and second specific questions

Step 6   Complete all the specific questions in this fashion,
           omitting nothing from the passage

Step 7   Read the closing 15 lines

Step 8   Answer the general questions

This method takes a little longer, but allows a student to read every word of the passage. For faster readers, this is perfect.

Reading the entire passage first
(for our fastest readers with the best memories)

Some students are gifted in reading and can read a Long Passage and keep it all in their heads for a short period of time. That's a gift! Students with such robust "working" memories will have no problem reading and retaining all the material in a Long Passage. If you fall into this category and you are a fast reader, there is no reason not to read the whole passage before going to the questions. Some students prefer this, and if you are fast enough to pull it off, this is an effective way to tackle a passage. But for the many students who get distracted or lose details when reading a long passage, breaking it up into parts is a better strategy.

The Scientific Approach

If you are not sure which approach will work for you, experiment! Take three timed sections using different strategies, and see which strategy is most comfortable for you. You want to shoot for the best time management and the greatest accuracy. Keep modifying your approach until you reach your optimal strategy and your best score.

Reading Comprehension Practice Problems

Short Passage 1

From Swiss Army knives to iPhones, it seems we just love fancy gadgets with as many different functions as possible. And judging from the ancient Greek Antikythera mechanism, the desire to impress
5 with the latest multipurpose must-have item goes back at least 2000 years. This mysterious box of tricks was a portable clockwork computer, dating from the first or second century BC. Operated by turning a handle on the side, it modeled the move-
10 ments of the Sun, Moon and planets through the sky, sported a local calendar, star calendar and Moon-phase display, and could even predict eclipses and track the timing of the Olympic games.

1. The author mentions the "Swiss Army knives" and "iPhones" (line 1) in order to suggest that

   (A) humans continue to be fascinated with multifunctional technology
   (B) humans value convenience over practical concerns
   (C) modern humans are more creative than their predecessors
   (D) ancient inventions continue to inspire today's inventors
   (E) technology has advanced continuously throughout history

2. The list of functions in lines 9-13 ("modeled... games)" primarily serves to

   (A) highlight the progressive nature of Greek thought
   (B) underscore the Greek's interest in celestial movements
   (C) emphasize the Antikythera's wide variety of features
   (D) illustrate the technological advances of early civilizations
   (E) highlight the mystery surrounding Greek invention

Short Passage 2

It's a dirty job, but someone's got to do it: for innovation to thrive on the internet, we must break up the very social networks that the web has made possible. Previous research has shown that certain patterns of
5 social interaction make radical innovation more likely. Bold ideas are typically incompletely formed when first conceived and easily shot down by criticism. Hence, they emerge more readily in communities in which individuals work mostly in small and relatively
10 isolated groups, giving their ideas time and space to mature. The problem, says social scientist Viktor Mayer-Schönberger of the National University of Singapore, is that today's software developers work in social networks in which everyone is closely linked to
15 everyone else. "The over-abundance of connections through which information travels reduces diversity and keeps radical ideas from taking hold," he suggests.

3. In lines 8-11 ("hence…mature') the author suggests that

   (A) small groups provide a more engaging intellectual environment than large groups
   (B) members of small groups are less critical than members of large groups
   (C) smaller groups provide more personalized attention to their members than do large groups
   (D) the diversity of larger groups stifles innovation and radical ideas
   (E) small groups create opportunities for new ideas to develop

4. The primary purpose of the passage is to

   (A) challenge a widely-held belief
   (B) explore a controversial technology
   (C) examine the nature of a problem
   (D) call attention to a crisis
   (E) highlight a common practice

Short Comparison Passages

Passage 1

On 3 March 2004, a group of 17 previously un-
contacted Ayoreo Indians emerged from the jungle
100 miles north-east of Filadelfia in Paraguay.
They were desperately thirsty, as cattle ranchers
5   had muscled in on their territory and taken control of their water supply. The group reluctantly
decided to approach some other Ayoreo who were
setting up a new community in the last sizeable
chunk of protected forest in the region and ask
10 for their help. This encounter may be the most
recent example of what anthropologists call "first
contact," but it certainly won't be the last. According to Survival International, there are still over a
hundred tribes around the world who still have no
15 sustained contact with outsiders.

Passage 2

My people, the Kuna, lived on islands near what
is now called Panama for generations before
the Spanish invasion. For centuries we lived in
relative isolation. Only recently, in the last few
20 decades, have our people been exposed to the
influences of non-Kuna Westerners. These outside influences have fueled divisions between the
elders and the youth of our tribe. Disagreements
concerning the preservation of our rituals and
25 the safeguarding of our culture have impacted
our community. Our time-honored practice of
conveying the wisdom of our people to the next
generation through the use of chants and dances
is now under attack. The younger generations
30 now prefer to read our history in books. While the
culture of my people is strong, no one knows what
long-term effects increased contact with non-Kuna
will have.

5. The author of Passage 1 would most likely
   view the scenario presented in Passage 2 with

   (A) cynical mistrust
   (B) objective curiosity
   (C) scholarly indifference
   (D) outright indignation
   (E) complete surprise

6. The authors of both passages would agree on
   which of the following points?

   (A) Outside influence has tangibly negative
       effects on a culture.
   (B) When outside influences present themselves,
       cultures must find ways to adjust.
   (C) Outside influence always results in cultural
       change.
   (D) The modern era has made it increasingly
       difficult for cultures to remain isolated.
   (E) All cultures will inevitably come into
       contact with outside cultures.

7. The tone of Passage 2 can best be characterized
   as

   (A) resentful
   (B) wistful
   (C) analytical
   (D) dismayed
   (E) concerned

8. Which of the following statements best captures
   the relationship between the two passages?

   (A) Passage 2 furnishes a larger context for the
       experiences described in Passage 1.
   (B) Passage 1 assesses the impact of a
       phenomenon, whereas Passage 2 offers a
       personal testament to that same phenomenon.
   (C) Passage 1 introduces the historical causes of
       an event, whereas Passage 2 considers that
       event from a personal perspective.
   (D) Passage 1 discusses a phenomenon whereas
       Passage 2 provides a personal reflection on
       the impact of a similar phenomenon.
   (E) Passage 1 presents a critical perspective,
       whereas Passage 2 presents the view of an
       impassioned observer.

Medium Passage 1

The following is from a short story about a Russian immigrant's trip to America at the turn of the nineteenth century.

As the steamship Lincoln pulled into its berth at the South Street Seaport, Pavel Fedorov couldn't believe his eyes. Beyond the harbor loomed New York City, the most enormous metropolis he had

5 ever seen. The massive edifices that made up the city's skyline seemed to reach for the clouds above, while the streets below teemed with bustling activity. Through a porthole of the Lincoln's lowest deck Pavel could see down the city's cobblestoned

10 streets, avenues overrun with the commotion of rushing pedestrians, overflowing carriages, horses and cattle, pushcarts and peddlers. Pavel eyed it all with wonder: America was the fulfillment of his lifelong dream. He couldn't believe that at last

15 he'd made it.

For more than six months Pavel had been on the road, first trudging on foot west across Europe, from his family's farm in the foothills of the Ural Mountains toward the ocean ports that would take

20 him to the United States. In the seaside city of Le Havre, lacking the money for even the cheapest steamship ticket, Pavel worked and slept on the docks until finally he could afford the fare. Once aboard the ship, Pavel and his fellow immigrants

25 were confined to the lower decks of the steerage class, so named for its location under the ship's steering apparatus. Together Pavel and the other hopeful immigrants journeyed across the Atlantic, sharing the same cramped spaces, the same stifling

30 air, the same unfettered optimism and same fears of the unknown. They all dreamed the United States would offer boundless new opportunities.

After weeks on the open sea, the Lincoln finally reached its destination. Through the porthole win-

35 dow Pavel could see New York's docks just twenty yards away, but as close as he was to the country physically, he had not yet arrived. Throughout the voyage the gossip below decks (translated haltingly into dozens of different languages) had been that

40 the steerage passengers would not even be allowed to disembark in New York City. It was said they would be ferried to a special place called "Ellis Island," a government outpost where the hopeful

immigrants would be processed and would have the

45 chance to prove their "right to land." The steerage-class passengers would have to pass a battery of tests administered by imposing federal officials, tests of their health, eyesight, sanity, and legality that would ensure the new Americans would not

50 become a burden to the U.S. government.

Pavel had doubted if the rumors about Ellis Island were true, but when the immigrants were finally let off the Lincoln it was not into the busy streets of New York City. Pavel had watched the

55 first- and second-class passengers disembark into the arms of their welcoming families and friends at the South Street Seaport, but he and his fellow steerage passengers were instead shepherded down gangplanks to a fleet of ferries waiting below.

60 "To Ellis Island," the Lincoln's crew shouted, "all aboard to Ellis Island."

9. The passage as a whole is best characterized as

   (A) an exploration of the impact of immigration on New York society
   (B) a personal anecdote describing a journey of great significance
   (C) a commentary on early American immigration policies
   (D) an extended metaphor of the power of hope to overcome adversity
   (E) an exploration of the economic struggles of immigrants

10. Pavel's attitude toward New York City in the first paragraph (lines 1-15) is primarily one of

   (A) awe
   (B) perplexity
   (C) skepticism
   (D) ambivalence
   (E) nostalgia

11. For Pavel, America represents

   (A) a myriad of new possibilities
   (B) freedom from oppression
   (C) a chance to reinvent himself
   (D) the hope for social equality
   (E) the promise of economic prosperity

12. In line 37 the phrase "had not yet arrived" emphasizes

    (A) New York City was not the Lincoln's final destination.

    (B) The Lincoln had not yet docked at the South Street Seaport.

    (C) Pavel had yet to disembark from the boat onto American soil.

    (D) Pavel was not quite ready to become an American citizen.

    (E) Pavel was intent on achieving success in New York.

13. In line 46 "battery" most nearly means

    (A) ordeal

    (B) series

    (C) list

    (D) burden

    (E) onslaught

14. The words "processed" (line 44) and "shepherded" (line 58) imply that the manner in which Pavel and the other steerage passengers were treated was

    (A) intended to discourage immigration

    (B) unpleasant but necessary

    (C) embarrassing to the prospective immigrants

    (D) both logical and comprehensive

    (E) highly impersonal

Medium Passage 2

The following is from a 2006 essay about transcendentalist author Henry David Thoreau's impact on non-violent civil disobedience.

Disgusted by his government's campaign in the Mexican-American War and its general complacency regarding slavery, American author Henry David Thoreau decided to hit the government where it
5 would hurt the most—in the pocket book. In July 1846, Thoreau was arrested for refusing to pay six years worth of delinquent poll taxes. Instead of paying taxes that would fund a war he abhorred and support a government he found morally bankrupt,
10 Thoreau willingly, almost gleefully, went to jail. Though Thoreau was released from prison the next day—a meddlesome aunt paid the delinquent fees against his wishes— this short-lived experience planted the seeds for Thoreau's future philosophy.
15 Two years later, still disheartened by the actions of his government, Thoreau penned an essay commonly known as *On Civil Disobedience*.

Formally published in 1849, *On Civil Disobedience* argues that citizens have a moral obligation to
20 refuse to support a government whose actions go against their individual consciences. Compliance with such a government would make the people themselves agents of injustice. When faced with an unjust government, Thoreau contended that
25 "the true place for a just man is in prison." He called for his countrymen to stand and join him in his "peaceable revolution," admonishing the men that simply wished for justice: "This is not to say that you have an obligation to devote your life to fighting for
30 justice, but you do have an obligation not to commit injustice and not to give injustice your practical support." With these words, a movement was born.

For the past 160 years, activists have been following Thoreau's example of non-violent
35 resistance, the active refusal to obey certain laws, demands and commands of a government without resorting to physical violence. His work has influenced religious and political leaders as well as countless social reformers. In fact, many scholars
40 consider *On Civil Disobedience* to be one of the most influential political tracts ever written by an American. Thoreau's convictions have inspired social reform movements ranging from India's fight for independence from Great Britain to the Ameri-
45 can Civil Rights Movement.

The Father of Indian Independence, Mohandas Gandhi, credited Thoreau as the "chief cause of the abolition of slavery in America." Galvanized by Thoreau's 19th century essay, Gandhi pioneered the
50 concept of satyagraha—the resistance of tyranny through mass civil disobedience. Gandhi promoted total non-violence and respectful disagreement, the civilest of civil disobedience. Equally influenced by Thoreau's writing about civil disobedience was
55 Dr. Martin Luther King, Jr. In his autobiography, the American civil rights leader wrote, "No other person has been more eloquent and passionate in getting this idea across than Henry David Thoreau. As a result of his writings and personal witness, we
60 are the heirs of a legacy of creative protest."

15. In line 10, the word "gleefully" implies what about Thoreau?

(A) He was eager to publicly express his dissent.
(B) He wanted to be an example for other dissidents.
(C) He was glad that he would no longer be expected to pay taxes.
(D) He felt that imprisonment would give him instant credibility.
(E) He knew that he would be quickly released from prison.

16. According to the passage, Thoreau believed his aunt (line 12) acted

(A) superficially
(B) ignorantly
(C) impractically
(D) intrusively
(E) impulsively

17. The passage suggests that one of the "actions" referred to in line 20 was

(A) arresting political dissenters
(B) condoning slavery
(C) releasing prisoners for a fee
(D) charging poll taxes
(E) exiting the Mexican-American War

18. The tone of Thoreau's statement, "This… support," (lines 28-32) is best described as

    (A) contemptuous
    (B) threatening
    (C) morose
    (D) earnest
    (E) sardonic

19. The phrase in line 25 ("the true…prison") suggests that

    (A) being imprisoned is a way to publicly express one's convictions
    (B) a true sense of morality can be expressed only through political action
    (C) the act of being arrested is an effective way to promote social change
    (D) moral leaders should be subject to the same laws as average citizens
    (E) complying with an unjust government compromises one's own morality

20. The mention of satyagraha (line 50) provides an example of

    (A) an educational movement embodying the same ideals as Thoreau
    (B) a concept that arose concurrently with Thoreau's ideas
    (C) a different culture's interpretation of Thoreau's ideas
    (D) a religious movement that lead to India's independence
    (E) a peaceful political movement that inspired Gandhi

21. In line 53 the phrase "civilest of civil" implies that Gandhi

    (A) was a political extremist with radical ideas
    (B) continued Thoreau's practice of organizing mass civil protest
    (C) adapted Thoreau's concept to better suit the needs of his people
    (D) successfully embellished upon Thoreau's original idea
    (E) advocated a complete rejection of violent forms of social protest

22. Martin Luther King, Jr.'s quotation in lines 56-60 primarily suggests that

    (A) he was inspired by Thoreau's legacy of nonviolent protest
    (B) he appreciated the international relevance of Thoreau's ideas
    (C) he was inspired by the creativity of Thoreau's writing
    (D) he believed Thoreau to be the most important author in American History
    (E) he acknowledged the tremendous debt that all social reformers owe to Thoreau

23. Which of the following situations most clearly exemplifies Thoreau's concept of civil disobedience?

    (A) Student protesters are arrested for holding rallies in the streets in protest of unfair, fraudulent elections.
    (B) The director of a non-profit organization refuses to pay payroll taxes to the IRS.
    (C) University students are jailed for defacing government property in protest of a newly-enforced military draft.
    (D) Environmentalists lobby their local legislature to pass a bill that would protect acres of natural swampland.
    (E) An animal-rights group barricades the entrance to a private research lab that conducts medical research on animals.

Medium Comparison Passages

The first of the following excerpts is adapted from a 1910 essay about the late nineteenth and early twentieth century American painter, Winslow Homer; the second is from a 1911 profile of Homer's life and work.

Passage 1

Winslow Homer, celebrated American seascape painter, felt more comfortable brushing elbows with fisherfolk and lobstermen on the coast than hobnobbing with art critics and reviewers in the bustling city.
5 The men at the docks had seen the world with their own eyes; the bourgeois critics in their cities could only see the world through Homer's paintings. So why would he listen to their pretentious blather, their demands for oil-brushed clichés on canvas? The es-
10 sence of his paintings is the relationship between the sea and the men who experience its strength and fury, its alternately cruel and benevolent roles in deciding their fates. The critics' chimerically tranquil ideal is overcome by Homer's stark portrayal of a harsh and
15 fickle mistress in such pictures as *The Lookout* and *The Life Line*.

When I first saw *A Northeaster*, I saw the anger of the sea through Homer's eyes. I had never seen the sea myself but I knew the full impact of the storm as
20 if I were in the middle of its vengeful fury. Looking at the rage upon the canvas, I could hear the wind roaring in my ears, smell the brooding storm, taste the saltwater as it whipped across my face, feel the boat lurch as it was buffeted by the waves. The full gamut
25 of sensations opened to me; Homer had captured a moment of the sea's power and energy in the frame. In his own way, Homer had achieved what no one else could: he had tamed the sea, if only for a moment, if only in an image. But the capture was incom-
30 plete; the sea rebelled even when preserved in paint. The white tips of the waves leapt off of the canvas. The water breaking over the black rocks alternately exhilarated and chilled me. I understood why he ignored the critics' puerile opinions and devoted himself
35 to the simplicity of his painting. Free from artifice, his work is great and inspiring in its candor.

Passage 2

When we say that Winslow Homer is an American

type of painter, fulfilling a national ideal that has singularly few exemplars in art, we think perhaps most
40 often of his coast and sea pictures, with their rugged naturalism, and their stern portrayal of the struggle between man and the elements. This is the temper we like to think of as expressive of our pioneer strength in establishing a new world on savage ground; this
45 is what we hope still typifies the firm sinew of our national character.

Homer's is the kind of painting that one would have expected to rise from the necessary purging of all inherited aesthetic influences as our young
50 nation strove to proclaim its own cultural identity. The American painters who preceded Homer had very little of his energy of innovation in their exceedingly academic paintings. The nation had not yet had time to grow young and develop its individuality in matters
55 of art. It was a bundle of imitations and traditions in that direction. Homer's early art has little in it that promises the freedom and breadth, the sense of nature strongly felt and strongly stated, the truly astonishing simplicity of his later work.

60 His *Sunday Morning in Old Virginia* has indeed ample simplicity of spirit in the grave candor of representation. The figures are given their true psychological value by the sheer honesty of the artist's objective point of view. But the execution is com-
65 monplace, hardly even skillful, yet always firm and lucid. What truly distinguishes this painting is the strength of its composition. It is here that Homer's greater qualities find consistent expression. When we look at *The Light on the Sea* or at *The Undertow* we
70 see clearly how the strong movement of the lines of direction establishes the splendid force of the picture's construction and how independent it is of the realism which is supposed to characterize Homer's work. And what could be finer in vigorous arrangement than
75 the *Cannon Rock*? Others have painted water with as successful an interpretation of its physical characteristics, its weight and liquidity and color and movement, but it took a bold architect to place that severe triangle like a wedge between the dark masses of the rocks
80 and under the long strip of dark sky unmodified by clouds. It is this masterful originality of composition that defines Homer's artistic legacy.

24. Both passages make use of which of the following

    (A) personal anecdote
    (B) rhetorical questioning
    (C) metaphorical language
    (D) appeal to emotion
    (E) literary allusion

25. Passage 1 suggests that Homer's critics

    (A) believed Homer to be a distinguished American painter
    (B) preferred more idealistic portrayals of nature
    (C) appreciated the sincerity of Homer's realistic portrayals
    (D) valued the calming effect of oil paintings
    (E) attacked his commonplace artistic execution

26. The "oil-brushed clichés" referenced in line 9 of Passage 1 are most similar to which of the following in Passage 2?

    (A) "his coast and sea pictures" (line 40)
    (B) "their exceedingly academic paintings" (lines 52-53)
    (C) "the astonishing simplicity of his later work" (line 58-59)
    (D) "the figures" (line 62)
    (E) "the *Light on the Sea*" (line 69)

27. The imagery in lines 20-24 ("Looking...waves") primarily serves to

    (A) illustrate the extraordinary level of realism Homer achieves in his painting
    (B) convey the unpredictability, starkness and fury of the sea
    (C) emphasize the struggle between men and the sea apparent in Homer's works
    (D) suggest that the realism of Homer's work compensates for his technical deficiencies
    (E) highlight the innovative qualities of Homer's realistic seascapes

28. The statement in lines 27-29 ("Homer...image") suggests that the author of Passage 1 believes that Homer

    (A) attempted a novel artistic experiment in his depiction of the sea
    (B) could not accurately represent the tempestuous nature of the sea in a painting
    (C) effectively and realistically portrayed the nature of the sea
    (D) was uncertain how to please the critics without compromising his artistic vision
    (E) artfully captured the relationship between men and the sea

29. In line 42, "temper" most nearly means

    (A) firmness
    (B) anger
    (C) bias
    (D) sentiment
    (E) personality

30. The author of Passage 2 refers to Homer's *Sunday Morning in Old Virginia* (line 60) primarily in order to

    (A) illustrate the spirit of rugged naturalism that characterizes many of Homer's paintings
    (B) emphasize the simplicity of execution and composition of Homer's earlier paintings
    (C) suggest that the compositional strength of Homer's paintings outweighs the limitations of his execution
    (D) provide and example of the character studies for which Homer became nationally recognized
    (E) convey the relationship between the figures and the composition of Homer's paintings

31. Unlike the author of Passage 1, the author of Passage 2

   (A) places Homer's work in a larger cultural context
   (B) focuses on the emotional impact of Homer's paintings
   (C) explores the relationship between Homer and his critics
   (D) references the simplicity and candor of Homer's paintings
   (E) discusses specific paintings created by Homer

32. Unlike Passage 1, Passage 2 focuses primarily on

   (A) Homer's innovative compositions
   (B) the emotional appeal of Homer's paintings
   (C) the American ideal of painting
   (D) the evolution of Homer's artistic technique
   (E) Homer's relationship to the sea

33. Compared to the tone of Passage 2, that of Passage 1 is more

   (A) impersonal
   (B) dramatic
   (C) severe
   (D) skeptical
   (E) academic

34. Which of the following can be found in both passages?

   I. Homer's portrayal of the relationship between man and the elements
   II. A reference to the simplicity of Homer's paintings
   III. Praise for the candor of Homer's work

   (A) I only
   (B) II only
   (C) I and III only
   (D) II and III only
   (E) I, II and III

35. Which statement about Homer is supported by both passages?

   (A) He realistically portrayed the nature of the sea.
   (B) He identified with the common man.
   (C) He preferred painting seascapes to portraits.
   (D) He was admired for his skillful composition.
   (E) He is considered a pioneer of American landscape painting.

Long Passage

The following passage is adapted from a 1920 novel about the life of a college student in post-World War I America.

Amory Blaine inherited from his mother every trait, except the stray inexpressible few, that made him worthwhile. His father, an ineffectual, inarticulate man with a taste for Byron and a hab-
5 it of drowsing over the Encyclopedia Britannica, grew wealthy at thirty through the death of two elder brothers, successful Chicago brokers, and in the first flush of feeling that the world was his, went to Bar Harbor and met Beatrice O'Hara.
10 In consequence, Stephen Blaine handed down to posterity his height of just under six feet and his tendency to waver at crucial moments, these two abstractions appearing in his son Amory. For many years he hovered in the background of his
15 family's life, an unassertive figure with a face half-obliterated by lifeless, silky hair, continually occupied in "taking care" of his wife, continually harassed by the idea that he didn't and couldn't understand her.
20 But Beatrice Blaine! There was a woman! Early pictures taken on her father's estate at Lake Geneva, Wisconsin, or in Rome at the Sacred Heart Convent—an educational extravagance that in her youth was only for the daughters of
25 the exceptionally wealthy—showed the exquisite delicacy of her features, the consummate art and simplicity of her clothes. A brilliant education she had—her youth passed in renaissance glory, she was versed in the latest gossip of the Older
30 Roman Families; known by name as a fabulously wealthy American girl to Cardinal Vitori and Queen Margherita and more subtle celebrities that one must have had some culture even to have heard of. All in all Beatrice O'Hara absorbed the
35 sort of education that will be quite impossible ever again; a tutelage measured by the number of things and people one could be contemptuous of and charming about; a culture rich in all arts and

traditions, barren of all ideas, in the last of those
40 days when the great gardener clipped the inferior roses to produce one perfect bud.

In her less important moments she returned to America, met Stephen Blaine and married him— this almost entirely because she was a little bit
45 weary, a little bit sad. Her only child was carried through a tiresome season and brought into the world on a spring day in 1896.

When Amory was five he was already a delightful companion for her. He was an auburn-
50 haired boy, with great, handsome eyes which he would grow up to in time, a facile imaginative mind and a taste for fancy dress. From his fourth to his tenth year he did the country with his moth-er in her father's private car, from Coronado down
55 to Mexico City, where she took a mild, almost epidemic consumption. This trouble pleased her, and later she made use of it as an intrinsic part of her atmosphere.

So, while more or less fortunate little rich boys
60 were defying governesses on the beach at New-port, or being spanked or tutored or read to from "Do and Dare," or "Frank on the Mississippi," Amory was biting acquiescent bell-boys in the Waldorf, outgrowing a natural repugnance to
65 chamber music and symphonies, and deriving a highly specialized education from his mother.

36. In context, the references to "Byron" (line 4) and the "Encyclopedia Britannica" (line 5) serve to indicate that Stephen Blaine is

(A) solemn
(B) intellectual
(C) introverted
(D) pretentious
(E) pompous

37. The quotation marks around the phrase "taking care" (line 17) primarily serve to

    (A) underscore a traditional definition
    (B) indicate a specialized term
    (C) question the appropriateness of a term
    (D) imply skepticism about a theory
    (E) defend a characterization

38. The description in lines 16-19, ("continually… her") primarily suggests that Steven Blaine

    (A) prefers not to be the center of attention
    (B) is typically indecisive
    (C) obsesses over his wife's health
    (D) is mystified by his wife's behavior
    (E) is physically and emotionally weak

39. The primary purpose of the second paragraph is to

    (A) highlight the importance of the O'Hara family fortune to Beatrice
    (B) explain why Beatrice was such a desirable wife for Stephen Blaine
    (C) establish Beatrice as a singularly unique and refined woman
    (D) celebrate Beatrice's sophistication and classical education
    (E) emphasize the breadth of Beatrice's education and experience

40. The phrase "consummate art and simplicity" (lines 26-27) most directly reflects Beatrice's

    (A) desire to remain fashionable, yet understated
    (B) interest in flaunting her wealth and status
    (C) attentiveness to all things artistic
    (D) wish to be noticed in a crowd
    (E) novel sense of style and fashion

41. The author mentions "Cardinal Vitori" and "Queen Margherita" (lines 31-32) in order to

    (A) emphasize the importance of Beatrice's European friendships
    (B) indicate the level of society with which Beatrice associated
    (C) illustrate that Beatrice had elite acquaintances in Europe as well as America
    (D) highlight Beatrice's widespread popularity in Europe
    (E) suggest the variety of social classes with which Beatrice had contact

42. In line 34, the word "absorbed" mostly nearly means

    (A) consumed
    (B) acquired
    (C) captivated
    (D) comprehended
    (E) involved

43. In the context of the passage, the metaphor in lines 40-41("great gardener…bud") primarily serves to

    (A) criticize a philosophy particular to an era
    (B) defend the complexity of a 19th century education
    (C) convey the importance of rank and status in a former time
    (D) emphasize the rich cultural traditions at the turn of the century
    (E) illustrate the process of the social refinement

44. The description of Beatrice's marriage to Stephen Blaine in the third paragraph implies that

    (A) marriage was not what Beatrice had hoped it would be
    (B) Stephen was more interested in getting married than Beatrice was
    (C) Beatrice's fear of being alone led her to marry at an early age
    (D) Beatrice was sad to leave behind the fashionable life of her youth
    (E) Beatrice married Stephen because she was discontented

45. In context, "tiresome" (line 46) most nearly means

   (A) somber
   (B) tedious
   (C) strenuous
   (D) lethargic
   (E) lengthy

46. The phrase "delightful companion" (line 49) suggests that

   (A) Amory was accustomed to being treated like an adult
   (B) Beatrice is lonely traveling without her husband
   (C) Beatrice views Amory more like a friend than a child
   (D) Beatrice and Amory have similar opinions about society
   (E) Amory enjoys traveling as much as his mother does

47. The phrase "this trouble pleased her" (line 56) primarily suggests that Beatrice

   (A) exploits her illness to gain her husband's attention
   (B) advances her social situation as a result of her illness
   (C) refuses to submit to her illness
   (D) uses this illness to her advantage
   (E) enjoys the sympathy of others

48. The final paragraph suggests that Amory's upbringing

   (A) was no different from that of other boys of his social class
   (B) hindered his social development
   (C) underscored the unusual relationship Amory had with his mother
   (D) failed to provide a necessary emphasis on academic learning
   (E) lacked childhood experiences typical of his peers

Critical Reading Mantras

Below is a series of Mantras or sayings that will help you remember the key strategies you have learned in this section. Mantras are meant to be repeated over and over in a soothing rhythm that will calm you and help trigger your memory. Repeat these to yourself when you are stuck in traffic, on your way to study hall or in the shower. Know them; love them; use them.

Sentence Completions

■ Find the **LOGIC** of the sentence.

■ **Solve it yourself first.**

■ For double-blankers, solve one blank at a time.

■ Use your **ROOTS**.

■ "Where have I heard this before?" **Use associations** with words to figure out their meanings.

■ Listen to your gut and select the best answer.

■ If you cross off two answer choices, **GUESS**.

■ For the last two problems, you must **knock off three choices** before you guess.

Reading Comprehension

- **Read ACTIVELY**.
- **FORGET** what you know.
- **IGNORE** your opinions.
- Make **NO ASSUMPTIONS**.
- Solve it yourself first.

Find the **THROW-AWAYS**.

Find the **SYNONYM CHAINS**.

Look for **EVIDENCE**.

- Put it in your own words: passages, questions and answer choices.

- Don't skip the *ITALICS*.

- Read 5 up and 5 down.

- Author's TONE: Don't slip on the

ICE

Critical Reading Answers

Sentence Completions

1. *A (E)*
2. *C (E)*
3. *E (E)*
4. *B (E)*
5. *C (E)*
6. *E (M)*
7. *B (M)*

8. *D (M)*
9. *A (M)*
10. *B (M)*
11. *A (M)*
12. *D (M)*
13. *A (M)*
14. *B (M)*

15. *D (M)*
16. *C (H)*
17. *E (H)*
18. *B (H)*
19. *B (H)*
20. *B (H5)*

Reading Comprehension

Short Passage 1

1. *A (M)*
2. *C (M)*

Short Passage 2

3. *E (H)*
4. *C (M)*

Short Comparison Passages

5. *B (H)*
6. *D (E)*
7. *E (E)*
8. *D (H)*

Medium Passage 1

9. *B (M)*
10. *A (E)*
11. *A (M)*
12. *C (E)*
13. *B (E)*
14. *E (H)*

Medium Passage 2

15. *A (M)*
16. *D (E)*
17. *B (M)*
18. *D (M)*
19. *E (H)*
20. *C (H)*
21. *E (H5)*

22. *A (E)*
23. *A (H5)*

Medium Comparison Passages

24. *C (M)*
25. *B (E)*
26. *B (H5)*
27. *A (H)*
28. *C (H)*
29. *E (H)*
30. *C (H)*
31. *A (M)*
32. *A (M)*
33. *B (H)*
34. *E (M)*
35. *A (M)*

Long Passage

36. *B (M)*
37. *C (H)*
38. *D (M)*
39. *E (H)*
40. *A (M)*
41. *B (H5)*
42. *B (E)*
43. *E (H5)*
44. *E (E)*
45. *B (H)*
46. *C (M)*
47. *D (H)*
48. *E (M)*

VOCABULARY

Vocabulary

The SAT test makers love to test your knowledge of words that few high school students have ever even seen. When was the last time your best friend dropped the P-bomb: **picayune** or **platitudinous**? Or broke out a high-C: **circumspect** or **compunction**?

Luckily you don't have to learn thousands of challenging and rarely used words to prepare for the CR section of the SAT. The test makers, for whatever reason, have a particular fondness for specific words, which they reuse again, and again and again. These are the words you need to learn. For example, the SAT authors adore **aesthetic**, love **loquacious** and are nuts about **nostalgia**. These three words occur on over 50% of SATs. Anyone prepping for the SAT had better learn these words!

To help you learn the frequently occurring SAT words, we have reviewed all the publicly released SATs and created an introductory vocabulary list for you. We have divided the top 350 words into seven blocks of 50 words with accompanying key word roots and practice exercises. Once you've knocked out the list of 350, move on to our extra list of 250 commonly occurring SAT words in our Overachiever List. And, while you are in SAT prep mode, don't limit yourself to our list. Whenever you come across an unfamiliar word—on the SAT, in a textbook, a newspaper or anywhere—write it down. You can build your vocabulary at any time of day: at school, at home, on the Internet. If you take on this challenge, you may end up with a Critical Reading score as high as your stack of flash cards!

How to use this list

One of the most effective ways to learn vocabulary is to make flash cards. Flash cards are great because they are portable and sortable. You may start with a stack of "working on it" words—those you are just becoming acquainted with—but you can quickly move the cards you've mastered to a new "I know it" stack. Some students are pressed for time and are not too thrilled at the prospect of making 350 flash cards. So we decided to do the work for them. We took the 350 words and 70 roots in the seven-week program and designed a set of funny, illustrated flash cards. They have been a big hit with our students and have helped raise many an SAT score. The flash card set is available online at www.applerouth.com.

Timely and Consistent Review

When you first learn a new word, review it within 24 hours to help transfer it to your long-term memory. Continue to review the word over numerous practice sessions. Soon you'll be able to recall the definition on your own. When you reach this point, continue to review the word during a few more practice sessions before you retire the word from the "working on it" stack to the "I know it" stack. A standard vocabulary review session should last 15-30 minutes. It's a better strategy to have several shorter sessions, spaced over days than to have one marathon review session.

Forced Recall Practice

When you are reviewing vocabulary, it is vastly more effective to force yourself to recall, or retrieve, the definition without any outside help. Reading through your vocabulary list, simultaneously seeing the word and the definition, is an ineffective way to commit words to memory. However, instead of just reading the word and definition side by side, quiz yourself. Cover up the definition, look only at the word, and try to retrieve the definition from memory. This "forced recall" is one of the best ways to lock things into your long-term memory, and flash cards are perfectly designed for this end.

Better Memorization Strategies

When you are trying to trap a new word in your long-term memory, you must find a way to make that word "sticky." Simply repeating the word and its definition again and again is one of the most commonly used and least effective ways to do this. There are better, more effective memorization strategies that you can use.

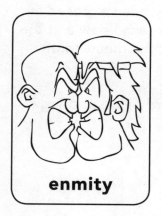

enmity

Make a picture in your mind

Associate the word with an image to help you remember.

Create a short phrase or saying

A *mnemonic* or memory device will help you learn the new word. ALEVE® helps to *alleviate* (relieve, lessen) headaches.

ALEVE® effectively alleviates most headaches.

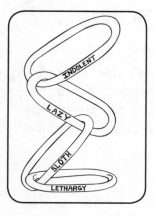

Link the new word with words you already know

By associating the unfamiliar word with familiar words that share the same meaning, you will have a better chance of recalling the new word. (Notice how we have linked words with similar meanings in the seven-week vocabulary list.)

If you personalize the meaning of the new word and find your own way to remember it, you will have a better chance of calling up the word from memory when you need it.

Use your Roots

One of the most effective ways to build your SAT vocabulary is to learn word roots, prefixes and suffixes. If you have taken Latin, Spanish, French, Italian or any other Romance language, you have already been exposed to many of the key SAT word roots. Using the roots you already know and the ones in our vocabulary list, you will be able to figure out the meaning of many new words on the SAT.

You may be able to figure out the meaning of a new word by associating it with words you already know, using word roots.

Let's try an example: CIRCUMSPECT

Let's break the word into its roots.

CIRCUM

What comes to mind? Circus, Circle, Circa. How about: circumnavigate, circumcise, circumference. My best guess is that this root has something to do with circle or around.

SPECT

What comes to mind? Respect, Spectacle, Inspect, Retrospect, Spectator. My best guess is that this root has something to do with looking.

AROUND   +   LOOKING

Circumspect must have something to do with looking in a circle, or looking around. Now we have enough information to go through a sentence completion and eliminate answer choices, even though we don't yet know the exact definition. It turns out circumspect means cautious, or careful or watchful: closely related to its "circle looking" roots.

For each root you learn, you will be able to decode many new SAT words. Learning roots is a great way to quickly expand your SAT vocabulary knowledge. Be sure to practice your roots each week.

Vocabulary: Week 1

Anal Retentive

fastidious possessing or displaying careful, meticulous attention to detail

meticulous extremely careful and precise; concerned with detail

scrutinize to examine carefully

vigilant alertly watchful

scrutinize

Ch-Ch-Ch-Changes

capricious impulsive; whimsical

fickle characterized by erratic changeableness or instability; capricious

vacillate to fluctuate or hesitate

whimsical unpredictable; erratic

erratic lacking consistency, regularity or uniformity

Do the Right Thing

apt appropriate; apropos; suitable

decorous proper; in good taste

discretion cautious reserve in speech; ability to make responsible decisions

tact acute sensitivity to what is proper and appropriate in dealing with others

discretion

Get Off Your High Horse!

condescend	to look down upon; to act superior toward
contemptuous	being scornful, hateful, or disdainful
disdain	n.) contempt or scorn v.) to look down upon with scorn
haughty	arrogant; proud; insolent (French haut = high, coming from above)
hubris	arrogant presumption or pride
insolent	contemptuously rude; insulting in manner or speech
narcissistic	self-absorbed; egotistical; self-centered
patronize	to treat condescendingly or haughtily; look down upon
presumptuous	overstepping due bounds (as of propriety or courtesy); taking liberties
pretentious	affected, fake, especially to exaggerate one's importance or status
smug	self-satisfied

narcissistic

Gotta Go Back In Time

nostalgic	longing for the past; wistful
retroactive	to apply a new law or condition to a time in the past
wistful	thoughtful but slightly sad, especially thinking about the past

How Do I Decide?

ambivalent	simultaneously feeling opposing feelings
cerebral	excessively rational; intellectual; brainy
impetuous	impulsive; without forethought; hotheaded
intuitive	knowing something instinctively rather than logically

ambivalent

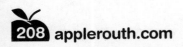

I Can See Clearly Now

cogent	convincing and reasonable
elucidate	make clear or plain, especially by explanation; clarify
lucid	clear; easily comprehended
unequivocal	clear; beyond controversy or doubt; unambiguous

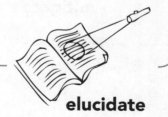

elucidate

Sing Some Praises!

adulation	excessive flattery or admiration
deference	submission or courteous yielding to the opinion of another; reverence
extol	to praise highly; exalt
exultant	overjoyed; rejoicing; elated; euphoric; jubilant
venerate	to regard with respect or reverence

Worn Out

hackneyed	worn-out through overuse; clichéd; trite
insipid	uninteresting, tasteless, not stimulating
jade	to wear out by overuse
monotony	tedious; boring because of sameness or repetition
mundane	commonplace; ordinary
prosaic	dull; unimaginative
tedious	boring; monotonous

tedious

Oooh Child, Things Are Gonna Get Easier

alleviate	relieve or improve; ease a pain or burden
ameliorate	to make or become better; improve
mitigate	make less severe; alleviate; become milder

Word Roots for the Week

ambi	both, around – ambidextrous, ambivalent, ambiguous
ami	friend – amicable, amity, amiable, amorous
arch	first – archetype, archangel, archaic, archrival
auto	self – autobiography, automatic, automaton, autonomy, autopsy
bell	war – belligerent, bellicose, antebellum South
ben	good – benign, beneficent, benefactor
chrono	time – chronology, anachronism
circum	around – circumscribe, circumvent
cis	cut – incision, decisive, incisive, precise

cis

Week 1 : Practice Exercises

Fill in the Blank

Use any appropriate form of the words in the box to fill in the blanks in the sentences below.

mundane   hackneyed   fickle   ambivalent   vacillate

narcissistic   extol   prosaic   tact   lucid

1. Though he really wanted to lick the frozen flagpole, Johnny was scared of the potential repercussions of his actions and felt _____ about the whole idea.

2. The press _____ the Nobel Peace Prize winner for his laudable efforts to achieve stability in Africa.

3. Laura, who changes her hairstyle every day, is the most _____ person I know; first she tried corn rows, then a perm, then a blue-green Mohawk!

4. The excuse "my dog ate my homework" is _____ and trite; better to try something innovative like "my dog ate my Honda Civic" or "I accidentally ate my dog."

5. After Zeke the Human Cannonball missed his landing mat and fell on his head, Ringleader Jack asked him simple questions to determine whether or not Zeke was _____.

6. If we do not take time to stop and marvel at life, it is easy to become weighed down by the _____ chores necessary to survive in this world.

7. Tired of his hum-drum, _____ life, James quit his job, joined the Merchant Marines and sailed to East Asia, where he married a beautiful goat-herder and opened a Blockbuster Video franchise.

8. As he prepared for his first tandem sky dive, Ben _____ between wanting to jump out of the plane immediately and wanting to lose his lunch.

9. Clara suddenly realized how _____ Marco was when she discovered he had been staring at his own reflection for the past hour instead of listening to her.

10. It wasn't very _____ of Marie to complain about the boss's halitosis in front of the new intern—his daughter!

Fill in the Blank

Use any appropriate form of the words in the box to fill in the blanks in the sentences below.

> exultant   ameliorate   unequivocal
>
> fastidious   wistful

11. My decision is final and _____; I will not be swayed from my plan to invest my lottery winnings in General Motors stock.

12. There is always a hint of _____ in Mary's gaze, as if she were longing for something just out of reach.

13. Aaron's mom _____ his punishment by allowing him to play video games and go on the Internet while he was grounded.

14. Baal was _____; he finally triumphed over the forces of darkness and was crowned Grand Pinball Wizard of Topeka, Kansas.

15. Thomas is _____ to the point of ridiculousness; he is practically addicted to his lint roller and shoe polish.

Word Association

Circle the word that does not belong.

> Example: laugh   chuckle   (sob)
>
> 1. patronize   mitigate   disdain
>
> 2. capricious   erratic   jade
>
> 3. tedious   apt   prosaic
>
> 4. adulate   alleviate   venerate
>
> 5. decorous   haughty   smug

Synonyms

Match each word on the right to its synonym on the left.

1. ameliorate	(a) fastidious
2. wistful	(b) cogent
3. veneration	(c) deference
4. discretion	(d) insipid
5. meticulous	(e) alleviate
6. prosaic	(f) nostalgic
7. lucid	(g) tact

Word Charge

Mark each word as positive (+), negative (−) or neutral (=).

1. impetuous _____   4. presumptuous _____   7. ameliorate _____

2. jade _____   5. vigilant _____   8. retroactive _____

3. hubris _____   6. pretentious _____   9. adulation _____

Sentence Completions

Choose the word that, when inserted in the sentence, best fits the meaning of the sentence as a whole.

1. Sister Mary Catherine was tired of Josiah's ------ attitude; he was always mocking her lisp and talking back.

   a. insolent
   b. whimsical
   c. cerebral
   d. prosaic

2. Biff was ------ at the age of 16; all he could do was listen to The Cure in the dark and wish the world weren't so disappointing.

   a. insipid
   b. contemptuous
   c. wistful
   d. jaded

3. Juana was ------ when she learned Bob's ------ decision left him tied to a tree in his underwear, just as she predicted.

   a. intuitive … cogent
   b. haughty … apt
   c. smug … impetuous
   d. nostalgic … capricious

4. Don't ------ me; I know my argument wasn't ------, and I was just grasping at straws.

   a. patronize … cogent
   b. disdain … erratic
   c. elucidate … cerebral
   d. ameliorate … lucid

Word Roots

Match the root words to their meanings.

1. ambi	(a) around
2. ami	(b) cut
3. arch	(c) first
4. auto	(d) friend
5. bell	(e) good
6. ben	(f) self
7. chrono	(g) time
8. circum	(h) two
9. cis	(i) war

Answers Week 1

Fill in the blank

*1. ambivalent 2. extolled 3. fickle 4. hackneyed 5. lucid 6. mundane 7. prosaic
8. vacillated 9. narcissistic 10. tactful 11. unequivocal 12. wistfulness 13. ameliorated
14. exultant 15. fastidious*

Word Association

1. mitigate 2. jade 3. apt 4. alleviate 5. decorous

Synonyms

1.(e) 2.(f) 3.(c) 4.(g) 5.(a) 6.(d) 7.(b)

Word Charge

1.(−) 2.(−) 3.(−) 4.(−) 5.(+) 6.(−) 7.(+) 8.(=) 9.(+)

Sentence Completions

1.(a) 2.(d) 3.(c) 4.(a)

Word Roots

1. (h) 2. (d) 3. (c) 4. (f) 5. (i) 6. (e) 7. (g) 8. (a) 9. (b)

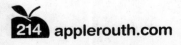

Vocabulary: Week 2

I Get So Emotional

demonstrative	emotional; displaying one's feelings openly
empathy	the ability to feel what you imagine another person feels; understanding
pathos	compassion; pity; sympathy

pathos

Things Fall Apart

cacophony	jarring, discordant sound; dissonance
debacle	a disaster or failure
deleterious	harmful; injurious; detrimental
desecrate	to violate the sacredness of; to make profane
discordant	conflicting; dissonant or harsh in sound
eradicate	to tear up by the roots
exacerbate	to aggravate; make worse; make more severe
mar	to ruin or spoil
raze	to destroy completely; demolish
sully	to soil or make dirty
virulent	extremely infectious, malignant, or poisonous

Listen To The Land

arid

arable	suitable for farming
arid	lacking moisture, especially due to insufficient rainfall
conflagration	a massive, destructive fire

Light & Lively

blithe	carefree and lighthearted
equanimity	composure; being calm, even-keeled, balanced
euphoric	extremely happy; elated; overjoyed
levity	lightness of manner or speech
placid	calm; peaceful; serene

levity

On The Sly

clandestine	kept or done in secret
furtive	characterized by stealth; surreptitious; sneaky
surreptitious	done, made or acquired by stealth; clandestine

One Smart Cookie

erudite	learned; scholarly
esoteric	understood by a small, specific group
profundity	depth; something intellectual or abstract; (the noun form of profound)
pundit	an authority who expresses his/her opinions; expert; learned person
sage	n.) one venerated for experience, judgment, & wisdom; adj.) wise

Good Times

felicitous	apt; pleasant; happy
serendipity	a lucky, chance occurrence

serendipity

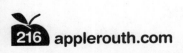

Something To Rely On

immutable	not subject or susceptible to change
innate	from birth; inherent
invariable	not subject to change; constant

invariable

A Little Out There

atypical	odd; different; unique; unusual; distinct
avant-garde	using experimental or new techniques
eccentric	strange; different; odd
idiosyncrasy	a unique character trait; eccentricity
maverick	an unbranded range animal; one that is independent in thought and action
novel	strikingly new, unusual, or different

Talkin' Trash

disparage

admonish	to warn or scold gently; give advice
censure	an expression of strong disapproval or harsh criticism
deride	to ridicule, mock, taunt
disparage	to speak of in a slighting or disrespectful way; belittle; decry
harangue	to deliver a pompous speech or tirade
impugn	to attack verbally; to challenge as false or questionable
malediction	a curse
scoff	to mock or disregard as ridiculous
vilify	to speak evil of

Word Roots for the Week

co/com/con	with – condescending, compliant, condemn, contemporary, context, convoke
cogn	know – cognition, recognize, incognito, cognizant, cognate
cred	trust, believe – incredible, incredulous, credit, credible
de	away, down, off – debilitate, decry, defame, devoid, desecrate, defenestrate
dict	say – dictate, dictator, dictum, indicative, edict
dis	not, away from – distance, discredit, disparity, digress
dur	hard – endure, durable, duration, obdurate
equi	equal – equivocate, equanimity, equidistant, equilibrium
ex	away from – exculpate, extract, exit, exhume, extinct, exonerate

de

Week 2 : Practice Exercises

Fill in the Blank

Use any appropriate form of the words in the box to fill in the blanks in the sentences below.

> pundit disparage innate desecrate immutable
> conflagration erudite cacophony equanimity arid

1. Death Valley, with very little rainfall each year, is one of the most _____ places in the United States.

2. When the zoo visitors entered the aviary, they were forced to cover their ears to muffle the _____ of birds' cries.

3. The _____ that destroyed over half of Chicago started when Mrs. O'Leary's cow kicked over a lantern.

4. The Romans _____ the Temple of Solomon when they erected a statue of the Roman Emperor inside its walls and played Twister in the sanctuary.

5. When Frank was caught licking the walls again for the fourth time in two weeks, his boss _____ him publicly so that all of Frank's co-workers could hear.

6. No matter what curveballs life threw at Elwood, he maintained his _____.

7. The Ph.D. candidate's _____ thesis was difficult to understand unless you were a scholar of Shakespeare.

8. Relatively unchanged since her creation, the Statue of Liberty has become a(n) _____ symbol of American values.

9. Somehow, birds have a(n) _____ sense of migratory patterns; even very young birds know when and where to fly south for the winter.

10. After six months in the Federal penitentiary, Martha Stewart became a(n) _____ on prison fashion and décor.

Fill in the Blank

Use any appropriate form of the words in the box to fill in the blanks in the sentences below.

> virulent   serendipitous   raze
>
> malediction   clandestine

11. Thousands of people ran to get flu shots this year when the CDC warned that this season's strand of the flu would be particularly _____.

12. Intent on utter destruction, Billy _____ his sister Sarah's carefully constructed Lego Town, much to her very vocal dismay.

13. Casting furtive glances down the hall while we gossiped about the new supervisor made us feel like spies conducting a _____ meeting.

14. How _____ for Mina to run into her old college roommate Jessica at the grocery store just as Mina was looking for someone to run for Chair of the Alumni Board.

15. My very superstitious Nana, who swears she has the second sight, put a _____ on the paperboy because he consistently threw *The Sunday Times* into her rose garden instead of onto her front porch.

Word Association

Circle the word that <u>does not belong</u>.

> Example: laugh chuckle (sob)
>
> 1. vilify   eradicate   admonish
>
> 2. clandestine   euphoric   blithe
>
> 3. eccentric   felicitous   idiosyncratic
>
> 4. immutable   impugn   innate
>
> 5. sage   pundit   pathos

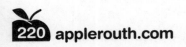

Synonyms

Match each word on the right to its synonym on the left.

1. furtive	(a) blithe
2. placid	(b) mar
3. sully	(c) scoff
4. cacophony	(d) surreptitious
5. euphoric	(e) invariable
6. immutable	(f) discordant
7. deride	(g) equanimity

Word Charge

Mark each word as positive (+), negative (–) or neutral (=).

1. vilify _____   4. innate _____   7. exacerbate _____

2. harangue _____   5. felicitous _____   8. deleterious _____

3. maverick _____   6. sage _____   9. novel _____

Sentence Completions

Choose the word that, when inserted in the sentence, <u>best</u> fits the meaning of the sentence as a whole.

1. The press should have been more ------
   with Jean Valjean and not ------ him; he
   stole the bread because he was starving.

   a. erudite ... scoffed
   b. empathetic ... vilified
   c. felicitous ... impugned
   d. sympathetic ... eradicated

2. Jen's birthday party was a ------; the cake was
   hard as a rock and the magician left the rabbit in
   his other pair of pants!

   a. debacle
   b. cacophony
   c. idiosyncrasy
   d. conflagration

3. Niles was no sheep; he fancied himself a
   ------ when it came to personalizing his
   remarkably drab school uniform.

   a. maverick
   b. sage
   c. debacle
   d. malediction

4. If you constantly ------ your friends with your
   new-found knowledge, they'll find you less of
   a(n) ------ and more of an irritant.

   a. censure ... eccentric
   b. sully ... pundit
   c. mar ... idiosyncrasy
   d. harangue ... sage

Word Roots
Match the root words to their meanings.

1. co/com/con	(a) away from
2. cog	(b) say
3. cred	(c) hard
4. de	(d) equal
5. dict	(e) not, away from
6. dis	(f) with
7. dur	(g) trust, believe
8. equi	(h) of, away, from
9. ex	(i) know

Answers Week 2

Fill in the Blank

1. arid 2. cacophony 3. conflagration 4. desecrated 5. disparaged 6. equanimity 7. erudite 8. immutable 9. innate 10. pundit 11. virulent 12. razed 13. clandestine 14. serendipitous 15. malediction

Word Association

1. eradicate 2. clandestine 3. felicitous 4. impugn 5. pathos

Synonyms

1.(d) 2.(g) 3.(b) 4.(f) 5.(a) 6.(e) 7.(c)

Word Charge

1.(–) 2.(–) 3.(+) 4.(=) 5.(+) 6.(+) 7.(–) 8.(–) 9.(=)

Sentence Completions

1.(b) 2.(a) 3.(a) 4.(d)

Word Roots

1.(f) 2.(i) 3.(g) 4.(h) 5.(b) 6.(e) 7.(c) 8.(d) 9.(a)

Vocabulary: Week 3

Stretchy

lithe   moves easily; flexible; supple

pliant   flexible; yielding; compliant

supple   flexible; compliant; pliant; easily yielding

lithe

Get 'Er Done

alacrity   cheerful willingness; eagerness; speed or quickness

assiduous   hard working; diligent

pragmatic   practical; concerned with the end results

Back To School

anthropology   the study of human cultures and origins

didactic   designed or intended to teach; preachy, moralizing, or sermonic

empirical   based on observation or experiment

epilogue   the final section of a piece of literature or music; conclusion

heterogeneous   mixed; consisting of many different parts

homogeneous   same; uniform; consisting of only one part

pedagogy   the art or profession of training, teaching, or instructing

rudimentary   elementary; basic

empirical

Gotta Keep 'Em Separated

discrepancy   an apparent contradiction or disagreement

disparity   the condition or fact of being unequal, as in age, rank, or degree

incongruous   not harmonious; disagreeing

partisan   not objective; firmly adhering to a party or cause

polarize   to break into opposing groups

disparity

Humor Me

facetious   jocular; joking; witty; playfully humorous

satirical   sarcastic; joking; tongue-in-cheek

Can You Back It Up?

ascertain   to prove; to know for certain

corroborate   to support with evidence; confirm

discern   to see; notice; make out; perceive; recognize

ostensible   outwardly appearing; apparent

substantiate   support with proof or evidence; verify

Can't Have Enough Of A Good Thing

augment   to make greater, as in size, extent, or quantity

copious   plentiful

disseminate   to spread

proliferate   to grow or increase rapidly

surfeit   excess; over-indulgence

proliferate

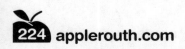

Hold Me Back

curtail	to cut short
deferment	a delay or postponement
preclude	to make impossible; block; stop; hinder
quell	to quiet or calm; pacify
temper	to moderate or restrain
thwart	to stop; block; hinder; preclude; oppose

quell

I'm Soooooooo Confused

abstruse	difficult to understand
ambiguous	open to multiple interpretations
convoluted	intricate; complex
cryptic	difficult to comprehend; obscure
dubious	doubtful; unlikely; questionable
enigma	one that is puzzling, ambiguous, or inexplicable

Judge Judy

arbitration	hearing and deciding a controversy or a legal case
equitable	fair; not favoring one party over another
exculpate	to free from guilt or blame
exonerate	to free from blame; to free from a burden
indict	to charge formally with a crime; accuse
objectivity	treating facts without personal feelings or biases; focusing on the object
perjure	to lie under oath

exculpate

Word Roots for the Week

fort strong – fortitude, fortuitous, effort, fortify

frac/frag break – fragment, fracture, fragile, fractious, refract

gen life – genesis, engender, gender, genital, gentle, regenerate

grat pleasing – congratulate, gratuitous, gratify, ingrate

gress step – progress, transgress, regress, digress, retrogress

hyper more than – hyperbole, hyper vigilant, hypertension, hyper-extend

hypo less than/under – hypothesis, hypodermic, hypothermia

in/im not – impossible, immutable, impartial, incessant, incoherent, indifferent

in with – intensify, inherent, innate, inspire, ingenious

frac/frag

Week 3 : Practice Exercises

Fill in the Blank

Use any appropriate form of the words in the box to fill in the blanks in the sentences below.

> abstruse   enigma   assiduous   exculpate   copious
>
> substantiate   didactic   pliant   discrepancy   pragmatic

1. _____ at its core, the story of *The Tortoise and the Hare* is intended to teach children the value of steady work and perseverance.

2. Perhaps the greatest thing about Play-Doh® is that it is so _____; it is easily formed into anything imaginable.

3. Lisa was not the most naturally gifted flautist in the band, but she was _____ and managed to practice her way into first chair.

4. Ever on the look out, Hasan was thrilled whenever he discovered a(n) _____ between a candidate's voting record and response in a debate.

5. Eric feared women would always remain a(n) _____; he just couldn't understand their general fascination with shoes and fluffy, white puppies.

6. In an attempt to maintain her impeccable vision, Marta ate _____ amounts of baby carrots, which only succeeded in adding a slightly orange cast to her skin.

7. Ava didn't have the courage to tell her husband that his children's book explaining the finer points of Wittegenstein's Poker was too _____ for her, let alone for the average six-year-old.

8. Maurice knew an alibi alone wouldn't _____ his client; he would have to find the key evidence himself.

9. The _____ senator agreed that the goals of the environmental bill were laudable, but he opposed the bill because he did not believe that it could ever be passed in the current Congressional environment.

10. The researcher _____ his claim that there was once water on Mars with compelling evidence based on years of research.

Fill in the Blank

Use any appropriate form of the words in the box to fill in the blanks in the sentences below.

> dubious   anthropology   rudimentary
>
> preclude   polarize

11. Only a _____ knowledge of baking is needed to apply for a job at Dunkin® Donuts since it has a very vigorous training program.

12. The issue of incorporating technology into traditional cookie sales _____ the Girl Scout® Troop mothers; some wanted to create web sites, while others advocated for the standard door-to-door approach.

13. Calleb found his sister's explanation of the theory of relativity a little _____; he really didn't think it had anything to do with marrying your second cousin.

14. Although Erin's guidance counselor told her it would be much easier to get a job in education than one in _____, she was always fascinated by the cultural development of societies and decided to take a chance and catch the next flight to Papua New Guinea.

15. A lack of skill doesn't necessarily _____ you from joining our knitting circle; all we do is eat coffee cake and gossip about the neighbors.

Word Association

Circle the word that <u>does not belong</u>.

> Example: laugh chuckle (sob)
>
> 1. facetious   satirical   pragmatic
>
> 2. discrepancy   deferment   disparity
>
> 3. ascertain   augment   discern
>
> 4. exonerate   corroborate   substantiate
>
> 5. supple   surfeit   copious

Synonyms

Match each word on the right to its synonym on the left.

1. abstruse	(a) thwart
2. corroborate	(b) supple
3. facetious	(c) satirical
4. pliant	(d) discern
5. ascertain	(e) exculpate
6. curtail	(f) substantiate
7. exonerate	(g) convoluted

Word Charge

Mark each word as positive (+), negative (−) or neutral (=).

1. copious _____   4. alacrity _____   7. didactic _____

2. indict _____   5. perjure _____   8. dubious _____

3. lithe _____   6. partisan _____   9. ambiguous _____

Sentence Completions

Choose the word that, when inserted in the sentence, <u>best</u> fits the meaning of the sentence as a whole.

1. Without the novel's humorous ------, it would be difficult to know the author was being ------.

   a. pedagogy ... facetious
   b. arbitration ... cryptic
   c. epilogue ... satirical
   d. discrepancy ... didactic

2. Reluctantly, Giuseppe bought the over-stuffed teddy bear in an attempt to ------ the torrent of tears running down his daughter's face.

   a. quell
   b. discern
   c. augment
   d. disseminate

3. I will not stand for the ------ of such propaganda; there's no ------ evidence that Bo's cat knocked over the trash bins.

   a. curtailment ... objective
   b. dissemination ... empirical
   c. tempering ... equitable
   d. proliferation ... abstruse

4. For someone who continually complained of his hatred for math, Marc agreed to work the problem on the board with surprising ------.

   a. alacrity
   b. deferment
   c. objectivity
   d. pedagogy

Word Roots
Match the root words to their meanings.

1. fort	(a) break
2. frac/frag	(b) less than/under
3. gen	(c) life
4. grat	(d) more than
5. gress	(e) not
6. hyper	(f) pleasing
7. hypo	(g) step
8. in	(h) strong
9. in/im	(i) with

Answers Week 3

Fill in the Blank

1. didactic 2. pliant 3. assiduous 4. discrepancy 5. enigma 6. copious 7. abstruse 8. exculpate 9. pragmatic 10. substantiated 11. rudimentary 12. polarized 13. dubious 14. anthropology 15. preclude

Word Association

1. pragmatic 2. deferment 3. augment 4. exonerate 5. supple

Synonyms

1.(g) 2.(f) 3.(c) 4.(b) 5.(d) 6.(a) 7.(e)

Word Charge

1.(+) 2.(–) 3.(+) 4.(+) 5.(–) 6.(–) 7.(=) 8.(–) 9.(=)

Sentence Completions

1.(c) 2.(a) 3.(b) 4.(a)

Word Roots

1.(h) 2.(a) 3.(c) 4.(f) 5.(g) 6.(d) 7.(b) 8.(i) 9.(e)

Vocabulary: Week 4

All About The Benjamins

magnanimous

affluent	wealthy; rich
altruism	generosity; magnanimity
magnanimous	generously noble in mind and heart
philanthropist	someone who is charitable or works for the betterment of humankind

Speak-Easy

articulate	well-spoken; able to communicate effectively
cajole	to urge with gentle and repeated appeals, teasing, or flattery
digress	to turn aside, especially from the main subject in writing or speaking
exhortation	speech intended to incite or move its audience
ineffable	too great or big to be put into words
loquacious	very talkative; garrulous
rhetoric	the art of using language effectively and persuasively
taciturn	habitually not talkative; not apt to talk or speak
tangent	digressing; irrelevant; straying from main point

Lazy Sunday

torpor

indolent	habitually lazy; slothful
languid	sluggish; slow; lethargic; weak
lethargic	deficient in alertness or activity
phlegmatic	possessing a calm, sluggish temperament; unemotional
torpor	a state of inactivity; lethargy

Bells And Whistles

embellish decorate; make more beautiful

florid describing flowery or elaborate language

opulent lavish; exhibiting a display of great wealth

ostentatious describing a showy, excessive or pretentious display

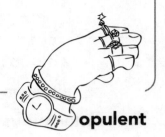

opulent

Ain't Nothing Gonna Break My Stride

formidable inspiring awe or dread; worthy

indomitable unable to be defeated; unconquerable

inexorable not letting up; relentless

intrepid courageous; fearless

resilient capable of easily bouncing back from adversity; tough

Not So Much

brevity the quality or state of being brief in duration

dearth smallness of quantity or number; scarcity; lack

diminution the process of diminishing or decreasing

modicum a small amount

negligible so small that it can be ignored

paucity scarcity; lack; dearth

wane to decrease; dwindle; dim

diminution

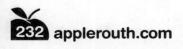

Mo' Money, Mo' Problems

avarice   greed; immoderate desire for wealth; cupidity

exorbitant   excessive; more than is necessary or reasonable

avarice

parsimony   unusual or excessive frugality; extreme economy or stinginess

penurious   penny-pinching; excessively thrifty; ungenerous

Eat, Drink And Be Merry

aesthete   one who cultivates an unusually high sensitivity to beauty

connoisseur   an expert; a discerning judge with extensive knowledge

hedonist   one devoted to pleasurable pursuits, especially pleasures of the senses

indulgent   giving into desires; lenient

Who's Got the Skills?

adept   skillful; deft; opposite of inept

adroit   dexterous; deft; skillful

facile   done or achieved with little effort or difficulty; easy

adept

inept   displaying a lack of judgment, sense, or reason; foolish

Removed From The World

ascetic   one who renounces material comforts for a life of austere self-discipline

insular   isolated; cut off

naïve   lacking in worldly wisdom; gullible; credulous

reclusive   solitary; cut off from the world

Word Roots for the Week

loc   place – locale, locus, allocate, dislocate, relocate

loqu/locut   talk, speech – elocution, loquacious

luc/lum   light – elucidate, translucent, luminous, lucid, illumine, luminary

magna   great – magnanimous, magnitude, magnificent

mal   bad – malign, malignant, malefactor, malice, malicious, malfeasance

med   middle – medieval, medley, meddle, mediate, meditate, remedial

meter/metr   measure – chronometer, metronome, geometry, commensurate

morph   shape – biomorphic, amorphous, anthropomorphic, morphology

mut   change – mutate, transmute, immutable, mutilate

luc/lum

Week 4 : Practice Exercises

Fill in the Blank

Use any appropriate form of the words in the box to fill in the blanks in the sentences below.

loquacious   indolent   avarice   insular   cajole

lethargic   digress   ostentatious   embellish   parsimony

1. While most of the people on the tour loved the ornate decoration and mammoth scale of Versailles's famous Hall of Mirrors, I found it _____.

2. In his chronic pursuit of bling, 50 Cent was accused of _____ when he announced to the world that he was going to get rich or die trying.

3. Josephina is so _____ that you often have to tune out her incessant chatter to get any work done around the office.

4. The students tried daily to get their physics teacher off of the topic, preferring his _____ about growing up in rural Kansas with his 2-legged horse and collection of pet groundhogs to his lectures about kinetic energy.

5. The author's style was too florid and full of rhetorical _____ for me; I prefer simple writing where ideas take precedence over style.

6. Because Guillermo would lazily watch sticks fly by without ever trying to go fetch, his owner complained that he was a(n) _____ dog.

7. Without access to television, radio, or internet in her home, Francine lived such a(n) _____ life that she thought *Dancing with the Stars* was an astronomical event.

8. Klaus often found it necessary to _____, even bribe his son Marx to clean his room.

9. On rainy days, I am overcome with a sense of _____, and I find that I'm unable to even get out of bed before my favorite Soaps are over.

10. Elmo's _____ destroyed his dating life; his dates tired quickly of cheap meals and hand-picked flowers from the side of the road.

Fill in the Blank

Use any appropriate form of the words in the box to fill in the blanks in the sentences below.

> naïve   ascetic   florid
>
> modicum   connoisseur

11. Sinbad's friends and family were shocked when he gave up his well-paying career as a stockbroker to adopt a(n) _____ lifestyle at a monastery.

12. The love letter Abelard sent Heloise was so full of _____ language that she couldn't understand what he was saying to her.

13. Edgar considered himself a _____ of Pez, able to distinguish between cherry and strawberry with a single glance.

14. Mary Kate and Ashley Olsen are not as _____ as they look; they've been in Hollywood for a long time.

15. Is it too much to ask you to show at least a _____ of decency? Please try to clean up your language around the Pope.

Word Association

Circle the word that <u>does not belong</u>.

> Example: laugh   chuckle   (sob)
>
> 1. paucity   dearth   torpor
>
> 2. cajole   embellish   exhort
>
> 3. aesthete   cacophony   hedonist
>
> 4. lethargic   languid   taciturn
>
> 5. ascetic   adroit   adept

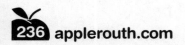

Synonyms

Match each word on the right to its synonym on the left.

1. altruism	(a) insular
2. reclusive	(b) dearth
3. formidable	(c) indomitable
4. parsimonious	(d) digress
5. paucity	(e) magnanimity
6. torpid	(f) penurious
7. tangent	(g) indolent

Word Charge

Mark each word as positive (+), negative (−) or neutral (=).

1. inept _____   4. brevity _____   7. didactic _____

2. intrepid _____   5. philanthropist _____ 8. opulent _____

3. adroit _____   6. avarice _____   9. ostentatious _____

Sentence Completions

Choose the word that, when inserted in the sentence, <u>best</u> fits the meaning of the sentence as a whole.

1. Mom always said Uncle Ted had a sluggish, ------ temperament, much like the giant ground sloth.

    a. phlegmatic
    b. hedonist
    c. adroit
    d. reclusive

2. No one expected the ------ Lily to make such an adamantly vocal stand against dissecting actual frogs in biology.

    a. loquacious
    b. taciturn
    c. articulate
    d. altruistic

3. The class was impressed when the professor ------ his argument with such eloquence and ------.

    a. embellished ... paucity
    b. waned ... altruism
    c. indulged ... ostentation
    d. articulated ... brevity

4. Eager to show off his new ------, Tony bought ------ gifts for family, friends, even strangers in department stores.

    a. avarice ... exorbitant
    b. magnanimity ... negligible
    c. torpor ... ostentatious
    d. affluence ... opulent

Word Roots

Match the root words to their meanings.

1. loc		(a) bad	
2. loqu/locut		(b) change	
3. luc/lum		(c) great	
4. magna		(d) light	
5. mal		(e) measure	
6. med		(f) middle	
7. meter/metr		(g) place	
8. morph		(h) shape	
9. mut		(i) talk	

Answers Week 4

Fill in the blank

*1. ostentatious 2. avarice 3. loquacious 4. digressions 5. embellishments
6. indolent 7. insular 8. cajole 9. lethargy 10. parsimony 11. ascetic 12. florid
13. connoisseur 14. naïve 15. modicum*

Word Association

1. torpor 2. embellish 3. cacophony 4. taciturn 5. ascetic

Synonyms

1.(e) 2.(a) 3.(c) 4.(f) 5.(b) 6.(g) 7.(d)

Word Charge

1.(–) 2.(+) 3.(+) 4.(=) 5.(+) 6.(–) 7.(=) 8. (+) 9. (–)

Sentence Completions

1.(a) 2.(b) 3.(d) 4.(d)

Word Roots

1.(g) 2.(i) 3.(d) 4.(c) 5.(a) 6.(f) 7.(e) 8.(h) 9.(b)

Vocabulary: Week 5

Candle In the Wind

elusive	hard to capture; evasive
ephemeral	lasting for a markedly brief time; short-lived
evanescent	tending to disappear like vapor; vanishing; fleeting
transitory	short-lived; temporary; of brief duration

evanescent

Feeling Scrappy

belligerent	bellicose; pugnacious; militant; war-like
querulous	prone to complaining or grumbling; quarrelsome
truculent	fierce and cruel; eager to fight; pugnacious

Here's A Quarter, Call Someone Who Cares

apathetic

aloof	distant physically or emotionally; reserved and remote
apathetic	not caring; showing little emotion
callous	emotionally hardened; unfeeling
complacent	contented to a fault; self-satisfied and unconcerned
impassive	revealing no emotion; expressionless
indifferent	not caring
nonchalant	carefree or laidback; unconcerned
perfunctory	done routinely and with little interest or care
remiss	negligent; careless
stoic	showing indifference to pain

It's Hard Being This Good

consummate	perfect or model example
emulate	to strive to equal or excel, especially through imitation
epitome	the model or embodiment of something
exemplify	to serve as an example; embody

epitome

Miss Congeniality

affable	easy to talk to; friendly
amiable	friendly; good-natured; kind; agreeable
amicable	friendly; agreeable; amiable
benevolent	generous; good natured
camaraderie	fellowship; friendship; good will
cordial	friendly; warmly welcoming; gracious

No Way, José

debunk	to expose as false
disillusion	to disabuse someone of their illusions; take away faith in something fake
futile	pointless; fruitless; ineffective
negate	to reject as false
nullify	to make inconsequential; negate; annul
repudiate	to reject emphatically as unfounded, untrue, or unjust

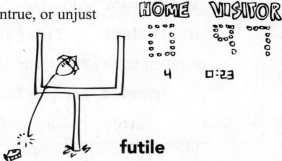

futile

My Way Or The Highway

obdurate stubbornly resistant; not flexible

obstinate stubbornly adhering to an opinion; unyielding

tenacity persistence; strength; holding fast

tenacity

Shaping Up

amorphous lacking definite form; shapeless

juxtaposition the placing of two things side by side

tactile relating to the sense of touch; tangible

tangible something capable of being touched; real; material

So Annoying!

hindrance impediment; obstruction; obstacle

miffed put out; annoyed; irritated; offended

onerous troubling; burdensome; oppressive

vexation annoyance; irritation

miffed

Thanks for Your Support

advocate to speak, plead, or argue in favor of; support

condone to overlook, forgive, or disregard a behavior without protest or censure

engender to bring into existence; give rise to

espouse to support or adopt

foster to support or encourage

heed to listen to; pay attention to; follow

Word Roots for the Week

nasc/nat born – native, natural, nascent, innate, neonatal

ob against – obdurate, obscure, obstinate, object, obstacle, obscure, obvious

pan all – panic, panacea, panorama, pantheistic, panoply

ped child – pedagogue, pediatrics, pedantic

peri around – perimeter, perinatal, periscope

phon sound – phonetics, phonics, cacophony, euphony, symphony

pro forward – profound, profuse, proliferate, protean

pro much, for, lots – prolific, profuse, prodigious, protracted, propensity

prot first – protagonist, protean, prototype, proton

phon

Week 5 : Practice Exercises

Fill in the Blank

Use any appropriate form of the words in the box to fill in the blanks in the sentences below.

> advocate   engender   callous   benevolent   debunk
>
> tenacity   belligerent   transitory   miffed   futile

1. When the nurse accidentally replaced the CD of Pachelbel's *Canon in D* with Alice Cooper's *Greatest Hits*, the patients became _____ and started trying to assault the hospital employees.

2. Dishwasher Pete leads a very _____ life, traveling from town to town washing dishes with only a P.O. Box to call home.

3. Crazy Duane has vowed to _____ the theory of relativity and prove Einstein was nothing more than a hack, even if it takes a lifetime.

4. Research confirms that Arts education strengthens student problem-solving and critical thinking skills, which is why many parents and teachers _____ for art, music and drama classes in schools.

5. Taylor Swift was _____ at Miley Cyrus for wearing a dress identical to hers to the Grammy Awards, especially since the designer swore it was one of a kind.

6. Resistance is _____, Earthlings! We do not come in peace.

7. The other mothers thought it _____ of Heide to let her baby cry alone in his crib, but she had read this was the best way to avoid spoiling a child.

8. Though the leader cultivated his image as a(n) _____ dictator, there is nothing generous about imprisoning people who disagree with you.

9. In the critically acclaimed *Pick of Destiny*, the assiduous protagonist pursued musical fame with a(n) _____ rarely seen in this age of quick celebrity and easy pickins'.

10. The general's courage in battle and unwillingness to leave his troops _____ respect among the soldiers.

Fill in the Blank

Use any appropriate form of the words in the box to fill in the blanks in the sentences below.

> ### nonchalant   juxtaposition   affable
> ### heed   camaraderie

11. Southerners have acquired a reputation as friendly, _____ people.

12. Only someone who has experienced war can understand the _____ that develops among the soldiers; they trust each other with their lives and will do anything to help one another.

13. Padamé refused to _____ the advice of the Magic 8 Ball® and shaved her head anyway.

14. You wouldn't naturally think that steak drenched in chocolate sauce would be a delicacy, but the unlikely _____ of these rarely combined flavors makes the dish exquisite.

15. Philemon acted _____ when his recent break-up was mentioned, but you could tell he was totally heartbroken.

Word Association

Circle the word that does not belong.

> Example: laugh chuckle (sob)
>
> 1. advocate espouse vindicate
>
> 2. affable indifferent apathetic
>
> 3. miffed vexed fostered
>
> 4. nonchalant ephemeral transitory
>
> 5. debunk delineate disillusion

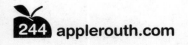

Synonyms

Match each word on the right to its synonym on the left.

1. advocate	(a) ephemeral
2. tangible	(b) espouse
3. negate	(c) obstinate
4. cordial	(d) tactile
5. impassive	(e) repudiate
6. transitory	(f) amiable
7. obdurate	(g) stoic

Word Charge

Mark each word as positive (+), negative (–) or neutral (=).

1. tenacity _____   4. amorphous _____   7. querulous _____

2. disillusion _____   5. onerous _____   8. evanescent _____

3. affable _____   6. engender _____   9. advocate _____

Sentence Completions

Choose the word that, when inserted in the sentence, <u>best</u> fits the meaning of the sentence as a whole.

1. An adept mediator, Mahendra believed he could help the union and management come to a(n) ------ agreement.

   a. tangible
   b. obdurate
   c. amicable
   d. futile

2. Famed photographer Nito von Nonenberg is the only one who has captured the ------ two-horned unicorn on film.

   a. stoic
   b. cordial
   c. complacent
   d. elusive

3. Georgina is a ------ professional, ------ all the traits needed to succeed in the fast-paced world of marketing.

   a. indifferent ... espousing
   b. consummate ... exemplifying
   c. benevolent ... engendering
   d. complacent ... epitomizing

4. Regardless of what your parents allow, I do not ------ that type of ------ behavior in my classroom.

   a. condone ... truculent
   b. negate ... onerous
   c. advocate ... perfunctory
   d. foster ... ephemeral

Word Roots

Match the root words to their meanings.

1. nasc/nat	(a) against
2. ob	(b) all
3. pan	(c) around
4. ped	(d) born
5. peri	(e) child
6. phon	(f) first
7. pro	(g) forward
8. prot	(h) sound
9. pro	(i) much, for, lots

Answers Week 5

Fill in the blank

*1. belligerent 2. transitory 3. debunk 4. advocated 5. miffed
6. futile 7. callous 8. benevolent 9. tenacity 10. engendered 11. affable
12. camaraderie 13. heed 14. juxtaposition 15. nonchalant*

Word Association

1. vindicate 2. affable 3. fostered 4. nonchalant 5. delineate

Synonyms

1.(b) 2.(d) 3.(e) 4.(f) 5.(g) 6.(a) 7.(c)

Word Charge

1.(+) 2.(−) 3.(+) 4.(=) 5.(−) 6.(=) 7.(−) 8.(=) 9.(+)

Sentence Completions

1.(c) 2.(d) 3.(b) 4.(a)

Word Roots

1.(d) 2.(a) 3.(b) 4.(e) 5.(c) 6.(h) 7.(g) or (i) 8.(f) 9.(i) or (g)

Vocabulary: Week 6

Bad, Mean And Low Down

egregious	flagrantly bad; conspicuously wrong
flagrant	extremely bad; deliberately shocking
heinous	terribly evil; abominable
nefarious	evil; wicked
reprehensible	deplorable; worthy of being hated

egregious

Come Together

amalgamate	to combine several elements into a whole
conciliation	regain friendship or goodwill by pleasant behavior
concordant	harmonious; being in accord or agreement

Dark Clouds Ahead

apprehension	fearful or uneasy anticipation of the future; dread
foreboding	a sense of dread about the future
ominous	threatening; menacing
wary	watchful; careful in guarding against danger

wary

Hard Times

adversity	a state of hardship or affliction; misfortune
arduous	strenuous; taxing; requiring significant effort
quandary	a state of uncertainty; perplexity

Don't Be A Player Hater

abhor	to hate or detest
animosity	hatred or enmity between people; ill-will
aversion	an intense dislike; repugnance
deplore	to find unacceptable
enmity	mutual hatred or ill-will
estrange	to remove or to alienate, especially from former loved ones
exasperate	to make angry; enrage; upset
indignation	anger incited by the unrighteousness or unfairness of something
malice	extreme ill-will
rancorous	marked with deep-seated hatred or ill-will
vindictive	vengeful; seeking revenge; spiteful

estrange

Dude, You Totally Rule!

autonomy	self-government or self-rule
demagogue	a leader who plays on people's emotions, fears, or prejudices
despotic	having absolute power; tyrannical
imperious	arrogant or domineering; bossy

Move Over Rover

antagonist	someone who opposes; opponent; adversary
encroach	to overstep boundaries
subversive	treasonous; attempting to secretly overthrow the government
supplant	to usurp; take the place of; supersede
undermine	to weaken or ruin
usurp	to wrongfully seize another's place, authority, or possession

subversive

Miscellaneous

catharsis   a release of emotional tension that restores or refreshes the spirit

eclectic   from a variety of sources and influences

emphatic   marked by emphasis or stress

innocuous   having no adverse effect; harmless

intemperate   extreme

maxim   a truism; a proverbial statement

vicarious   to live through someone else's experiences

vocation   an occupation; a calling

intemperate

Ye Of Little Faith

cynical   distrustful; disbelieving

irreverent   not showing proper respect or deference

nihilism   a philosophy that denies any absolute truth, meaning or purpose

You Better Bring It!

elicit   to draw out; to bring forth

evoke   to draw out; conjure

procure   to gain possession of; attain

evoke

Word Roots for the Week

que   ask, seek – inquisitive, query, inquiry, quest, request

re   again – reiterate, reclamation, repulse, recognize

sanct/sacr   holy – sanctify, sanctum, sanction, sacrosanct, desecrate, sacrament

scrib/scrip   write – describe, circumscribe, postscript, ascribe, inscribe

sens/sent   feel, think – sentimental, sensitive, sentient, sensible, dissent, assent

sequ/secu   follow – sequel, consequence, sequester, consecutive

son   sound – sonic, consonant, dissonant, resonant, sonorous

spec/spic   look, see – aspect, spectacle, speculate, circumspect, introspect

spir   breath – inspire, conspire, respiration, spirit

sens/sent

250 applerouth.com

Week 6 : Practice Exercises

Fill in the Blank

Use any appropriate form of the words in the box to fill in the blanks in the sentences below.

ominous   wary   eclectic   flagrant   indignant

despotic   vocation   adversity   encroach   irreverent

1. When Shaq picked up his coach and threw him into the stands, he was fined by the NBA for a(n) _____ violation of the NBA rules of conduct.

2. We sought shelter inside when _____ clouds filed the sky.

3. In Pink Floyd's *The Wall*, the school children resented their teacher's _____ rule over them and rebelled against the tyranny.

4. Gilgamesh's _____ music collection featured everything from Rob Zombie to Kanye West to Earl Scroggins.

5. Yoko was suspended for drawing and distributing a(n) _____ cartoon which likened her math teacher, Father Bearden, to an unflattering farm animal.

6. A passionate, if taciturn, mime, Marcel insisted that performance art was not a job but a(n) _____.

7. Although he professed to be above sibling bickering, Iliya was the first to holler when Svetlana's oversized pillow appeared to be _____ on his side of the backseat.

8. Ever since that fateful day in Grant Park when she was attacked by a rabid pigeon, Tess has been _____ of any member of the avian community.

9. Maya Angelou has overcome much _____ in her life to become one of the most popular poets of her time.

10. The _____ was evident on Rosa's face as the principal incorrectly introduced her to the PTA as her sister Roberta.

Fill in the Blank

Use any appropriate form of the words in the box to fill in the blanks in the sentences below.

> emphatic   procure   antagonist
>
> quandary   vicarious

11. Caitlin was convinced that Tiffany was the _____ in the melodrama that was her high school life.

12. The President's _____ acceptance of the treaty was signaled by his exuberant, if tasteless, victory dance in lieu of a handshake.

13. To complete the mission, it was Hector's job to _____ 30lbs of flour, a copy of the *Oxford English Dictionary*, an inflatable giraffe, a bucket of wolf toenail clippings and a 9-volt battery.

14. Living the unfulfilling life of an office temp, Siobhan found it easy to live _____ through her favorite celebrity who, oddly enough, played an office temp in her newest movie.

15. Sanchez found himself in the middle of a moral _____: should he tell his girlfriend that he didn't like her hair cut or should he lie?

Word Association

Circle the word that <u>does not belong</u>.

> Example: laugh   chuckle   (sob)
>
> 1. abhor   deplore   evoke
>
> 2. ominous   foreboding   nefarious
>
> 3. wary   despotic   imperious
>
> 4. malice   adversity   enmity
>
> 5. subvert   usurp   estrange

Synonyms

Match each word on the right to its synonym on the left.

1. supplant	(a) deplore
2. abhor	(b) usurp
3. enmity	(c) subvert
4. apprehension	(d) nefarious
5. heinous	(e) foreboding
6. undermine	(f) evoke
7. elicit	(g) malice

Word Charge

Mark each word as positive (+), negative (−) or neutral (=).

1. reprehensible _____   4. rancorous _____   7. arduous _____

2. amalgamate _____   5. innocuous _____   8. concordant _____

3. exasperate _____   6. intemperate _____   9. cynical _____

Sentence Completions

Choose the word that, when inserted in the sentence, <u>best</u> fits the meaning of the sentence as a whole.

1. A(n) ------ between the two mob bosses promised peace on the streets even if only for a short while.

   a. conciliation
   b. estrangement
   c. catharsis
   d. enmity

2. Lady Bracknell found the pirate Sharp Tooth Pete's marriage proposal to her daughter Gwendolyn utterly ------ .

   a. concordant
   b. rancorous
   c. reprehensible
   d. vindictive

3. As a Lutheran minister, Ann found her teen-age son's persistent belief in ------ completely ------.

   a. catharsis ... innocuous
   b. autonomy ... imperious
   c. animosity ... cynical
   d. nihilism ... exasperating

4. Despite the long, ------ winter, Dexter was able to ------ the supplies necessary to survive the cold, bitter season.

   a. innocuous ... supplant
   b. ominous ... elicit
   c. arduous ... procure
   d. emphatic ... amalgamate

Word Roots

Match the root words to their meanings.

1. que	(a) again
2. re	(b) ask
3. sanct/sacr	(c) breath
4. scrib/scrip	(d) feel
5. sens/sent	(e) follow
6. sequ/secu	(f) holy
7. son	(g) look
8. spec/spic	(h) sound
9. spir	(i) write

Answers Week 6

Fill in the blank

*1. flagrant 2. ominous 3. despotic 4. eclectic 5. irreverent 6. vocation
7. encroaching 8. wary 9. adversity 10. indignation 11. antagonist 12. emphatic
13. procure 14. vicariously 15. quandary*

Word Association

1. evoke 2. nefarious 3. wary 4. adversity 5. estrange

Synonyms

1.(b) 2.(a) 3.(g) 4.(e) 5.(d) 6.(c) 7.(f)

Word Charge

1.(–) 2.(=) 3.(–) 4.(–) 5.(=) 6.(–) 7.(–) 8.(+) 9.(–)

Sentence Completions

1.(a) 2.(c) 3.(d) 4.(c)

Word Roots

1.(b) 2.(a) 3.(f) 4.(i) 5.(d) 6.(e) 7.(h) 8.(g) 9.(c)

Vocabulary: Week 7

Pretty Sneaky Sis

belie	to be false; disguise; contradict
dissemble	disguise or conceal behind a false appearance
equivocate	to avoid making a definite statement
fallacy	a statement or argument based on a false or invalid inference
feign	to pretend; to fake
specious	seeming true, but actually being false, fallacious
spurious	false, illegitimate
wily	cunning; crafty; artful

dissemble

A Fine Line

circumscribe	to form a boundary around; contain; limit
delineate	to describe or draw out; depict
depict	to show or illustrate; describe
underscore	to emphasize or underline

Can't Escape Father Time

anachronism	something out of place in time
contemporary	from the same time; current
dilatory	always late; delaying; not prompt
exigency	pressing or urgent situation; crisis
expedite	to speed up the progress of; accelerate; to execute quickly and efficiently

anachronism

Doubtful At Best

implausible   not feasible or practical

quizzical   questioning or confused; gently teasing

tenuous   flimsy or weak; having little substance

implausible

Feeling Blue

condolence   an expression of sympathy for a mourner

lament   mourn; express grief over

morose   sullenly melancholy; gloomy

penitent   being sorry for one's misdeeds

resignation   unresisting acceptance of something as inescapable; giving in

somber   sad; gloomy; melancholy; morose

Miscellaneous

fidelity   faithfulness; loyalty

grandiose   characterized by greatness of scope or intent

gratuitous   given freely; unwarranted

inadvertent   without intention; especially resulting from heedless action

propensity   a natural inclination or tendency; penchant

renowned   well-known in a positive way; famous

solicitous   anxious or concerned

synergy   a phenomena where the whole is greater than the parts; combined effect

solicitous

Laying Low...

diffident	shy; timid; reserved in manner
docile	tame; obedient; calm
servile	submissive, like a servant
sycophant	a flatterer; a suck-up
timorous	timid; fearful
tremulous	fearful; timid; timorous

tremulous

More Than Words

connotation	the meaning of a word beyond its definition; association; implication
implicit	not directly stated; implied
tacit	implied; not explicitly stated

Straight Talk

candor	frankness or sincerity of expression; openness; the noun form of candid
incisive	penetrating; clear; sharp
poignant	moving; touching and powerful

Old School Like an Old Fool

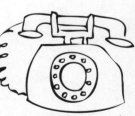

archaic

arcane	obscure; mysterious; unknown
archaic	from an earlier period in history; antiquated; old-fashioned
obscure	relatively unknown; mysterious
obsolete	no longer in use; outdated

Word Roots for the Week

sub	under – subdue, substantiate, subsistent, subterfuge, subliminal
super	more than – superficial, superlative, superfluous, supercilious
syn/sym	with – synthesis, sympathy, syndicate, synergy, symbiotic
tenu/tent/tend	thin – attenuate, tenuous, distend, tentative, extend
tort	twist – contort, distort, torture, torsion, tortuous
trans	across, through – transport, transit, transmutation, transient, transitory
ven/vent	come – advent, convene, prevent
vert/vers	turn – controversy, revert, divert, aversion, introvert, inadvertent, versatile
via/vita	life – vitamin, viable, vitality, vitiate, revitalize
voc	voice – vocal, equivocate, convoke, provocative, revoke, vocation

sub

Week 7 : Practice Exercises

Fill in the Blank

Use any appropriate form of the words in the box to fill in the blanks in the sentences below.

archaic   depict   anachronism   servile   implicit

tenuous   equivocate   timorous   lament   wily

1. Though he never admitted it, Nixon's silence and then resignation seemed to signal his _____ approval of the Watergate happenings.

2. After only one semester of science, Tabitha's understanding of marine biology was _____, which explains why she thinks catfish are the result of cross-breeding kittens with gold fish.

3. The language of Shakespeare, replete with words like thou and thy, is_____.

4. Gareth's _____ behavior, always volunteering to wash the chalkboards and straighten the desks after class, did little more than irritate his teachers.

5. Many fans agreed that *Man on the Moon*, starring Jim Carrey, was a fairly accurate _____ of comedian Andy Kaufman's short life.

6. We feared that the _____ puppy, who ran and hid under a table whenever anyone raised his voice, had been abused by his previous owners.

7. The entire class _____ the loss of 36 Krispy Kreme® donuts that fell on the floor and were covered with dirt, never to be eaten.

8. President Clinton _____ when he refused to answer questions about his relationship with Monica Lewinsky, preferring, instead, to focus on his relationship with Bob Dole.

9. In *The Great Escape*, Steve McQueen plays a(n) _____ prisoner of war who is always concocting some new and intricate plan for escape.

10. One of my favorite _____ is the wrist-watch worn by Moses—Charleton Heston—in the classic movie *The Ten Commandments*.

Fill in the Blank

Use any appropriate form of the words in the box to fill in the blanks in the sentences below.

> morose   grandiose   propensity
>
> implausible   gratuitous

11. Ambrosine was a big fan of Kung-fu movies, which offered plenty of scenes full of _____ violence.

12. The stereotype of llamas as _____, moody beings is unfair; many are actually quite cheerful.

13. Since her mother was an opera singer and her father a classical pianist, it wasn't _____ to predict a musical career for Ursula.

14. It is ridiculous to think Usher's house is anything but _____; it has two pools and has been featured on MTV *Cribs* and Robin Leach's *The Fabulous Life*.

15. A world class, competitive jigsaw puzzler, Endymion seemed to have a natural _____ for seeing patterns.

Word Association

Circle the word that <u>does not belong</u>.

> Example: laugh   chuckle   (sob)
>
> 1. fallacious   spurious   quizzical
>
> 2. morose   docile   somber
>
> 3. implicit   tacit   wily
>
> 4. arcane   obscure   autonomous
>
> 5. diffident   timorous   tenuous

Synonyms

Match each word on the right to its synonym on the left.

1. obsolete	(a) dissemble
2. diffident	(b) archaic
3. implicit	(c) expeditious
4. exigent	(d) spurious
5. depict	(e) tremulous
6. belie	(f) tacit
7. fallacious	(g) delineate

Word Charge

Mark each word as positive (+), negative (−) or neutral (=).

1. specious _____   4. implausible _____   7. renowned _____

2. dilatory _____   5. lament _____   8. fidelity_____

3. circumscribe _____   6. sycophant _____   9. connotation_____

Sentence Completions

Choose the word that, when inserted in the sentence, <u>best</u> fits the meaning of the sentence as a whole.

1. Students who are ------ and indolent in their SAT preparation rarely improve their scores.

   a. diffident
   b. exigent
   c. specious
   d. dilatory

2. Chen found the symbols on the decoder ring ------ and mysterious until he realized they were just letters printed backward.

   a. anachronistic
   b. tacit
   c. arcane
   d. grandiose

3. The commentator's remarks were both witty and ------; the audience appreciated his ------ and honesty.

   a. incisive ... candor
   b. morose ... poignancy
   c. spurious ... synergy
   d. quizzical ... anachronism

4. The ------ of the moment was ------ when Eva realized her mother had said her own wedding vows 30 years ago at the same altar.

   a. resignation ... depicted
   b. synergy ... expedited
   c. poignancy ... underscored
   d. fidelity ... lamented

Word Roots

Match the root words to their meanings.

1. sub	(a) across
2. super	(b) come
3. syn/sym	(c) life
4. tenu/tent/tend	(d) more than
5. tort	(e) thin
6. trans	(f) turn
7. ven/vent	(g) twist
8. vert/vers	(h) under
9. via/vita	(i) voice
10. voc	(j) with

Answers Week 7

Fill in the blank

*1. implicit 2. tenuous 3. archaic 4. servile 5. depiction 6. timorous 7. lamented
8. equivocated 9. wily 10. anachronisms 11. gratuitous 12. morose 13. implausible
14. grandiose 15. propensity*

Word Association

1. quizzical 2. docile 3. wily 4. autonomous 5. diffident

Synonyms

1.(b) 2.(e) 3.(f) 4.(c) 5.(g) 6.(a) 7.(d)

Word Charge

1.(−) 2.(−) 3.(=) 4.(−) 5.(−) 6.(−) 7.(+) 8.(+) 9.(=)

Sentence Completions

1.(d) 2.(c) 3.(a) 4.(c)

Word Roots

1.(h) 2.(d) 3.(j) 4.(e) 5.(g) 6.(a) 7.(b) 8.(f) 9.(c) 10.(i)

Vocabulary: Overachiever Words

acquiesce	to assent tacitly; submit or comply silently or without protest; agree; consent
acrid	sharp or biting to the taste or smell; bitterly pungent
affected	assumed artificially; unnatural; feigned
allure	to attract or tempt by something flattering or desirable
allusion	a passing or casual reference; an incidental mention of something
anecdote	a short, interesting or amusing account of a particular incident often biographical
arboreal	of or pertaining to trees; treelike
aspersion	a damaging or derogatory remark or criticism; slander
assuage	to make milder or less severe; relieve; ease; mitigate
astute	of keen penetration or discernment; sagacious
atrophy	degeneration, decline, or decrease, as from disuse
audacity	boldness or daring; confident or arrogant disregard for conventional thought
austere	severe in manner or appearance; uncompromising; strict; forbidding
bafflement	to confuse, bewilder, or perplex
banal	devoid of freshness or originality; hackneyed; trite
bane	a person or thing that ruins or spoils; a source of persistent annoyance
bemusement	bafflement, befuddlement, bewilderment, confusion
benefactor	a person who confers a benefit; one that gives aid, especially financial aid
bereavement	state of sorrow over the death or departure of a loved one
bereft	deprived
bewilder	to confuse or puzzle completely; perplex
bourgeois	conventional; middle-class; dominated or characterized by materialistic concerns
burnished	bright, polished; made to shine with luster
buttress	external support built to steady a structure
cadence	rhythmic flow of a sequence of sounds or words
calamity	a great misfortune or disaster, as in a flood or serious injury

cantankerous	disagreeable to deal with; contentious; peevish
carp	to find fault or complain querulously or unreasonably
castigate	to criticize or reprimand severely
cataclysmic	a violent upheaval causing great destruction or a fundamental change
catalyst	a person or thing that brings about an event or change
cathartic	purging of the emotions or relieving of emotional tensions
caustic	severely critical or sarcastic
charlatan	one who pretends to be more knowledgable or skillful than he/she is; quack
chauvinist	biased devotion to any group, attitude, or cause
circuitous	roundabout; indirect
circumspect	watchful and discreet; cautious; prudent
cloying	overly ingratiating or sentimental
colloquial	characteristic of ordinary or familiar conversation; informal
concur	to accord in opinion; agree
conducive	helpful; favorable
confound	to perplex or amaze; bewilder; confuse
conjecture	to guess; to offer an opinion or theory without sufficient evidence or proof
consecrate	to make or declare sacred; set apart or dedicate to the service of a deity
consign	to hand over or deliver formally or officially; commit
conspicuous	easily seen or noticed; readily visible or observable
conundrum	a riddle or difficult problem
convivial	friendly; agreeable
cosmopolitan	at home all over the world; sophisticated; urbane; worldly
credence	belief as to the truth of something
curative	serving to cure or heal; pertaining to curing or remedial treatment
decry	to speak disparagingly of; denounce as faulty or worthless; express censure
deduce	to derive as a conclusion from something known or assumed; infer
defunct	no longer in effect or use; not operating or functioning

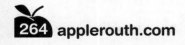

dejection	depression or lowness of spirits
deliberate	to weigh in the mind; consider
demographic	relating to the characteristics of human population
demure	characterized by shyness and modesty; reserved
deprecate	to express earnest disapproval of
desolate	barren or laid waste; devastated
despondent	feeling or showing profound hopelessness, dejection, or gloom
diffuse	adj. characterized by great length or discursiveness in speech or writing; wordy
diligent	constant in effort to accomplish something; attentive and persistent
disaffected	discontented and disloyal, as toward the government or toward authority
disavow	to disclaim knowledge of, connection with, or responsibility for; disown
disconcert	to cause to lose one's composure; perturb; ruffle
disingenuous	lacking in frankness, candor, or sincerity; falsely or hypocritically ingenuous
dispassionate	free from passion; devoid of personal feeling or bias; impartial; calm
dispatch	a written message sent with speed
disrepute	the state of being held in low esteem; low regard; disfavor
dissipate	1). to scatter in various directions; disperse; 2). to spend or use wastefully; squander
dissonance	inharmonious or harsh sound; discord; cacophony
divining	to discover or declare by prophesy; to perceive by intuition or insight
dogmatic	asserting opinions in a doctrinaire or arrogant manner; opinionated
dupe	a person who is easily deceived or fooled
economical	avoiding waste or extravagance; thrifty
edifice	a building, especially one of large size or imposing appearance
edify	to instruct or benefit, especially morally or spiritually; uplift
efficacious	capable of having the desired result or effect; effective
effusive	unduly demonstrative; with unrestrained enthusiasm
eminent	high in station, rank, or repute; prominent; distinguished
encumbrance	something burdensome, useless, or superfluous; burden; hindrance

enervated	without vigor, force, or strength; languid
enthrall	to captivate or charm
entreat	to ask earnestly; beseech; implore; beg
enumerate	to mention separately as if in counting; name one by one; to specify; to list
euphemism	a mild or indirect expression substituted for another that is thought to be offensive
excise	to cut out or off
explicit	fully and clearly expressed or demonstrated; leaving nothing implied; unequivocal
expropriation	to take possession of for public use by the right of eminent domain
expurgation	to amend by removing words or passages deemed offensive or objectionable
exuberance	effusively and almost uninhibitedly enthusiastic; lavishly abundant
fatalistic	accepting all things and events as inevitable; submitting to fate
fathom	to penetrate the meaning or nature of; comprehend; understand
filial	of, pertaining to, or befitting a son or daughter
flippant	frivolously disrespectful or lacking in seriousness; characterized by levity
folly	the state or quality of being foolish; lack of understanding or sense
foppish	excessively refined and fastidious in taste and manner
forgo	to abstain or refrain from; do without
forlorn	desolate or dreary; unhappy or miserable
forthright	going straight to the point; frank; direct; outspoken
frank	direct and unreserved in speech; straightforward; sincere
frivolous	characterized by lack of seriousness or sense
frugal	economical in use or expenditure; prudently saving or sparing; not wasteful
gargantuan	gigantic; enormous; colossal
garish	crudely or tastelessly colorful, showy, or elaborate, as in clothes or decoration
garner	to get; acquire; earn
garnish	to provide or supply with something ornamental; adorn; decorate
glacial	bitterly cold; icy; happening or moving extremely slowly
gullible	easily deceived or cheated

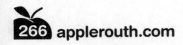

habituate	to accustom (a person, the mind, etc.) to a particular situation
halting	faltering or hesitating, especially in speech
hapless	unlucky; luckless; unfortunate
holistic	emphasizing the importance of the whole and the interdependence of its parts
impede	to slow in movement or progress by means of obstacles; obstruct; hinder
impute	to relate to a particular cause or source; attribute the fault or responsibility to
inarticulate	lacking the ability to express oneself, especially in clear and effective speech
incontrovertible	not open to question or dispute; indisputable
incorrigible	bad beyond correction or reform
incredulous	disinclined or indisposed to believe; skeptical
indeterminate	not clear; vague; not settled or decided
indigenous	originating in and characteristic of a particular region or country; native
indigent	lacking food, clothing, and other necessities of life because of poverty; needy
indiscriminate	lacking in care, judgment, selectivity
induce	to lead or move by persuasion or influence to some action or state of mind
industrious	working energetically and devotedly; hard-working; diligent
inordinate	not within proper or reasonable limits; immoderate; excessive
inscrutable	incapable of being investigated, analyzed, or scrutinized; impenetrable
insidious	intended to entrap or beguile
insinuate	to suggest or hint slyly
insurgent	a person who rises in forcible opposition to lawful authority; rebel
intermittent	stopping or ceasing for a time; alternately ceasing and beginning again
intrinsic	belonging to a thing by its very nature; innate, natural
inundate	to flood; cover or overspread with water; deluge
inviolable	secure from destruction, violence, infringement, or desecration
invocation	the act of calling upon a deity, spirit for aid, protection or inspiration
irresolute	not resolute; doubtful; infirm of purpose; vacillating
jocular	characterized by joking or jesting; waggish; facetious

laud	to praise; extol
libel	defamation by written or printed words, pictures
libertine	a person who is morally or sexually unrestrained; a profligate; rake
lurid	gruesome; horrible; revolting
machinations	crafty schemes; plots; intrigues
malevolence	ill will; malice; hatred
malfeasance	wrongful conduct by a public official that is legally unjustified or harmful
malign	to speak harmful untruths about; speak evil of; slander; defame
marginal	barely within a lower standard or limit of quality
mendicant	begging; practicing begging; living on alms
mercenary	working or acting merely for money or other reward; a hired soldier
mollify	to soften in feeling or temper, as a person; pacify; appease
moribund	in a dying state; near death
munificent	extremely liberal in giving; very generous
myopic	lacking tolerance or understanding; narrow-minded
nemesis	something that a person cannot conquer which causes misery or death; enemy
nondescript	of no recognized, definite, or particular type or kind
notoriety	the state, quality, or character of being notorious or widely known
nuance	a subtle difference or distinction in expression, meaning, response
obsequious	attentive in an ingratiating, deferential or servile manner; fawning
obtuse	not quick or alert in perception, feeling, or intellect; not sensitive or observant
omnipotent	almighty or infinite in power
outmoded	gone out of style; no longer fashionable
palpable	readily or plainly seen, heard, perceived; obvious; evident
pander	to cater to the lower tastes and desires of others or exploit their weaknesses
paramount	chief in importance or impact; supreme; preeminent
pedestrian	lacking in vitality, imagination, distinction; commonplace; prosaic or dull
pejorative	having a disparaging, derogatory, or belittling effect or force

penchant	a strong inclination, taste, or liking for something
peril	exposure to injury, loss, or destruction; grave risk; jeopardy; danger
periphery	the external boundary of any surface or area
permeate	to pass into or through every part of
perspicacity	keenness of mental perception and understanding; discernment; penetration
peruse	to read through with thoroughness or care
petulant	showing sudden, impatient irritation over some trifling annoyance
platitudes	flat, dull, or trite remarks, especially uttered as if they were fresh or profound
plaudits	enthusiastic expressions of approval
ponder	to consider something deeply and thoroughly; meditate
portent	an indication or omen of something, most likely momentous, about to happen
potentate	a person who possesses great power, as a sovereign, monarch, or ruler
precipitous	extremely or impassably steep
precocious	unusually advanced or mature in development, especially mental development
preeminence	character of being superior to or notable above all others; outstanding
prescribe	to lay down rules; direct; dictate
pretext	something that is put forward to conceal a true purpose or object; excuse
prodigious	extraordinary in size, amount, extent, degree, force
prognosis	a forecasting of the probable course and outcome of a disease
promulgate	to make known by open declaration; publish; proclaim formally
prostrate	to cast (oneself) face down on the ground in humility, submission, or adoration
protégé	one whose welfare, training, or career is promoted by an influential person
prudent	wise or judicious in practical affairs; sagacious; discreet or circumspect
pugnacious	inclined to quarrel or fight readily; quarrelsome; belligerent; combative
punctilious	extremely attentive; strict or exact in the observance of formalities of conduct
punctuate	to give emphasis or force to; emphasize; underline; to interrupt at intervals
purported	reputed or claimed; alleged
qualify	modify or limit in some way; make less strong or positive; to make less; moderate

query a question; an inquiry

rambunctious difficult to control or handle; wildly boisterous, unpleasantly loud and harsh

raucous harsh; strident; grating

reductive characterized by or causing diminution or reduction

refurbish renovate; brighten; redecorate

reproof an expression of censure or rebuke

respite a delay for a time especially of anything distressing or trying; an interval of relief

resplendent shining brilliantly; gleaming; splendid

resuscitate to revive, especially from apparent death or from unconsciousness

rigor strictness, severity, or harshness, as in dealing with people

sacrilege the violation or profanation of anything sacred or held sacred

sanctimonious making a hypocritical show of religious devotion, piety, righteousness

sardonic characterized by bitter or scornful derision; mocking; cynical; sneering

scrupulous having scruples; having or showing a strict regard for what is considered right; principled

shrewd astute or sharp in practical matters

shroud an expression of censure or rebuke; to cover; hide from view

slipshod careless, untidy, or slovenly

spare frugally restricted or meager; scanty or scant, as in amount or fullness

steadfast fixed in direction; steadily directed

stilted stiffly dignified or formal, as in speech or literary style; pompous

stipulate to make an express demand or arrangement as a condition of agreement

strident making or having a harsh sound; grating; creaking

stringent rigorously binding or exacting; strict; severe

subjective pertaining to or characteristic of an individual; personal

subordinate n. belonging to a lower order or rank

subterfuge something intended to misrepresent; to evade a rule; escape a consequence

succulent full of juice; juicy

suffrage the right to vote, especially in a political election

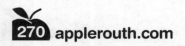

sullen showing irritation or ill humor by a gloomy silence or reserve

sumptuous entailing great expense from choice materials, fine work; costly

supercilious haughtily disdainful or contemptuous

superfluous being more than is sufficient or required; excessive

tenet an opinion, principle, or doctrine; especially one held as true to a profession or movement

transcribe to make a written copy of dictated material, notes from a lecture, or other spoken material

truncate to shorten by cutting off a part; cut short

tumultuous marked by disturbance and uproar

ubiquity the state or capacity of being everywhere, especially at the same time; omnipresence

unassuming modest; unpretentious

uncanny having or seeming to have a supernatural or inexplicable basis; extraordinary

unpalatable unpleasant to the taste

unstinting bestowed liberally; very generous

unwarranted having no justification; groundless

vacuity the state of being vacuous or without contents; vacancy; emptiness

vapid lacking liveliness, sharpness, or flavor; insipid; flat

verbose characterized by the use of many or too many words; wordy

verdant green with vegetation; covered with growing plants or grass

vestige a mark, trace, or visible evidence of something that is no longer present or in existence

viable practicable; workable, capable of being done

vindicate to clear, as from an accusation, imputation or suspicion

visceral characterized by or proceeding from instinct rather than intellect

vituperative using, containing, or marked by harshly abusive criticism

vivacious lively; animated

voluminous large in number, quantity, volume or bulk

vulnerable capable of or susceptible to being wounded or hurt, as by a weapon

wry bitterly or disdainfully ironic or amusing, humorously sarcastic or mocking

zeal passion, enthusiastic devotion to a cause, ideal, or goal

Key SAT Word Roots

ambi	two – ambidextrous, ambivalent, ambiguous
ami	friend – amicable, amity, amiable, amorous
arch	first – archetype, archangel, archaic, archrival
auto	self – autobiography, automatic, automaton, autonomy, autopsy
bell	war – belligerent, bellicose, antebellum South
ben	good – benign, beneficent, benefactor
chrono	time – chronology, anachronism
circum	around – circumscribe, circumvent
cis	cut – incision, decisive, incisive, precise
co/com/con	with – condescending, compliant, condemn, contemporary, context, convoke
cogn	know – cognition, recognize, incognito, cognizant, cognate
cred	trust, believe – incredible, incredulous, credit, credible
de	away, down, off – debilitate, defraud, decry, defame, devoid, desecrate
dict	say – dictate, dictator, dictum, indicative, edict
dis	not, away from – distance, discredit, disparity, digress
dur	hard – endure, durable, duration, obdurate
equi	equal – equivocate, equanimity, equidistance, equilibrium
ex	away from – exculpate, extract, exit, exhume, extinct, exonerate
fort	strong – fortitude, fortuitous, effort, fortify
frac/frag	break – fragment, fracture, fragile, fractious, refract
gen	life – genesis, engender, gender, genital, gentle, regenerate
grat	pleasing – congratulate, gratuitous, gratify, ingrate
gress	step – progress, transgress, regress, digress, retrogress
hyper	more than – hyperbole, hyper vigilant, hypertension, hyper-extend
hypo	less than/under – hypothesis, hypodermic, hypothermia
in	with – intensify, inherent, innate, inspire, ingenious
in/im	not – impossible, immutable, impartial, incessant, incoherent, indifferent

Key SAT Word Roots

loc	place – locale, locus, allocate, dislocate, relocate
loqu/locut	talk, speech – elocution, loquacious
luc/lum	light – elucidate, translucent, luminous, lucid, illumine, luminary
magna	great – magnanimous, magnitude, magnificent
mal	bad – malign, malignant, malefactor, malice, malicious, malfeasance
med	middle – medieval, medley, meddle, mediate, meditate, remedial
meter/metr	measure – chronometer, metronome, geometry, commensurate
morph	shape – biomorphic, amorphous, anthropomorphic, morphology
mut	change – mutate, transmute, immutable, mutilate
nasc/nat	born – native, natural, nascent, innate, neonatal
ob	against – obdurate, obscure, obstinate, object, obstacle, obscure, obvious
pan	all – panic, panacea, panorama, pantheistic, panoply
ped	child – pedagogue, pediatrics, pedantic
peri	around – perimeter, perinatal, periscope
phon	sound – phonetics, phonics, cacophony, euphony, symphony
pro	forward – profound, profuse, proliferate, protean,
pro	much, for, lots – prolific, profuse, prodigious, protracted, propensity
prot	first – protagonist, protean, prototype, proton
que	ask, seek – inquisitive, query, inquiry, quest, request
re	again – reiterate, reclamation, repulse, recognize
sanct/sacr	holy – sanctify, sanctus, sanction, sacrosanct, desecrate, sacrament
scrib/scrip	write – describe, circumscribe, postscript, ascribe, inscribe
sens/sent	feel, think – sentimental, sensitive, sentient, sensible, dissent, assent, resent
sequ/secu	follow – sequel, consequence, sequester, consecutive
son	sound – sonic, consonant, dissonant, resonant, sonorous
spec/spic	look, see – aspect, spectacle, speculate, circumspect, introspect
spir	breath – inspire, conspire, respiration, spirit

Key SAT Word Roots

sub   under – subdue, substantiate, subsistent, subterfuge, subliminal

super   more than – superficial, superlative, superfluous, supercilious

syn/sym   with – synthesis, sympathy, syndicate, synergy, symbiotic

tenu/tent/tend   thin – attenuate, tenuous, distend, tentative, extend

tort   twist – contort, distort, torture, torsion, tortuous

trans   across – through, transport, transit, transmutation, transient, transitory

ven/vent   come – advent, convene, prevent

vert/vers   turn – controversy, revert, divert, aversion, introvert, inadvertent, versatile

via/vita   life – vitamin, viable, vitality, vitiate, revitalize

voc   voice – vocal, equivocate, convoke, provocative, revoke, vocation, vociferous

WRITING

The Writing Section

The Writing portion of the SAT will count for all students. To find out how the schools on your list use your Writing score in admissions decisions, go to the websites of particular colleges or use The College Board's (www.collegeboard.com) college search feature.

Good news

Of the three sections on the SAT, Writing is the easiest and most coachable section by leaps and bounds. In order to achieve tremendous score gains on the Writing section, you only have to master a discrete set of skills.

Structure

Writing has two components: the 25-minute essay and two multiple choice sections that test rules of grammar. The SAT always starts with the essay and always ends with the short, 14-question multiple choice Writing section. And somewhere in between you will run into a longer, 35-question multiple choice Writing section.

The Essay

The essay is formulaic. To succeed on the Essay, learn what the SAT readers are looking for and give them exactly that. We will explain the SAT essay grading rubric in detail and provide examples of high scoring essays.

The Grammar Section

The grammar section tests a very limited number of grammar concepts. SAT writers are highly consistent in their choice of grammar concepts that will appear on the SAT Writing test.

If you memorize the most frequently occurring rules, you can achieve a very significant score increase. We will outline all the key concepts that are assessed by the SAT and give you a head start on achieving your best possible Writing score.

The Essay

Don't fret! This essay is one of the easiest things you will have to do on the SAT. The question is not, "are you Ernest Hemingway or Emily Bronte?"—the question is whether you can think and write in a structured, logical fashion.

The graders have gone through a quick grading workshop sponsored by the College Board. They know the criteria for each essay grade intimately, and most graders can glance at an essay and differentiate between a 4, a 5 and a 6 in less than 30 seconds. They know what a 6 looks like, what a 5 looks like, etc... They are instructed never to spend more than 3 minutes reading your essay, and the graders we have spoken with report that the actual time spent per essay is closer to the 1-2 minute mark. Most of the graders are English teachers looking to make some quick weekend cash.

The SAT graders will rarely read your entire essay. That isn't the point; these graders have to knock out hundreds of these essays per day, all covering the same topic—fun job, eh? The job of a grader is to tear through his/her pile of essays as expediently as possible and assign each essay a number 1-6.

You must keep in mind that your essay will not be read—it will be glanced at, quickly assessed, and portions will be read in a cursory fashion. The introduction and conclusion will be read, and those have to be good. The grader may also look at one paragraph or the paragraph transitions. It will be a quick pass either way. Your job is to give the graders what they want. Let them check the boxes for 5 or 6 and then move on to the next essay.

SAT Essay Grading Process

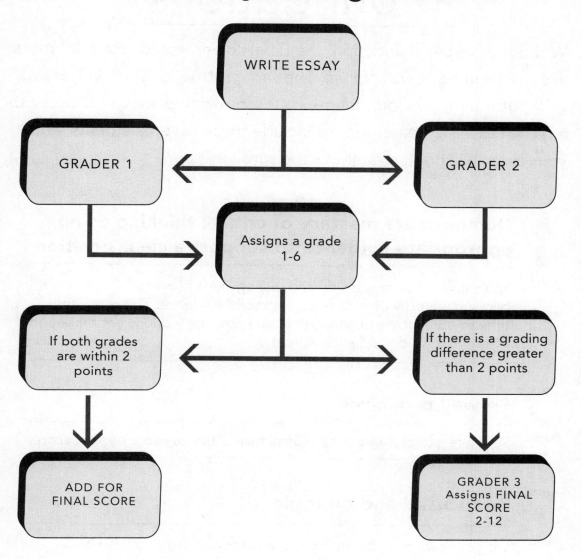

If you receive a score of 8 on your essay, most likely each of your graders scored your essay as a 4. If you receive a 9, one grader probably gave you a 5 and the other gave you a 4. It is unlikely that two graders will differ in their assessment of your essay by more than two points. If this does occur, another grader will be called in to assign a final score between 2 and 12.

Foundations

Without a proper foundation, the Eiffel Tower would look a lot more like the Leaning Tower of Pisa. The same is true for your SAT Essay. Without the proper foundation, your score would lean a lot closer to a 5 than to a 12. Remember to include these seven elements, and your essay will point straight to the sun.

1 Demonstrate mastery of critical thinking using appropriate evidence to support a clear position

You will need to take a side and, acting like a lawyer in a courtroom, back up your decisive position with solid evidence. This is not the time to equivocate or show that you know the world is not black and white. Pick a side and stick with it!

2 Be well-organized

Structure, structure, structure. *Structure is the key to a perfect score*.

3 Be focused and on topic

Let your grader know that you are on topic—again and again—keep hitting him/her with your thesis until he/she is blue in the face. Once per paragraph is recommended.

Lucky 7

Remember these 7 elements for a strong foundation

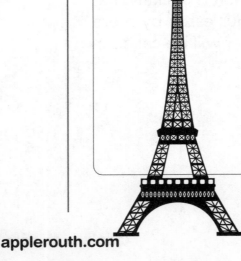

4 Have smooth transitions between paragraphs

The flow is important—have good segues and transitions that lead from one paragraph or example to the next.

Keep your grader engaged with varied and unique sentence structures. Stand out from the crowd!

5 Demonstrate skillful and appropriate use of vocabulary

Use vocabulary skillfully! This is the key. Better to use simple words than try to show off and sound ridiculous. Use words that you know and love. Avoid too many $20 words like circumambulate, obfuscate, or ratiocination—they will actually hurt your cause. Be smart with your words, sound intelligent, but don't try too hard. Really push your verbs—get away from the "to be" verbs and shake it up some. This demonstrates, clarifies, delineates, displays, provides evidence of, exemplifies…Be creative.

- In spite of this…

- Refuting the claim…

- No matter how persistently they tried, the team members were unable to…

6 Utilize a variety of sentence structures

Too much simplistic subject–predicate sentence construction will hurt your score. You need some dependent clauses, introductory phrases and alternative sentence structures.

- Facing defeat, the coach opted to…

- They gave it all they could; by the third quarter the team…

7 Minimize grammar, usage and punctuation errors

Some errors will certainly occur. Graders expect this. They are looking more for patterns of errors, consistent lapses in a given area.

- It all came down to determination: the desire to win and …

1 Critical Thinking	5 Skillful Language
2 Structure	6 Varied Sentences
3 Remain on Target	7 Correct Grammar
4 Smooth Transitions	

Structure, Structure, Structure

The primary element graders want to see is **STRUCTURE**! It makes their jobs quicker and easier and leaves them feeling warm and fuzzy inside. Structure is the basis for your grade on the Essay section.

The Pyramid Principle

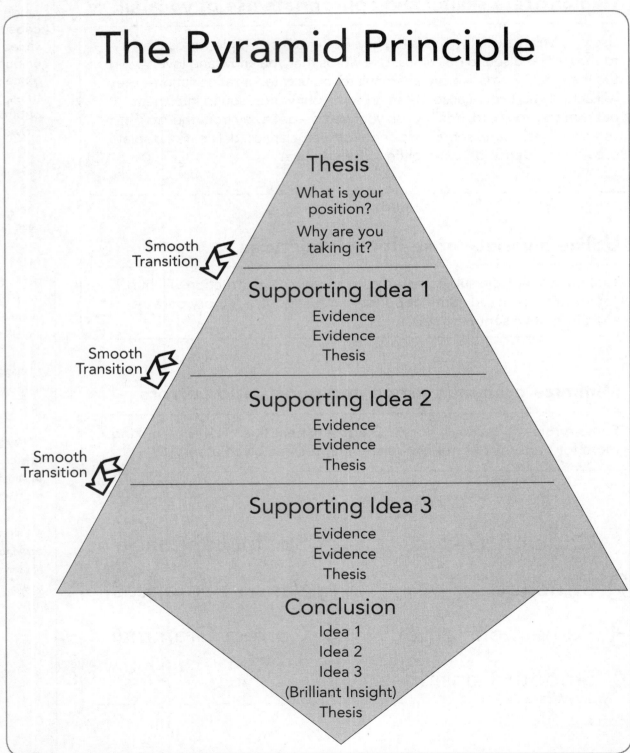

Thesis

What is your position?

Why are you taking it?

Smooth Transition

Supporting Idea 1

Evidence
Evidence
Thesis

Smooth Transition

Supporting Idea 2

Evidence
Evidence
Thesis

Smooth Transition

Supporting Idea 3

Evidence
Evidence
Thesis

Conclusion

Idea 1
Idea 2
Idea 3
(Brilliant Insight)
Thesis

Building the Essay

We've given you all the tools you'll need to write a perfect-scoring essay. But how do you get started? Below is a step-by-step strategy to put all your good words to use.

1 Read the assignment

Be very clear: the assignment is the key, and it is more important than the prompt. The prompt is the background. The assignment is **what you are responsible** for addressing.

2 Read the prompt if needed

The prompt is there to stimulate your thoughts. Generally it will advocate the affirmative or negative position on a given assignment.

3 Assume your position

Time to put on your lawyer's cap and pick your side. Affirmative or negative. "I agree or disagree with the statement." Don't forget: **No one cares if you are right or wrong.** For you perfectionists—there is no right answer, and you get no points for answering the question correctly. The grader just wants to see if you know **how to write** and doesn't have much interest in your position, as long as you take one.

It's okay to qualify your statement some, such as "I agree, but there is an exception." Most rules have an exception. You can tee that up later, but in the beginning all that matters is that you take a definite position that you will be able to defend with evidence. **It is generally easier to take and defend the affirmative stance.**

4 Brainstorm your examples

The assignments are generally abstract and fluffy such as:

- Do our greatest strengths contribute to our downfall?

- Does technology enhance or diminish the quality of our lives?

- Is honesty always the best policy?

You can probably see how some people could see these prompts and immediately begin rambling and spewing paragraphs of drivel and inconsistent swill. Fluff and more fluff. The key here is to take the abstract assignments and **get concrete. Get specific.** Get to solid examples and you begin to build the foundation of your argument.

Once you take your position, you will need to brainstorm examples to defend your position.

Veracity- Tellin' it straight or tellin' it slant

When you are writing from personal experience, the graders don't know a thing about you; you have complete artistic license to concoct any story that serves your thesis. **Make things up; have fun.** Invent your friend Steve who was on MTV's *The Real World*, your Grandma Bessie who jumps out of airplanes, your dog Herman that ate 3 pounds of chocolate and a flank steak before noon.

When you cannot remember historical details, come as close as you can. The readers want to see how you think; they know you would get the actual names and dates right if you could access the Internet or your text books. Again, this is not about the content—it's about showing off your writing skills.

The Great Scavenger Hunt

Where exactly are you supposed to find your concrete examples? Well, feel free to pull from History, Literature, Pop Culture, Current Events and Personal Narrative. Don't stress out trying to find a cultured or sophisticated example. Use one that fits! It doesn't matter if your example is about an aunt, the President or a Hollywood star.

It is all right to fudge some details when supporting your thesis. But remember, this is not a creative writing exercise.
Don't lose track of your thesis!

5 Select the Big 3

Next you must choose the three examples that you will use to support your thesis. At the minimum you need two examples, but three is best. Choose the 3 examples that you can **best support** and that are the **most specific.**

Mix and Match

Your 3 examples can come from any of the following categories: History, Literature, Current Events, Pop Culture, Personal Narrative. Branch out, mix it up a little. Have fun!

I.   Pick all 3 examples from one category
II. Pick an example from each category
III. Pick one example—one event in history— and flesh it out with 3 distinct supporting points

Macro to Micro

A general rule is that it's better to go from the general to the specific—from the macro to the micro—beginning with a historical example and ending with a personal example.

History / Literature

Pop Culture / Current Events

Personal Narrative

This is the natural flow of things. If all your examples are in the same category—you can prioritize by **starting with your strongest example** and ending with the weakest. This is just in case you run out of time and need to skip Supporting Idea 3.

Transitions

Below are some simple transitional phrases for you to use in between paragraphs.

• The next example is...(yes, it can be that simple)

• Another area that exemplifies this...

• Providing further evidence for this point...

• On a more personal level, I have experienced...

• Although this phenomenon exists in the world of politics, the world of... also demonstrates...

• Beyond the experience of... that of... also illustrates the point that...

6 Write Your Essay

Introduction
Body Paragraph 1
Body Paragraph 2
Body Paragraph 3
Closing

Introduction

The grader **will** read your entire introduction. Count on that. The grader needs to see two things: 1) Your thesis statement. 2) The rationale behind your thesis. Following the Pyramid principle, it's not a bad idea to hit your grader with your thesis first. Some students prefer to end the introduction with the thesis statement. Both are appropriate methods. *The Intro should be short and sweet.* This is not the time to flesh things out. Save your evidence for the body paragraphs.

Body Paragraphs 1, 2, 3

In each paragraph you need three things:

   I.   A transition from the preceding paragraph
   II. Evidence to support your point
   III. A reiteration of your thesis statement

You have lots of freedom within the confines of these three rules, but you need to provide evidence, hit your thesis and create a smooth transition between points.

Transitions
Every good essay has a logical flow, a natural development from one point to the next. Reiterating early points and incorporating transitional phrases will help you create this effortless progression from one idea to the next.

Evidence
You need to reinforce your Supporting Ideas with **concrete examples and details.**

Thesis
You need to reiterate your thesis. Often this is easiest at the beginning or the end of each body paragraph.

Closing

Your reader will most likely read your entire closing. **You absolutely need a closing.** Ending mid-sentence is a no-no. If you only have two minutes left and you are smack in the middle of Supporting Idea 2, end that paragraph, scratch Supporting Idea 3, and immediately write a two-sentence closing. Short closings are preferable. This is not the time to add new evidence.

In the closing, you have 2 tasks:

    I.   Hit your thesis one more time
    II.   Add your personal insight or a bit of wisdom

Thesis
Re-phrase your thesis one last time.

Insight/Wisdom
Regarding the chunk of personal wisdom or insight, you have several options. You can either qualify your thesis or take it to a deeper level expanding to a broader application.

Ex:

As evidenced by S1, S2, S3, it is obvious that... (Thesis).

You want to end well and persuasively.

End with a BANG, not a whimper.

7 Review if time permits

If there is time, take a quick crack at proofing your essay. Check your transitions and look for errors. If you accidentally run out of time and are only able to cover Supporting Idea 1 and Supporting Idea 2, go back and cross off Supporting Idea 3 from your intro paragraph.

Conclusions

Just in case you have trouble saying goodbye, we've given you a list of snappy ways to introduce the conclusion of your essay.

• Although it is true that we all have strengths that can become weaknesses…

• Looking beyond this, our lives cannot be limited to…

• Knowing this, we must ensure that we maintain focus on…to guarantee…

• However much we may try, as humans we are limited to…

• If all people followed this counsel, humanity would certainly benefit by…

• On a global level, every country needs to take into account…

Final Review

Step 1	Understand the assignment and take a position	1 Minute
Step 2	Brainstorm examples	2 Minutes
Step 3	Prioritize and sequence your examples	2 Minutes
Step 4	Write your essay	18 Minutes
Step 5	Proof the essay	2 Minutes

What is Perfect?

The following essay was written for a REAL SAT and received a perfect score. According to the College Board, a level 12 essay "demonstrates clear and consistent mastery, although it may have a few minor errors." Below, we have identified all the parts that helped put this essay over the top.

Is it easier to achieve success through cooperation or through competition?

Though Western Civilization celebrates the efforts of the solitary

(str.)　(vocab.)

individual, professing determination and rugged individualism as the keys

[thesis]

to success, **the collaborative efforts of great teams have yielded**

some of the greatest results in history. If we can find a way to unite

behind a cause, putting our differences aside, **we can achieve more**

[thesis]

than if we work in isolation and competition.

(trans.)　　　　　　　　　　　[detail]

<u>One of the greatest collaborative efforts</u> of the *20th century* was the

[detail]

remarkable *Manhattan Project*. Led by the brilliant nuclear physicist,

[detail]

Robert J. Oppenheimer, the Manhattan Project brought together

(str.)

the greatest minds in America to achieve a common goal: create a

weapon that would end the Second World War and save hundreds of

thesis

You will see this symbol over the bolded thesis every time it appears.

detail

You will see this symbol over specific details that have been italicized.

(str.)

You will see this symbol over punctuation that signals advanced sentence structure.

(trans.)

You will see this symbol over every underlined transition.

(vocab.)

You will see this symbol over the skillfully used vocabulary words.

thesis

detail

str.

trans.

vocab.

thesis

You will see this symbol over the bolded thesis every time it appears.

detail

You will see this symbol over specific details that have been italicized.

str.

You will see this symbol over punctuation that signals advanced sentence structure.

trans.

You will see this symbol over every underlined transition.

vocab.

You will see this symbol over the skillfully used vocabulary words.

thousands of American lives. Dozens of scientists, **previously working** [thesis]

in competition at their respective universities, were called together

to join efforts to serve their country. Brilliant minds, the likes of *Enrico* [detail]

Fermi and *Albert Ellis*, joined forces, putting their egos aside to **col-** [detail]

laborate and achieve a greater success than they could in isolation [thesis]

or competition. For *three years* this team of scientists toiled in the [detail] [vocab.]

New Mexico desert, testing their theories of *atomic energy and nucle-* [detail] [detail]

ar fusion. By *1943*, this **collaborative effort** produced the first atomic [detail] [thesis]

bomb, which allowed the United States to save the lives of *500,000* of [detail]

its own soldiers, *avoiding a direct invasion of Japan.* [detail]

Collaboration, rather than competition, was the key to success in [thesis]

the Second World War. Faced with the spectre of the rise of the Third [vocab.]

Reich, the *United States, Britain, and Russia* joined ranks to defeat the [detail]

German military force. The Russians had initially resisted collaboration

with the allies, but after *Hitler* invaded Russia, *Stalin* quickly saw the [detail] [detail]

advantage of a unified effort against Hitler. At *Yalta, Churchill, Stalin* `[detail] [detail]`

and Roosevelt settled on a **collaborative strategy and chose to work** `[thesis]`

together to achieve the end of the war. **Again this illustrates that**

collaboration is a more effective means of achieving success. `[thesis]`

(trans.) In the 21st century, **collaboration is the genius of the age.** You `[thesis]`

cannot compete alone and survive in this world of partnerships, joint

ventures, and shared interests. Companies are leading the way, **work-**

ing together to survive and thrive, rather than working alone. `[thesis]`

Though it's tempting to work alone and gratify your own desires and (vocab.)

needs, if **we can collaborate with others we will achieve greater and** (str.) `[thesis]`

more durable successes. (vocab.)

`[thesis]`

You will see this symbol over the bolded thesis every time it appears.

`[detail]`

You will see this symbol over specific details that have been italicized.

(str.)

You will see this symbol over punctuation that signals advanced sentence structure.

(trans.)

You will see this symbol over every underlined transition.

(vocab.)

You will see this symbol over the skillfully used vocabulary words.

Level 10 Essay

The College Board describes an essay that receives a score of 10 as demonstrating "reasonably consistent mastery, although it will have occasional errors or lapses in quality." The following essay still has a strong thesis and supporting examples; however, you will notice that the vocabulary is not as strong and sentence sturcture is not as varied as the level 12 essay. The examples are also not as detailed nor are the transitions as clear.

Is it easier to achieve success through cooperation or through competition?

Though Western Civilization celebrates the efforts of isolated in-dividuals, **the collaborative efforts of great teams have yielded some of the greatest results** in history. If we can find a way to unite behind a cause, **we can achieve more than if we work in isolation and competition**.

One of the greatest team-led efforts of the 20th century was the *Manhattan Project*. Led by the *nuclear physicist, Robert J. Oppen-heimer*, the Manhattan Project brought together the greatest minds in America to achieve the goal of creating a weapon that would end the *Second World War*. Scientists across the country were called together to

Sidebar symbols:

thesis
You will see this symbol over the bolded thesis every time it appears.

detail
You will see this symbol over specific details that have been italicized.

str.
You will see this symbol over punctuation that signals advanced sentence structure.

trans.
You will see this symbol over every underlined transition.

vocab.
You will see this symbol over the skillfully used vocabulary words.

join efforts and create the ultimate, war-ending weapon. These brilliant

【thesis】

scientists put their egos aside to **collaborate and achieve a success**

that none of them could have achieved independently of one an-

（vocab.） 【detail】

other. For years this team of scientists worked diligently in the *desert*,

【detail】

testing their theories of atomic energy. By *1943* this extraordinary team

produced the first atomic bomb, which allowed the United States to

【detail】

end the war *without a direct invasion of mainland Japan*. **Cooperation**

【thesis】

proved infinitely powerful in this effort.

【thesis】

Collaboration was the key to success in the Second World

【detail】   【detail】

War. Faced with the rise of the *Third Reich, the United States, Brit-*

ain, and Russia joined ranks to defeat the German military force. The

（str.）

Russians had initially resisted working with the allies, but after Hitler

【detail】

invaded Russia, *Stalin* saw the advantage of a unified effort against Hit-

ler. The leaders of the three allied countries settled in on a **collaborative**

【thesis】

strategy and chose to work together to successfully end the war.

【thesis】

You will see this symbol over the bolded thesis every time it appears.

【detail】

You will see this symbol over specific details that have been italicized.

（str.）

You will see this symbol over punctuation that signals advanced sentence structure.

（trans.）

You will see this symbol over every underlined transition.

（vocab.）

You will see this symbol over the skillfully used vocabulary words.

thesis

You will see this symbol over the bolded thesis every time it appears.

detail

You will see this symbol over specific details that have been italicized.

str.

You will see this symbol over punctuation that signals advanced sentence structure.

trans.

You will see this symbol over every underlined transition.

vocab.

You will see this symbol over the skillfully used vocabulary words.

thesis

In the 21st century **collaboration is the genius of the age.**

Companies and business interests all work together, in partnerships, to achieve advantages in the marketplace. If you do not collaborate with others, it is almost impossible to succeed in today's competitive market.

trans.

Though it's tempting to work alone and focus on advancing your

str. **thesis**

own interests, **collaboration is a better strategy**. As revealed by the efforts of the scientists of the Manhattan project and the allied powers in the Second World War, **whenever we put our energies and talents**

thesis

together, we can achieve more than if we work in competition with one another.

Level 8 Essay

The College Board describes an essay that receives a score of 8 as demonstrating "adequate mastery, although it will have lapses in quality." The following essay has a clear thesis, though it isn't as complex as the previous two theses. You'll also notice very few advanced vocabulary words, virtually no transitions and simple setence structures. However, this essay does have examples to support its thesis. It also has a decent conclusion.

Is it easier to achieve success through cooperation or through competition?

Any student of history knows that individuals have contributed greatly ⬭str.⬭ ▢thesis▢ to our civilization. However, **when individuals work together in**

teams, they have accomplished even greater things. Whenever ▢thesis▢ **people can unite and work together, they will accomplish more**

than if they work independently of one another. ⬭trans.⬭
        One of the most successful team efforts of the 20th century was ▢detail▢
the Manhattan Project. The Manhattan Project brought together the

greatest minds in America to build a weapon that would end the

---

thesis
You will see this symbol over the bolded thesis every time it appears.

detail
You will see this symbol over specific details that have been italicized.

⬭str.⬭
You will see this symbol over punctuation that signals advanced sentence structure.

⬭trans.⬭
You will see this symbol over every underlined transition.

⬭vocab.⬭
You will see this symbol over the skillfully used vocabulary words.

thesis

You will see this symbol over the bolded thesis every time it appears.

detail

You will see this symbol over specific details that have been italicized.

str.

You will see this symbol over punctuation that signals advanced sentence structure.

trans.

You will see this symbol over every underlined transition.

vocab.

You will see this symbol over the skillfully used vocabulary words.

detail   **detail**

Second World War. Dozens of scientists gathered together in the *desert*

thesis

to serve their country. **Together these scientists achieved the kind**

of success that none of them could have attained on their own. For

years this team of scientists worked in the desert, experimenting with

the new theories of atomic energy. Eventually their efforts produced

detail   **str.**

the *first atomic bomb*, which allowed the United States to save the

lives of thousands of its own soldiers and successfully end the war.

vocab.

During the Second World War, collaboration was essential. Faced

detail

with the rise of the *Third Reich, the United States, Britain, and Russia*

joined ranks to defeat the growing German military force. The Rus-

sians had initially resisted cooperating with the allies, but after Hitler

detail

invaded *Russia, Stalin* quickly saw the advantage of a unified effort

thesis

against Hitler. Eventually all three allied countries **came together** to

defeat Germany and end the war.

Though it's tempting to work alone and focus on your individual

(str.) [thesis] (vocab.)

success, **cooperation is a far better way to achieve lofty goals.**

[thesis]

Throughout history, teams have **worked together to achieve** great

things. **Teams who work in cooperation will always achieve more**

[thesis]

than those who work in competition with one another.

Perfect 12 Essays

The following 3 essays are essays that were written for REAL SAT tests and were graded by REAL SAT graders. Each one scored a perfect 12. Look for the following components in each essay that will help you get a perfect score, too!

1 Length

Max out the 2 pages—come as close as you can to filling up all the space. Longer essays achieve higher scores.

2 Structure

Good essays have an introduction and a conclusion. The thesis is repeated again, and again, and again—in every single body paragraph, often multiple times. Let there be no confusion that you are clearly on topic and answering the question.

3 Specific, Concrete, Detailed Examples

Give them names, dates, figures, events. Make them up! This is not the AP exam; content does not count. The readers will not check your facts on Wikipedia. They simply want to see you are using details to support an abstract thesis.

4 Sentence Structure

Give me a **:** or a **;** or even a **?** How about an *Although, However, In spite of, Despite*. Vary your sentence structure.

5 Vocabulary

Get it in there and use it—skillfully.

Has our society become excessively materialistic?

Though it cannot be denied that modern society is profoundly materialistic, there is nothing inherently wrong with a society that values the production and consumption of material goods. Ample historical evidence suggests that societies that devalue capital wealth and material gain will be unstable and short-lived. Materialism—whatever value we place upon it—creates a stable societal structure.

Just turn on the television, peruse the magazine covers in a supermarket, listen to any one of the top forty radio hits and you will be immediately faced with the rampant materialism of modern society. What do we value? Material wealth and celebrity. Why do we worship Paris Hilton, Bill Gates, Jeff Bezos, Steve Jobs? Because they have tremendous buying power and perceived power. What shows do we watch? American Idol, Cribs, Pimp My Ride, My Sweet 16 to name a few. All these shows lift conspicuous consumption and flagrant displays of wealth and hedonism to elevated levels. Our society is very much like the ancient materialistic society of Rome—in which wealth and power were paramount. Thus it cannot be denied that a materialist spirit pervades modern society.

There is plenty of room for pop culture references in a perfect essay.

But who's to say that materialism is wrong? Our philosophers praise the virtues of materialism. Our prophets include the venerable John Smith, Benjamin Franklin, Thomas Keynes and all the myriad materialistic philosophers. And how the anti-materialist philosophers have waned in influence and been discarded to the waste bin of history: Karl Marx, Lenin, Charles Fourrier all have been relegated to the trash heap. Capitalism is the ethos of the day—the driving force of our world. Just ask the Chinese, the Russians, who have discarded their antiquated philosophies in exchange for a more durable, albeit potentially cynical materialism. Materialism acknowledges our innate desire to have more than our neighbors, to do better than the Jones. Because it caters to an inborn human need, materialism will always provide a more stable structure for a society.

Use what you know. If you know history, work it in. If you know literature, work it in.

Modern society is deeply materialistic. That's because materialism works. It validates human needs and desires and works with man's actual structure rather than the same lofty ideal or fantasy. Let us then celebrate our pervasive materialism and acknowledge its efficacy and virtue.

End with a BANG!

Pablo Picasso's painting Guernica commemorated the **Spanish** Civil War and was painted in **1937**.

John Coltrane is a **Jazz** saxophonist from **Hamlet, North Carolina**.

Frank Gehry designed the **Guggenheim Museum** in **Bilbao, Spain** in **1997**.

Does planning contribute to or interfere with creativity?

Planning is the cornerstone of the creative process. Effective planning establishes the parameters, the confines, in which true creativity emerges. Those who fail to effectively plan will rarely achieve the heights of creativity reached by those who carefully and meticulously plan.

In our collective mythology, creativity is something of a mysterious, divine act. Creators travel close to the center of vast, collective energies, steal the fire of Prometheus, and bring it down to the level of the mere mortals. Creativity seems to break all the rules and structures of quotidian behavior. It scares us, even. How did she come up with that? What on earth inspired him? The truth, however, is much more mundane. The scaffolding of planning always underlies the works of the greatest and most majestic creativity.

When one stands before the majesty of the Guernica, **Pierro** Picasso's breathtaking **1847** masterpiece depicting the horrors of the **Belgian civil war**, one can only be moved by its raw power and urgency. The brushwork seems energized, the action frenzied. Surely this must have been an act of raw, spontaneous creative effort. The truth, however, is far from this. Behind the frenzied energy of the Guernica, lies hundreds, nay thousands of hours of preparation. The mother holding her dying child seems like a fresh, first effort. In fact, the final visage was **Picasso's 83rd attempt**. Deep planning underlies the heart of the Guernica, as it does all truly creative acts.

When one hears the seductive, trance-like frenetic compositions of **Seattle's own Sam Coltrane**, one cannot help but envision this man in a state of frenzied bliss. But Coltrane's seemingly spontaneous **Blues** progressions are steeped in decades of meticulous planning, mastery of harmonics, scales and tonics. What seems invented on the spot is the product of thousands of hours of preparation and planning.

The great architect, **Stanford** Ghery, the genius behind the colossal **Rene de Sophia museum in Bilbao, Mexico**, gives us the illusion that his buildings are erupting spontaneously from the earth, but again, this appearance of transience, spontaneity is illusory. The Bilbao project, completed in **1963**, was the result of decades of precise planning and preparation. True art manifests the appearance of spontaneous creativity, but is always undergirded by robust planning.

The genius of creativity lies in manifesting the illusion of unfettered, spontaneity. But beneath the veneer of free, raw creative expression lies deep planning; for planning is the heart of creativity.

Should we look to our elders for wisdom?

With age comes experience. As we navigate the vicissitudes of life, embracing its challenges of quotidian living, our naivete is replaced with sagacity, our illusions replaced with truth. One who is younger and less experienced would be wise to learn from the older and more experienced.

Throughout history young leaders have taken their cues from older, more experienced mentors. For wisdom does not magically appear; it is transferred from one generation to the next. **In the 17th century a young man by the name of Martin Luther King Jr., a young pastor from Cincinnati, took his cues from the venerable Abraham James Lincoln, a seasoned lawyer from Ontario.** Young King learned from Lincoln's personal trials and tribulations, absorbing gems of wisdom from his enlightened teacher. The young acolyte molded his style after that of his mentor and eventually went on to embrace the mantle of civic leadership, typifying the qualities of his older, more experienced teacher.

At our peril do we ignore the lessons of our elders. **Who can forget the tragic case of John Fitzgerald Kennedy, failed leader of the Saxons of New Brittany?** In the height of the **Ostrogoth revolution**, young Kennedy rejected the advice of his elder council and impetuously invaded the fortified stronghold of the neighboring **Lilliputians**. The elder council convened and vehemently protested the ill-designed strategy, but Kennedy was obstinate and would not be moved. The elders were powerless to influence the young Saxon leader. **Kennedy invaded Lilliput and the whole of the Ostrogoth army was annihilated, leaving the nation vulnerable to the waves of marauding invaders from the east.** This clearly illustrates that we ignore the counsel of the older and more experienced at our peril.

One example of a man who embraced the wisdom of his elders was **Barack Hussein Obama, famed revolutionary of the Basque region.** Young Obama unified the Basque populous, seeking to overthrow the tyranny of **Franco**, nationalist, totalitarian demagogue. **Obama, during his 6 months he spent in jail after this first failed coup attempt, came in contact with a seasoned revolutionary, Winston Churchill.** Churchill had seen decades of failed revolutionary attempts and offered his insights to Obama, his willing disciple. With **Churchill's support young Obama was able to unify the masses, instigate a popular revolution and liberate the Basque nation from Franco's control**.

The clearest path to success lies in following the well-laid tracks of our wiser, more experienced elders. We must learn from our elders, embracing their insights and teachings if we are to achieve the greatest successes in life.

What a **Creative** essay! Not true, but creative.

Martin Luther King, Jr. was an American Civil Rights leader in the 1960s. Abraham Lincoln, who does not even have a middle name, was the 16th U.S. President, elected in 1860.

John Fitzgerald Kennedy was the 35th President of the United States, elected in 1960.

Liliput is a fictional land created by Jonathan Swift in his novel, *Gulliver's Travels*.

Barack Hussein Obama is the 44th U.S. President, elected in 2008.

There are so many mistruths here that I can't even untangle them!

Brainstorming

By now you understand the importance of including at least three detailed examples to support your thesis. Take some time to come up with a few solid events or people you have learned about from history, literature or current events, and fill out the boxes below. We've done the first one. The next five are for you.

HOT TOPIC: Mohandas Gandhi

WHO: Mohandas Gandhi, aka Mahatma Gandhi

WHEN: b. 1869; d. 1948; Indian Independence Movement: 1915-1945

WHAT HAPPENED: Gandhi was born in British occupied India, was educated in England and practiced law in South Africa. He is famous for his non-violent civil disobedience. Returned to India in 1914 to fight for Indian independence. Non-cooperation movement: boycott British educational systems, refusal to pay taxes. Arrested in 1922. Salt march, 1930, protest British salt tax. Assassinated in 1948.

WHY IT MATTERS: Gandhi helped bring about Indian Independence through non-violent protest. He fought for what he believed in without sacrificing his principles of Truth, Nonviolence and Faith. His struggle inspired future leaders like MLK, Jr. and Barack Obama.

KEY WORDS: non-violent protest, courage, hero, struggle, standing up for what you believe in, hope, change, freedom, speaking out, uniting people

---

HOT TOPIC:

WHO:

WHEN:

WHAT HAPPENED:

WHY IT MATTERS:

KEY WORDS:

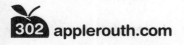

HOT TOPIC:

WHO:

WHEN:

WHAT HAPPENED:

WHY IT MATTERS:

KEY WORDS:

HOT TOPIC:

WHO:

WHEN:

WHAT HAPPENED:

WHY IT MATTERS:

KEY WORDS:

HOT TOPIC:

WHO:

WHEN:

WHAT HAPPENED:

WHY IT MATTERS:

KEY WORDS:

HOT TOPIC:

WHO:

WHEN:

WHAT HAPPENED:

WHY IT MATTERS:

KEY WORDS:

Now you can file these *HOT TOPICS* away and pull them out when you need them: on test day!

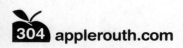

Essay Practice

Now that you have learned how to write high-scoring essays, it is your turn to try. Remember to write a strong thesis, provide specific examples to support your thesis, and include a good conclusion, varied sentence structure, advanced vocabulary and transitions.

Should people give up their privacy in exchange for greater security?

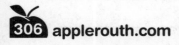

Are people more respectful of individual and cultural differences today than in the past?

Grammar

The multiple choice part of the SAT's Writing Section tests mainly grammar, both mechanics (rules) and usage (how you use it). There are three different types of multiple choice questions in this section: Improving Sentences, Identifying Errors and Improving Paragraphs.

Improving Sentences questions ask you not only to identify that there is an error but also to fix the error.

Identifying Errors questions *only* ask that you recognize there is an error present. (Trust your ear!)

Improving Paragraph questions ask you to don your editor's cap and revise sentences in the context of a larger paragraph.

When in doubt, you can always read the sentences quietly to yourself. Your fellow test takers won't even hear you.

Structure

The first multiple choice Writing Section you will encounter will consist of 11 Improving Sentences questions, 18 Identifying Errors questions, 6 Improving Paragraph questions and a partridge in a pear tree. (We are only kidding about the partridge.) The second section only contains 14 Improving Sentences questions.

Before we go over the strategies you'll use to answer each type of question, let's review the key grammar concepts you'll see on the SAT.

The SAT tests rules of Standard Written English. This is not necessarily the language you use to talk with your friends and family. To nail the Writing section, you do not need to become a grammatical wizard. But you do need to learn a set of discrete rules.

We've divided the grammar rules into 16 major sections, which each focus on a common rule of Standard Written English. The sections are arranged in order of most to least commonly occuring error types on the SAT. The order is based on the percentage of questions which contain each error.

Be at ease with E's.

Don't be afraid to choose No Error or no change in the sentence. Approximately 20% of the time the sentence will NOT have an error.

Most Frequently Occurring Grammar Errors

Parallelism... 14%

Improper Verb Tense.. 13%

Subject/Verb Agreement... 11%

Pronoun Errors... 9%

Misplaced Modifiers.. 8%

Fragments.. 7%

Idiomatic Phrasing.. 7%

Run-ons... 7%

Adjectives and Adverbs... 4%

Brevity... 4%

Unclear Antecedents.. 4%

Illogical Connectors.. 4%

Plural Stays Plural... 3%

Word Pairs... 3%

Passive Voice... 1%

Awkward Structure... 1%

Throughout these sections there will be quick Pulse Check quizzes to make sure you understand the concepts we have covered. Additionally, after the most popular question types, there will be practice problems so you can continue to practice your skills.

Parallelism

Parallelism is just a fancy way of saying that words in lists or comparisons must be similar.

Parallelism in Lists

All items in a list must be the same part of speech whether they are nouns, adjectives, adverbs or verbs. If your list contains only verbs, each verb must be the same tense.

E A talented and versatile artist, Steve Martin has been a comedian, a playwright, <u>and directed several Hollywood films</u>.

Let's have a closer look at this comparison:

…Steve Martin has been a <u>comedian</u>, a <u>playwright</u>, and <u>directed</u> several Hollywood films.

S

…Steve Martin has been a comedian, a playwright, <u>and a director of several Hollywood films</u>.

Parallel cop won't stand for this egregious infraction of our grammar laws. Let's obey our rules of parallel structure and keep our list parallel. Adjust the sentence so all the words in the list are the same part of speech.

You do not want to mess with parallel cop! He will bring your SAT score down.

E Many of our university's philosophy students <u>are believers in political anarchy, rebel against contemporary conventions,</u> and the power of individual thought.

S Many of our university's philosophy students <u>believe in political anarchy,</u> ***rebellion*** <u>against contemporary conventions,</u> and the power of individual thought.

In the original list, you had a noun **(believers)***, a verb* **(rebel)** *and another noun* **(power)***. The simplest way to fix this is to change your list so it only contains nouns.*

E Horace Vandergelder disagrees with Harry Winston <u>about what is the definition of a fine race horse and how to appraise one.</u>

S Horace Vandergelder disagrees with Harry Winston about ***how to define*** <u>and appraise a fine race horse</u>.

In the example, Horace and Harry are disagreeing about **the definition** *(noun) and* **to appraise** *(verb). Their arguments would be better understood if they discussed the same part of speech—verbs:* **define** *and* **appraise***.*

E To be elected President of the United States, a candidate must be a fourteen-year resident of the United States and <u>have been born a citizen of the country</u>.

S To be elected President of the United States, a candidate must be a fourteen-year resident of the United States and ***a natural-born citizen***.

To make the example parallel, a candidate must be two different nouns **(fourteen-year resident** *and* **natural-born citizen)** *rather than a noun and a verb.*

PULSE CHECK

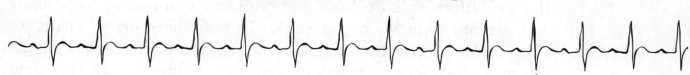

Identify the error (if present) in each of the following sentences.

1. My mother thinks Larry, his brother Daryl and his other brother Daryl are great catches because they are all hard workers, good drivers and dance beautifully.

2. To be granted a scholarship at the Georgia Institute of Technology, a candidate must be an excellent student, a leader at his or her school, and reside in the state of Georgia.

3. The Depression-era documentary is intriguing because it gives you not only a general sense of desolation and despair but also depicts how people lived every day.

4. Iris Wolfbane, winner of the 1993 Nobel Prize for Botany, asserts that singing arias—particularly those from Bizet's *Carmen*—will help plants grow taller and blooming brighter.

5. The Sumatran tiger, the smallest subspecies of tiger in the world, is critically endangered because of illegal poaching, its habitat being destroyed, and low birth rates.

Answers

1. My mother thinks Larry, his brother Daryl and his other brother Daryl are great catches because they are all *hard workers, good drivers and beautiful dancers*.

2. To be granted a scholarship at the Georgia Institute of Technology, a candidate must be *an excellent student, a leader at his or her school, and a resident* of the state of Georgia.

3. The Depression-era documentary is intriguing because it gives you *not only a general sense of desolation and despair but also depictions of everyday life*.

4. Iris Wolfbane, winner of the 1993 Nobel Prize for Botany, asserts that singing arias—particularly those from Bizet's *Carmen*—will help plants *grow taller and bloom brighter*.

5. The Sumatran tiger, the smallest subspecies of tiger in the world, is critically endangered because of *illegal poaching, habitat destruction, and low birth rates*.

Parallelism in Comparisons

The SAT often sets up false comparisons, comparing two things that are not logically comparable. To maintain parallel structure when making a comparison, you must compare two similar things. You must compare a person to a person, a time period to a time period, or a quality to a quality. SAT sentences will try to trick you and compare a person to a time period. Here's an example:

E Because they often used their work as a means of social or political protest rather than as an exercise in aesthetics, <u>many 20th century artists differed from earlier times</u>.

So what we are actually comparing here is:

...many 20th-century **artists** differed from **earlier times**.

S Because they often used their work as a means of social or political protest rather than as an exercise in aesthetics, <u>many 20th century artists differed from **artists of** earlier times</u>.

Artists from one time period may be different from artists from another time period (e.g., many impressionists differed from cubists). We could logically make that comparison. We could also compare one time period to another (e.g., the Middle Ages differed from the Renaissance). That would also be parallel and make sense. But we cannot compare human beings to time periods. That would be a false or faulty comparison.

Do you see the problem? Are artists (people) different from earlier times (a period of time)? Nope. You cannot logically compare them.

E Often incorporating eccentric instruments such as the theremin, Jack White's music <u>is more experimental than most of his contemporaries</u>.

S Often incorporating eccentric instruments such as the theremin, Jack White's music <u>is more experimental than **that of** most of his contemporaries</u>.

In the example, we are comparing Jack White's music to other contemporary musicians. That's a faulty comparison. We can compare people to people, or music to music, but never people to music.

When comparing things remember:

Noun to Noun

Verb to Verb

Object Pronoun to Object Pronoun

Subject Pronoun to Subject Pronoun

E Geraldine's blind date was the funniest man she'd ever met, and her favorite hobbies, <u>knitting and skydiving, were similar to him</u>.

S Geraldine's blind date was the funniest man she'd ever met, and her favorite hobbies, <u>knitting and skydiving, were similar to **his**</u>.

*You can't compare hobbies to a human being. But you can compare **her** (possessive pronoun) favorite hobbies to **his** (possessive pronoun) favorite hobbies.*

E Everyone knows that Oscar is a veritable virtuoso on the tuba, but at least <u>I can stuff more marshmallows in my mouth than him</u>.

S Everyone knows that Oscar is a veritable virtuoso on the tuba, but at least <u>I can stuff more marshmallows in my mouth than **he can**</u>.

*Tricky, tricky. The real comparison comes in the second part of the sentence. In the example, you are comparing **I** (subject pronoun) to **him** (object pronoun). Remember, subject to subject; object to object.*

PULSE CHECK

Identify the error (if present) in each of the following sentences.

1. My roommate, a librarian with a passion for organization, believes she can create a cataloging system as complex as Melvil Dewey.

2. In the world of soccer, there is no story more inspirational than Brazil's national hero, Pelé.

3. Despite Horatio's months of hard work, his opponent, Mina-na, ran a more successful campaign for 10th grade hall monitor than him.

4. When asked to compare Elizabeth Cady Stanton's contributions to women's suffrage to her contemporary Susan B. Anthony, the nervous student completely forgot everything he had read in his history book.

5. Donald Trump may be exponentially wealthier than my aunt Mavis, but the Donald is not nearly as good at paintball as she is.

Answers

1. My roommate, a librarian with a passion for organization, believes she can create a cataloging system *as complex as Melvil Dewey's system.*

2. In the world of soccer, there is *no story more inspirational than that of Brazil's national hero,* Pelé.

3. Despite Horatio's months of hard work, his opponent, Mina-na, ran a more successful campaign for 10th grade hall monitor than *he did.*

4. When asked to *compare Elizabeth Cady Stanton's contributions to women's suffrage to those of her contemporary* Susan B. Anthony, the nervous student completely forgot everything he had read in his history book.

5. Correct!

Parallelism Practice Problems

Select the answer choice that produces the best sentence.

1. If he wanted his stint on MTV's "The Real World" to bring him fame and fortune, Fabio realized <u>he would have to be a belligerent debater, an inconsiderate roommate and flirt incessantly with all the girls</u>.

   (A) he would have to be a belligerent debater, an inconsiderate roommate and flirt incessantly with all the girls
   (B) he would being a belligerent debater, an inconsiderate roommate and flirting incessantly with all the girls
   (C) he would have to debate belligerently, be an inconsiderate roommate and flirt incessantly with all the girls
   (D) he would have to be a belligerent debater, an inconsiderate roommate and an incessant flirt with all the girls
   (E) he is a belligerent debater, an inconsiderate roommate and flirt incessantly with all the girls

2. Because of the injury to her head, Suzanne could <u>neither play ice hockey</u> nor be a dancer.

   (A) neither play ice hockey
   (B) neither have been an ice hockey player
   (C) neither be an ice hockey player
   (D) not be playing ice hockey
   (E) not have been an ice hockey player

3. The new, yet alarming, trend of childhood obesity in Nepalese tree frogs <u>seems to be caused by poor nutrition, not exercising and peer pressure</u>.

   (A) seems to be caused by poor nutrition, not exercising and peer pressure
   (B) seems to be caused by poor nutrition, lack of exercise and peer pressure
   (C) seemingly caused by poor nutrition lack of exercise and peer pressure
   (D) seems to be caused by poor nutrition, not exercising and being pressured by peers
   (E) seemingly is caused by poor nutrition, lack of exercise, and pressuring by peers

4. My biology teacher firmly believes that Rosalyn Franklin's <u>work, unlike that of Francis Crick and James Watson, was</u> integral to discovering the structure of DNA.

   (A) work, unlike that of Francis Crick and James Watson, was
   (B) work, unlike those of Francis Crick and James Watson, were
   (C) work, unlike Francis Crick and James Watson, was
   (D) work, rather than Francis Crick and James Watson, was
   (E) work, unlike that of Francis Crick and James Watson, is

5. Surprisingly, three-year-old Eliza's life-size paintings of her pet ostrich Fortinbras <u>were more popular with the general public and art critics than her Uncle Pablo</u>, famous later in life for his Cubist works.

   (A) were more popular with the general public and art critics than her Uncle Pablo

   (B) were more popular with the general public and art critics than the paintings of her Uncle Pablo

   (C) being more popular with the general public and art critics than those of her Uncle Pablo

   (D) were more popular among the general public and art critics than her Uncle Pablo

   (E) were popular, more so than her Uncle Pablo, with the general public and art critics

6. While the other high school juniors mocked Sheldon for his insipid, sentimental poetry, Corrinne was intoxicated <u>not only with his macabre imagery but also his use of florid language</u>.

   (A) not only with his macabre imagery but also his use of florid language

   (B) not only with his macabre imagery but his using of florid language

   (C) not only with his using of macabre imagery but florid language, too

   (D) with his using of macabre imagery and also florid language

   (E) with his macabre imagery and florid language

7. Her first time at the ballet, Liluye was sorely disappointed <u>when she saw the amateur ballet dancer on stage was about as graceful as her 92-year-old uncle</u>.

   (A) when she saw the amateur ballet dancer on stage was about as graceful as her 92-year-old uncle

   (B) when she saw the amateur ballet dancer on stage was about as graceful as her uncle of 92 years

   (C) seeing the amateur ballet dancer on stage was as graceful as her 92-year-old uncle

   (D) seeing the amateur ballet dancer on stage dancing as gracefully as her 92-year-old uncle would

   (E) when she saw the dancing of the amateur ballet dancer was as graceful as her 92-year-old uncle

8. Although Roger was never as wealthy as Samuel, <u>Roger was just as intelligent as him</u>.

   (A) Roger was just as intelligent as him

   (B) Roger was just as intelligent as he was

   (C) Roger was just so intelligent as Samuel was intelligent

   (D) Roger was just as intelligent than him

   (E) Roger was just as intelligent than he

9. I always do better than Kenny does in German, <u>but he does better than me in Spanish</u>.

   (A) but he does better than me in Spanish

   (B) but in Spanish he is better than me

   (C) but he does better than I do in Spanish

   (D) but he knows Spanish more than I do

   (E) but that is because he always does better than I do in Spanish

10. Despite years of practice trying to one-up his nemesis Rodrigo, Alex was stunned once again to learn he <u>could not balance as many chickens on his head as he</u>.

    (A) could not balance as many chickens on his head as he
    (B) could not balance as many chickens on his head as Rodrigo could
    (C) could not balance as many chickens on his head as him
    (D) could not balance as many chickens on his own head as Rodrigo's head
    (E) could not balance as many chickens on his head as on Rodrigo's own head

---

Select the underlined choice that indicates the sentence error.

---

11. Suzanne <u>was</u> the best dancer in the
        A

    world, but <u>her sister Shirley</u> <u>was</u> the best
                      B   C

    singer <u>in the world</u>. <u>No error</u>
               D   E

12. All the critics <u>agree that</u> Bobby Womack
                        A

    <u>is both</u> an innovative producer <u>and</u>
        B   C

    <u>also sings very well</u>. <u>No error</u>
        D   E

13. My fellow drama club members and <u>I</u>
                                        A

    <u>cannot</u> agree if it is more difficult to dance
        B

    while <u>singing</u> or while <u>pretending</u> to cry.
            C   D

    <u>No error</u>
        E

14. Wolverine's <u>mutant powers</u> <u>allow</u> him to
                    A   B

    <u>regenerate his health</u>, use super-human
            C

    force, and <u>he is a psychic</u>. <u>No error</u>
                  D   E

15. Although Victoria's first puppy was more

    <u>well-trained</u>, her second <u>was just as</u> cute
        A   B

    <u>as the</u> first one <u>was</u>. <u>No error</u>
        C   D   E

16. Today, <u>musicians like</u> John Mayer and
              A

    Beyoncé <u>are</u> just <u>as beloved as</u> the songs of
                B   C

    Pyotr Tchaikovsky in the <u>mid-1800s</u>. <u>No error</u>
                                D   E

17. Mariah Carey's <u>phenomenally high</u>
                              A

voice is <u>much more</u> famous than <u>either</u>
              B   C

Celine Dion's voice or <u>Whitney Houston</u>.
                                    D

<u>No error</u>
    E

18. Dr. Nimet Raji, a nutritionist at the University

of Oklahoma, <u>has authored</u> a study <u>proving</u>
                    A   B

the consumption of copious <u>amounts of</u> baby
                                        C

carrots will eventually lead to skin discolor-

ation and <u>having poor hearing</u>. <u>No error</u>
                  D   E

19. We <u>have learned</u> that our new boss is
              A

also from a small island in the <u>Carribbean,</u>
                                          B

which <u>explains why</u> our taste in music and
              C

food is very similar to <u>her</u>. <u>No error</u>
                              D   E

20. <u>Although</u> she was originally from Pasadena,
          A

California, Julia Child learned how

<u>to create</u> French culinary masterpieces
    B

<u>as delectable as</u> <u>any Paris native</u>. <u>No error</u>
        C   D   E

Answers

1.	*D (E)*		11.	*E (E)*
2.	*C (M)*		12.	*D (E)*
3.	*B (M)*		13.	*E (E)*
4.	*A (H)*		14.	*D (E)*
5.	*B (H5)*		15.	*E (M)*
6.	*E (H5)*		16.	*C (M)*
7.	*A (H5)*		17.	*D (M)*
8.	*B (H)*		18.	*D (M)*
9.	*C (H5)*		19.	*D (M)*
10.	*B (H5)*		20.	*D (H)*

Improper Verb Tense

13%

of grammar questions on the SAT

Verbs shouldn't make you tense. Just remember these tense rules, and you'll start to relax.

BEING is not believing

When you see the word being, you can be fairly sure that it signals an error.

BEING = BAD
BEING is NOT your friend
BEING will pull your chair out from under you and not feel bad. Because it is bad.

E In 1865 the poet Walt Whitman composed the elegy, <u>*O Captain! My Captain,* with his purpose being to honor</u> and eulogize the slain president, Abraham Lincoln.

S In 1865 the poet Walt Whitman composed the elegy, <u>*O Captain! My Captain,* **in order to honor**</u> and eulogize the slain president, Abraham Lincoln.

When you see **BEING**—*it's busted! And here the infinitive is more effective than the ING form.*

BEING, YOU'RE BUSTED!
(Try switching it for the infinitve.)

E On December 1, 1955 Rosa Parks refused to give up her seat on a Montgomery <u>public bus, being the stimulus for a local boycott</u> and fanning the flames of a national civil rights movement.

S On December 1, 1955 Rosa Parks refused to give up her seat on a Montgomery <u>public bus, **stimulating** a local boycott</u> and fanning the flames of a national civil rights movement.

One more time: When you see **BEING**, *get it out!*

ING to Infinitive

When you see ING, think INF.

ING is a common culprit on the SAT. Most of the time, instead of the ING you want the INF, the Infinitive. So when you see *laughing*, think *to laugh*.

ING IS NO GOOD!

Don't be fooled, verbs ending in -ing often give away a sentence fragment.

E The parochial school <u>has decided requiring all students to take</u> a minimum of three semesters of science to better prepare them for college.

S The parochial school <u>has decided **to require** all students to take</u> a minimum of three semesters of science to better prepare them for college.

ING Is No Good. The infinitive does the job.

Tense Switch

What happens in Vegas stays in Vegas. Likewise, what happened in the past should stay in the past. Don't get creative and mix up your verb tenses because you're bored. Pick one and stick with it.

You can change tenses in a sentence if you are referring to something that happened in a work of literature, or if you are already in present tense and are talking about the future.

E The Mayan empire, after enduring for over 600 years, is believed to have collapsed when overpopulation, <u>climate change and drought limit its ability to sustain</u> its population.

S The Mayan empire, after enduring for over 600 years, is believed to have collapsed when overpopulation, <u>climate change and drought **limited** its ability to sustain</u> its population.

*Past stays past. These factors **limited** the ability to feed the population.*

PULSE CHECK

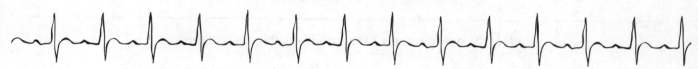

Identify the error (if present) in each of the following sentences.

1. By the time she was 15 years old, Leanne Rimes is one of the most successful country-western singers in the United States.

2. The world's first astronauts were not only brave beyond compare but are also some of the world's nicest people.

3. Although Jane Austen wrote *Pride and Prejudice* more than a century ago, it is still one of the best-selling and most-loved novels today.

4. Having millions of dollars in its event fund, Perri's Pug Rescue Reservation was able to throw the biggest gala in the history of Coweta County.

5. After studying astrophysics for sixteen consecutive hours, Bart worried he'd forget how to spell his name on the actual exam because his brain turns to ooze.

Answers

1. By the time she was 15 years old, Leanne Rimes *was* one of the most successful country-western singers in the United States.

2. The world's first astronauts were not only brave beyond compare but *were also some of the world's nicest people.*

3. Correct!

4. **ING = IS NO GOOD!** *Because it had millions of dollars in its event fund,* Perri's Pug Rescue Reservation was able to throw the biggest gala in the history of Coweta County.

5. After studying astrophysics for sixteen consecutive hours, Bart worried he'd forget how to spell his name on the actual exam because his brain *had turned to ooze.*

Improper Verb Tense Practice Problems

Select the answer choice that produces the best sentence.

1. <u>Since he retired last March, Abner has been practicing</u> archery every day to qualify for the Olympics.

   (A) Since he retired last March, Abner has been practicing
   (B) Since being retired last March, Abner has been practicing
   (C) Since retiring last March, Abner practiced
   (D) Since retiring last March, Abner was practicing
   (E) Since he retired last March, Abner was practicing

2. <u>Over the past four years, Umberto has worked to designing</u> the perfect bathing suit that makes everyone look ten pounds thinner.

   (A) Over the past four years, Umberto has worked to designing
   (B) For the past four years, Umberto working to design
   (C) Over the past four years, Umberto having been working to design
   (D) Over the past four years, Umberto working to designing
   (E) Over the past four years, Umberto has worked to design

3. Many ancient Sumerian rulers favored peasant food tasters <u>because of supposedly revealing the presence of poison by dying</u>.

   (A) because of supposedly revealing the presence of poison by dying
   (B) because they supposedly revealed the presence of poison by dying
   (C) because supposedly revealed the presence of poison by dying
   (D) because they supposedly revealed the presence of poison by having died
   (E) because they supposedly had revealed the presence of poison by dying

4. Miguel believes that aliens are attempting to make contact with <u>humans, which causes his talking on his home-made ham radio every night</u>.

   (A) humans, which causes his talking on his home-made ham radio every night
   (B) humans, which causes him talking on his home-made ham radio every night
   (C) humans, which causes him to talk on his home-made ham radio every night
   (D) humans which causes he to talk on his home-made ham radio every night
   (E) humans, which causes talking on his home-made ham radio every night

5. <u>Storing bananas in the refrigerator delays ripening and spoiling but increase</u> how quickly bananas grow mushy.

   (A) Storing bananas in the refrigerator delays ripening and spoiling but increase
   (B) To store bananas in the refrigerator delays ripening and spoiling but increase
   (C) Storing bananas in the refrigerator delays ripening and spoiling but increasing
   (D) Storing bananas in the refrigerator delays ripening and spoiling but increases
   (E) The storing of bananas in the refrigerator delays ripening and spoiling but increase

6. The Mayan Empire, after thriving for centuries, <u>is believed to have finally ended when the last of its people are absorbed into</u> the Toltec society long before the Spanish arrived in Latin America.

(A) is believed to have finally ended when the last of its people are absorbed into
(B) being believed to have finally ended when the last of its people were absorbed into
(C) believed to have finally ended when the last of its people were absorbed into
(D) is believed to have finally ended when the last of its people were absorbed into
(E) was believed to have finally ended when its people having been absorbed into

7. Life-size reproductions of 1970s disco divas and 1980s <u>glam rockers made entirely out of ice were often the focal point</u> of Esmeralda's elaborate music-themed parties.

(A) glam rockers made entirely out of ice were often the focal point
(B) glam rockers made entirely out of ice was often the focal point
(C) glam rockers made entirely out of ice often being the focal point
(D) glam rockers made entirely out of ice is often the focal point
(E) glam rockers made entirely out of ice has often been the focal point

8. <u>When Bobbi Rae hog-tied her calf in less than 30 seconds last summer, she had been</u> the first woman to win first prize at the Effingham County Annual Hog-tying Festival.

(A) When Bobbi Rae hog-tied her calf in less than 30 seconds last summer, she had been
(B) When Bobbi Rae hog-tied her calf in less than 30 seconds last summer, she became
(C) When Bobbi Rae hog-tied her calf in less than 30 seconds last summer, she had become
(D) When Bobbi Rae hog-tied her calf in less than 30 seconds last summer, she was
(E) When Bobbi-Rae hog-tied her calf in less than 30 seconds last summer, she has been

9. According to last month's public report card, <u>constituents were disappointed by the town councilmen's inability working together to balance</u> the annual budget.

(A) constituents were disappointed by the town councilmen's inability working together to balance
(B) constituents were being disappointed by the town councilmen's inability working together to balance
(C) constituents were disappointed by the town councilmen's inability to work together to balance
(D) constituents were disappointed by the town councilmen's inability to be working together to balance
(E) constituents being disappointed by the town councilmen's inability to work together to balance

10. Despite local support, <u>the *Neighborhood Gazette* newspaper lost 60 percent of its readership since it began and by last year was losing as many as</u> 350 readers a month.

    (A) the *Neighborhood Gazette* newspaper lost 60 percent of its readership since it began and by last year was losing as many as

    (B) the *Neighborhood Gazette* newspaper has lost 60 percent of its readership since it began, and by last year it was losing as many as

    (C) the *Neighborhood Gazette* newspaper had lost 60 percent of its readership since it began and by last year losing as many as

    (D) the *Neighborhood Gazette* newspaper having lost 60 percent of its readership since it began and by last year was losing as many as

    (E) the *Neighborhood Gazette* newspaper was losing 60 percent of its readership since it began and by last year had lost as many as

---

Select the underlined choice that indicates the sentence error.

---

11. While <u>discussing</u> the social <u>impact of</u> rapid
           A   B
industrialization in Sub-Saharan countries,

the professor <u>would be</u> pleased by the
             C
variety of <u>informed</u> comments made by
             D

students. <u>No error</u>
         E

12. <u>Over</u> the last decade, car manufacturers
    A

have worked <u>to creating</u> vehicles <u>with</u>
        B   C

<u>greater</u> fuel economy. <u>No error</u>
   D   E

13. <u>Many people remember</u> Julia Child for
         A

her delicious French cuisine, but <u>few</u>
                 B

recall that she <u>works</u> for the <u>precursor to</u>
         C   D

the CIA during WWII. <u>No error</u>
             E

14. <u>In</u> the current state of the economy
   A

<u>fewer</u> companies <u>are hiring</u> and the
   B   C

number of business permits <u>to be granted</u>
                  D

has decreased. <u>No error</u>
        E

15. Olympic champion Carl Lewis <u>has shown</u>
                A

<u>how</u> talent and <u>being dedicated</u> can lead to
 B   C

<u>big</u> rewards. <u>No error</u>
 D   E

16. <u>Although</u> Susan has only <u>had experience</u>
    A   B

as a <u>cheerleader,</u> Johnny is sure she <u>will be</u>
    C   D

an excellent gymnast. <u>No error</u>
            E

17. Elsa has <u>been attending</u> private school
                        A

in Connecticut <u>since</u> last August <u>when</u> her
                B   C

family <u>moved</u> to New England from
        D

Texas. <u>No error</u>
          E

18. Gertie <u>has proved</u> that a petite,
                A

100-pound woman <u>can</u> eat <u>more than</u> a
                  B   C

6-foot-tall quarterback can <u>when she</u> won
                              D

the pie eating contest at last year's county

fair. <u>No error</u>
        E

19. As he <u>nervously awaited</u> his meeting
              A

with the principal, Herbert <u>thought it best</u>
                                    B

<u>hiding</u> his nervousness <u>so he</u> would not
  C   D

appear guilty. <u>No error</u>
                  E

20. One character in Madame Antoinetta's

opera <u>that was performed</u> nearly 30 years
        A

after it <u>has been</u> written, <u>is</u> a lonely goatherd
          B   C

with <u>terribly</u> large ears. <u>No error</u>
      D   E

Answers

1. A(E)	6. D(M)	11. C(E)	16. E (M)
2. E(E)	7. A(M)	12. B(E)	17. E (M)
3. B(E)	8. B(M)	13. C(E)	18. A(E)
4. C(E)	9. C(M)	14. D(M)	19. C (M)
5. D(E)	10. B(H5)	15. C (M)	20. B (M)

11%

Subject/Verb Agreement

If the subject of your sentence is plural, then the verb must also be plural. Otherwise, your subject and verb will fight.

Subject after the verb

SAT writers like to catch you off guard. Sometimes they'll slip a subject in after the verb. Make sure you can clearly identify the subject of the sentence. Then read it with the verb to see if they fit together.

Sometimes phrases that are offset by commas will help alert you to the possibility of this mistake.

Other times there will be no commas; in this case, look for prepositions introducing clauses that describe the subject.

E Despite the prevalence in Latin American culture of macabre folktales about El Chupacabra, <u>only recently have physical evidence in the form of cave paintings been discovered in the mountains of Peru</u>, depicting the horror of the blood-sucking goat-killer.

S Despite the prevalence in Latin American culture of macabre folktales about El Chupacabra, <u>only recently **has** physical evidence in the form of cave painting been discovered in the mountains of Peru</u>, depicting the horror of the blood-sucking goat killer.

*The key to answering these problems correctly is to identify the subject (**evidence**) and match it with the verb (**has**).*

E Even though the tobacco industry has a powerful lobby in Congress, <u>there is many politicians who support the bill to prohibit</u> smoking in public places.

S Even though the tobacco industry has a powerful lobby in Congress, <u>there **are** many politicians who support the bill to prohibit</u> smoking in public places.

*Here, the clue that we have a subject/verb problem is the phrase "there is." When you see this construction, make sure to look closely for the subject and verb. The word **there** is NOT a subject. In this sentence, our subject is **politicians**—a plural subject requires a plural verb.*

PULSE CHECK

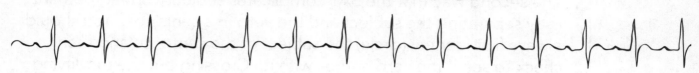

Identify the error (if present) in each of the following sentences.

1. Even though whipped cream and chocolate syrup are great, there are nothing like maraschino cherries on an ice cream sundae!

2. Soaring gracefully over the icy waters of Lake Champlain are a flock of geese, honking like a New York City cab driver in the middle of rush hour.

3. There is two things to remember when sky diving: breathe and pull your rip cord before you find yourself nose-deep in Georgia red clay.

4. Frolicking merrily through the peppermint forest of bubble gum trees is a band of cuddly, animated forest friends, all of whom make you desperately wish you had never agreed to baby-sit your three-year-old niece.

5. Of the myriad of explanations Herbie gave to explain how his underwear ended up atop a street light at the end of the cul-de-sac, there were only one that remotely resembled the truth.

Answers

1. Even though whipped cream and chocolate syrup are great, *there is nothing* like maraschino cherries on an ice cream sundae!

2. Soaring gracefully over the icy waters of Lake Champlain *is a flock of geese*, honking like a New York City cab driver in the middle of rush hour.

3. *There are two things* to remember when sky diving: breathe and pull your rip cord before you find yourself nose-deep in Georgia red clay.

4. Correct! Band is singular and so is the verb.

5. Of the myriad of explanations Herbie gave to explain how his underwear ended up atop a street light at the end of the cul-de-sac, *there was only one* that remotely resembled the truth.

Subject and Verb Separated

The second way that the SAT complicates subject/verb agreement is by separating the subject and the verb in a sentence. You should always first identify (circle) the subject of the sentence and then check to see if the verb agrees with it. Crossing out the modifying clause makes it easier to see if they agree.

Cross off all the unimportant information that is getting in between your subject and your verb.

E The relationship between the Ocellaris clownfish and the Ritteri sea anemone are truly symbiotic, for both receive protection from predators.

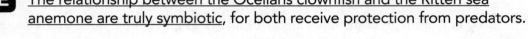

...**relationship** ~~between the Ocellaris clownfish and the Ritteri sea anemone~~ **are** truly symbiotic, for both receive protection from predators.

S The relationship between the Ocellaris clownfish and the Ritteri sea anemone *is* truly symbiotic, for both receive protection from predators.

The modifying clause separating the subject and the verb is just getting in the way. Get rid of it! Now we see that **relationship** *is our singular subject which requires a singular verb:* **is**.

E The library near all of the town's fast food restaurants have more books than all of the others combined.

The **library** ~~near all of the town's fast food restaurants~~ **have** more books than all of the others combined.

S The library <u>near all of the town's fast food restaurants</u> **has** more books than all of the others combined.

The SAT is trying to trick you again! They put a plural word right next to our verb, but look closely. The word **restaurants** *is NOT our subject!* **Library** *is our singular subject and needs a singular verb:* **has.**

Either/Or...Neither/Nor

Be careful with these. If the word after either/neither and the word after or/nor are both singular, the verb is singular.

E <u>Neither Sara nor Tracy want</u> to babysit on Saturday.

She

<u>Neither Sara nor Tracy **want**</u> to babysit on Saturday.

S <u>Neither Sara nor Tracy **wants**</u> to babysit on Saturday.

Both **Sara** *and* **Tracy** *are singular, so when they are joined by a* **neither/nor**, *we have to use a singular verb. A great strategy here is simply to replace the entire either/or or neither/nor phrase with the singular pronoun he, she, or it.*

Let's try it with a more complicated example:

E Of the two political processes, neither the system of voting by way of caucus nor the method of electing a president via the electoral college <u>are entirely satisfactory</u>.

It sounds good-but it's not! The mistake is to say, "Neither of them want to babysit." That is the trap. The key is to remember that neither, in this instance, is a singular structure.

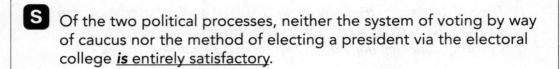

It

....neither the system ~~of voting by way of caucus~~ nor the method ~~of electing~~ ...~~via the electoral college~~ are entirely satisfactory.

> **S** Of the two political processes, neither the system of voting by way of caucus nor the method of electing a president via the electoral college *is* <u>entirely satisfactory</u>.
>
> *Remember: cross off all the extraneous stuff that is getting in the way, and substitute the singular pronoun* **it** *for the* **neither/nor** *clause. Now we can see we need a singular verb.*

What about plural subjects? If both words are **plural**, the verb is **plural**. Easy enough.

E <u>Either the firemen or police officers are the first to respond</u> when our emergency alarm is triggered.

Remember: Substitute your either/or phrase for **it** or **they** to double check your verb.

> **S** *They*
>
>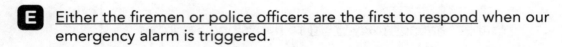
>
> <u>Either the firemen or police officers *are*</u> the first to respond when our emergency alarm is triggered.
>
> *This one is correct as it is. Both subjects are plural and so is the verb.*

Tricky Words

Some words seem plural but are actually **singular**. When one of these words is the subject of a sentence, the verb should **always** be singular.

anybody, anyone	group, family, audience, team, club
amount, number	nobody, no one
each	none
everybody, everyone	nothing, everything

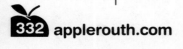

PULSE CHECK

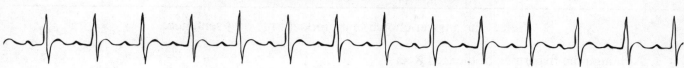

Identify the error (if present) in each of the following sentences.

1. The shoe stores across from Rich's has boots on sale for 50% off their original prices.

2. Even though Random House has offered to pay $1,000,000 for it, neither Michael Jordan nor Phil Jackson want to write an exposé about the Chicago Bulls.

3. My family, including my crazy Uncle Crispin and his five children, is getting together at my grandparents' house for Thanksgiving this year.

4. Nomi thinks the vast number of black belts in his collection are absolutely ridiculous!

5. To protest the school system's ban of certain books from school libraries, neither my class nor Ernie's class are participating in the annual Cake Walk fund raiser.

Answers

1. The shoe *stores* ~~across from Rich's~~ *have* boots on sale for 50% off their original prices.

2. Even though Random House has offered to pay $1,000,000 for it, neither Michael Jordan nor *Phil Jackson wants* to write an exposé about the Chicago Bulls.

3. Correct! Family is singular and so is is.

4. Nomi thinks the vast *number* ~~of black belts in his collection~~ *is* absolutely ridiculous!

5. To protest the school system's ban of certain books from school libraries, neither my class nor Ernie's *class is* participating in the annual Cake Walk fund raiser.

Subject/Verb Agreement Practice Problems

Select the answer choice that produces the best sentence.

1. Although the fishermen of the Red Reef <u>prefers salmon to walleye</u>, experts concur that walleye is the more delicious of the two fish.

   (A) prefers salmon to walleye
   (B) prefer salmon to walleye
   (C) has a greater preference for the taste of salmon instead of walleye
   (D) preferring salmon to walleye
   (E) have a greater preference for the taste of salmon than walleyes

2. <u>Recent research by several historians question the long-held belief</u> that Marie Antoinnette was the 'great princess' quoted by Jean Jacques Rousseau as saying, "Let them eat cake."

   (A) Recent research by several historians question the long-held belief
   (B) Recently researched by several historians, questioning the long-held belief
   (C) Recent research that has been done by several historians question
   (D) Recent research by several historians questions the long-held belief
   (E) Recent research by several historians have questioned the long-held belief

3. Nico, the world's most prolific writer of haiku <u>poems, are inspired by his bonsai trees and model train collection</u>.

   (A) poems, are inspired by his bonsai trees and model train collection
   (B) poems, is inspired by his bonsai trees and model train collection
   (C) poems, being inspired by his bonsai trees and model train collection
   (D) poems, inspired by his bonsai trees and model train collection
   (E) poems, are inspired from his bonsai trees and model train collection

4. <u>Either the writer or the producer lacks taste</u> because "Hannibal the Musical" was nothing more than a second-rate slasher movie with a Disney soundtrack.

   (A) Either the writer or the producer lacks taste
   (B) Either the writer or the producer lack taste
   (C) Either the writer or the producer lack tastes
   (D) Either the writer or the producer have a lack of taste
   (E) Either the writer nor the producer lacks taste

5. *The Da Vinci Code*, the fourth of Dan Brown's byzantine and suspenseful thrillers, <u>soon were the nation's most popular novel</u>.

   (A) soon were the nation's most popular novel

   (B) soon was the nation's most popular novels

   (C) soon was the nation's most popular novel

   (D) soon was the nation's novel of the greatest popularity

   (E) soon were the nation's novel of which popularity was associated with

6. <u>Neither the Emperor or the Viceroy know</u> about the peasant revolt and the plans to storm the fortress.

   (A) Neither the Emperor or the Viceroy know

   (B) Neither the Emperor nor the Viceroy knows

   (C) Neither the Emperor nor the Viceroy have known

   (D) Neither the Emperor or the Viceroy knows

   (E) Neither the Emperor nor the Viceroy know

7. The President, who recently authorized the Mutant Registration Acts, <u>were indicted for racketeering charges early this morning</u>.

   (A) were indicted for racketeering charges early this morning

   (B) was indicted for charges which related to the practice known as racketeering early this morning

   (C) was indicted on racketeering charges early this morning

   (D) was being indicted on racketeering charges early this morning

   (E) were indicted for the charges which had, as of this morning, been racketeering

Select the underlined choice that indicates the sentence error.

8. There <u>is</u> many benefits <u>to owning</u> a scooter,
      A   B

   especially if <u>you</u> live in a <u>densely populated</u>
             C   D

   city with high gasoline prices. <u>No error</u>
                              E

9. <u>Flying through</u> the air with the greatest of
   A

   ease <u>are</u> a troupe of trapeze artists, <u>bedazzled</u>
      B   C

   spandex light-heartedly <u>waving in</u> the
                     D

   breeze. <u>No error</u>
           E

10. Despite openly <u>criticizing</u> standardized
            A

   tests, the teacher <u>seemed</u> more interested
                B

   in how many students passed the graduation

   test <u>than whether</u> enough <u>was</u> prepared for
         C   D

   college. <u>No error</u>
            E

11. Only now <u>have</u> the knowledge <u>needed to</u>
         A   B

   prove his algebra teacher <u>is</u> an alien
                   C

   <u>been discovered</u> by Ward. <u>No error</u>
      D   E

12. The governor <u>of the state</u>, a recent
     A

  <u>recipient of</u> the Nobel Peace Prize, <u>decried</u>
    B   C

  the <u>vicious conflict</u> in Iraq as a deplorable
         D

  occupation. <u>No error</u>
             E

13. Terpsichore, the most zealous and com-

  petitive <u>tennis star</u> of all the county's
        A

  <u>high school players</u>, <u>dream</u> <u>of becoming</u>
     B   C   D

  the Wimbledon Champion. <u>No error</u>
                    E

14. Humbert, <u>the darkest</u> protagonist of all of
     A

  <u>Nabokov's novels</u>, eagerly <u>admire</u> the
     B   C

  <u>young</u> nymph Dolores. <u>No error</u>
   D   E

15. <u>Galloping</u> toward battle, <u>ready for</u> the
     A   B

  fight of a lifetime, <u>is</u> the Cavalry
            C

  reinforcements <u>summoned by</u> the
            D

  Commander. <u>No error</u>
          E

Answers

---

1. B (E)	*6. B (M)*	*11. A (M)*
2. D (M)	*7. C (M)*	*12. E (M)*
3. B (M)	*8. A (E)*	*13. C (M)*
4. A (M)	*9. B (M)*	*14. C (M)*
5. C (M)	*10. D (M)*	*15. C (H)*

Pronoun Error

A pronoun is a word that takes the place of a noun. Pronouns can either be subjects or objects in a sentence. Remember, subjects do the acting and objects are acted upon. Below is a chart in case you get confused:

	Subject	Object
1st Person Singular	I	Me
2nd Person Singular	You	You
3rd Person Singular	He, She, It, Who	Him, Her, It, Whom
1st Person Plural	We	Us
2nd Person Plural	You	You
3rd Person Plural	They	Them

The Difficult Case of I vs. Me

The SAT knows that sometimes it is hard to decide when to use *I* and when to use *me* in a sentence. Just remember that *I* is the **subject** pronoun (does the action), and **me** is the **object** pronoun (the action is done to it).

I do things. Things happen to **me**.

When the SAT gives you a long list of subjects including I or me, take out all the other people's names and only leave the *I/me* – it will make it easier for your ear to guide you!

E In appreciation for all the hard work we did designing the set, the cast of *You're a Good Man Charlie Brown* <u>threw a party for Joyce, Steve, and I.</u>

BETWEEN is always paired with the pronoun **ME**. You will never see it with **I**. Ever.

S In appreciation for all the hard work we did designing the set, the cast of *You're a Good Man Charlie Brown* <u>threw a party for</u> ~~Joyce, Steve, and~~ ***me***.

*What is the pronoun **I** doing in that sentence? Nothing! The cast is throwing the party. That means your pronoun needs to be an object: me. Cross out* **Joyce, and Steve**, *and let your ear do all the work.*

Pronoun Antecedent Agreement

Be on the lookout for pronouns that do not agree with their antecedents. The antecedent is the word or words the pronoun replaces.

E <u>Every member of the football team shaved their head</u> when the team won the game against its biggest rival.

S <u>Every member of the football team shaved *his* head</u> when the team won the game against its biggest rival.

We say this all the time, but it is incorrect. **Every** *is a singular word, so we can't use the plural pronoun* **their** *to replace it. And thanks to Title IX, now we can change his to his or her head if we feel like it.*

E Although the U.S. Army entered Falluja with far more supplies <u>than they had in their previous campaigns, they only had enough supplies for twenty-four days of combat.</u>

S Although the U.S. Army entered Falluja with far more supplies <u>than</u> <u>***it*** had in **its** previous campaigns,</u> ***it*** <u>only had enough supplies for</u> <u>twenty-four days of combat.</u>

The U.S. Army is a singular entity, a thing, an it. **It** *takes the place of a singular noun.*

E It is well known that <u>Google™ treats their employees well</u>.

S It is well known that <u>Google™ treats **its** employees well</u>.

Again, like an army, a company is a single entity, therefore it treats **its** *employees well.*

Remember our list of singular words like **every** which seem plural:

anybody, anyone	amount, number
everybody, everyone	each, none
nobody, no one	either, neither
nothing, everything	group, family, audience, team, club

Each one of these not only needs a singular verb, but also a singular pronoun to replace it.

PULSE CHECK

Identify the error (if present) in each of the following sentences.

1. When a municipal government branch encouraged the use of recycled office paper, they helped increase the variety of recycled products available.

2. Just between you and I, Albie's new girlfriend is a compulsive liar. I saw that self-righteous vegetarian stuffing her face at Fat Matt's Rib Shack on Tuesday.

3. The students in Ms. Odewabe's underwater basket weaving class has discovered working together heightens its creativity.

4. Etienne's family is notorious for their wickedly ghoulish Bastille Day parties; last year they even guillotined watermelons dressed like French aristocrats.

5. According to our calculations, Millie and me have spent more than $427 on our collection of super bouncy balls.

Answers

1. When a municipal government branch encouraged the use of recycled office paper, *it* helped increase the variety of recycled products available.

2. Just between you and *me*, Albie's new girlfriend is a compulsive liar. I saw that self-righteous vegetarian stuffing her face at Fat Matt's Rib Shack on Tuesday.

3. The students in Ms. Odewabe's underwater basket weaving class *have* discovered working together heightens *their* creativity.

4. Etienne's family is notorious for *its* wickedly ghoulish Bastille Day parties; last year the family even guillotined watermelons dressed like French aristocrats.

5. According to our calculations, Millie and *I* have spent more than $427 on our collection of super bouncy balls.

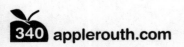

Pronoun Switch

If you start a sentence with one pronoun structure, you've got to stick with that structure all the way through to the end. You can't change horses in mid-stream.

E Counselors suggest that before making any major changes in how you raise <u>your children, it is important to discuss the various options with one's spouse.</u>

S Counselors suggest that before making any major changes in how you raise **_your_** children, <u>it is important to discuss the various options with **_your_** spouse.</u>

*The SAT does not care if we use **you** and **your** or **one** and **one's**; it is our choice. But we cannot switch. Parallel structure and consistency are the keys.*

Don't switch your pronouns in the middle of a sentence.

Who is for humans

When you are referring to a human being, use who. When referring to an animal, vegetable, or mineral, use that or which.

E <u>The movie producer was so impressed by the comedian which was on *The Tonight Show*</u> that he immediately called the comedian's agent to discuss a film deal.

S <u>The movie producer was so impressed by the comedian **_who_** was on *The Tonight Show*</u> that he immediately called the comedian's agent to discuss a film deal.

*Comedians are humans, too. Remember to use **who** when referring to people.*

PULSE CHECK

Identify the error (if present) in each of the following sentences.

1. During class, the teacher admonished the students which were louder and more disruptive than the quieter students.

2. When you are considering updating your wardrobe, women should be careful not to choose impractical clothing that doesn't fit their lifestyle.

3. As a business owner, you need to keep detailed financial statements and records of people one has hired.

4. Natalya nearly cried when the band who she saw on her first date with her husband showed up to play a song at her wedding reception.

5. It wasn't Nora that broke the priceless Ming vase in Nana Henderson's drawing room; it was Nora's cousin Bambi who broke it.

Answers

---

1. During class, the teacher admonished the students *who* were louder and more disruptive than the quieter students.

2. When you are considering updating your wardrobe, *you* should be careful not to choose impractical clothing that doesn't fit *your* lifestyle.

3. As a business owner, you need to keep detailed financial statements and records of people *you have* hired.

4. Natalya nearly cried when the band *that* she saw on her first date with her husband showed up to play a song at her wedding reception.

5. It wasn't Nora *who* broke the priceless Ming vase in Nana Henderson's drawing room; it was Nora's cousin Bambi who broke it.

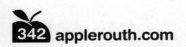

Pronoun Error Practice Problems

Select the answer choice that produces the best sentence.

1. Wind-up mechanical tin toys, once inexpensive collectors' items, grow ever more valuable as it becomes older and more popular among collectors.

   (A) grow ever more valuable as it becomes older
   (B) growing ever more valuable as they become older
   (C) have grown ever more valuable as it becomes older
   (D) have grown ever more valuable by them becoming older
   (E) grow ever more valuable as they become older

2. In the mid-eighteenth century, the English emphasis on ancient Greek and Roman arts and ideals, allowed it to create a neo-classical movement that carried on well into the next century.

   (A) the English emphasis on ancient Greek and Roman arts and ideals, allowed it
   (B) by emphasizing ancient Greek and Roman arts and ideals, this allowed England
   (C) English emphasis on ancient Greek and Roman arts and ideals allowed them
   (D) an emphasis in England on the ancient Greek and Roman arts and ideals allowed them
   (E) an emphasis on ancient Greek and Roman arts and ideals allowed the English

3. Due to continuous budget shortfalls, a new law requires state politicians to pay for his or her own transportation from now on without the hope for reimbursement.

   (A) requires state politicians to pay for his or her own transportation
   (B) requires state politicians to pay for one's own transportation
   (C) requires state politicians to pay for their own transportation
   (D) requires a state politician to pay for their own transportation
   (E) requires a state politician to pay for one's own transportation

4. Maurice has expanded one's notion of what makes a car ideal to include not only a steering wheel and a gas pedal but also working brakes.

   (A) has expanded one's notion of what makes a car ideal to include
   (B) has expanded one's notion of an ideal car including
   (C) expand his notion of what makes a car ideal, he includes
   (D) expanding the notion of what makes a car ideal to include
   (E) has expanded his notion of what makes a car ideal to include

5. There was a good working relationship <u>between my coach and I because each of us had</u> respect for the other.

    (A) between my coach and I because each of us had
    (B) between my coach and me because we each had
    (C) between my coach and me because each of us has
    (D) between my coach and me, each having
    (E) between my coach and I because we had

6. Polls indicated that the <u>public thought the political candidate that gave</u> out red, white and blue gumballs reading "Vote for Me" was too immature to seriously consider for public office.

    (A) public thought the political candidate that gave
    (B) public thinks the political candidate that gave
    (C) public thinks the political candidate that gives
    (D) public thought the political candidate who gave
    (E) public thought the political candidate who gives

7. Experienced bakers advise that before frosting <u>your cake, a person needs to allow one's cake to cool</u>.

    (A) your cake, a person needs to allow one's cake to cool
    (B) their cake, a person needs to allow their cake to cool
    (C) their cakes, allow the cake to cool
    (D) one's cake, you need to allow it to cool
    (E) your cake, you need to allow it to cool

Select the underlined choice that indicates the sentence error.

8. <u>Seemingly</u> dormant volcanoes, like Mt.
   A

   Rainier in Washington, <u>what</u> have not
   B

   erupted in 200 <u>years, still</u> pose a significant
   C

   threat if <u>they</u> were to erupt today. <u>No error</u>
   D   E

9. <u>Although he</u> acknowledged that last year's
   A

   winner of the National Spelling Bee was

   a <u>formidable opponent,</u> Derek was
   B

   confident <u>that he</u> could spell <u>better than her</u>.
   C   D

   <u>No error</u>
   E

10. <u>Seeing</u> the dark figure <u>leap out</u> of the
    A   B

    woods, Jorge, Francois, and <u>me</u> were
    C

    so scared <u>we</u> ran the last three miles
    D

    home without looking back. <u>No error</u>
    E

11. The soldiers of the rebel militia

    have discovered the many benefits
        A

    of following the often illogical orders of
        B   C

    the general whether it does so happily or
                         D

    unhappily. No error
            E

12. During auditions, the casting director
        A

    critiqued the actors which had less experience
                  B

    more harshly than those with more substantial
        C   D

    résumés. No error
          E

13. Because we practiced for hours every day,
        A   B

    both Rachel and me qualified to compete in
          C   D

    the national gymnastics finals. No error
                       E

14. After the final performance of Romeo
                         A

    and Juliet, each of the cast members got

    their scripts signed by everyone else in the
        B   C

    cast before going out to celebrate. No error
           D   E

15. It is important for one to find a job if
               A   B

    one wants to have money with which to
        C   D

    buy a bright yellow Ford Mustang. No error
                           E

Answers

1. E (M)	6. D (M)	11. D (M)
2. E (M)	7. E (H5)	12. B (M)
3. C (M)	8. B (E)	13. C (M)
4. E (M)	9. D (E)	14. B (H)
5. B (M)	10. C (M)	15. E (H5)

Misplaced Modifier

A clause is always looking for something to modify. It will indiscriminately modify whatever it is touching. To avoid some ridiculous events, make sure the modifier is as close as possible to the noun/pronoun it is modifying. Otherwise, you end up with some pretty strange sentences. Always identify your modifiying clause first, and see if it is doing its job.

E Ripping through her street, Emily was terrified of the tornado.

Modifier   **Object**

Ripping through her street, Emily was terrified of the tornado.

Object   **Modifier**

S *Emily was terrified of the tornado ripping through her street.*

Modifier   **Object**

Ripping through the street, the tornado terrified Emily.

First, you have to identify the modifier and see if it is acting appropriately.

As the sentence was originally written, we have Emily ripping through her street. Is that what we are really trying to say? No. We want the tornado to rip through the street. "Ripping through the street" should be modifying the tornado, rather than poor Emily.

E Timmy found his stray gerbil cleaning his room.

> **S** ***While cleaning his room, Timmy found his stray gerbil.***
>
> *We would like to know how Timmy trained his gerbil to clean his room, wouldn't you? However, it is much more likely that Timmy, not his gerbil, was cleaning his room. Remember, place your modifier right next to the noun it is working on.*

E Loved for their small size and chipper dispositions, more and more people are breeding Chiweenies, which are Chihuahua and Daschund mixes.

> **S** ***More and more people are breeding Chiweenies, Chihuahua and Daschund mixes, loved for their small size and chipper dispositions.***
>
> *It has been said that owners begin to look like their pets after they have lived together for many years. Even so, we doubt the **people** who are breeding are loved for **their small size and chipper dispositions**. We suspect the modifier was meant to refer to the cheeky little **Chiweenies** themselves.*

E When I walked into the kitchen, <u>I saw that Rex was cooking lasagna, not his mom.</u>

S *<u>When I walked into the kitchen, **I saw that Rex, not his mom, was cooking lasagna.**</u>*

I certainly hope Rex wasn't cooking his mother! Unless there is another Hanibal Lector in the making, Rex was cooking the lasagna. Remember, the adjective clause will modify what is closest to it.

E <u>Flying out the window, Naomi spotted her errant parrot</u>.

S *<u>**Naomi spotted her errant parrot flying out the window.**</u>*

*Do we even need to address this? Unless Naomi is from Krypton like Superman, it was the **errant parrot** that was **flying out the window**.*

E Nhuy-i found her lost diamond ring searching under her couch cushions.

S *<u>**While searching under her couch cushions, Nhuy-i found her lost diamond ring**</u>.*

*Perhaps the diamond ring was looking for loose change. It is more likely that **Nhuy-i** was the one **searching under her couch cushions**.*

PULSE CHECK

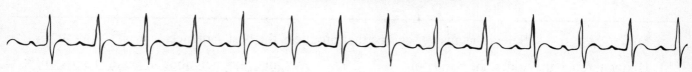

Identify the error (if present) in each of the following sentences.

1. Leaning too closely to her birthday candles, Eunice's hair burst into flames.

2. Last Halloween our dentist passed out toothbrushes dressed as Napoleon Bonaparte instead of candy.

3. Harold tripped over his pet turtle dancing across his room.

4. The spy plane spotted our secret hideout flying through the sky.

5. Running through the woods to escape Sasquatch, the brambles tore Ida's skirt.

Answers

1. *Eunice's hair burst into flames while she was leaning too closely to her birthday candles.*

2. *Last Halloween our dentist, dressed as Napoleon Bonaparte, passed out toothbrushes instead of candy.*

3. *Dancing across his room, Harold tripped over his pet turtle.*

4. *Flying through the sky, the spy plane spotted our secret hideout.*

5. *The brambles tore Ida's skirt as she was running through the woods to escape Sasquatch.*

Misplaced Modifier Practice Problems

Select the answer choice that produces the best sentence.

1. Hiking through the Andes, <u>the beauty of the high peaks and verdant valleys, which we photographed, was stunning</u>.

   (A) the beauty of the high peaks and verdant valleys, which we photographed, was stunning
   (B) the beauty of the high peaks and verdant valleys being stunning, we photographed them
   (C) we photographed the stunning beauty of the high peaks and verdant valleys
   (D) we photographed the beauty of the high peaks and verdant valleys which we found stunning
   (E) finding the high peaks and verdant valleys stunning, we photographed their beauty

2. Unique among the artists of his time, <u>Leonardo da Vinci's works illustrate a remarkable understanding of both anatomy and physiology</u>.

   (A) Leonardo da Vinci's works illustrate a remarkable understanding of both anatomy and physiology
   (B) Leonardo da Vinci and his works illustrating a remarkable understanding of both anatomy and physiology
   (C) Leonardo da Vinci illustrating a remarkable understanding of both anatomy and physiology
   (D) Leonardo da Vinci illustrates through his works that he had a remarkable understanding of both anatomy and physiology
   (E) Leonardo da Vinci's remarkable understanding of both anatomy and physiology is illustrated in his works

3. <u>Our crazy neighbor Josephus hands out oranges to children dressed as Santa Claus</u> every year on July 26.

   (A) Our crazy neighbor Josephus hands out oranges to children dressed as Santa Claus
   (B) Our crazy neighbor Josephus hands out oranges dressed as Santa Claus to children
   (C) Our crazy neighbor Josephus, being dressed as Santa Claus, hands out oranges to children
   (D) Dressing as Santa Claus, our crazy neighbor Josephus handing out oranges to children
   (E) Dressed as Santa Claus, our crazy neighbor Josephus hands out oranges to children

4. <u>Prized for their uniqueness and rarity, collectors will pay thousands of dollars for Bacarat perfume bottles designed by Salvador Dalí.</u>

   (A) Prized for their uniqueness and rarity, collectors will pay thousands of dollars for Bacarat perfume bottles designed by Salvador Dalí.
   (B) Prized for being unique and rare, collectors will pay thousands of dollars for Bacarat perfume bottles designed by Salvador Dalí.
   (C) Collectors will pay thousands of dollars for unique and rare Bacarat perfume bottles designed by Salvador Dalí.
   (D) Collectors will pay thousands of dollars for Bacarat perfume bottles designed by Salvador Dalí for being rare and unique.
   (E) Paying thousands of dollars, collectors prize Bacarat perfume bottles having been designed by Salvador Dalí for their rarity and uniqueness.

5. <u>Finding his older sister's diary fascinating, all the pages were read thoroughly by Horatio.</u>

(A) Finding his older sister's diary fascinating, all the pages were read thoroughly by Horatio.
(B) Finding his older sister's diary fascinating, Horatio thoroughly read all the pages.
(C) Being that his older sister's diary was fascinating, Horatio read all the pages.
(D) Horatio found his older sister's diary fascinating, he read all the pages.
(E) In that he found his older sister's diary fascinating, he read all the pages of it.

6. <u>We believe we have found Amelia Earhart's crashed Lockheed 10E exploring the Pacific Ocean</u> off the coast of New Britain Island near New Guinea.

(A) We believe we have found Amelia Earhart's crashed Lockheed 10E exploring the Pacific Ocean
(B) While exploring the Pacific Ocean, we believe we found Amelia Earhart's crashed Lockheed 10E
(C) We believed we had found Amelia Earhart's crashed Lockheed 10E exploring the Pacific Ocean
(D) Having explored the Pacific Ocean, we believe we have found Amelia Earhart's crashed Lockheed 10E
(E) While exploring the Pacific Ocean, we had believed to find Amelia Earhart's crashed Lockheed 10E

7. Although he was always very resourceful, <u>the answer to the criminal's riddle was not discovered by the detective.</u>

(A) the answer to the criminal's riddle was not discovered by the detective
(B) the answer to the riddle of the criminal was not to be discovered by the detective
(C) the detective could not discover the answer to the criminal's riddle
(D) the answer to the criminal's riddle that the detective sought was not discovered by him
(E) the detective not discovering the answer to the criminal's riddle

8. <u>Running swiftly through the school's largest field, Brad caught</u> the football squarely in his arms.

(A) Running swiftly through the school's largest field, Brad caught
(B) Running swiftly through the school's largest field, Brad catching
(C) Brad had been running swiftly through the school's largest field and caught
(D) Having run swiftly through the school's largest field, Brad catches
(E) Brad, who had been running swiftly through the school's largest field, caught

9. Because of their ability to provide inexpensive produce, some people are shopping at local farmers' markets.

    (A) Because of their ability to provide inexpensive produce, some people are shopping at local farmers' markets.
    (B) Some people are shopping at local farmers' markets because of the markets' ability to provide inexpensive produce.
    (C) Markets have the ability to provide inexpensive produce so some people are shopping at local farmers' markets.
    (D) Because local farmers' markets are able to provide inexpensive produce, some people are shopping at them.
    (E) Local farmers' markets can provide inexpensive produce, because of this some people are shopping at them.

10. Known for their delicious fruit, many backyard gardeners are planting blueberry bushes.

    (A) Known for their delicious fruit, many backyard gardeners are planting blueberry bushes.
    (B) Being known for their delicious fruit, many backyard gardeners plant blueberry bushes.
    (C) Many backyard gardeners plant blueberry bushes, known for its delicious fruit.
    (D) Many backyard gardeners are planting blueberry bushes, being known for their delicious fruit.
    (E) Many backyard gardeners plant blueberry bushes, known for their delicious fruit.

Answers

1. C (E)	*6. B (M)*
2. D (M)	*7. C (M)*
3. E (M)	*8. A (M)*
4. C (M)	*9. B (M)*
5. B (M)	*10. E (H5)*

Fragments

When it comes to spotting fragments, the main question you need to ask yourself is:

Where's the verb?

The SAT will give you extraordinarily long and boring sentences filled with multiple phrases and commas. But don't be fooled! Just because a sentence is long doesn't mean it is complete. For every sentence in the Writing Section, make sure you can identify a subject and a verb.

Looking closer, you must ask yourself: what's my subject and what's the corresponding verb?

E <u>All the demands on the president for resolving international crises, mediating foreign conflicts and addressing global economic issues, leading him to ignore domestic issues and minimized his effectiveness.</u>

S All the (demands) ~~on the president for resolving international crises, mediating foreign conflicts and addressing global economic issues,~~ | leading | him to ignore domestic issues and minimized his effectiveness.

If you cross off all the distracting clauses you are left with:

All the (demands) … | leading | him to ignore domestic issues and minimized his effectiveness.

*Now it is much easier to see that this is a fragment. There is no active verb. The problem is the ING. We need an active verb to pair with **the demands. Led.** Led would work well. Now we have an independent phrase.*

EVERYBODY NOW:

ING IS NO GOOD!

Don't be fooled, verbs ending in -ing often give away a sentence fragment.

ING

-*ING* verbs are the big winner: 50% of SAT fragments are caused by ING.

E Since art classes in elementary schools are central to cultivating creativity, art education <u>deserving continuing</u> support.

S Since art classes in elementary schools are central to cultivating creativity, art education ***deserves*** <u>continuing</u> support.

ING is no good! *All you need here is a present tense verb to make it a complete sentence.*

BEING is a liar, a cheater, and a heartbreaker. You can't trust it!

Being

Being is almost always wrong. And it is very common on the SAT—easy points here.

E Although wireless radio transmissions were popular after Marconi's invention of the wireless radio, systematic regulation of <u>this method of communication not being established until</u> the Communications Act of 1934.

S Although wireless radio transmissions were popular after Marconi's invention of the wireless radio, systematic regulation of <u>this method of communication **was** not established until</u> the Communications Act of 1934.

Here, the past tense verb makes this a complete sentence.

The Wicked Which

We're not in Kansas anymore, Toto! *Which* will quickly turn an independent clause into a dependent one, leaving you with a fragment.

E John Cage has said that <u>his music, which was powerfully influenced</u> by the soundscape of modern life, but the works of earlier composers also provided a strong structural foundation for his compositions.

S John Cage has said that ***his music was powerfully influenced*** by the soundscape of modern life, but the works of earlier composers also provided a strong structural foundation for his compositions.

Banish that **which***! It does not belong here.*

Beware of **whiches**, especially those without brooms and pointy hats.

Missing Helping Verb

We all need a little help sometimes. The past participle form of verbs needs help, too. Remember these helpers: *be, being, been, am, are, is, was, were, may, might, must, do, does, did, should, could, would, have, had, has, will, can, shall.*

E One of the most <u>majestic birds of prey in North America, the bald eagle brought to the brink</u> of extinction in the 1960s due to excessive use of harmful pesticides like DDT.

S One of the most <u>majestic birds of prey in North America, the bald eagle *was* brought to the brink</u> of extinction in the 1960s due to excessive use of harmful pesticides like DDT.

The helping verb **was** *is missing in action. Read each problem sentence carefully so you're sure not to miss something.*

Who
These three little letters can equal one big problem.

E Charlie <u>Chaplin, one of the most versatile performers of the 20th century, who acquired fame</u> as an actor, writer, director, producer, composer and choreographer.

S Charlie <u>Chaplin, one of the most versatile performers of the 20th *century, acquired fame*</u> as an actor, writer, director, producer, composer and choreographer.

Who *is unnecessary in this sentence; it just destroys your perfectly good independent clause.*

The Sneaky Since
The word *since* should be a signal to you that a fragment is looming.

E <u>Since some people are convinced that Tarot card reading, a method of divining the future, is a legitimate way</u> to make sound decisions, but others consider it antiquated, superstitious, and ridiculous.

S <u>*Some people are convinced that Tarot card reading, a method of divining the future, is a legitimate way*</u> to make sound decisions, but others consider it antiquated, superstitious, and ridiculous.

Once you oust that sneaky **since**, *you have a complete sentence.*

That

When you see *that* in a sentence, double check to make sure you have a complete sentence with a subject and verb.

E <u>The teacher that planned a trip to the botannical gardens because she thought it would be educational</u> for students to see all the different varieties of local flowering plants.

S ***The teacher planned a trip to the botannical gardens because she thought it would be educational*** for students to see all the different varieties of local flowering plants.

The **that** *strikes again! Once you remove* **that**, *you have a complete sentence.*

And

Last but not least, *and* is not always your friend. Double check to make sure it isn't trying to trip you up.

E Because budgetary limitations will compel some municipalities to <u>lay off police officers, and so the state legislature must determine</u> whether to provide additional financial support to those cities.

S Because budgetary limitations will compel some municipalities to ***lay off police officers, the state legislature must determine*** whether to provide additional financial support to those cities.

And so *is usually wrong. Most of the time, one conjunction will do the job for you. In this case, we didn't even need a conjunction.*

Keep your eyes open for these classic fragment-makers:

-ING
BEING
WHICH
Missing Helping Verb
WHO
SINCE
THAT
AND

PULSE CHECK

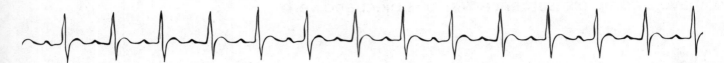

Identify the error (if present) in each of the following sentences.

1. Revered by millions for his role in ending Apartheid in South Africa, and Nelson Mandela was awarded the Nobel Peace Prize in 1993.

2. To protect the gray wolf from extinction in North America, regulations having been created by the Federal Government to keep the wolves' habitats intact.

3. Senior citizens on fixed incomes in the United States face a challenge, being that they must reconcile high prescription medication prices with their limited budgets.

4. Frequently out of town on business, Melina's father, treated like a king every time he returns home.

5. Anton von Leeuwenhoek, often referred to as the "Father of Microbiology," who created over 400 different types of microscopes.

Answers

1. Revered by millions for his role in ending Apartheid in *South Africa, Nelson Mandela* was awarded the Nobel Peace Prize in 1993.

2. To protect the gray wolf from extinction in North America, regulations *were created* by the Federal Government to keep the wolves' habitats intact.

3. Senior citizens on fixed incomes in the United States face a challenge *because they must reconcile* high prescription medication prices with their limited budgets.

4. Frequently out of town on business, Melina's father *is treated* like a king every time he returns home.

5. Anton von Leeuwenhoek, often referred to as the "Father of Microbiology," *created* over 400 different types of microscopes.

Fragments Practice Problems

Select the answer choice that produces the best sentence.

1. Facing a great challenge, Lacey, who is the first woman to attempt to fly across the English Channel without any pilot training.

   (A) Facing a great challenge, Lacey, who is
   (B) To face a great challenge, Lacey, who is
   (C) Being faced with a great challenge, Lacey who is
   (D) Facing a great challenge, Lacey is
   (E) Being faced with a great challenge, Lacey is

2. My favorite book by Vladimir Nabokov, *The Real Life of Sebastian Knight, which was his first book written in English*.

   (A) Nabokov, *The Real Life of Sebastian Knight*, which was his first book written in English
   (B) Nabokov, *The Real Life of Sebastian Knight*, being his first book written in English
   (C) Nabokov is *The Real Life of Sebastian Knight*, being his first book written in English
   (D) Nabokov is *The Real Life of Sebastian Knight*, which was his first book that had been written in English
   (E) Nabokov is *The Real Life of Sebastian Knight,* which was his first book written in English

3. Because Eileen had poor vision and even worse balance, and she was always falling over.

   (A) and she was always falling over
   (B) she was always falling over
   (C) she was always to fall over
   (D) and so she was always falling over
   (E) and so always was falling over

4. Since many people believe dancing can be an intense and entertaining aerobic work out.

   (A) Since many people believe dancing can be an intense
   (B) Since many people believing dancing can be an intense
   (C) Many people believe to dance can be an intense
   (D) Because many people believe dancing to be an intense
   (E) Many people believe dancing can be an intense

5. David Lynch's cult classic, _Twin Peaks,_ <u>that is so complicated with multiple confusing plot twists and character changes that most people</u> have trouble following the storyline.

    (A) _Twin Peaks_, that is so complicated with multiple confusing plot twists and character changes that most people

    (B) _Twin Peaks_, is so complicated with multiple confusing plot twists and character changes that most people

    (C) _Twin Peaks_, is so complicated with multiple confusing plot twists and characters changing, most people

    (D) _Twin Peaks_, that is so complicated with multiple confusing plot twists and character changes, most people

    (E) _Twin Peaks_, is so complicated having multiple confusing plot twists and character changes and most people

---

Select the underlined choice that indicates the sentence error.

---

6. Elmer was <u>unanimously</u> elected Prom
                A

King <u>this</u> year <u>which was</u> because we all
      B   C

think he is the <u>cat's</u> pajamas. <u>No error</u>
             D   E

7. Ronald Reagan's mediocre <u>film career</u>
                      A

<u>eclipsed</u> by his <u>later career</u> <u>as</u> President
  B   C   D

of the United States. <u>No error</u>
                E

8. Captain Planet <u>was</u> an eco-friendly
              A

cartoon superhero <u>in the early</u> 90s and
               B

<u>who</u> was my hero for <u>most of</u> my child-
 C   D

hood. <u>No error</u>
      E

9. In 1973, <u>to protect</u> certain <u>species of</u>
         A   B

endangered plants and animals, laws

<u>having been</u> passed by the United States
  C

government <u>to preserve</u> threatened ecosys-
            D

tems. <u>No error</u>
     E

10. Teenaged girls often <u>finding</u> <u>fictional</u>
              A   B

vampires <u>romantic, forgetting</u> <u>that</u> they are
         C   D

bloodsucking monsters. <u>No error</u>
               E

Answers

1. D (E)   6. C (E)
2. E (M)   7. B (M)
3. B (E)   8. C (E)
4. E (M)   9. C (M)
5. B (M)   10. A (M)

7%

of grammar questions on the SAT

Idiomatic Phrasing

The hardest grammar problems on the SAT test your knowledge of idiomatic expressions; these involve pairing particular words with the appropriate prepositions. For example, you **abide by** the law, rather than *to* or *with* the law. Your actions may be **consistent with** your beliefs, rather than *consistent to* them. Luckily, you probably have been listening to spoken English for quite a while. This training will help you recognize awkward phrasing that just doesn't sound right.

-ING Verbs

The SAT will often use the infinitive of a verb (to dance) instead of the -ing verb (dancing).

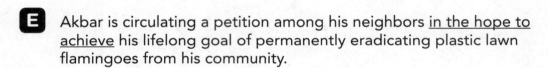 Akbar is circulating a petition among his neighbors <u>in the hope to achieve</u> his lifelong goal of permanently eradicating plastic lawn flamingoes from his community.

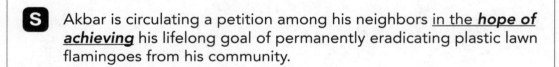 Akbar is circulating a petition among his neighbors <u>in the **hope of achieving**</u> his lifelong goal of permanently eradicating plastic lawn flamingoes from his community.

In this instance, the -ing verb of achieve is the proper verb form. Don't be afraid to read the sentences quietly to yourself. Your fellow test takers won't even hear you.

Preposition pairs

In English there are certain prepositions that pair with verbs. You've heard these pairs all your life. Now it is time to pick them out on the SAT.

E Zoltan's sunny disposition is <u>inconsistent to</u> the neo-gothic clothing he wears to the mall.

S Zoltan's sunny disposition is ***inconsistent with*** the neo-gothic clothing he wears to the mall.

The word **inconsistent** *is always paired with the preposition* **with**—*no exceptions. Following are other common verb/preposition pairs.*

Common Prepositional Phrases

verb	preposition
abide	by
accuse	of
agree	to/with/on/upon
apologize	for
apply	to/for
approve	of
argue	with/about/over
arrive	at
believe	in
blame	for
care	about/for
charge	for/with
compare	with/to

verb	preposition
complain	about/of/to
consist	of
contribute	to
count	upon/on
cover	with
decide	upon/on
depend	upon/on
differ	about/from over/with
discriminate	against
distinguish	from/between
dream	of/about
escape	from

Trust your instincts if you get stuck on this type of question. Chances are you have heard these combinations many times in you life.

verb	preposition		verb	preposition
excel	in		recover	from
excuse	for		rely	upon/on
forget	about		rescue	from
forgive	for		respond	to
hide	from		stare	at
hope	for		stop	from
insist	upon/on		subscribe	to
object	to		subsititute	for
participate	in		suceed	in
prevent	from		thank	for
prohibit	from		vote	for/on/against
protect	against/from		wait	for/on
provide	for/with		worry	about

PULSE CHECK

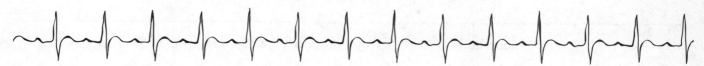

Identify the error (if present) in each of the following sentences.

1. My neighbor Ben Dover will never forgive his parents about their terrible choice in naming him.

2. Southern by birth, Dixie has suffered with terrible teasing about her accent by her fellow classmates in New York.

3. After further investigation, it appears that Samson falsely accused Delilah with chopping off his luscious locks.

4. Three weeks after his parents suspended his allowance and in desperate need of funds, Rigoberto finally realized he needed a summer job and applied at Ed's World of Twinkies.

5. Despite their families' objections to their union, Tyrone and Pamela succeeded with getting married in a private ceremony last month.

Answers

1. My neighbor Ben Dover will never forgive his parents *for* their terrible choice in naming him.

2. Southern by birth, Dixie has *suffered from* terrible teasing about her accent by her fellow classmates in New York.

3. After further investigation, it appears that Samson falsely *accused Delilah of* chopping off his luscious locks.

4. Three weeks after his parents suspended his allowance and in desperate need of funds, Rigoberto finally realized he needed a summer job and *applied to* Ed's World of Twinkies.

5. Despite their families' objections to their union, Tyrone and Pamela *succeeded in* getting married in a private ceremony last month.

Idiomatic Phrasing Practice Problems

Select the answer choice that produces the best sentence.

1. <u>My younger brother's opinions on everything differ so greatly with mine that it is</u> hard to believe we are even related.

   (A) My younger brother's opinions on everything differ so greatly with mine that it is
   (B) My younger brother's opinions on everything differ so greatly from mine that it is
   (C) My younger brother's opinions on everything, differing so greatly from mine, it is
   (D) My younger brother's opinions on everything differing so greatly with mine, it is
   (E) My younger brother's opinions on everything differ so greatly with mine; it is

2. Tired of his neighbor's cats invading his property and falling asleep inside his garage, <u>Orlando finally succeeded in keeping them away by</u> gluing a strongly-worded note to an unlucky orange tabby.

   (A) Orlando finally succeeded in keeping them away by
   (B) Orlando finally succeeded with keeping them away by
   (C) Orlando finally succeeded to keep them away by
   (D) Orlando finally succeeded in keeping them away and
   (E) Orlando finally succeeds in keeping them away with

3. <u>The term "silkscreening" comes from a nineteenth-century technique for which specific parts of a screen of porous fiber, silk or polyester, are blocked off</u> with non-permeable material to create a stencil to be inked onto cloth or paper.

   (A) The term "silkscreening" comes from a nineteenth-century technique for which specific parts of a screen of porous fiber, silk or polyester, are blocked off
   (B) The term "silkscreening" comes from a nineteenth-century technique whereby specific parts of a screen of porous fiber, silk or polyester, are blocked off
   (C) The term "silkscreening" comes from a nineteenth-century technique that means specific parts of a screen of porous fiber, silk or polyester, are blocked off
   (D) The term "silkscreening" comes from a nineteenth-century technique for which specific parts of a screen of porous fiber, silk or polyester, is blocked off
   (E) The term "silkscreening" comes from a nineteenth-century technique and specific parts of a screen of porous fiber, silk or polyester, are blocked off

4. Miss Bliss was standing by, ready to help Maximus complete his dried macaroni sculpture <u>even though he had refused earlier offers for assistance</u>.

(A) even though he had refused earlier offers for assistance
(B) although he had refused earlier offers for assistance
(C) even though he had refused earlier offers of assistance
(D) even though he had refused earlier offers for assisting
(E) even though he had refused earlier offers of assisting

5. <u>Not very particular in the restaurants where we go for our weekly lunch meetings, our boss allowed Tatum to choose</u> the venue since she has so many food allergies.

(A) Not very particular in the restaurants where we go for our weekly lunch meetings, our boss allowed Tatum to choose

(B) Not very particular in the restaurants where we have our weekly lunch meetings, our boss allowed Tatum to choose

(C) Not very particular about the restaurants where we go for our weekly lunch meetings, our boss allowing Tatum to choose

(D) Not very particular about the restaurants where we have our weekly lunch meetings, our boss allowed Tatum to choose

(E) Not very particular with the restaurants where we have our weekly lunch meetings, our boss allowed Tatum to choose

Select the underlined choice that indicates the sentence error.

6. <u>Having</u> never been to France before,
     A

   Stella and McKenna <u>created</u> a detailed,
               B

   <u>day-by-day</u> trip itinerary the moment
     C

   they <u>arrived to</u> Paris. <u>No error</u>
       D   E

7. <u>Opposite to</u> most math majors at our
     A

   school, Bruno <u>is</u> <u>surprisingly good at</u>
           B   C

   writing long, complex research papers

   that <u>explore</u> abstract philosophical
        D

   concepts. <u>No error</u>
         E

8. Although <u>famous for building</u> the British
           A
   Empire, Queen Victoria <u>is</u> often
              B
   <u>remembered for</u> her <u>tendency of gaining</u>
     C   D
   weight easily. <u>No error</u>
           E

9. <u>Ten years in the making,</u> his new skyscraper
        A

<u>is</u> both a response to a dramatic change
B

in popular aesthetics and to his critics'

<u>mistrust with</u> his <u>earlier</u> structural
    C   D

hypotheses. <u>No error</u>
          E

10. The morning show host <u>has received</u>
            A

numerous complaints about Wednesday's

segment, which many listeners

<u>condemned to be</u> tasteless and <u>offensive to</u>
     B   C

women <u>who</u> choose to stay home and
       D

raise families. <u>No error</u>
         E

Answers

1. B (M)	6. D (M)
2. A (M)	7. A (H)
3. B(H5)	8. D (H5)
4. C (H5)	9. C (H5)
5. D (H5)	10. B (H5)

Run-ons

A run-on or comma splice is a series of independent clauses stuck together without the appropriate punctuation. Quite often, the SAT will send in a comma to do a semi-colon or a period's job.

E The flying squirrel had not eaten in two days, it was famished.

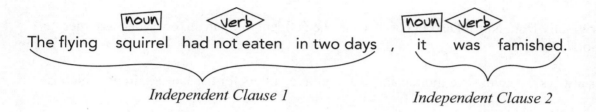

Independent Clause 1   *Independent Clause 2*

As you can see, we have 2 independent clauses separated by a comma. A comma cannot do that!

There are four ways to fix a run-on.

S The flying squirrel had not eaten in two days. It was famished.

Add a period. Separate the two independent clauses with a period, and the problem is solved.

The flying squirrel had not eaten in two days; it was famished.

Use a semi-colon. A comma cannot stand in the middle of two independent clauses; a semi-colon, on the other hand, was designed for the job.

The flying squirrel had not eaten in two days, **SO** it was famished.

Drop in a conjunction. You know the function. Drop in a conjunction and our two independent clauses will be sitting pretty. To remember the conjunctions, think FANBOYS: **for, and, nor, but, or, yet, so.**

Because the flying squirrel had not eaten in two days , it was famished.

Dependent Clause   *Independent Clause*

Subordinate one of the clauses. A comma cannot separate two **independent** *clauses, but it can easily handle a dependent and an independent clause. If we subordinate one of the clauses and make it dependent, life will be complete.*

PULSE CHECK

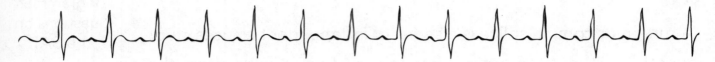

Identify the error (if present) in each of the following sentences.

1. Maura, a veritable recluse, has a terrible sense of style, when she does leave the house, she only wears ancient flannel pajamas.

2. Singing the sweetest notes I've ever heard, the nightingale outside my window woke me up this morning, she does every day.

3. Santiago is originally from North Dakota but, because he is fluent in Spanish, everyone assumes he was born in South America.

4. Wilhelmina is always trying to save money and she paid five dollars for her latest haircut, which is hideous.

5. Studies show that eating a bowl of oatmeal adds a healthy dose of fiber to your diet, it can also significantly lower your cholesterol, decreasing your risk for heart disease.

Answers

1. Maura, a veritable recluse, has a terrible sense of *style; when* she does leave the house, she only wears ancient flannel pajamas.

2. Singing the sweetest notes I've ever heard, the nightingale outside my window woke me up this morning *as she does every day*.

3. Santiago is originally from *North Dakota, but* because he is fluent in Spanish, everyone assumes he was born in South America.

4. Wilhelmina is always trying to save *money. She* paid five dollars for her latest haircut, which is hideous.

5. Studies show that eating a bowl of oatmeal adds a healthy dose of fiber to your *diet, and it* can also significantly lower your cholesterol, decreasing your risk for heart disease.

Run-on Practice Problems

Select the answer choice that produces the best sentence.

1. As a cake decorator, <u>Trenton Trenilson has enriched the world of baked goods, he uses as his work's inspiration</u> Monet's early oil paintings.

   (A) Trenton Trenilson has enriched the world of baked goods, he uses as his work's inspiration
   (B) Trenton Trenilson has enriched the world of baked goods, using as his work's inspiration
   (C) Trenton Trenilson having enriched the world of baked goods, he uses as his work's inspiration
   (D) Trenton Trenilson has enriched the world of baked goods, but he uses as his work's inspiration
   (E) Trenton Trenilson has enriched the world of baked goods, he used as his work's inspiration

2. A recent report from the Olympic Committee indicates that sleep-deprived divers <u>caused numerous accidents in last summer's Olympic Games, they frequently fell asleep</u> in the middle of a reverse 2 ½ pike.

   (A) caused numerous accidents in last summer's Olympic Games, they frequently fell asleep
   (B) causing numerous accidents in last summer's Olympic Games, they frequently fell asleep
   (C) causing numerous accidents in last summer's Olympic Games, frequently falling asleep
   (D) caused numerous accidents in last summer's Olympic Games; they frequently fell asleep
   (E) caused numerous accidents in last summer's Olympic Games; because, they frequently fell asleep

3. Last year, my mother became the first woman in our family <u>to earn a master's degree, moreover, she is the first family member</u> to go on to study for a doctorate degree.

   (A) to earn a masters degree, moreover, she is the first family member
   (B) to earn a master's degree; moreover, she is the first family member
   (C) earning a master's degree, moreover, she is the first family member
   (D) to earn a master's degree, moreover, she was the first family member
   (E) who earned a master's degree; moreover she was the first family member

4. Occasionally teenage girls must leave the safety of the hive <u>to forage for designer jeans and tacky jewelry, they are risking being labeled social pariahs</u> if they are caught in last season's styles.

   (A) to forage for designer jeans and tacky jewelry, they are risking being labeled social pariahs
   (B) foraging for designer jeans and tacky jewelry, they are risking being labeled social pariahs
   (C) to forage for designer jeans and tacky jewelry; they are risking being labeled social pariahs
   (D) having to forage for designer jeans and tacky jewelry; they are risking being labeled social pariahs
   (E) to forage for designer jeans and tacky jewelry because they risk being labeled social pariahs

5. <u>It has taken my mother 30 years of creative and persistent effort to finally convince me</u> the universe never intended me to be a platinum blond.

(A) It has taken my mother 30 years of creative and persistent effort to finally convince me
(B) It has taken my mother 30 years of creative and persistent effort, her finally convincing me
(C) Taking my mother 30 years of creative and persistent effort, she finally convinced me
(D) Taking my mother 30 years of creative and persistent effort, but she finally convinced me
(E) It took my mother 30 years of creative and persistent effort, but she finally convinces me

_____

Select the underlined choice that indicates the sentence error.

_____

6. This year, the <u>president of</u> the PTA
                  A

<u>will be chosen</u> by <u>committee, it</u> <u>will include</u>
    B   C   D

parents, teachers, and school administrators.

<u>No error</u>
  E

7. <u>Built in the late 1600s,</u> Castillo de San
        A

Marcos is the oldest fort still standing in the

<u>United States, its</u> bastioned, stone structure
       B

<u>is</u> surrounded by a <u>now-dry</u> moat. <u>No error</u>
C   D   E

8. <u>Running</u> for Congress <u>is</u> a long and arduous
    A   B

process requiring a lot of patience and

<u>perseverance, but</u> the chance <u>to make</u> a
     C   D

difference in the lives of others is priceless.

<u>No error</u>
  E

9. <u>Paying</u> for the wedding <u>is traditionally</u>
  A   B

the responsibility of the bride's

<u>parents; however</u> the groom's parents
      C

usually <u>pay for</u> the honeymoon. <u>No error</u>
      D   E

10. Although she <u>had to wake up</u> every
           A

morning before sunrise <u>to practice, Mona</u>
                     B

was thrilled when <u>she passed</u> the first
              C

round of Olympic Qualifying <u>trials, this</u>
                   D

is something only 20 out of 537 people

were able accomplish. <u>No error</u>
                E

Answers

---

1. B (E)	6. C (E)
2. D (E)	7. B (E)
3. B (M)	8. E (E)
4. E (H)	9. C (M)
5. A (H)	10. D (M)

4%

of grammar
questions
on the SAT

Adjectives and Adverbs

The SAT consistently uses adjectives when an adverb is required. It is essential that you first identify what is being modified in the sentence to determine whether you need an adjective or an adverb. An adjective describes a noun or a pronoun. An adverb describes a *verb*, an *adjective*, or another *adverb*, and the vast majority of adverbs end in *–ly*.

The most common SAT question incorrectly uses an adjective to describe another adjective.

E In 2007, Steve Jobs proudly <u>announced the release of the iPhone, a clever designed mobile phone,</u> that would go on to rock the telecommunications industry and send technophiles running to Apple outlets.

S

...release of the iPhone, **a clever designed mobile phone**...

Clever *is not modifying the phone, but how it was designed. It may have been a clever phone, but it was* **cleverly** *designed. We need an adverb to describe the adjective.*
All about the **-ly***!!*

E <u>Come quick!</u> I think I see a dead body over there!

S <u>Come **quickly**!</u> I think I see a dead body over there!

Quick *describes the verb* **come***, therefore it needs to be an adverb. Just add* **-ly***!*

E After years of being ignored, Jorgen was surprised when the cute girl next door commented <u>on how good he played the bassoon</u>.

> **S** After years of being ignored, Jorgen was surprised when the cute girl next door commented <u>on how **well** he played the bassoon</u>.
>
> *Here, it is Jorgen's playing that is being complimented. Since **played** is a verb, we need an adverb, **well**, to describe it.*

Good is an adjective. Well is an adverb!!

Standard, run-of-the-mill adjectives normally don't give students too much trouble. It is trying to decide whether to use a comparative adjective—one that ends in **-er** like smart**er** or is paired with **more** like **more** beautiful—or a superlative adjective—one that ends in **-est** like smart**est** or is paired with **most** like **most** beautiful. You should use **comparative** adjectives when you are **comparing** only 2 things, and use **superlative** adjectives when you are talking about 3 or more things.

E Between my Coach and Chanel purses, <u>I like the Chanel one best</u>.

> **S** Between my Coach and Chanel purses, <u>I like the Chanel one **better**</u>.
>
> *We are only comparing two things here, a Coach and a Chanel purse. Since there are only two purses, we have to use the comparative adjective.*

PULSE CHECK

Identify the error (if present) in each of the following sentences.

1. Before I registered for Dr. Platnic's Advanced Theories of Cultural Rhetoric and Protest seminar, my roommate warned me that it was surprising difficult.

2. Wealthy women have no problem paying exorbitant amounts for designer shoes because these shoes are not only stunning but also beautiful hand-made.

3. I was shocked when I went to the organic produce market and found that Chinese eggplants were priced so high.

4. Of my two brothers, Jonas is definitely the strongest.

5. Despite being light seasoned, the tripe Olga made was delicious.

Answers

1. Before I registered for Dr. Platnic's Advanced Theories of Cultural Rhetoric and Protest seminar, my roommate warned me that it was *surprisingly* difficult.

2. Wealthy women have no problem paying exorbitant amounts for designer shoes because these shoes are not only stunning but also *beautifully* hand-made.

3. I was shocked when I went to the organic produce market and found that Chinese eggplants were priced so *highly*.

4. Of my two brothers, Jonas is definitely the *stronger*.

5. Despite being *lightly* seasoned, the tripe Olga made was delicious.

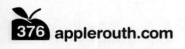

Adjectives and Adverbs Practice Problems

Select the answer choice that produces the best sentence.

1. Terry <u>played swift and vicious</u> on the basketball court, yet he never won a championship.

   (A) played swift and vicious
   (B) played swiftly with much viciousness
   (C) played swift and viciously
   (D) played with a swiftness and viciously
   (E) played swiftly and viciously

2. Cletus feared he had <u>scored poor on his while Berdine assured him he had done very well</u>.

   (A) scored poor on his test, while Berdine assured him he had done very well
   (B) scoring poorly on his test with Berdine assuring him he had done very well
   (C) scored poorly on his test, and Berdine assuring him he had done very well
   (D) scored poorly on his test, while Berdine assured him he had done very well
   (E) scored poor-like on that there test, while Berdine been assurin' him he had gone and done mighty good

3. Despite early predictions of clear skies all day, <u>by noon the snow had begun to fall quite heavily</u>.

   (A) by noon the snow had begun to fall quite heavily
   (B) by noon the snow had begun to fall quite heavy
   (C) by noon the snow began to fall quite heavy
   (D) by noon the snow is falling quite heavily
   (E) by noon the snow falling quite heavily

Select the underlined choice that indicates the sentence error.

4. No matter how <u>diligent</u> Bob monitored the
              A

   two <u>monstrous volcanoes</u>, the town <u>was</u>
        B   C

   still fated <u>for</u> utter annihilation. <u>No error</u>
          D   E

5. Running <u>quickly</u> toward the <u>outfield,</u>
          A   B

   <u>almost colliding</u> with the second baseman
      C

   in the process, Marquez <u>caught</u> the baseball
                  D

   squarely in his mitt. <u>No error</u>
              E

6. The King's <u>armed guard slaughtered</u> the
             A

   insurgency so <u>quick</u> that <u>no one</u> realized
            B   C

   the crown was <u>in</u> jeopardy. <u>No error</u>
           D   E

Answers

---

1. E (M)   4. A (E)
2. D (M)   5. E (M)
3. A (M)   6. B (M)

Brevity

4%

of grammar questions on the SAT

Short, sweet and to the point: that is the SAT's motto. If you come across a sentence that seems too long for its own good, it probably is. Just remember: less is more.

E When you see the flashing blue lights approaching in your rear view mirror, <u>this is when you know it's time to change your radio station from Hard Rock to NPR</u>.

S When you see the flashing blue lights approaching in your rear view mirror, ***you know it's time to change your radio station from Hard Rock to NPR***.

This is when *is a dead giveaway that there are too many words in the sentence. Why say* **this is when** *when we can just say "when"? The same goes for "this is what" and "this is where."*

The Number 1 Rule for the Grammar Section is:

Short is Sweet!

E <u>Joan was worried that her annual property tax, which is due every year in January,</u> would be more expensive this year.

S <u>Joan was worried that her annual property tax, ***which is due in January,***</u> would be more expensive this year.

In this sentence, the **property tax** *is described as* **annual**, *which means "happens every year." So, the words* **every year** *are redundant or repetitive in the sentence. We don't need both* **annual** *and* **every year**. **Annual** *by itself is sufficient.*

PULSE CHECK

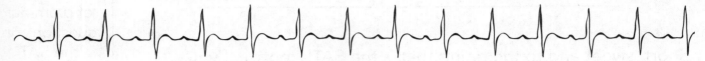

Identify the error (if present) in each of the following sentences.

1. On February 9, 1964, The Beatles appeared live on *The Ed Sullivan Show* being the inauguration of both the band and a new type of rock and roll in America.

2. In the early morning of May 20, 1927, Charles Lindbergh left Roosevelt Field in New York in his monoplane, The Spirit of St. Louis, with his purpose being to complete the first transatlantic flight.

3. All of Edward's lifelong dreams to become a ballet dancer with the American Ballet Company came to an end last Thursday; this is when he knocked over the other dancers during his final pirouette in *Swan Lake*.

4. Sharon found it nearly impossible to rent a car in Reykjavik, this being because she does not speak Icelandic.

5. Rodney took great pride in his lush, grass lawn.

Answers

1. On February 9, 1964, The Beatles appeared live on *The Ed Sullivan Show thus inaugurating* both the band and a new type of rock and roll in America.

2. In the early morning of May 20, 1927, Charles Lindbergh left Roosevelt Field in New York in his monoplane, The Spirit of St. Louis, *to complete* the first transatlantic flight.

3. All of Edward's lifelong dreams to become a ballet dancer with the American Ballet Company came to an end last Thursday *when* he knocked over the other dancers during his final pirouette in *Swan Lake*.

4. Sharon found it nearly impossible to rent a car in Reykjavik *because* she does not speak Icelandic.

5. Rodney took great pride in his *lush lawn*.

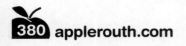

Brevity Practice Problems

Select the answer choice that produces the best sentence.

1. Norton is morally opposed to killing anything, insects included, <u>the reason being he has recently converted to Buddhism</u>.

   (A) the reason being he has recently converted to Buddhism
   (B) because he has recently converted to Buddhism
   (C) because of recently converting to Buddhism
   (D) the reason why being he has recently converted to Buddhism
   (E) the reason being because he has recently converted to Buddhism

2. Jamarion was reading Edgar Allan Poe's *The Tell-Tale Heart*, <u>this is when he heard a loud thump down the hall which nearly scared him to death</u>.

   (A) *The Tell-Tale Heart*, this is when he heard a loud thump down the hall which nearly scared him to death
   (B) *The Tell-Tale Heart*, this is when he heard a loud thump down the hall, nearly scaring him to death
   (C) *The Tell-Tale Heart*, which is when he heard a loud thump down the hall, nearly scaring him to death
   (D) *The Tell-Tale Heart* when he heard a loud thump down the hall, nearly scared him to death
   (E) *The Tell-Tale Heart* when he heard a loud thump down the hall that nearly scared him to death

3. Jazlyn installed new energy-efficient insulation in her attic <u>the purpose of which is to lower her heating and cooling bills</u>.

   (A) the purpose of which is to lower her heating and cooling bills
   (B) the purpose being to lower her heating and cooling bills
   (C) in order to lower her heating and cooling bills
   (D) in order to have her heating and cooling bills lowered
   (E) the purpose of that is to lower her heating and cooling bills

Select the underlined choice that indicates the sentence error.

4. Rocco was thrilled <u>at the time</u> he
                       A
   discovered he not only <u>was accepted to</u>
                           B
   his top choice university <u>but also</u> <u>received</u>
                             C   D
   a scholarship. <u>No error</u>
                   E

5. Tobias <u>did</u> not ask Francesca to dance at
          A

Prom, not because he disliked her, but

<u>the reason was</u> he <u>had never learned</u> <u>to dance</u>.
          B   C   D

<u>No error</u>
    E

6. Dayanara and Cyrus <u>climbed</u> Mt. Everest
                              A

<u>to prove</u> to <u>themselves</u> and their families
      B   C

that they had not <u>been beaten</u> by their
                        D

near-fatal diagnoses of cancer. <u>No error</u>
                                      E

Answers

---

1. B (M)   4. A (E)

2. E (E)   5. B (E)

3. C (H)   6. E (M)

Unclear Antecedents

Sometimes a pronoun reference is ambiguous, creating confusion regarding to whom the pronoun is referring.

E Mr. Miyagi and Daniel-san were surprised that his front snap kick, a classic move, proved to be too much for the Cobra Kai's star athlete Johnny Lawrence.

S Mr. Miyagi and Daniel-san were surprised that **Daniel-san's** front snap kick, a classic move, proved to be too much for the Cobra Kai's star athlete Johnny Lawrence.

Whose front kick? Mr. Miyagi's? Or Daniel-san's? You have to be specific to avoid pronoun confusion. When your subjects are the same gender, you will have to specify by name who is doing what in the second half of the sentence.

E When Ingrid and Helga visited the Ikea bakery, she noticed her favorite cupcake, KYPKKÄKKEN, was no longer on the menu.

S When Ingrid and Helga visited the Ikea bakery, **Helga** noticed her favorite cupcake, KYPKKÄKKEN, was no longer on the menu.

*There's no question about the error in the above example. Both ladies may have visited the bakery, but only one noticed the absent cupcake. The pronoun **she** is too vague. You have to clarify who is noticing the absent dessert.*

PULSE CHECK

Identify the error (if present) in each of the following sentences.

1. Despite her dislike of sand and surf, Mary Ellen and Meredith went to the beach on their vacation.

2. Nathaniel and Marcus, best friends since they were in kindergarten, were disconsolate when his parents decided to move to Cairo, Egypt.

3. She had always dreamed of making it big in Hollywood, like Shirley Temple or Audrey Hepburn, which is why Cordelia and her mother went to every open call audition they could find.

4. Needing an A on his final physics project to pass the course, Otis and Bob worked on it together all night long.

5. Yessenia and Yasmina decided to try speed dating because she refused to go on another blind date.

Answers

1. Despite *Mary Ellen's* dislike of sand and surf, *she* and Meredith went to the beach on their vacation.

2. Nathaniel and Marcus, best friends since they were in kindergarten, were disconsolate when *Nathaniel's* parents decided to move to Cairo, Egypt.

3. *Cordelia* had always dreamed of making it big in Hollywood, like Shirley Temple or Audrey Hepburn, which is why *she* and her mother went to every open call audition they could find.

4. *Otis, needing an A on his final physics project to pass the course, worked on it with Bob* all night long.

5. Yessenia and Yasmina decided to try speed dating because *Yasmina* refused to go on another blind date.

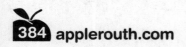

Unclear Antecendents Practice Problems

Select the answer choice that produces the best sentence.

1. <u>Because he has always wanted to be an Olympic swimmer, Herbert and Wyatt trained</u> every morning at six for over thirteen years.

   (A) Because he has always wanted to be an Olympic swimmer, Herbert and Wyatt trained
   (B) Because Herbert has always wanted to be an Olympic swimmer, him and Wyatt trained
   (C) Because he has always wanted to be an Olympic swimmer, Herbert and Wyatt had trained
   (D) Because Herbert has always wanted to be an Olympic swimmer, he and Wyatt trained
   (E) Because Herbert has always wanted to be an Olympic swimmer, him and Wyatt had trained

2. <u>Aldo and Geoff were surprised when Aldo was elected</u> vice president of the student body even though it was an uncontested race.

   (A) Aldo and Geoff were surprised when Aldo was elected
   (B) Aldo and Geoff were surprised when he was elected
   (C) Aldo and Geoff being surprised when Aldo was elected
   (D) Aldo and Geoff was surprised when Aldo was elected
   (E) Aldo and Geoff was surprised when he was elected

3. <u>The Great Blue Heron is larger than it but just as graceful as the swan</u>.

   (A) The Great Blue Heron is larger than it but just as graceful as the swan
   (B) The Great Blue Heron is larger than but just as graceful as the swan
   (C) The Great Blue Heron, being larger than the swan, is still as graceful
   (D) The Great Blue Heron is larger than the swan but just as graceful
   (E) The Great Blue heron is larger than the swan; however, just as graceful

Select the underlined choice that indicates the sentence error.

4. <u>Among</u> the events <u>recounted</u> in *The*
   A   B

   Histories by Herdotus <u>he described</u> the
                                  C

   King Cyrus of <u>Persia's childhood</u>. <u>No error</u>
                         D   E

5. Liam and Dominic, both classically

trained storytellers, <u>were shocked</u> when
  A   B

<u>he</u> lost the annual "Big Liars" competition
C

in West Virginia <u>to a</u> high school student
                  D

with an overactive imagination. <u>No error</u>
                                E

6. When Pablo Picasso <u>unveiled</u> *Les*
                     A

Demoiselles d'Avignon in 1907, <u>it</u>
                              B

established himself <u>as one</u> of the <u>leaders of</u>
                  C   D

the Cubist movement. <u>No error</u>
                        E

Answers

1. D (E)	4. C (M)
2. A (M)	5. C (M)
3. D (H5)	6. B (M)

Illogical Connectors

When you're combining two independent clauses with a conjunction, make sure you're making a logical connection. Not all FANBOYS—for, and, nor, but, or, yet, so—are interchangeable. Pick the one that makes the most sense for your sentence.

E <u>Because Bjorn covered his principal's car with bacon, eggs and hashbrowns,</u> he was not suspended.

S ***Even though*** <u>Bjorn covered his principal's car with bacon, eggs and hashbrowns,</u> he was not suspended.

Logically, covering the principal's car with various breakfast items will not prevent one's suspension. We could choose a better connector, one that illustrates the contrasting relationship between the two events. Luckily, the principal revealed his apparent sense of humor and did not throw the book at Bjorn.

E <u>For months the public had eagerly anticipated the reunion tour of Led Zeppelin, and popular opinion changed quickly</u> when the band's lead singer was unable to hit the high notes in the first concert of the tour.

S

positive direction

For months the public had eagerly anticipated...

but popular opinion changed quickly...

negative direction

Logically, there is a contrast, or change of direction in this sentence. People were initially excited. Then people were not so excited. The ideal connector would be **but**, *rather than* **and**, *which conveys a sense of continuation.*

PULSE CHECK

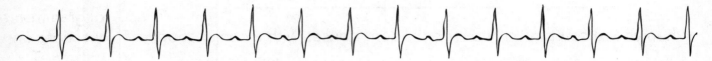

Identify the error (if present) in each of the following sentences.

1. Most people thought that Auntie Gladys, with her thick cockney accent, was born in London's West End, and she had never even left Kansas!

2. Maurice became personally responsible for the start of my shoe obsession, and, ten years ago, he bought me my first pair of Christian Louboutin heels.

3. Elmer's meticulously planned outdoor wedding had to be moved inside at the last minute, and it started to rain.

4. Abjit diligently trained for 8 months, but he was able to finish all 26 miles of the Boston Marathon.

5. According to the review of Guillermo's new novel, the plot was muddled and confusing, and the book was redeemed by its insightful character developments.

Answers

1. Most people thought that Auntie Gladys, with her thick cockney accent, was born in London's West End *even though* she had never even left Kansas!

2. Maurice became personally responsible for the start of my shoe obsession *when*, ten years ago, he bought me my first pair of Christian Louboutin heels.

3. Elmer's meticulously planned outdoor wedding had to be moved inside at the last minute *because* it started to rain.

4. Abjit diligently trained for 8 months, *so* he was able to finish all 26 miles of the Boston Marathon.

5. According to the review of Guillermo's new novel, the plot was muddled and confusing, *but* the book was redeemed by its insightful character developments.

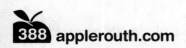

Illogical Connectors Practice Problems

Select the answer choice that produces the best sentence.

1. Gertrude Stein, famed American writer, <u>spent her final years and wrote novels,</u> plays and poetry in Paris.

   (A) spent her final years and wrote novels
   (B) spent her final years writing novels
   (C) spent her final years having written novels
   (D) spent her final years with writing novels
   (E) spent her final years in writing novels

2. In the movie *Titanic*, actress Kate Winslet <u>speaks with a convincing blue-blooded American accent even though she was</u> born in Reading, England.

   (A) speaks with a convincing blue-blooded American accent even though she was
   (B) speaks with a convincing blue-blooded American accent and she was
   (C) speaks with a convincing blue-blooded American accent but she was
   (D) speaks with a convincing blue-blooded American accent even having been
   (E) speaks with a convincing blue-blooded American accent though being

3. Breakdancing originated in South Bronx in the 1970s, <u>and many people assume that it originated in the 1980s.</u>

   (A) and many people assume that it originated in the 1980s
   (B) and many people assume it originating in the 1980s
   (C) but many people assuming it originated in the 1980s
   (D) and yet many people assume that it originated the 1980s
   (E) but many people assume that it originated in the 1980s

---

Select the underlined choice that indicates the sentence error.

---

4. The roadside fortune teller at the annual

   County Fair <u>told</u> Jarvis he would be
   　　　　　　　 A

   <u>exceedingly</u> <u>successful</u> in business <u>and</u>
   　　B　　　　　　 C　　　　　　　　　　 D

   he'd never be truly happy. <u>No error</u>
   　　　　　　　　　　　　　　　　 E

5. <u>Regardless</u> of her singular <u>talent for</u>
   　 A　　　　　　　　　　　　 B

   training pygmy hedgehogs <u>to play</u> the
   　　　　　　　　　　　　　　 C

   harmonica, Hortense <u>was invited</u> to host
   　　　　　　　　　　　　 D

   Animal Planet's new reality television

   series about exotic pet trainers. <u>No error</u>
   　　　　　　　　　　　　　　　　　 E

6. We generally <u>think of</u> Labradoodles as
   　　　　　　　 A

   <u>friendly, muppet-like</u> dogs <u>and</u> recent
   　　 B　　　　　　　　　　 C

   reports <u>have exposed</u> an underground
   　　　　　 D

   Labradoodle fighting ring in Vidalia, Georgia.

   <u>No error</u>
   　 E

Answers

1. B (E)   4. D (M)
2. A (M)   5. A (M)
3. E (H5)   6. C (M)

Plural Stays Plural

3%

As attractive as cold fusion seems, two things will never become one at any temperature on the SAT. Don't worry; it's not rocket science. The examples below will clue you in.

E According to Mr. Pentazopolous, both Stiva and Oleg are extremely talented at manipulating clay and <u>have a great future as a ceramic artist</u>.

S According to Mr. Pentazopolous, both Stiva and Oleg are extremely talented at manipulating clay and ***have great futures as ceramic artists***.

Unless Mr. P is also a geneticist and plans to splice Stiva and Oleg together, they will have their own futures as two, separate artists.

Modern technology has yet to discover how to turn two people into one.

E My history teacher is <u>constantly reminding us that as a student, only we are responsible</u> for what we learn from him.

S My history teacher is <u>constantly reminding us that **as students,** only we are responsible</u> for what we learn from him.

No matter how close you are with your classmates, you are still an individual. I'm sure the history teacher is fully aware of this, which is why he addresses all students in the plural form.

PULSE CHECK

Identify the error (if present) in each of the following sentences.

1. Wanting to become rich and famous, Seamus and Sinaede decided to run away from home to join the circus, learn the ancient art of fire-eating, and become a pop culture icon thanks to their new-found, fiery knowledge.

2. A model of perseverance, 19th-century Siamese twins Chang and Eng Bunker managed their own professional career, married, and had over 20 children between them.

3. As a senior member of the math team, Marco and Fatime were able to attend the annual High School Math Olympics in Lake Havasu City for free.

4. A first-time visitor to Disney World, the Smiths were thrilled to have earned enough money recycling soda cans to pay for their trip to the Magic Kingdom.

5. The son of a world-renowned Romanian haberdasher, Michel and Otis were afraid their fedoras would always be sub-par because they could not live up to their father's skill with felt.

Answers

1. Wanting to become rich and famous, Seamus and Sinaede decided to run away from home to join the circus, learn the ancient art of fire-eating, and become *pop culture icons* thanks to their new-found, fiery knowledge.

2. *Models of perseverance,* 19th-century Siamese twins Chang and Eng Bunker managed their own *professional careers*, married, and had over 20 children between them.

3. *As senior members of the math team,* Marco and Fatime were able to attend the annual High School Math Olympics in Lake Havasu City for free.

4. *First-time visitors* to Disney World, the Smiths were thrilled to have earned enough money recycling soda cans to pay for their trip to the Magic Kingdom.

5. *The sons of a* world-renowned Romanian haberdasher, Michel and Otis were afraid their fedoras would always be sub-par because they could not live up to their father's skill with felt.

Word Pairs

3%

of grammar
questions
on the SAT

Certain things just go together—like chocolate and peanut butter or popcorn and gummy bears. Below is a list of words that are as inseparable as Laurel and Hardy, Sonny and Cher, John and Yoko.

If you don't know who these famous couples are, you should look them up on Wikipedia.

Consider these words co-dependent:

> Either…Or
> Neither…Nor
> Both…And
> Not Only…But Also

E Wilbur not only plays the harmonica with his toes, <u>but he bakes a mean cherry streusel in addition</u>!

S Wilbur not only plays the harmonica with his toes, ***but he also bakes a mean cherry streusel*** !

Remember, **not only** *needs a* **but also** *to complete the recipe.*

E <u>Both my cousin Ona as well as her boyfriend Milo are</u> morally opposed to eating walnuts, claiming they are tiny bits of trees' souls.

S <u>***Both my cousin Ona and*** her boyfriend Milo are</u> morally opposed to eating walnuts, claiming they are tiny bits of trees' souls.

The simple, three-letter word **and** *is the perfect match for the* **both** *at the beginning of the sentence.*

PULSE CHECK

Identify the error (if present) in each of the following sentences.

1. For my nephew Lev's bar mitzvah we will have either a paintball party after the service and a trip to the zoo to see his favorite animals, the flamingoes.

2. Neither Panina or her twin sister Aninap would be in the school production of *Annie Get Your Gun* because they felt the choreography for the group dance numbers was too pedestrian.

3. Marie Curie was not only the first woman to win the Nobel Prize, and she is the only woman ever to win it twice.

4. Elizabeth Cady Stanton was both a suffragist but also a women's rights activist, fighting for property, income and employment rights for the women of her generation.

5. Both my uncle Herbert as well as his second wife Gertrude are fruititarians, refusing to eat anything but nuts and berries so as not to harm plants.

Answers
---

1. For my nephew Lev's bar mitzvah we will have *either* a paintball party after the service *or* a trip to the zoo to see his favorite animals, the flamingoes.

2. *Neither* Panina *nor* her twin sister Aninap would be in the school production of *Annie Get Your Gun* because they felt the choreography for the group dance numbers was too pedestrian.

3. Marie Curie was *not only* the first woman to win the Nobel Prize, *but also* the only woman ever to win it twice.

4. Elizabeth Cady Stanton was *both* a suffragist *and* a women's rights activist, fighting for property, income and employment rights for the women of her generation.

5. *Both* my uncle Herbert *and* his second wife Gertrude are fruititarians, refusing to eat anything but nuts and berries so as not to harm plants.

Passive Voice

1%

of grammar questions on the SAT

Don't be so passive! Write with conviction. In life, you'd rather **do** things than have them **done** to you. The same is true in writing.

E Rocco was unprepared for the negative response his first screenplay received <u>because of believing the dialogue was witty and incisive.</u>

S Rocco was unprepared for the negative response his first screenplay received <u>because **he believed** the dialogue was witty and incisive</u>.

Keep the verbs active. Verbs ending in –ing, should make bells go off in your head. They often indicate passive voice.

The SAT hates **passive voice**! So get off your couch and go do something!

E Performed first in 1913, <u>audiences were shocked by the rhythmic score and primitive setting of Igor Stravinsky's ballet *The Rite of Spring*</u>.

S Performed first in 1913, <u>***Igor Stravinsky's ballet The Rite of Spring shocked audiences with its rhythmic score and primitive setting***</u>.

Of course you were so distracted by the participle dangling within an inch of its life that you failed to notice the passive voice. Luckily if you fix one, you usually fix the other.

PULSE CHECK

Identify the error (if present) in each of the following sentences.

1. The word quixotic, from Cervantes' Spanish knight Don Quixote, is often attributed to dreamers of impossible dreams by skeptics.

2. The famous impressionist painting is being displayed by the local art gallery.

3. The safe door, lined with three feet of bullet-proof lead, was opened by the thief in a matter of seconds, thanks to industrial explosives.

4. After failing to adhere to curfew for the fourth night in a row, Toshiko was chastised and reprimanded by her mother.

5. The rigorous audition required for admittance into the highly competitive music program was failed by nearly seventy percent of applicants.

Answers

1. *Skeptics often attribute the word quixotic, from Cervantes' Spanish knight Don Quixote, to* dreamers of impossible dreams.

2. *The local art gallery is displaying the famous impressionist painting.*

3. *Thanks to industrial explosives, the thief opened the safe door, lined with three feet of bullet-proof lead, in a matter of seconds.*

4. *Toshiko's mother chastised and reprimanded Toshiko* for failing to adhere to curfew for the fourth night in a row.

5. *Nearly seventy percent of the applicants failed* the rigorous audition required for admittance into the highly competitive music program.

Awkward Structure

1%

of grammar
questions
on the SAT

Sometimes a sentence just sounds wrong; learn to trust your ear. If a sentence reminds you more of a cacophonous elementary school orchestra than an elegant philharmonic, chances are something is out of tune.

E Brutus advanced to the final round of the ice skating competition because <u>two consecutive triple axels were completed without flaws by him.</u>

S Brutus advanced to the final round of the ice skating competition because ***he flawlessly completed two consecutive triple axels.***

Remember: **short is sweet**. *Say what you have to say with as few words as possible without changing the meaning of the sentence.*

Words, words, words — and too many of them.

E Pavarti easily won the underwater basket weaving contest held by the local YMCA <u>the reason being she practiced diligently four hours every day.</u>

S Pavarti easily won the underwater basket weaving contest held by the local YMCA ***because she diligently practiced four hours every day.***

Don't be afraid to be simple, and watch the placement of your adverbs.

E Now that most of this year's tomato crop has been infected with salmonella, <u>Antonia has a problem what to make for her annual Spaghetti-fest.</u>

S Now that most of this year's tomato crop has been infected with salmonella, ***Antonia has a problem deciding what to make for her annual Spaghetti-fest***.

In this example, the SAT simply omitted a key word, making the structure awkward. Add it back in, and the sentence is complete.

PULSE CHECK

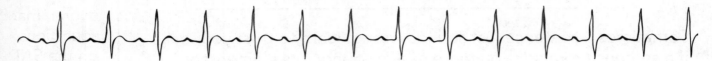

Identify the error (if present) in each of the following sentences.

1. The reason Chieu was elected is that of all the students who had run he had the cleverest and brightest posters.

2. Being that Santiago has won the Ballroom Dance Competition at the Elks Lounge for five years running, it is expected that he will be this year's favorite.

3. A strong, howling wind whipped the back porch door open; that is when Noori woke up.

4. Despite not wishing to be a published poet, Emily Dickinson remains one of America's favorite poets writing during the 19th century.

5. The reason being that there is a lack of interest in it, the seminar on the mating habits of the Congolese fruit fly has been canceled.

Answers

1. *Chieu was elected because, of all the students running,* he had the cleverest and brightest posters.

2. **Just say no to being. It is usually wrong.** *Having won the Ballroom Dance competition at the Elks Lounge for the past five years, Santiago is expected to be this year's favorite.*

3. **"That is when" and "that is why" will only bring you tears.** Noori woke up *when* a strong, howling wind whipped open the back porch door.

4. *Even though Emily Dickinson did not wish to be published,* she remains one of America's favorite 19th century poets.

5. The seminar on the mating habits of the Congolese fruit fly *has been canceled due to a lack of interest.*

Strategy

Improving Sentences

There will be 25 Improving Sentences questions on the SAT. This is more than any other type of grammar question. With these questions, you will have a sentence that will be partially underlined. You are to find the mistake in the underlined part and select that answer choice that best corrects the mistake. Answer choice (A) will always be a reproduction of the original sentence, and you should choose this answer only if there is no mistake in the sentence.

The key to these is to be skilled at listening. Do not rely on the answer choices. Cover up the answer choices. Read the sentence and listen closely for the error. If you hear it, ask yourself, "How would I correct this sentence?" Once you determine that, look to the options. If you do not hear an error, you will only look to see if the sentence can be stated in a shorter, more concise way.

The most essential thing to remember for this section is a simple, little rule:

> ## Shorter is sweeter. Simplicity is Golden.

When in doubt: if you are down to two answers and can't make the final decision, always go with the shorter answer.

65% of the time, the answer choice is either the shortest or the 2nd shortest answer. This is extremely mathematically significant. 65% is an incredible edge. Use it when in doubt.

If shorter wasn't sweeter, the shortest 2 choices would be correct only 40% of the time.

Tricks to remember

1 BE BRIEF! Often the shorter answers are correct.

2 DO NOT pick answers that change the meaning of the sentence.

3 ING IS NO GOOD! Be wary of words ending in '-ing'.

4 IF THERE IS NO ERROR, pick A. 'A' is correct 20% of the time.

How to Solve Improving Sentences Questions

Step 1   COVER the answers.

Step 2   Read the sentence and LISTEN FOR THE MISTAKE (if there is one) in the underlined part of the sentence. If you find a mistake, you can eliminate (A) as an answer choice.

Step 3   GIVE YOUR OWN CORRECTION for the mistake, and look for answers that closely match your correction. If none do, go to step 4.

Step 4   CROSS OUT answers that repeat the mistake in the original sentence.

Step 5   READ the sentence with the remaining answers, and CHOOSE the one that sounds best.

E   Michelangelo was celebrated in his time not only as a great sculptor and painter but also <u>he was celebrated for his writing of poetry</u>.

(A) he was celebrated for his writing of poetry
(B) having been celebrated for writing poetry
(C) celebrated for his writing poetry
(D) being a celebrated poet
(E) as a poet

S   Michelangelo was celebrated in his time not only as a great sculptor and painter but also **_as a poet_**.

(A) Awkward and wordy
(B) "ING" is generally wrong (80% of the time)
(C) Getting better
(D) Being is almost always wrong!
(E) is the best answer—and it is the shortest answer

Identifying Sentence Errors

There are 18 Identifying Sentence Error questions on the SAT. Identify the underlined section of the sentence that contains an error, and then bubble in the letter that corresponds to that section. All parts of a sentence that are not underlined are to be taken as correct. If there is no mistake in a sentence, bubble in (E). (E) will be the answer about 20% of the time (so expect 3-4 (E)s!).

Be at ease with Es.

How to Solve Identifying Sentence Errors Questions

Step 1 Read the sentence and LISTEN for the mistake. If you hear it, choose it and move on.

Step 2 Check the UNDERLINED parts for grammatical errors (look for the common errors discussed in the grammar review). When you find one, choose it and move on.

Step 3 If you've listened to the sentence and checked all underlined parts without finding an error, SELECT (E). Remember, "No error" will be the correct answer about 20% of the time!

The same rules apply for both sections. You have to work a little harder in the Improving Sentences section; all you have to do is find the error in the Identifying Errors section.

E Each of the poems <u>attributed to</u> William Shakespeare <u>has</u> <u>their own</u>
                             A   B   C

unique imagery and <u>application</u> of literary devices. <u>No error</u>
                           D   E

S *The correct answer is (**C**). (A) has no mistake ("to" is the correct preposition to be paired with attributed). (B) may sound funny, but the subject of our sentence is "Each," not poems. This means a singular verb is correct. (C), however, is a plural pronoun. If the pronoun is replacing "each," this is not correct—**their** should be **its**. We can stop here!*

Improving Paragraphs

There are only 6 of these questions on the SAT, and they tend to be pretty easy. They test no additional grammar other than that tested in the Identifying Errors/Improving Sentences sections, and they should be approached much as you would approach revising your own essays. Be especially careful to think about things like logical flow and use of conjunctions.

How to Solve Improving Paragraphs Questions

Step 1   READ the line before and after the line referenced in the question.

Step 2   COVER the answers and READ the first question.

Step 3   PROVIDE your own answer/revision.

Step 4   SEARCH for the answer that most nearly matches yours.

Big Picture Questions

The only exceptions are the Summary Questions such as "what would be the best way to end this paragraph?" or "what would be the best introduction for this paragraph?" Just like in Reading Comprehension—circle these questions and come back to them at the end after you have finished the other 5 questions.

E **Questions 30-35 are based on the following passage.**

(1) My mother has the uncanny ability to detect when someone is lying. (2) She can sniff out a liar a mile away. (3) When people try to stretch the truth or tell my mother a tall tale, appearing as if she is taking the bait, but in reality she is five steps ahead of them. (4) She always knows when deception is rearing its ugly head.

(5) Whether we tried to hide a report card with a failing grade or conceal a vase shattered by an errant baseball, she caught us every time. (6) She always knew, before we even opened our mouths, that we were lying. (7) At first I thought this ability was some kind of maternal super power. (8) I believed the talent extended only as far as our family. (9) Eventually, however, I became convinced that she could use her power on anybody.

(10) I remember the first time she would turn her nose for falsehoods to a complete stranger, something I would never forget. (11) We were waiting for our car at the local garage. (12) The mechanic spent 20 minutes presenting my mother with an expensive bill. (13) My mother knew it was way too high. (14) Then, looking the mechanic dead in the eye, she said, "You must be mistaken; I insist you go back and look again." (15) Five minutes later he returned with some rambling explanations and a significantly lower bill.

30. Which of the following is the best version of the underlined portion of sentence 3 (reproduced below)?

When people try to stretch the truth or <u>*tell my mother a tall tale, appearing*</u> *as if she is taking the bait, but in reality she is five steps ahead of them.*

(A) (as it is now)
(B) tell my mother a tall tale; it appears
(C) tell my mother a tall tale, it may appear
(D) telling my mother a tall tale, it appears
(E) telling my mother a tall tale, it may appear

31. In context, which of the following sentences is best inserted at the beginning of the second paragraph?

(A) My mother was always disappointed when my sister and I lied to her.
(B) My sister and I always told the truth in our house when we were younger.
(C) My mother believed honesty was always the best policy.
(D) As children, my sister and I experienced my mother's impressive talent first hand, and we never stood a chance.
(E) My sister and I made up stories when we were younger to pass the time.

32. An important strategy used in the second paragraph is to

    (A) elaborate a position that contradicts the essay's main point
    (B) use descriptive detail to support an earlier claim
    (C) objectively analyze a past situation
    (D) introduce a lighthearted digression
    (E) investigate a familial relationship

33. In context, which is the best version of sentence 10 (reproduced below) ?

    I remember the first time she would turn her nose for falsehoods to a complete stranger, something I would never forget.

    (A) I soon discovered she could turn her nose for falsehoods to a complete stranger, it was highly memorable for me.
    (B) Discovering that she could turn her nose for falsehoods to a complete stranger, this was memorable for me.
    (C) I will never forget the first time I watched her turn her nose for falsehoods to a complete stranger.
    (D) I was soon to discover how memorable it is when she first turned her nose for falsehoods to a complete stranger.
    (E) Watching her turn her nose for falsehoods to a complete stranger, which is something I will always remember.

34. In context, which version of sentences 12 and 13 best combines them into a single sentence (reproduced below) ?

    (12) The mechanic spent 20 minutes presenting my mother with an expensive bill.
    (13) My mother knew it was way too high.

    (A) The mechanic spent 20 minutes presenting my mother with an expensive bill, being way too high.
    (B) The mechanic, having spent 20 minutes presenting the expensive bill to my mother, which she knew was way too high.
    (C) Knowing it was way too high, the bill was presented to my mother by the mechanic in 20 minutes.
    (D) The mechanic spent 20 minutes presenting my mother with an expensive bill, which she knew was way too high.
    (E) The mechanic spent 20 minutes presenting my mother with an expensive bill, she knew it was way too high.

35. Which of the following if placed after sentence 15 would be the most effective concluding sentence for the essay?

    (A) It seemed there were some errors and miscalculations, which needed correcting.
    (B) In the future we would find a different kind of repair shop, where the customer was always right.
    (C) I was incredibly curious to know how my mom was able to recognize deception in complete strangers.
    (D) My mother paid for the lower-priced repairs, and we got in the car and made it home in time for dinner.
    (E) The mechanic found out what we knew all along: no one can pull one over on our mother.

S Questions 30-35 are based on the following passage.

(1) My mother has the uncanny ability to detect when someone is lying. (2) She can sniff out a liar a mile away. (3) When people try to stretch the truth or tell my mother a tall tale, appearing as if she is taking the bait, but in reality she is five steps ahead of them. (4) She always knows when deception is rearing its ugly head.

(5) Whether we tried to hide a report card with a failing grade or conceal a vase shattered by an errant baseball, she caught us every time. (6) She always knew, before we even opened our mouths, that we were lying. (7) At first I thought this ability was some kind of maternal super power. (8) I believed the talent extended only as far as our family. (9) Eventually, however, I became convinced that she could use her power on anybody.

(10) I remember the first time she would turn her nose for falsehoods to a complete stranger, something I would never forget. (11) We were waiting for our car at the local garage. (12) The mechanic spent 20 minutes presenting my mother with an expensive bill. (13) My mother knew it was way too high. (14) Then, looking the mechanic dead in the eye, she said, "You must be mistaken; I insist you go back and look again." (15) Five minutes later he returned with some rambling explanations and a significantly lower bill.

30. Which of the following is the best version of the underlined portion of sentence 3 (reproduced below)?

> **When people try to stretch the truth or tell my mother a tall tale, appearing as if she is taking the bait, but in reality she is five steps ahead of them.**

This is a straightforward sentence correction. Nothing fancy. We have a predictable ING issue to deal with.

(A) (as it is now)
The ING is the wrong way to begin this clause. Nix it.

(B) tell my mother a tall tale; it appears
*Semi-colons are good for separating 2 **Independent Clauses**, but our first clause is dependent, lacking a stand-alone Subject-Predicate Combo. Nix this one.*

(C) tell my mother a tall tale, it may appear
Dependent, Independent. Commas can do this. Looks good!

(D) telling my mother a tall tale, it appears
Another ING issue and a parallel issue. "When people try to stretch...and telling." We are mixing infinitives with -ings. Nix it.

(E) telling my mother a tall tale, it may appear
Same issue as (D). Not parallel. Nix it.

(C)

31. In context, which of the following sentences is best to inserted at the beginning of the second paragraph?

This question requires a deeper level of understanding of the content of the passage. This goes beyond grammar. We need to understand the flow of the paragraph and logical transitions.

Whenever you are working with transitions in a paragraph, you must take into account the logical links or "tags" that exist, connecting parts of a paragraph.

For example:
Sentence 1. We enjoyed our time with the Smiths.
Sentence 2. Their hospitality was legendary.

We have a link between these two sentences.
Sentence 1. We enjoyed our time with the Smiths.

Sentence 2. Their hospitality was legendary.

The word "Their" is a tag, and it is tied to previous content, "Smiths'." Whenever you are working with transition sentences, you must be very aware of the tags, the logical links to content before and after the transition sentence.

For Question 31—we are looking at the transition between the first and second paragraph, so we must naturally look at the last sentence of Paragraph 1 and the first sentence of Paragraph 2 to look for these tags.

She always knows when deception is rearing its ugly head.

TRANSITION Tags: She, we, deception

Whether we tried to hide a report card with a failing grade or conceal a vase shattered by an errant baseball, she caught us every time.

So our transition sentence needs to connect the tags. It needs to account for the "we" and the "she," and it needs to make a connection between the "deception" in the first sentence and the content ("hide" and "conceal") in the second sentence.

S *Let's see which sentences hold all of the tags and have no throw-aways.*

~ (A) My mother was always disappointed when my sister and I lied to her.
This accounts for the "she" and the "we" and the "deception", but adds a new element, disappointment. Maybe

(B) My sister and I always told the truth in our house when we were younger.
We have the "we" tag, but no "deception." Nix it.

(C) My mother believed honesty was always the best policy.
We don't have the "we" tag. Nix it.

~ (D) As children, my sister and I experienced my mother's impressive talent first hand, and we never stood a chance.
We have the "she" and the "we" tags. And we are referring to mother's talent. Not sure about the deception. Let's keep looking.

(E) My sister and I made up stories when we were younger to pass the time.
We don't have the "she" tag and there is no "deception". Nix it.

We must choose between (A) and (D). Let's read them in context and see which is a better transition.

(A) She always knows when deception is rearing its ugly head. **My mother was always** disappointed **when my sister and I lied to her.** Whether we tried to hide a report card with a failing grade or conceal a vase shattered by an errant baseball, she caught us every time.
We have "mother" which matches up with our "she," and we have "sister and I" which matches up with "we." We also have "lied to" which goes with "deception." However, we have "disappointed," which we don't see in either of our two original sentences.

(D) She always knows when deception is rearing its ugly head. **As children, my sister and I experienced my mother's impressive talent first hand, and we never stood a chance.** Whether we tried to hide a report card with a failing grade or conceal a vase shattered by an errant baseball, she caught us every time.
This is a much better transition. Everything matches up and we don't have any missing parts or throw-aways.

(D)

S 32. An important strategy used in the second paragraph is to

This type of question is straight out of Reading Comprehension. We've seen this before! We simply need to look at the second paragraph, identify the strategies used, and cross out all the throw-aways.

Let's look at the second paragraph to see what's happening.

(5) Whether we tried to hide a report card with a failing grade or conceal a vase shattered by an errant baseball, she caught us every time. (6) She always knew, before we even opened our mouths, that we were lying. (7) At first I thought this ability was some kind of maternal super power. (8) I believed the talent extended only as far as our family. (9) Eventually, however, I became convinced that she could use her power on anybody.

OK. The narrator and her sister hid "report cards" and "shattered vases," and "mom" always found out. They thought one thing—mom's power only worked on the family—but then discovered they were wrong. That's it; what a simple paragraph! Let's go to our choices.

(A) elaborate a position that contradicts the essay's main point
It does not contradict the essay's main point, that mom can detect lying. The paragraph actually continues to build on that theory. Nix it.

(B) use descriptive detail to support an earlier claim
It does use detail—"vases," "report cards," "maternal super power." And it also supports the claim that mom is hard to fool. Keep it.

(C) objectively analyze a past situation
The paragraph does look to the past, but there is clearly no objective analysis. There is our throw-away! Cross this one off!

(D) introduce a lighthearted digression
The content is neither lighthearted, nor is it a digression. Double throw-away.

(E) investigate a familial relationship
Investigate is a stretch, and it's not truly exploring the relationship. Nix it.

(B)

33. In context, which is the best version of sentence 10 (reproduced below) ?

I remember the first time she would turn her nose for falsehoods to a complete stranger, something I would never forget.

This is very much like a sentence correction question. Let's go to the choices.

S   (A) I soon discovered she could turn her nose for falsehoods to a complete stranger, it was highly memorable for me.

Independent, Independent = Run-on! Comma Splice! Cross it off!

(B) Discovering that she could turn her nose for falsehoods to a complete stranger, this was memorable for me.

"Discovering...this was"—wrong. Our modifier is dangling! It would be correct if it looked like "Discovering...I found this to be memorable." Kick it to the curb!

(C) I will never forget the first time I watched her turn her nose for falsehoods to a complete stranger.

There is nothing blatantly incorrect grammar-wise in this sentence. Let's keep it.

(D) I was soon to discover how memorable it is when she first turned her nose for falsehoods to a complete stranger.

*Verb Tense error! Remember the past stays past tense. It would be correct if it were, "How memorable it **was**. Nix it.*

(E) Watching her turn her nose for falsehoods to a complete stranger, which is something I will always remember.

*This is a total sentence fragment. Dependent, Dependent means there is no complete sentence. Remember: Watch out for the **wicked which**! We don't have a stand-alone sentence here. This answer cannot be correct either.*

(C)

34. In context, which version of sentences 12 and 13 best combines them into a single sentence (reproduced below)?

(12) The mechanic spent 20 minutes presenting my mother with an expensive bill. (13) My mother knew it was way too high.

This is another sentence correction type of question. Let's dive in.

(A) The mechanic spent 20 minutes presenting my mother with an expensive bill, being way too high.

BEING!!! This is hardly ever right, and it is definitely not right here. Next!

(B) The mechanic, having spent 20 minutes presenting the expensive bill to my mother, which she knew was way too high.

*Watch out for the -ING and the **wicked which**! This is a fragment. Nix it.*

(C) Knowing it was way too high, the bill was presented to my mother by the mechanic in 20 minutes.

Our modifier is dangling! "Knowing..., the bill." The bill did not know anything. It is the mother who knows something. Cross it off!

(D) The mechanic spent 20 minutes presenting my mother with an expensive bill, which she knew was way too high.

Nothing grammatically wrong here.

(E) The mechanic spent 20 minutes presenting my mother with an expensive bill, she knew it was way too high.

Independent clause, Independent clause. This is a comma splice and a run-on.

(D)

S 35. Which of the following if placed after sentence 15 would be the most effective concluding sentence for the essay?

A good conclusion must be on topic and wrap things up. What's our focus: mother knows how to spot deception. So a concluding sentence would connect to this idea.

(A) It seemed there were some errors and miscalculations, which needed correcting.

This one leaves you hanging. It closes the incident in the last paragraph with the mechanic, but it does not conclude the whole passage. We can do better.

(B) In the future we would find a different kind of repair shop, where the customer was always right.

This does not even address the topic. Nix it.

(C) I was incredibly curious to know how my mom was able to recognize deception in complete strangers.

This sentence is on the topic of deception, but it really is not a great summary or conclusion. Let's keep looking.

(D) My mother paid for the lower-priced repairs, and we got in the car and made it home in time for dinner.

Again—this closes the incident, but it gives no summary statement or conclusion for the whole passage. Let's keep looking.

(E) The mechanic found out what we knew all along: no one can pull one over on our mother.

Perfect! It's about deception—"pulling one over"—and it also addresses the incident with the mechanic. This effectively closes the final paragraph and brings us back to our main point—Mom's ability to spot deception. This is a perfect concluding sentence.

(E)

Revising Paragraphs Practice Problems

Select the best answer to the questions below.

Questions 30 – 35 refer to the following passage.

(1) A strange thing is happening at the edge of Poul Bjerge's forest; a remote and modest grove near Narsarsuaq, Greenland. (2) Its four oldest trees, in fact the four oldest pine trees in Greenland, are waking up. (3) Having lapsed into stately, sleepy old age over 100 years ago, these pines exhibited new sprinklings of green at their tops, as if someone has glued on fresh needles. (4) Botanists are surprised at this new growth since Greenland has historically been a relatively infertile country. (5) Despite its massive size, Greenland only has 51 farms. (6) They are all sheep farms, although one man is trying to raise cattle; he has 22 cows. (7) Because there are so few farms, the majority of vegetables consumed in Greenland are imported from Denmark.

(8) In addition, farmers and researchers in Greenland alike are now beginning to have success in growing vegetables on the large island north of sixty degrees latitude. (9) Thanks to increasing temperatures in Greenland, the New York Times reports, "A Greenlandic supermarket is stocking locally grown cauliflower, broccoli and cabbage this year for the first time."

(10) Eight sheep ranchers have begun growing potatoes commercially, while five more are experimenting with other vegetables. (11) And Kenneth Hoeg, the region's chief agriculture adviser, says he does not see why southern Greenland cannot eventually be full of vegetable farms and viable forests." (12) I suppose Greenland's blooming agricultural activity ought to be added to the list of advantages of global warming.

30. Which of the following is the best version of the underlined portion of sentence 1 (reproduced below)?

    A strange thing is happening at the edge of Poul Bjerge's <u>forest; a remote and modest grove</u> near Narsarsuaq, Greenland.

    (A) (as it is now)
    (B) forest. A remote and modest grove
    (C) forest, being a remote and modest grove
    (D) forest, a remote and modest grove
    (E) forest, and it is a remote and modest grove

31. Which is of the following revisions is most needed in of sentence 3 (reproduced below)?

    Having lapsed into stately, sleepy old age over 100 years ago, these pines exhibited new sprinklings of green at their tops, as if someone has glued on fresh needles.

    (A) Insert "Despite" at the beginning
    (B) Change "exhibited" to "are exhibiting"
    (C) Change "Having lapsed into stately" to "After lapsing into stately"
    (D) Change "new sprinklings of green" to "new green sprinklings"
    (E) Insert "now" before "glued"

32. In context, which of the following is the best replacement for "In addition" in sentence 8?

    (A) As a result
    (B) Therefore
    (C) Alternately
    (D) Consequently
    (E) However

33. Which of the following sentences would most effectively be placed after sentence 9 ?

    (A) The higher temperatures are tempting long-time ranchers to try their hand at growing vegetables.
    (B) Greenlanders are able to buy a greater variety of local, organically grown produce these days.
    (C) Greenland's supermarket industry is thriving now that there is greater demand for exotic vegetables.
    (D) Over the past five years, the quantity of produce imported into Greenland has fallen sharply.
    (E) The benefits of recent warmer temperatures are not limited to farming alone; Greenland has seen an increased interest in outdoor youth activities as well.

34. Of the following, which is the best revision of sentence 13 (reproduced below) ?

    I suppose Greenland's blooming agricultural activity ought to be added to the list of advantages of global warming.

    (A) Correct as is.
    (B) Change "I suppose" to "In general,"
    (C) Change "ought to" to "will"
    (D) Change "I suppose" to "Perhaps"
    (E) Delete "I suppose"

35. Of the following, which sentence should be deleted because it interrupts the logical development of the passage?

    (A) Sentence 1
    (B) Sentence 2
    (C) Sentence 6
    (D) Sentence 9
    (E) Sentence 10

Answers

---

30. D (E)	33. A (M)
31. B (E)	34. D (M)
32. E (E)	35. C (E)

The Short List

So, now you know all of the grammar concepts consistently tested on the SAT. Before you move on to Math, however, take a moment and look over The Short List on the following pages. It's a quick review of the main grammar tricks/rules you'll need and some catchy phrases to help you remember them easily.

1 Short is **SWEET**. Simple is Golden.

2 ING **Is No Good**. Most of the time if you see a verb with an ING, it is incorrect. Very often ING is tied to passive voice or sentence fragments, and it would be far simpler to swap it for the infinitive.

3 **BEING** is not believing. The word Being is wrong nearly every time. Cross it off!

4 Beware of the Ambiguous **IT** or the unclear **THEY**. These are often tied to pronoun reference errors. You will ask yourself: What the heck is it? And who are they?

5 **Watch your SUBJECT/VERB AGREEMENT!** What is your subject? Cross out all the subordinate junk in the way.

6 **PLURAL** subjects stay **PLURAL**. You won't find students becoming a teacher. You will find students becoming teachers.

7 **I** do things to you. You did this to **ME**. I is the subject; me is the object.

8 Compare Apples to Apples and Oranges to Oranges. You must have **PROPER COMPARISONS**. People to People; Things to Things.

9 **WHERE'S THE VERB?** Watch out for the fragments where there is no independent predicate but a dependent one instead. ING is often the culprit here.

10 **Proper lists** are essential. You can list nouns or verbs, but you can't mix it up (N,N,N, or V,V,V, never N,N,V).

11 **THIS IS WHEN, THIS IS WHERE**: These are almost always wrong.

12 Keep your past outta my present – watch your **VERB TENSES.**

13 **PARALLEL** structure is the rule for verbs, prepositions, and lists. The majority of parallel mistakes deal with –ING verbs and Infinitives (To ___).

14 Avoid **FALSE CAUSALITY**: What is causing what? Check your logic.

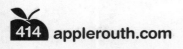

Writing Mantras

Below is a series of Mantras or sayings that will help you remember the key strategies you have learned in this section. Mantras are meant to be repeated over and over in a soothing rhythm that will calm you and help trigger your memory. Repeat these to yourself when you are stuck in traffic, on your way to study hall or in the shower. Know them; love them; use them.

Essay

- Focus on the **ASSIGNMENT**, not the prompt.

- Structure your thoughts before you write.

- **PICK** a side and **STICK** with it.

- The AFFIRMATIVE is usually the easiest side to argue.

- Rephrase your **THESIS** in every paragraph.

- Use **SPECIFIC, CONCRETE DETAILS**: names, dates, events, figures.

- Fill both pages.

- Vary your **SENTENCE STRUCTURE**.
- Use your **VOCABULARY** skillfully.
- **INTRO** and **CLOSING** are a must.

Grammar

- **CROSS OUT** all unnecessary information.

- When in doubt, **TRUST YOUR EAR.**

- **BE AT EASE WITH Es**. Sometimes there is No Error.
- **SHORTER** answers have an edge.
- SOLVE IT YOURSELF FIRST.
- For paragraph revisions, go straight to the questions.

- In paragraph revisions, look for **LOGICAL TAGS** to keep the order straight.

MATH

Math

Just as logic and analysis are the keys to success on SAT Reading Comprehension, critical reading skills are essential to success on SAT Math.

The actual math assessed by the SAT is not particularly difficult: Algebra 1, Geometry, a handful of Algebra 2 concepts. Most of these concepts you learned in 8th and 9th grade. What makes the math so challenging is the manner in which it is presented. You must decode each problem and translate the words into equations you can work with.

After you've worked a few math problems, you will notice the SAT is trying to trick you with *reading* errors as well as math errors. Did you catch that underlined word? Did you realize you are solving for everything EXCEPT the variable or that you are solving for $x + 2$ rather than for x? The SAT is so sneaky! Reading traps are stealthily hidden throughout the Math section.

Active Reading

Just as with Reading Comprehension, you will never sit back and passively read a problem on the Math section. You read a line, and then you translate it onto paper in a structured, organized way. You move on to the next line. You stop and translate. One line at a time you make your way through the problem, translating, structuring and setting things up as you go. The set-up is more than 50% of the formula for success.

Anytime you come across an <u>underlined</u>, ALL CAPS (EXCEPT, NOT), or **bold word**, circle it.

Anytime you are given new data for a **diagram** or **chart**, immediately fill that information in.

When you find out what you are **solving** for, circle it.

$$3x + y = ?$$

When you come across a **number** or a **variable** in the problem text, write it down.

The key is to move as quickly as possible from the cumbersome SAT text to your own efficient problem solving space. Narrow down those six lines of text into a structured two line mathematical equation and never look back to that confusing pile of words designed to distract and delay you.

Structure is key: Set up and solve problems systematically

Solve each problem in a linear fashion, working left to right, top to bottom, always keeping in mind what you are solving for. Do all of your work in your problem solving space and refrain from doing any computations in your head.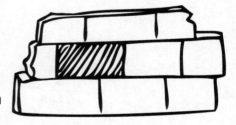
Leave a perfect, written record of your work on the page: this is the surest way to avoid costly careless errors.

Be more flexible and creative in your approach

Every SAT problem can be solved using a number of different approaches. There is no "right way" to solve any SAT problem. Learn to experiment and find the approach that works best for you. You can tackle a problem head on with algebra, or graph it on your calculator, or pick numbers and move away from the variables, or work backwards, plugging in the answer choices. If you get stuck, simply move to the next approach, rather than spinning your wheels and wasting valuable time.

Decode the language of the SAT

Learn the short cuts and problem cues of the SAT. When you see

- "in terms of," that translates to "pick numbers"
- a bizarre shape, look for a right triangle
- $a^2 - b^2$, instantly translate that to $(a + b) \times (a - b)$
- "average," you must find the sum of the terms
- 2 fractions across an equal sign, you must cross multiply

These are a small sample of the clues you must come to anticipate on the SAT. Once you learn the familiar patterns, you will see them again and again.

Look for the elegant solution

On most problems, the SAT writers set you up for elegant solutions that will save you lots of time and effort. To find the elegant solution you must adjust your thinking. Practice seeing the problem differently. Instead of writing out 30 terms, see if there's a more efficient way to solve the problem. Keep you eyes open for the one pivotal step that will allow you to skip all the other steps.

> "Wait! These two equations are multiples of each other."
> "If I drop in a line here, I'll create a 3, 4, 5 triangle: I know how to solve that!"

"If I plug the point back into the equation, I'll have the answer."
"Do I really need to write out 20 terms? No, wait. There's the repeat in the pattern. Aha!"

When you find that elegant step, all of your work is done almost instantly. Thinking creatively will help you save time and attain a higher score.

Use your resources

- Write all over your test booklet.
- Use the answer choices to work backwards and solve the hardest problems.
- Fill in and use all of your charts, tables and graphs.
- When diagrams are drawn to scale, you can use them to measure and solve problems.
- Your Scantron sheet can become a ruler or help you measure angles!
- Use your calculator whenever you can: for graphing, converting fractions, computing, remembering exponent rules and much more.

Use common sense to check your answers

Review your answers to ensure they make sense. You can get so caught up in your own problem solving that you don't realize you have strayed way off course. You may take one wrong turn early in the problem and arrive at an answer that is utterly impossible. Do a quick **sanity check**.

Ask yourself:

- "Does this make sense?"
- "Is this logical?"
- "Is this possible?"

Taking a moment to step back and shift your perspective can help you avoid many careless errors.

Focus on the math concepts you need: Be strategic with this book

The test writers tend to privilege certain math concepts and test them more frequently than others. You will see very few square roots on the SAT, but numerous exponents; few composite functions, but many triangle problems. We tried to be exhaustive in our approach, covering 43 concepts you could potentially see on the SAT. However, many of these concepts will not occur on every single SAT.

Know your goal

Your score goal should help you determine where to invest your time and energy. If you are aiming for a 770, you must be ready for even the rarest of problem type. However, if you are aiming for a 550, don't worry about Distance = Rate × Time questions: these account for only 0.4% of the questions on the SAT

(you'll see one every 5 tests). Instead, go for the big hitters: triangles, translation, sequences, picking numbers, etc. The top 15 concepts account for 82% of questions on the SAT; the top 8 concepts account for over 50% of the questions. Be discriminating and strategic in how you invest your time and which sections you study. Use your practice tests as your guides. Focus where you are weak and where you will get the most bang for your study buck.

Math Problem Type Breakdown

Most Frequently Occuring Problem Types	Percentage of Problems*	Average Number per Test
Arithmetic	**40%**	**21.60**
Properties of Numbers	6%	3.24
Art of Translation	6%	3.24
Sequences	4%	2.16
Percentages	4%	2.16
Exponents	4%	2.16
Fractions	3%	1.62
Ratios	2%	1.08
Absolute Value	2%	1.08
Inequalities	2%	1.08
Probability	2%	1.08
Logic	2%	1.08
Miscellaneous	3%	1.62
Algebra	**31%**	**16.74**
Charts, Tables and Graphs	8%	4.32
Complex Word Problems	5%	2.70

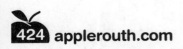

Most Frequently Occuring Problem Types	Percentage of Problems*	Average Number per Test
Multiple Equations	4%	2.16
Mean, Median and Mode	4%	2.16
Function Notation	4%	2.16
Wacked-Out Functions	2%	1.08
Miscellaneous	4%	2.16
Geometry	**44%**	**23.76**
Perimeter, Area and Volume	10%	5.40
Triangles	7%	3.78
Circles	6%	3.24
Angles	5%	2.70
Coordinate Systems	5%	2.70
Slope	4%	2.16
Number Lines	3%	1.62
Miscellaneous	4%	2.16
Strategy	**19%**	**10.26**
Picking Numbers	12%	6.48
Working Backwards	7%	3.78

*Problem percentages do not sum to 100% as certain problems test multiple concepts, e.g. a triangle problem that tests algebra concepts would be counted in both the algebra and geometry categories.

Student-produced Response Questions

These questions, also referred to as *grid-in* questions, require you to bubble in your own answer instead of choosing an answer (A) through (E). Below are the SAT instructions for answering these questions. Familiarize yourself with these directions before you sit down to take the test. Also, remember to **ALWAYS GUESS** on these questions. You lose no points for getting one of these wrong. **ALWAYS GUESS!**

Directions: For Student-Produced Response questions 9-18, use the grids at the bottom of the answer sheet page where you have already answered questions 1-8.

The last 10 questions require you to solve the problem and record your answer by bubbling the circles in the special grid on the answer sheet. You may use any fee space for scratchwork.

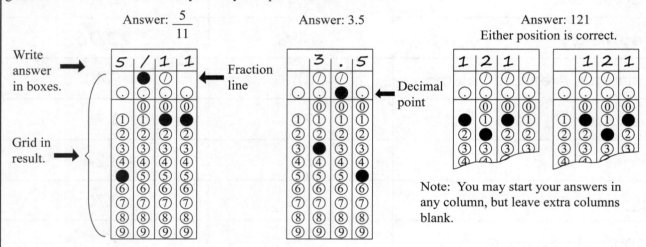

• Bubble only one circle in any column.

• The machine will only give you credit if you fill in the circles correctly.

• Although not required, you should write your answer in the boxes at the top of the columns. This will help you fill in the circles accurately.

• Some problems may have more than one correct answer. However, only grid one answer.

• All answers except zero (0) are positive.

• Mixed Numbers such as $4\frac{1}{2}$ must be gridded as 4.5 or 9/2. (If [4|1|/|2] is gridded, it will be interpreted as $\frac{41}{2}$ not $4\frac{1}{2}$.)

Note: You may start your answers in any column, but leave extra columns blank.

Decimal Answers: If your answer is a decimal with more digits than spaces on the grid you can either round or shorten it, but it must fill up the entire grid. For example, if your answer is 0.6666…, you should mark your result as either .666 or .667. A less accurate answer such as .66 or .67 will be scored as incorrect.

Acceptable ways to grid $\frac{2}{3}$ are:

Angles

5%

of all math
questions
on the SAT

General Rules:

For lines: On line A, $\angle 1 + \angle 2 + \angle 3 = 180°$.
There are 180° on each side of a straight line.

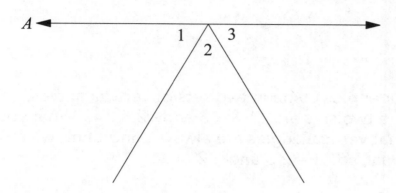

For triangles: In triangle *EFG*, $\angle e + \angle f + \angle g = 180°$.
There are 180° in any triangle.

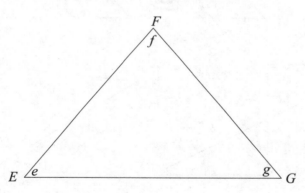

For four-sided figures: In quadrilateral *ABCD*, $\angle a + \angle b + \angle c + \angle d = 360°$.
There are 360° in any quadrilateral.

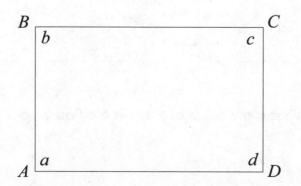

Vertical Angles

Vertical angles occur whenever two lines cross and form four angles.

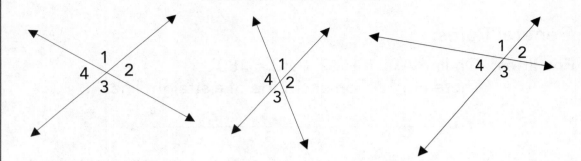

Those four angles come in two sets of vertical angles. In these figures, the two sets are ∠1 & ∠3 and ∠2 & ∠4. What you must know is that vertical angles are always congruent, which just means equal, so ∠1 = ∠3 and ∠2 = ∠4.

That goes for line segments that cross in shapes as well. So in the diagrams below,

$$\angle a = \angle b$$

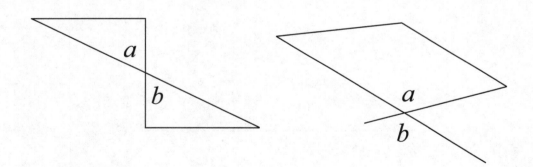

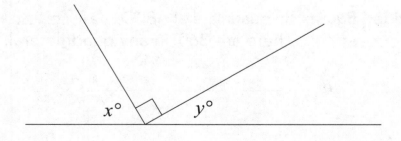

What is the value of x + y in the figure above?

S Because a line always has 180° on either side, $x + y = 180 - 90 =$ **(90°)**.

E

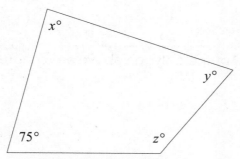

In the quadrilateral above, $x + y + z = $?

S All quadrilaterals (four-sided figures) have four angles that always add up to 360°.

So: $x + y + z + 75 = 360°$

$x + y + z = 360° - 75°$

$x + y + z =$ **(285°)**

Good news! There's no need to worry about complex shapes; if you can remember that triangles have 180° and quadrilaterals have 360°, all you have to do is split complex shapes into triangles and rectangles.

Or you can simply use the formula

$$(n - 2) \times 180$$

where n is the number of sides, to find the total internal degrees for any shape! Solve whichever way is easiest for you.

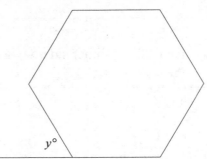

If all interior angles of the polygon above are congruent, what is the value of *y*?

For all you math machines:

We can use the formula for the sum of the interior angles of a polygon with *n* sides.

$(n - 2) \times 180$

(A) 60
(B) 72
(C) 75
(D) 105
(E) 120

S We can use the fact that there are 180° on one side of a line to get *y*. All we have to do is find the measure of the interior angle on the same line as *y*.

If you can't remember the formula we just learned, we can simply break the shape into triangles and rectangles.

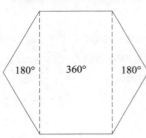

Now it's easy.
The sum of the interior angles:
$180° + 360° + 180° = \boxed{720°}$

We know that all interior angles of the polygon above are **congruent** (AKA the same).

$a = b = c = d = e = f$

We also know that:

$a + b + c + d + e + f = 720°$

So, $\dfrac{720}{6} = 120°$

The measure of each interior angle is 120°.

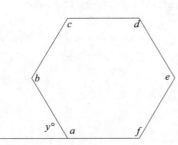

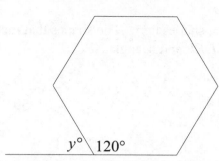

Degrees on a line   –   degrees of interior angle   = y

    $180°$ – $120°$ = $\boxed{60°}$

Our answer is **(A)**.

One note about breaking up polygons: the lines you draw CANNOT cross. When your lines intersect they create central angles that are not part of the original shape.

This would give us six triangles.
$6(180°) = 1080°$, which is $360°$ too many because of those pesky central angles.

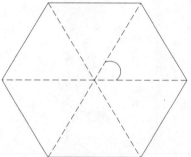

E

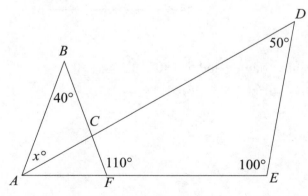

Note: Figure not drawn to scale.

In the figure above, what is the value of *x* ?

Remember, vertical angles are congruent, so the third angle in triangle *ABC* is 100°.

S We've got to see all of the shapes here. The shapes that include angles we know are quadrilateral *CDEF* and triangle *ABC*.

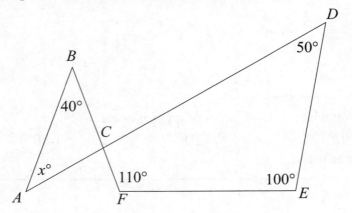

The angles in any quadrilaterals add to 360°.
The missing angle in quadrilateral *CDEF* is

$$360° - 50° - 100° - 110° = \boxed{100°}$$

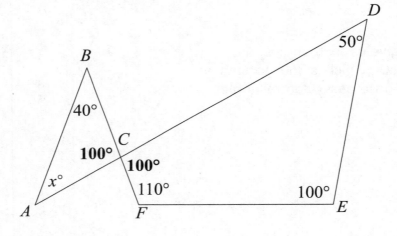

The angles in any triangle add to 180°.

$$x = 180° - 40° - 100° = \boxed{40°}$$

E

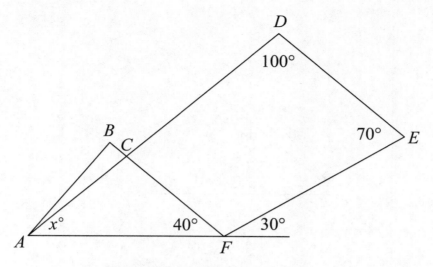

Note: Figure not drawn to scale.

What is the value of *x* in the figure above?

(A)   40°
(B)   75°
(C)   80°
(D) 100°
(E) 110°

S This one incorporates pretty much everything we've covered.

$$\angle CFE = 180° - 40° - 30° = 110°.$$

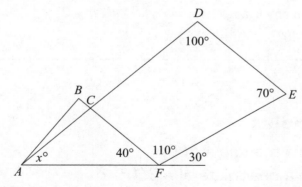

The missing angle, $\angle DCF$, in quadrilateral *CDEF* is

$$360° - 70° - 100° - 110° = \boxed{80°.}$$

All quadrilaterals have 360°.

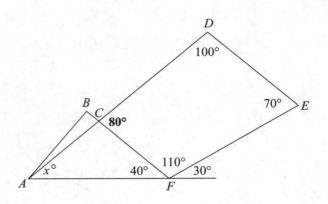

The missing angle, $\angle ACF$, in triangle ACF is
$$180° - 80° = \boxed{100°}$$

$\angle ACF$ is adjacent to $\angle DCF$, and adjacent angles add up to 180°.

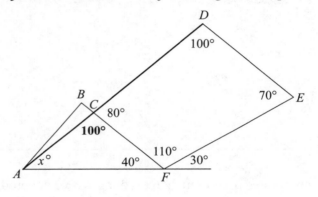

There are 180° in any triangle, so
$$x = 180° - 40° - 100° = \boxed{\textbf{40°}}, \textbf{(A)}$$

Summary of Angles

1. Total of angles in a triangle = 180°
2. Total of angles in a quadrilateral = 360°
3. Angles on one side of a line = 180°
4. Vertical angles are equal

Parallel Lines and Corresponding Angles

The rules are easy:
When Line $l \parallel m$

$\angle 1 = \angle 3 = \angle A = \angle C$

$\angle 2 = \angle 4 = \angle B = \angle D$

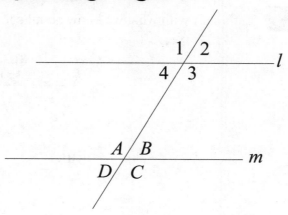

small = small

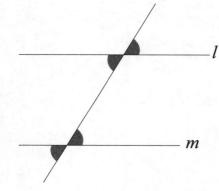

BIG = BIG

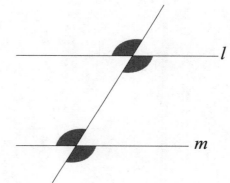

E

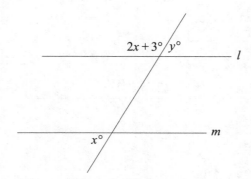

Note: Figure not drawn to scale.

In the figure above, $l \parallel m$. What is the value of y?

(A) 40
(B) 59
(C) 72
(D) 177
(E) 180

S Let's start with what we know about parallel lines:

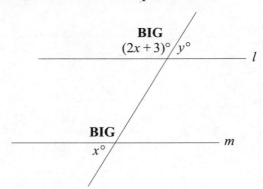

BIG = BIG, so all of the big angles = (2x + 3)°.

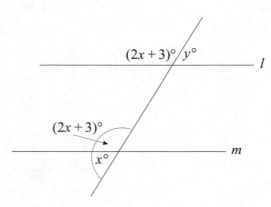

There are 180° on one side of a line, so

$$(2x + 3) + x = 180$$
$$3x + 3 = 180$$
$$3x = 177$$
$$x = \boxed{59}$$

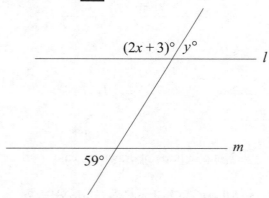

What is the value of *y* ?

small = small
$$x = y = \enclose{circle}{59} , \textbf{(B)}$$

Angles Practice Problems

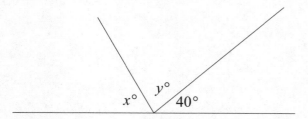

1. What is the value of $x + y$ in the figure above?

(A) 120
(B) 140
(C) 150
(D) 160
(E) 170

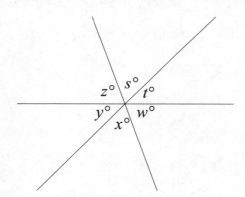

Note: Figure not drawn to scale.

2. In the figure above, $t = 45$ and $z = 70$. What is the value of x ?

(A) 50
(B) 65
(C) 90
(D) 135
(E) 165

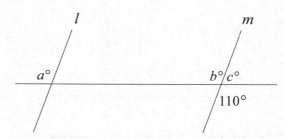

Note: Figure not drawn to scale.

3. In the figure above, $l \parallel m$. What is the value of $a + b + c$?

(A) 180
(B) 240
(C) 260
(D) 290
(E) 300

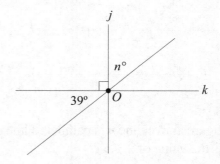

4. In the figure above, line j is perpendicular to line k, and the two intersect at O. What is the value of n ?

(A) 39
(B) 47
(C) 51
(D) 53
(E) 61

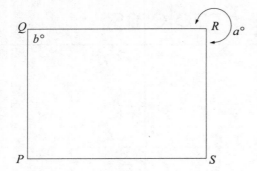

5. In the figure above, *PQRS* is a parallelogram. If *a* = 271, what is the value of *b* ?

(A) 85
(B) 89
(C) 90
(D) 91
(E) 95

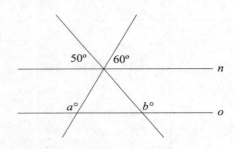

6. In the figure above, line *n* is parallel to line *o*. What is the value of *a* + *b* ?

(A) 110
(B) 180
(C) 210
(D) 230
(E) 250

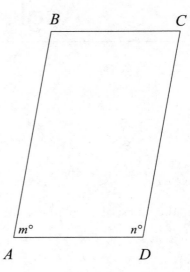

7. In the figure above, *ABCD* is a parallelogram. What is the value of *m* + *n* ?

(A) 90
(B) 115
(C) 180
(D) 270
(E) 360

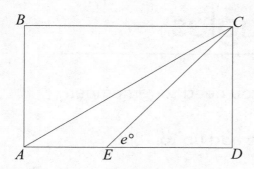

8. In the figure above, *ABCD* is a rectangle and *CD* = *ED*. What is the value of *e* ?

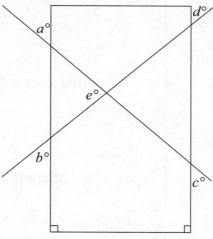

9. In the figure above, which of the following must equal 360°?

(A) $a + b + c + d$
(B) $a + b + c + d + e$
(C) $a + b + c + d + 2e$
(D) $2a + 2b + 2c + 2d$
(E) $2a + 2b + 2c + 2d + 2e$

Triangles

There are some triangle basics you need to remember.

1 The three angles of a triangle add up to 180°.

2 The longest side is always opposite the largest angle.

3 The area is ½ base × height.

Isosceles Triangle

Isosceles Triangles have two equal sides. The key is to remember that if two sides are equal, then the angles opposite them are equal (and if two angles of a triangle are equal, you know the two sides opposite them are also equal).

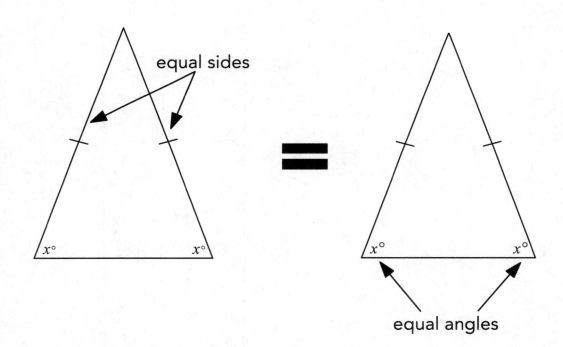

Equilateral Triangle

Equilateral Triangles have 3 equal sides and 3 equal angles. Each angle measures 60°.

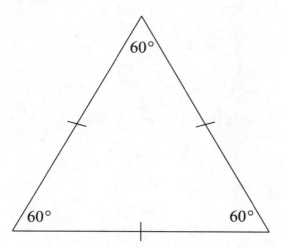

Side Lengths

If you add the lengths of two of the sides of any triangle together, they are always bigger than the length of the third side. Or, in math: $A + B > C$ for every triangle.

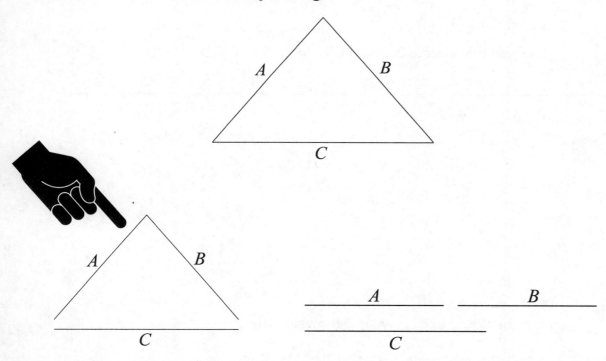

Imagine pushing the triangle down and flattening the sides. Two sides added together must be longer than the third side.

E

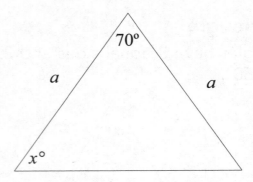

What is the value of x in the triangle above?

S Because 2 sides have length *a*, we know this is an isosceles triangle, which means the tirangle also has 2 equal angles.

$$x + x + 70 = 180$$
$$2x = 110$$
$$x = \frac{110}{2}$$
$$x = \circled{55}$$

Use your calculator to double check. 55 + 55 + 70 = 180.

Isosceles triangle: two equal sides, two equal angles.

E

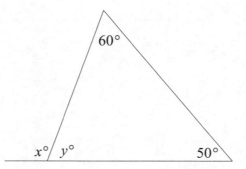

In the figure above, what is the value of x ?

(A) 30
(B) 50
(C) 60
(D) 110
(E) 120

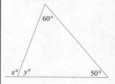

S

$$180 - 60 - 50 = 70 = y$$

x and y share a line, so:

$$x + y = 180°.$$
$$x + 70 = 180$$
$$x = \boxed{110}$$

E

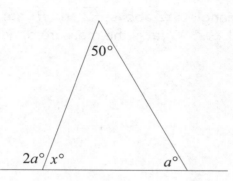

What is the value of x in the figure above?

S For our triangle,

$$180° = 50° + x + a$$

For our line,

$$180° = x + 2a$$
$$50° + x + a = 180° = x + 2a$$

Remember, when you have two equations that are equal to the same thing, you can set them equal to each other.

$$50° + x + a = x + 2a$$
$$50° + x + a = x + a + a$$
$$\boxed{50°} = a$$

$$180° = 50° + x + 50°$$
$$180 - 100 = x$$
$$\boxed{80} = x$$

E

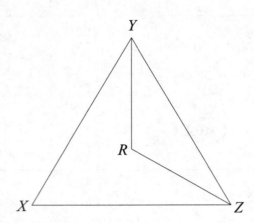

In equilateral triangle *XYZ* above, $\overline{RZ}$ and $\overline{RY}$ are the angle bisectors of angles *XZY* and *XYZ*. What is the measure of angle *YRZ*?

(A) 30°
(B) 60°
(C) 70°
(D) 90°
(E) 120°

S *XYZ* is equilateral, so all three angles are 60°.

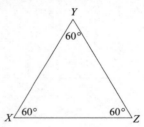

$\overline{RZ}$ and $\overline{RY}$ are angle bisectors, which mean they cut angle *XZY* and angle *XYZ* in half, so angles *RZY* and angle *RYZ* are both 30°.

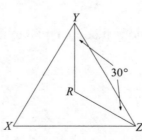 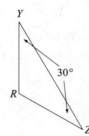

Like all triangles, △*RYZ* has 180°.

Angle *YRZ* = 180 − 30 − 30 = **120°**, **(E)**

Right Triangles

When you see the right angle symbol, think Pythagorean Theorem!

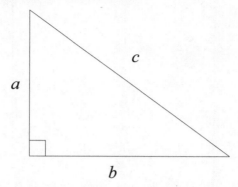

Pythagorean Theorem

$$a^2 + b^2 = c^2$$

There are some special right triangles you must know.

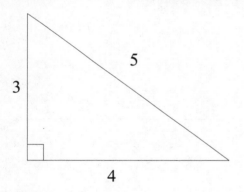

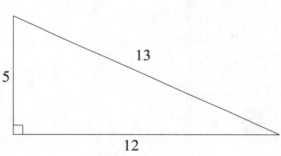

Look out for multiples of these (e.g. 6:8:10 or 10:24:26).

There are also special side relationships created by certain angles.

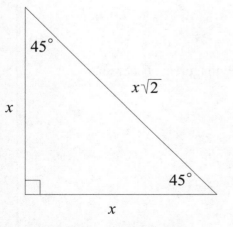

45°– 45°– 90° Triangle

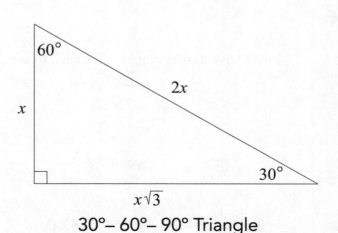

30°– 60°– 90° Triangle

The SAT gives you these triangles at the beginning of every Math section.

So, if x = 2

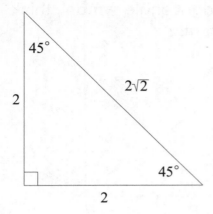

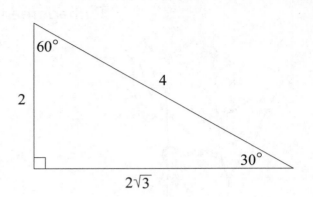

E What is the perimeter of a right triangle whose legs have lengths 12 and 16?

(A) 12
(B) 16
(C) 20
(D) 48
(E) 428

If you see that this is just a multiple of the 3-4-5 right triangle, you can multiply each side by 4, and you have c = 5(4) = 20.

S First, let's draw the triangle.

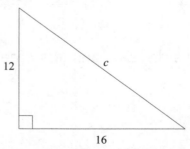

We have a right triangle. We need to use the Pythagorean Theorem.

$$a^2 + b^2 = c^2$$
$$12^2 + 16^2 = c^2$$
$$144 + 256 = c^2$$
$$400 = c^2$$
$$\sqrt{400} = \sqrt{c^2}$$
$$20 = c$$

Perimeter = 12 + 16 + 20 = $\boxed{48}$, **(D)**

E

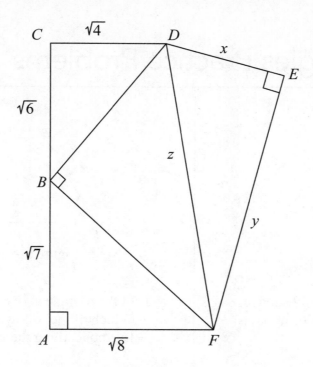

In the figure above, what is the value of $x^2 + y^2$?

S Find a starting point and begin.

We see that $x^2 + y^2 = z^2$. So we need to find z^2.

Step 1: $(\sqrt{6})^2 + (\sqrt{4})^2 = \overline{BD}^2$

$ 6 + 4 = \overline{BD}^2$

$ 10 = \overline{BD}^2$

$ \boxed{\sqrt{10}} = \overline{BD}$

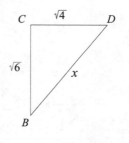

Step 2: $(\sqrt{7})^2 + (\sqrt{8})^2 = \overline{BF}^2$

$ 7 + 8 = \overline{BF}^2$

$ 15 = \overline{BF}^2$

$ \boxed{15} = \overline{BF}$

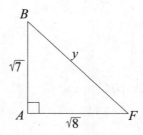

Step 3: $ \overline{BD}^2 + \overline{BF}^2 = z^2$

$ (\sqrt{10})^2 + (\sqrt{15})^2 = z^2$

$ 10 + 15 = z^2$

$ \textcircled{25} = z^2 = x^2 + y^2$

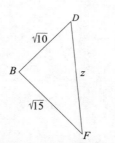

Note that you don't need to solve for either x or y. You don't even need to solve for z. All you need is z^2 and you are done.

Triangles Practice Problems

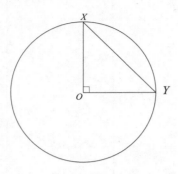

1. Point O is the center of the circle above, and the radius of the circle is 6. What is the length of $\overline{XY}$?

(A)   3
(B) $3\sqrt{3}$
(C)   6
(D) $6\sqrt{2}$
(E) $6\sqrt{3}$

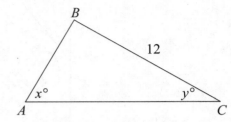

Note: Figure not drawn to scale.

3. In the triangle above, $x = 30$ and $y = 60$. Which of the following statements must be true concerning the figure above?

I. $AC > 12$
II. $AB > 12$
III. $AC > AB$

(A) I only
(B) II only
(C) III only
(D) I and III only
(E) I, II and III

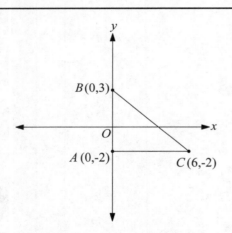

2. What is the area of $\triangle ABC$ in the figure above?

(A) 12
(B) 15
(C) 24
(D) 28
(E) 30

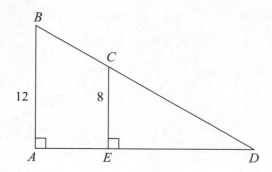

4. In the figure above, what is the value of $\dfrac{\overline{AE}}{\overline{AD}}$?

(A) $\dfrac{1}{4}$

(B) $\dfrac{1}{3}$

(C) $\dfrac{1}{2}$

(D) $\dfrac{2}{3}$

(E) $\dfrac{3}{4}$

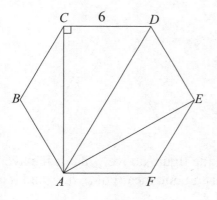

5. All interior angles of the polygon above are congruent, and $\overline{AD}$ bisects angle CDE. If the length of $\overline{CD}$ is 6, what is the area of $\triangle ACD$?

(A) $36\sqrt{3}$
(B) $36\sqrt{2}$
(C) 36
(D) $18\sqrt{3}$
(E) $18\sqrt{2}$

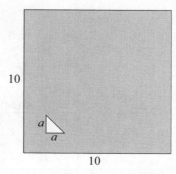

6. In the figure above, a small triangle is inside a square. What is the area of the shaded region in terms of a?

(A) $a - 20$
(B) $20 - a$
(C) $100 - a^2$
(D) $50 - a^2$
(E) $100 - (\dfrac{a^2}{2})$

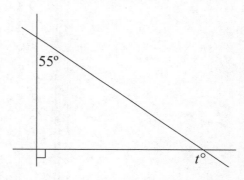

7. In the figure above, three lines intersect as shown. What is the value of t?

(A) 125
(B) 135
(C) 145
(D) 155
(E) 165

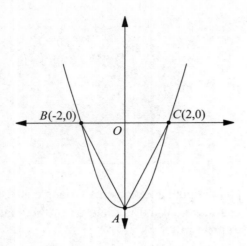

8. In the figure above, ABC is a triangle, and points B and C lie on the graph of $y = x^2 - k$, where k is a constant. If the area of $\triangle ABC$ is 8, what is the value of k?

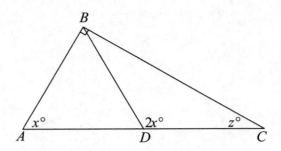

9. In the figure above, $\triangle ABD$ is equilateral. What is the value of z?

(A)   30
(B)   45
(C)   75
(D)   90
(E)   120

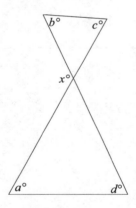

10. In the figure above, what is the average (arithmetic mean) of a, b, c, and d in terms of x?

(A) $\dfrac{180 - x}{4}$

(B) $\dfrac{360 - 2x}{4}$

(C) $\dfrac{360 - x}{8}$

(D) $\dfrac{x}{2}$

(E) x

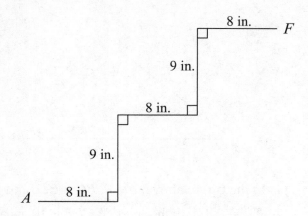

11. The figure above shows a staircase with the height and depth of each stair as indicated. If the stairs are to be replaced with a ramp from A to F, what will be the length, in inches, of the ramp?

(A) 17
(B) 30
(C) 36
(D) 42
(E) 51

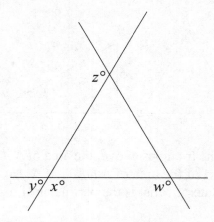

Note: Figure not drawn to scale.

12. In the figure above, $2y = x$. What is the value of $z + w$?

(A) 120
(B) 180
(C) 220
(D) 240
(E) 360

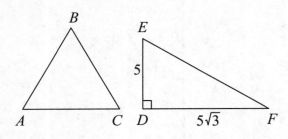

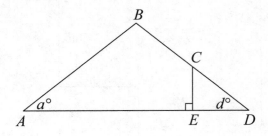

13. For the triangles above, the area of $\triangle ABC$ is half of the area of $\triangle DEF$. If $\triangle ABC$ is equilateral, what is the perimeter of $\triangle ABC$?

(A) 15

(B) $15\sqrt{2}$

(C) $15\sqrt{3}$

(D) $25\sqrt{3}$

(E) 30

14. In the figure above, $a = d$, $BC = CD$, and $ED = \frac{1}{4}AD$. If the area of $\triangle CDE$ is 10, what is the area of $\triangle ABD$?

(A)   40

(B)   50

(C)   60

(D)   80

(E)   100

Circles

6%

of all math
questions
on the SAT

There are some circle basics you need to remember.

1 Circles have 360°

2 Diameter = d

3 Radius (r) = $\dfrac{d}{2}$

4 Area = πr^2

5 Circumference = $2\pi r$ or πd

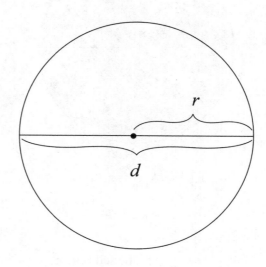

E

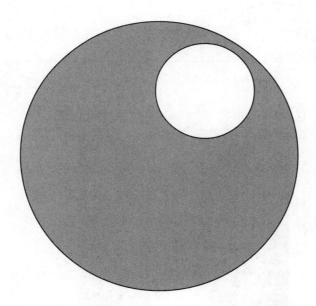

In the figure above, a smaller circle with radius 3 is inside a larger circle with radius x. What is the area of the shaded region in terms of x ?

(A) $x - 3$
(B) $x^2 - 3\pi$
(C) $\pi x^2 - 9$
(D) $\pi(x^2 - 3)$
(E) $\pi(x^2 - 9)$

S Our first step is to label everything.

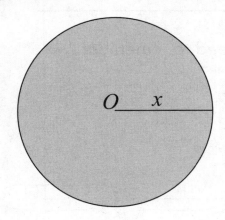

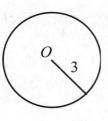

$$A_{Small} = \pi r^2$$
$$A_{Small} = \pi(3)^2$$
$$A_{Small} = 9\pi$$

$$A_{Big} = \pi r^2$$
$$A_{Big} = \pi x^2$$

$$A_{Big} - A_{Small} = \text{shaded region}$$

$$\pi x^2 - 9\pi = \boxed{\pi(x^2 - 9)}$$

Our answer is (**E**).

E

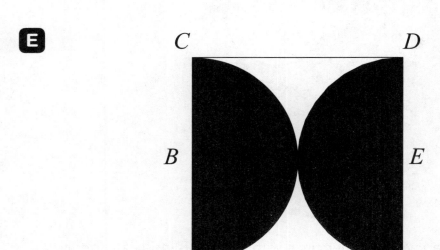

In square *ACDF* arcs $\overarc{AC}$ and $\overarc{DF}$ are semicircles with centers at *B* and *E*, respectively. If the radius of each semicircle is 2, what is the area of the unshaded region?

S Let's start by labeling what we know.

The radius of each semicircle is 2.

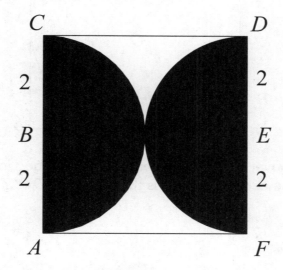

We can now see that the length of each side of the square is
$$2 + 2 = 4.$$
So, the area of square $ACDF$ is
$$\text{side}^2 = 4^2 = 16.$$
But, we are looking for the area of the unshaded region. To find that, we need to subtract the area of shaded parts from the area of the square. Now we need to find the area of the shaded parts.

Remember: Area of a circle = πr^2. Be careful not to use the diameter here.

If we put these two semi-circles together, they form one complete circle with diameter 4.

The area of our circle = πr^2
$$= \pi(2)^2$$
$$A = 4\pi$$

Now, to get to our final answer, we need to subtract the shaded area from the total area.

Total area – shaded area = unshaded area

$\boxed{16 - 4\pi}$ = unshaded area

"Inscribed in" simply means one shape is drawn within another shape.

Usually one of the shapes is a circle.

E

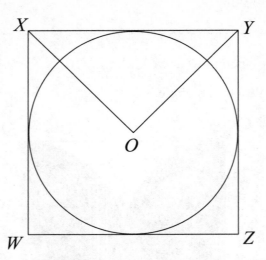

In the figure above, a circle with center O is inscribed in square $WXYZ$. If the radius of the circle is 4, what is the area of $\triangle OXY$?

S Our first step is to label everything.

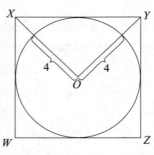

We also know that every radius of this circle is equal to 4. We need to label some additional radii:

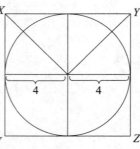

By adding the radii together, we see that the side length of the square $WXYZ$ is:

$$4 + 4 = 8$$

The area of square $WXYZ$ is side^2

$$8^2 = 64$$

We need the area of triangle OXY ½ $b(h)$:

$$½ (8)(4) = \boxed{16}$$

Note that 16 = ¼ of the area of our square. Doing a visual check, this looks right.

Arcs and Wedges

The key for arcs and wedges is this: think of the WHOLE CIRCLE first, and then compare the pieces to that.

Piece

Whole

An interior angle is just a piece of the whole 360°.

An arc is just a piece of the whole circle circumference.

A wedge is just a piece of the whole circle area.

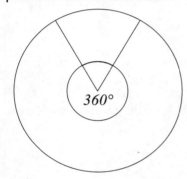

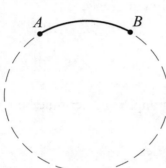

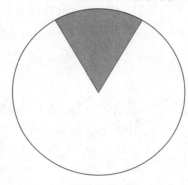

Remember that the circumference = $2\pi r$, and area = πr^2. So, if you have the radius, you can solve for anything.

$$\frac{\text{Piece}}{\text{Whole}} = \frac{\text{Angle measure}}{360°} = \frac{\text{Arc length}}{\text{Circumference}} = \frac{\text{Wedge area}}{\text{Circle area}}$$

E

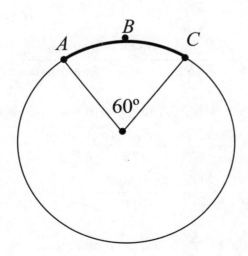

If the area of the circle above is 36π, what is the length of the darkened arc ABC?

Whenever we are talking about an arc, remember that we're just talking about a piece of the circumference. So **when you see the word arc, think circumference**. And to find a part, you have to find the whole.

Step 1: Determine the circumference of the entire circle.

$$C = 2\pi r$$

To find the circumference, we need to know what r is. Thankfully, we are given the area (36π); we can use this to find r:

$$A = \pi r^2$$
$$\pi r^2 = 36\pi$$
$$r^2 = 36$$
$$r = \boxed{6}$$

Now we can find the circumference:

$$C = 2\pi r$$
$$C = 2\pi(6)$$
$$C = 12\pi$$

Step 2: Use the interior angle to determine how much of the circumference the arc covers.

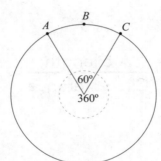

Interior Angle = 60°

Whole Circle = 360°

$$\frac{\text{Piece}}{\text{Whole}} = \frac{\text{Angle measure}}{360°} = \frac{\text{Arc length}}{\text{Circumference}}$$

The entire circle is 360°. Our piece of the circle is 60°.

$$\frac{60°}{360°} = \frac{\text{Arc length}}{12\pi}$$

$$\frac{1}{6} = \frac{\text{Arc length}}{12\pi}$$

Our arc is equal to $\frac{1}{6}$ of the circumference.

$$\overset{\frown}{ABC} = \frac{1}{6}(12\pi)$$
$$= \boxed{2\pi}$$

Cross multiply.

Tangent

One last thing about circles: a common term that you might come across when you work with circles is tangent. A line is tangent to a circle when the two shapes intersect at 1 and only 1 point on the circumference of the circle. An example is shown below.

Circles inscribed in shapes are tangent to the sides of that shape.

This is really important because the intersection of a circle's radius and a line tangent to the circle creates a right angle. This usually sets up a Pythagorean Theorem problem that can easily be solved if you know two sides of the triangle. Here's a common setup:

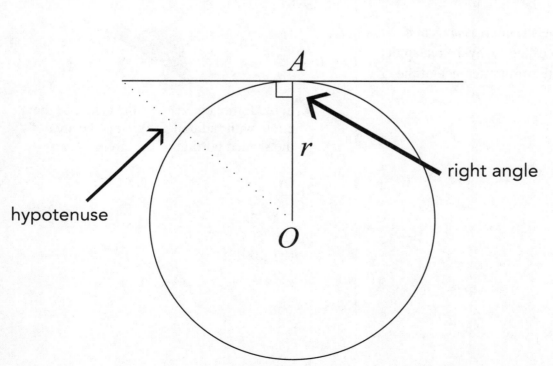

Circles Practice Problems

1. If the circumference of a circle is 8, what is the radius of the circle?

(A) 8π

(B) $\dfrac{8}{\pi}$

(C) 4π

(D) $\dfrac{4}{\pi}$

(E) 2π

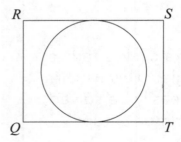

2. In the figure above, the circle is tangent to sides $\overline{QT}$ and $\overline{RS}$ of the 12-by-16 rectangle, *QRST*. What is the circumference of the circle?

(A) 8π
(B) 12π
(C) 16π
(D) 24π
(E) 36π

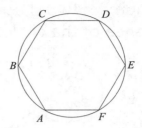

3. In the figure above, regular hexagon *ABCDEF* is inscribed in the circle. What is the degree measure of arc $\overset{\frown}{ABE}$?

(A) 360
(B) 270
(C) 240
(D) 180
(E) 120

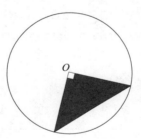

4. In the figure above, *O* is the center of the circle with radius 10. What is the area of the shaded portion of the circle?

(A) 25
(B) 50
(C) 25π
(D) 50π
(E) 100

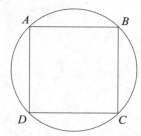

5. In the figure above, square *ABCD* is inscribed in the circle. If the area of the circle is 64π, what is the length of arc $\overset{\frown}{BC}$?

(A) 2π
(B) 4π
(C) 8π
(D) 16π
(E) 32π

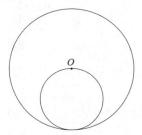

6. In the figure above, the circles are tangent as shown, and *O* is the center of the larger circle. If the radius of the larger circle is 12, what is the area of the smaller circle?

(A) 6π
(B) 9π
(C) 12π
(D) 16π
(E) 36π

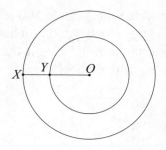

7. In the figure above, *O* is the center of both circles. If *YO* = 3 and *XY* = 2, what is the ratio of the area of the smaller circle to the area of the larger circle?

(A) 2:5
(B) 3:5
(C) 2:3
(D) 9:25
(E) 4:9

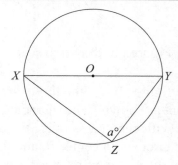

8. In the figure above, Δ *XYZ* is inscribed in the circle with center *O*. What is the value of *a* ?

(A) 60
(B) 75
(C) 80
(D) 90
(E) It cannot be determined from the information provided.

9. A bicycle wheel made 500 revolutions while travelling 9000π inches in a straight line along a trail. What is the diameter, in inches, of the wheel?

(A)   9
(B) 9π
(C)   18
(D) 18π
(E)   27

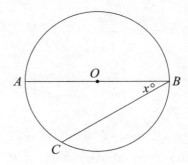

11. In the figure above, $\overline{AB}$ is the diameter of the circle with center O. If $AO = 6$, and the length of arc $\overarc{BC}$ is 4π, what is the value of x?

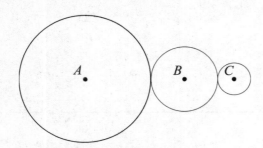

Note: Figure not drawn to scale.

10. In the figure above, the three circles are tangent as shown. The diameter of the circle with center A is twice the diameter of the circle with center B, and the diameter of the circle with center B is twice the diameter of circle with center C. What is the ratio of the area of the smallest circle to the area of largest circle?

(A) 1:4
(B) 1:8
(C) 1:12
(D) 1:16
(E) 1:64

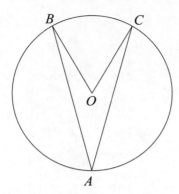

12. In the figure above, point O is the center of the circle. If arc $\overarc{BC}$ is one-sixth of the circumference of circle O, what is the degree measure of inscribed $\angle BAC$?

13. Five spheres, each of radius 2, are placed together so that each sphere is tangent to at least one other sphere. If A is the center of one of the spheres and B is the center of another of the spheres, what is the greatest possible length of $\overline{AB}$?

(A) 7
(B) 8
(C) 9.5
(D) 11
(E) 16

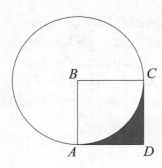

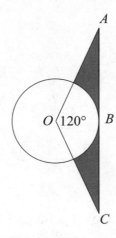

14. In the figure above, point B is the center of the circle, and $ABCD$ is a square. If $\overline{AB}$ has length r, what is the area of the shaded region in terms of r ?

(A) $\pi r^2 - r^2$

(B) $\dfrac{(3\pi r^2)}{4}$

(C) $r^2 - \dfrac{(\pi r^2)}{4}$

(D) $\dfrac{(\pi r^2)}{4}$

(E) $r^2 - \pi r^2$

15. In the figure above, the center of the circle is O, and $\overline{AC}$ is tangent to the circle at B. If B is the midpoint of $\overline{AC}$ and the area of the circle is 81π, what is the total area of the shaded region?

(A) $27\pi - 18\sqrt{3}$
(B) $81\sqrt{3} - 27\pi$
(C) $81\sqrt{3}$
(D) $162\sqrt{3} - 27\pi$
(E) $162\sqrt{3}$

Perimeter, Area and Volume

10%

of all math
questions
on the SAT

Perimeter

Perimeter is simply the distance around the **outside** edge of a shape.

The perimeter of this square is
$$4 + 4 + 4 + 4 = \textbf{16}$$
$$\textbf{NOT}$$
$$4 + 4 + 4 + 4 + 4\sqrt{2} = 16 + 4\sqrt{2}$$

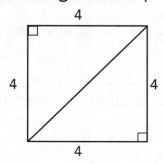

Make sure not to count any internal lines as part of the perimeter. Even if the diagonal of a square is shown, it is not part of the perimeter.

E

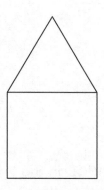

In the figure above, the triangle is equilateral and the area of the square is 25. What is the perimeter of the triangle?

S

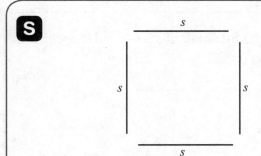

Area $\square = s^2$
$$25 = s^2$$
$$\sqrt{25} = \sqrt{s^2}$$
$$s = 5$$

Perimeter $\Delta = 3s$
$$3(5) = \text{⑮}$$

Area

Here are some tricks to remember when trying to solve for the area of a 2-D shape.

1 Area of a triangle = $\frac{1}{2} b \times h$

2 Area of a rectangle = *length × width*

3 Unusual quadrilaterals: Break unfamiliar shapes into shapes you know: rectangles, right triangles, circles and semicircles.

E

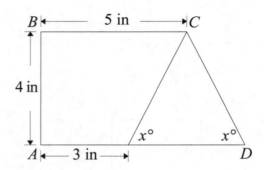

What is the area of trapezoid *ABCD* in the figure above?

(A) 18 square inches
(B) 24 square inches
(C) 28 square inches
(D) 32 square inches
(E) 60 square inches

S This definitely qualifies as an unusual quadrilateral. It's a 4-sided shape that isn't a rectangle.

Drop a line straight down from *C* to $\overline{AD}$, creating a rectangle and cutting the triangle in half into two right triangles.

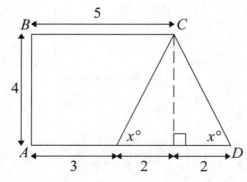

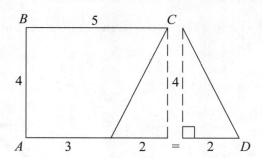

The base of the triangle on the left is 2 because $5 - 3 = 2$. The base of the one on the right is also 2 because we cut the original triangle in half when we drew our line.

The Area of the new rectangle is

$$(5)(4) = \boxed{20}$$

The Area of the newly formed triangle is

$$\frac{1}{2}(2)(4) = \boxed{4}$$

Total Area of *ABCD* is

$$20 + 4 = \boxed{\textbf{24 square inches}}, \text{ answer (B)}.$$

E

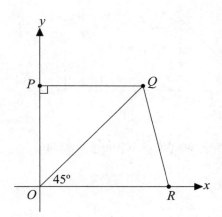

In the *xy*-plane above, the length of $\overline{OR}$ is 5, and the coordinates of point *P* are (0, 4). What is the area of quadrilateral *OPQR* ?

(A) 9
(B) 12
(C) 18
(D) 20
(E) 22

S Drop a line down from Q to $\overline{OR}$, creating a rectangle and a new triangle.

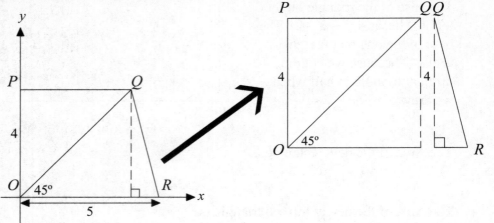

By the coordinates of point P, we learn that $OP = 4$. LABEL.
The middle triangle is a 45°, 45°, 90° isosceles triangle.

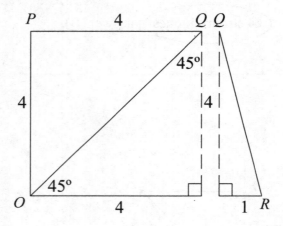

That means the rectangle above is actually a square.
The area of the square is

$$4 \times 4 = 16$$

The area of the newly formed triangle is $\frac{1}{2}(b)(h)$

The base is $5 - 4 = 1$, and the height is the same as the side of the square.

$$A = 0.5(1)(4)$$
$$A = 2$$

Now we add the two areas together:

$$16 + 2 = 18$$

Total area of $OPQR$ is ⑱. **(C)** is our answer!

Volume

Volume is the space occupied by a three dimensional shape. A simple example is the space inside a box. Let's look at some common shapes the SAT uses to test this concept.

Cubes

Most of the solid geometry problems test your knowledge of the cube. You must be able to visualize in 3-D and draw all of the information you are given.

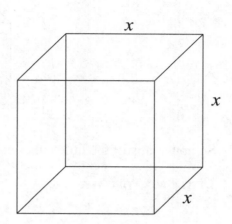

Here are two important things to remember about cubes.

1 All 6 sides are the same, and each side is a perfect square.

2 Volume of a cube = side³ or x^3

Volume = length × width × height for a rectangular solid.

 E

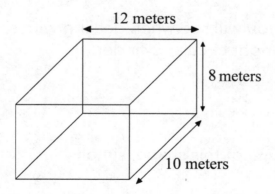

What is the maximum number of cubes with side length 2 meters that will fit into the rectangular box shown above?

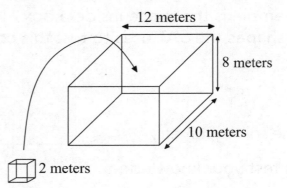

S Shapes fitting inside shapes—think volume; we're in 3-D here!

12 meters

8 meters

10 meters

2 meters

So how many of the little cubes can we fit into the big box?

LITTLE BOX VOLUME = side³   **BIG BOX VOLUME** = length × width × height
$$s^3 = 2^3$$ $$l \times w \times h = 10(12)(8)$$
$$= 8$$ $$= 960$$

To figure out how many little cubes fit in the bigger box, we need to divide.

$$\frac{\textbf{BIG BOX VOLUME}}{\textbf{LITTLE BOX VOLUME}} = \frac{960}{8} = \boxed{120}$$

We can fit 120 of the small cubes into the figure.

This only works if each of the sides of the larger object are divisible by the sides of the smaller object. Luckily, the SAT always creates problems to work this way.

Cylinders

Another shape you will see when dealing with solid geometry problems is the right circular cylinder.

To find the volume of this shape, simply use the formula:

$$V = \pi r^2 h$$

where r is the radius and h is the height of the cylinder.

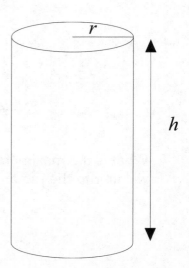

More about Volume

For the 3-D shapes on the SAT, you can just think of the volume as the area of the shape on the end multiplied by the height. For the **box shapes**, find the **area of the rectangle** on the end and multiply by the height; for the **cylinders**, find the **area of the circle** on the end and multiply by the height.

Common Formula

Volume = area of shape on end × height

Surface Area

To find the surface area of any three-dimensional shape, find the area of each side individually, and then add them all together.

To find the surface area of a cube, all you need to do is find the area of one side, which is a square, and multiply by 6 (the number of sides on a cube).

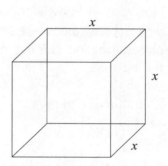

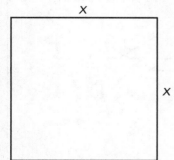

The area of one side of a cube is x^2. Surface area = $6x^2$. (Add the areas of all of the sides to get the surface area.)

E

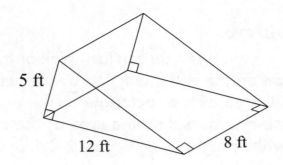

What is the surface area, in square inches, of the solid wedge shown above?

(A) 104
(B) 200
(C) 204
(D) 270
(E) 300

S The only measurement we are missing is the hypotenuse of side *A*, which is a 5 – 12 – 13 right triangle (one of the special right triangles we discussed earlier in the TRIANGLES section).

Now that we know all of our measurements, we can break the whole shape into smaller pieces, then add their individual areas together for the total:

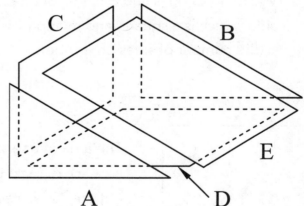

Side *A*: Right triangle
$\frac{1}{2}$ (12)(5) = 30

Side *B*: Right triangle
$\frac{1}{2}$ (12)(5) = 30

Side *C*: Back rectangle
(5)(8) = 40

Side *D*: Bottom rectangle
(12)(8) = 96

Side *E*: Top rectangle
(13)(8) = 104

Total is 30 + 30 + 40 + 96 + 104 = **300**
Our answer is **(E)**.

Perimeter, Area and Volume Practice Problems

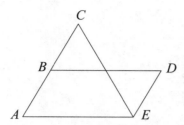

1. In the figure above, $\triangle ACE$ is an equilateral triangle and $ABDE$ is a parallelogram. If B is the midpoint of $\overline{AC}$ and the perimeter of $\triangle ACE$ is 12, what is the perimeter of parallelogram $ABDE$?

   (A)   6
   (B)   8
   (C)   12
   (D)   16
   (E)   18

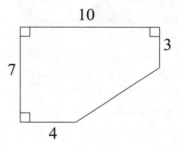

2. What is the area of the five-sided figure above?

   (A)   32
   (B)   46
   (C)   58
   (D)   70
   (E)   84

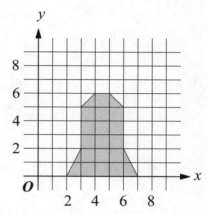

3. What is the area of the shaded region in the figure above?

   (A) 16
   (B) 17
   (C) 18
   (D) 19
   (E) 20

4. If there is no waste, how many square feet of linoleum are needed to cover a floor that is 6 yards by 9 yards? (1 yard = 3 feet)

   (A)   18
   (B)   27
   (C)   54
   (D) 162
   (E) 486

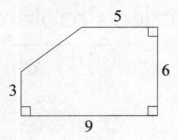

5. What is the perimeter of the figure above?

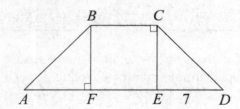

6. In the figure above, $AF = FE = ED$, and the area of the trapezoid $ABCD$ is 98 square inches. What is the perimeter of the trapezoid?

(A) $14 + 7\sqrt{2}$

(B) 28

(C) $28 + 7\sqrt{2}$

(D) $28 + 14\sqrt{2}$

(E) 42

7. The perimeter of a certain rectangle is 5 times its width. What is the ratio of the length of the rectangle to the width of the rectangle?

(A) 1:2

(B) 1:5

(C) 2:3

(D) 2:5

(E) 3:2

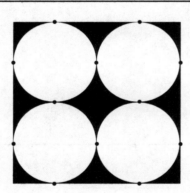

8. In the square above, the circles are tangent at the points shown. If the radius of each circle is 2, what is the total area of the shaded regions?

(A) $16 - 4\pi$

(B) $16 - 16\pi$

(C) $64 - 4\pi$

(D) $64 - 8\pi$

(E) $64 - 16\pi$

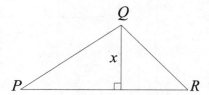

9. In the figure above x is the length of the altitude of $\triangle PQR$. If $x = \frac{2}{5}\,PR$, what is the area of $\triangle PQR$ in terms of x ?

(A) $\dfrac{5x^2}{4}$

(B) $\dfrac{5x^2}{2}$

(C) $\dfrac{x^2}{5}$

(D) $\dfrac{x}{4}$

(E) $\dfrac{5x}{4}$

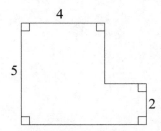

Note: Figure not drawn to scale.

10. The area of the figure above is 24. What is the perimeter of the figure?

(A) 17
(B) 20
(C) 22
(D) 24
(E) It cannot be determined from the information provided.

11. A certain hardware store sells bathroom tiles in rectangular boxes with inside dimensions 8 inches by 14 inches by 20 inches. What is the maximum number of tiles that will fit inside each box if each tile has outside dimensions of 2 inches by 5 inches by $\frac{1}{2}$ inch?

12. If the height of a triangle is increased by 20% and the base of the same triangle is decreased by 20%, what is the effect on the area of the triangle?

(A) The area is increased by 40%.
(B) The area is increased by 20%.
(C) The area is unchanged.
(D) The area is decreased by 10%.
(E) The area is decreased by 4%.

13. Ahmad fills a spherical beach ball which has a diameter of 6 inches with air until it is full. How many such beach balls could he fill using the amount of air in a spherical beach ball with diameter 18 inches? (The volume of a sphere with radius r is given by $\frac{4}{3}\pi r^3$.)

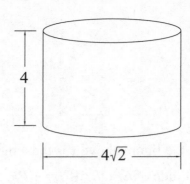

14. What is volume of the largest rectangular box that will fit completely in the right circular cylinder shown above?

(A) $12\sqrt{2}$
(B) 16
(C) $16\sqrt{2}$
(D) 64
(E) $64\sqrt{2}$

Proportional Shapes

0.6%

of all math
questions
on the SAT

Proportional shapes are all about ratios. Shapes that are proportional have a fixed relationship.

Similar triangles

Similar triangles are the most common proportional shapes on the SAT. These are triangles that have the same angle measures; any time you see them, think ratios.

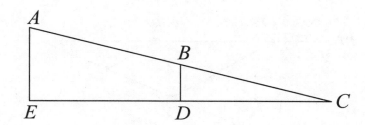

Note: Figure not drawn to scale

In the triangle above, $\overline{AE} \parallel \overline{BD}$. If $EC = 40$, $AE = 10$, and $ED = 20$, what is the value of $\overline{BD}$?

S ALWAYS label first.

This is a proportional shape: a **locked ratio**.

Step 1: The ratio for $\triangle AEC$:

$$\frac{\text{Length}}{\text{Height}} = \frac{40}{10} = \boxed{\frac{4}{1}}$$

This is our locked ratio for both shapes.

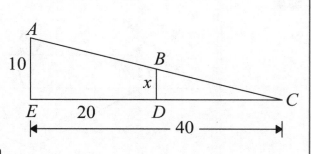

Step 2: $EC - ED = DC$
$40 - 20 = DC$
$20 = DC$

Step 3: The ratio for $\triangle BDC$:

$$\frac{\text{Length}}{\text{Height}} = \frac{20}{x} = \frac{4}{1}$$

$$4x = 20$$

$$x = \boxed{5}$$

E

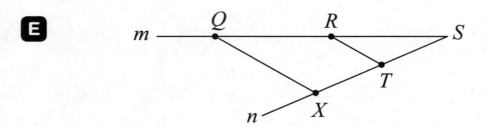

In the figure above, Q, R, and S lie on line m, and X, T, and S lie on line n. R is the midpoint of $\overline{QS}$ and T is the midpoint of $\overline{XS}$. If $QS = 8$, $TS = 3$, and $RT = 2$, what is the perimeter of quadrilateral $QRTX$?

S Our first step is to label what we know:

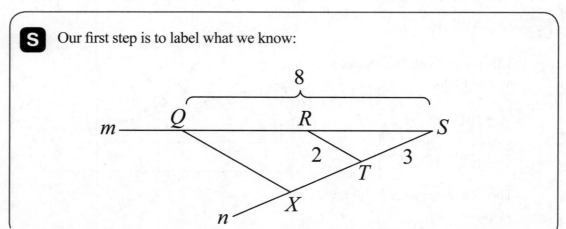

If $TS = 3$, then $XT = 3$ because T is the midpoint of $\overline{XS}$. And if $QS = 8$, then $QR = 4$ and $RS = 4$ because R is the midpoint of $\overline{QS}$.

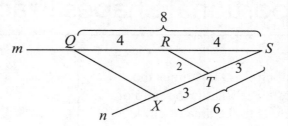

Now we can clearly see the relationship between the larger shape and the smaller proportional shape.

Large Shape

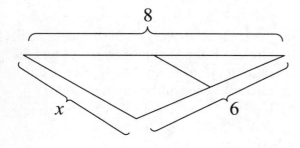

Small Shape

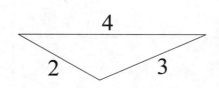

Let's look at our ratios:

$$\frac{\text{Large}}{\text{Small}} = \frac{8}{4} = \frac{6}{3} = \frac{x}{2}$$

Using our fixed proportion, or locked ratio, we can solve for x.

$$\frac{6}{3} = \frac{x}{2}$$
$$12 = 3x$$
$$4 = x$$

Our final step is to add up all the sides of quadrilateral $QRTX$.

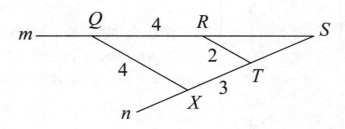

$$4 + 4 + 3 + 2 = \boxed{13}$$

Proportional Shapes Practice Problems

1. The diameter of circle O is 4 times the diameter of circle P. What is the ratio of the area of circle O to the area of circle P?

(A) 2:1
(B) 3:8
(C) 4:1
(D) 8:1
(E) 16:1

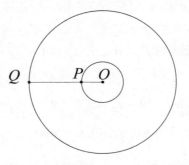

Note: Figure not drawn to scale.

3. In the figure above, O is the center of both circles. If the length of $\overline{QO}$ is 14 and the ratio of $\overline{QP}$ to $\overline{PO}$ is 4 to 3, what is the circumference of the smaller circle?

(A) 8π
(B) 12π
(C) 24π
(D) 32π
(E) 64π

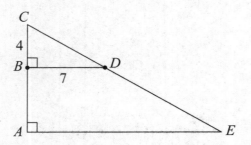

Note: Figure not drawn to scale.

2. In the figure above, $\overline{AE}$ and $\overline{BD}$ are each perpendicular to $\overline{AC}$. If the length of $\overline{AC}$ is 10, what is the length of $\overline{AE}$?

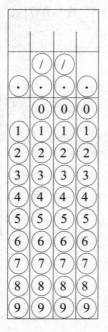

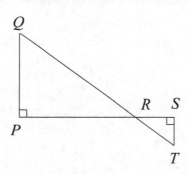

4. In the figure above, $\overline{PQ}$ and $\overline{TS}$ are each perpendicular to $\overline{PS}$. If $PR = 12$, $RS = 4$, and $ST = 3$, what is the length of $\overline{QT}$?

(A) 10
(B) 12
(C) 15
(D) 16
(E) 20

Number Lines

3%

of all math
questions
on the SAT

The key to solving number line questions is to draw a number line. Don't just try to imagine it in your head. Use your pencil and paper to make things more concrete.

E Points L and M lie on a line in that order. The coordinate of point L is -6 and the coordinate of point M is 10. If N is located $\frac{1}{4}$ of the way from L to M, what is the coordinate N?

S Let's go and populate our number line and draw the full distance.

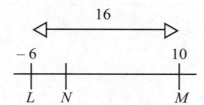

Total distance $= 10 - (-6) = 16$
$\frac{1}{4} \times 16 = 4$; we need to travel 4 units from -6.

Rest assured 4 will be an answer, and it will be the most commonly selected wrong answer. The question did NOT ask for $\frac{1}{4}$ of the distance from L to M; it asked for the coordinate of N.

Coordinate of $L = -6$.
$(-6) + 4 = -2$, so the coordinate of the point we're looking for is $\boxed{-2.}$

E

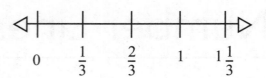

0    $\frac{1}{3}$ $\frac{2}{3}$ 1 $1\frac{1}{3}$

On the number line above, the tick marks are equally spaced, and their coordinates are indicated above. How many tick marks would lie on this number line (between) the coordinates 11 and 14?

S Let's go populate our number line and draw the full distance.

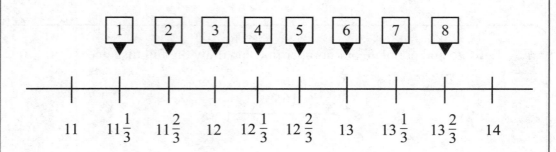

So if we remember to count between the tick marks on either end, we get ⑧.

Number Line Practice Problems

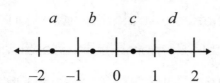

1. The letters *a, b, c,* and *d* are coordinates of the points shown on the number line above. Which of the expressions below has the least value?

(A) $a + b$
(B) $a + c$
(C) $b + c$
(D) $c + d$
(E) $a \times c$

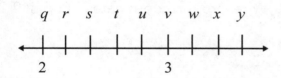

2. On the number line above, the tick marks are evenly spaced. What is the value of (y^x) rounded to the nearest tenth?

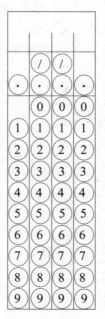

$$-7 \leq 2y + 1 < 9$$

3. Which of the following represents all values of *y* that satisfy the inequality above?

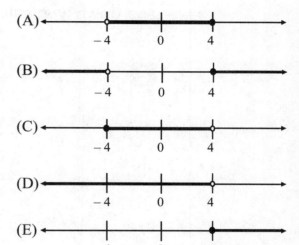

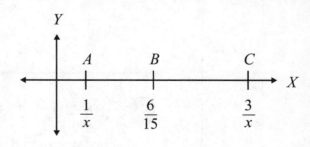

Note: Figure not drawn to scale.

4. In the coordinate system above, segment $\overline{AB}$ is equal to segment $\overline{BC}$. What is the length of segment $\overline{AC}$?

(A) 15
(B) 5
(C) 0.6
(D) 0.4
(E) 0.2

Coordinate Systems

5%

of all math
questions
on the SAT

Coordinate system problems are relatively straightforward on the SAT, but they ALL require a visual. Remember, in coordinate systems, the x-axis goes across (horizontal) and the y-axis goes up and down (vertical).

E

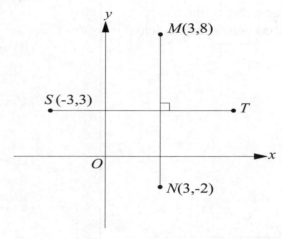

In the figure above, $ST = MN$. What are the coordinates of point T?

S The length of $\overline{MN}$ is 10 because we are going up from -2 to $+8$.

Since we are told $ST = MN$ in the problem, $ST = 10$

To find the x-coordinate of T, begin at -3 (x-coordinate of point S), and add the length of $\overline{ST}$ (10):

$$-3 + 10 = +7$$

$\overline{MN}$ is a vertical line segment because M and N have the same x-coordinate. Because $\overline{ST}$ is perpendicular to $\overline{MN}$, we know it is a horizontal line segment. That means that any point on $\overline{ST}$ must have the same y-coordinate as S. So the y-value at T is $+3$.

Thus, the coordinates of T are $(7, 3)$.

E In the *xy*-coordinate plane, what is the perimeter of a rectangle with opposite vertices at (– 3, 3) and (2, – 3)?

S This is a very simple problem if you graph it.

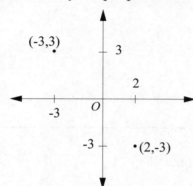 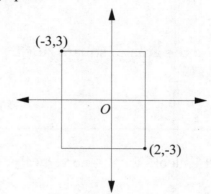

These are opposite vertices. Draw the lines to complete the rectangle, then find and label the side lengths.

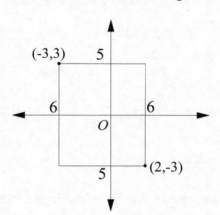 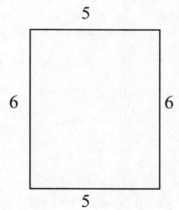

Add the lengths of the sides to find the perimeter.

5 + 5 + 6 + 6 = **22**

The perimeter is ⟨**22**⟩.

E

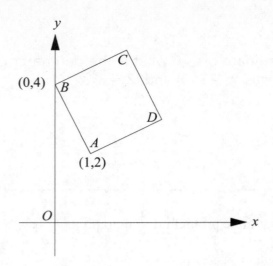

Find the area of square *ABCD*.

Remember: Right triangles mean use the Pythagorean Theorem!

$$a^2 + b^2 = c^2$$

S This looks tough—no verticals or horizontals!

Step 1: Draw shapes we know. See the right triangle? One great thing that coordinate systems always allow you to do is create right triangles. Any diagonal line can be made into a right triangle with two other lines, one parallel to the *x*-axis and one parallel to the *y*-axis.

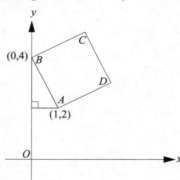

With these two points, you can find the length of the sides of the legs of the right triangle. Subtract the *y*-coordinates of the two points to find the vertical leg, and subtract the *x*-coordinates of the two points to find the horizontal leg.

$y_1 - y_2 \rightarrow 4 - 2 = 2$
$x_1 - x_2 \rightarrow 0 - 1 = -1$
(really 1 because there is no such thing as a negative distance)

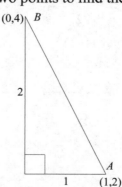

Now, use the Pythagorean Theorem to find the hypotenuse, which is the length of $\overline{AB}$.

$$1^2 + 2^2 = AB^2$$
$$1 + 4 = AB^2$$
$$5 = AB^2$$
$$\sqrt{5} = AB$$

AB is also one side of the square.

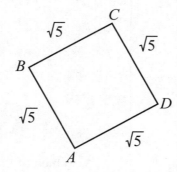

Since it's a square, the area is simply the length of the side, squared.

area $= (\sqrt{5})^2 = \boxed{5}$

You may have noticed by now that graphs set you up to draw right triangles. Any diagonal line can be the hypotenuse of a right triangle if you just make one leg a horizontal line and the other leg a vertical line.

Coordinate Systems Practice Problems

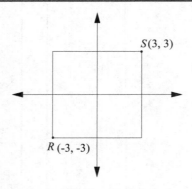

1. In the *xy*-coordinate system above, points *R* and *S* are opposite vertices of a square. Which of the following points could be another vertex of the square?

(A) $(3, -3)$
(B) $(-3, 2)$
(C) $(3, -2)$
(D) $(0, -3)$
(E) $(0, 3)$

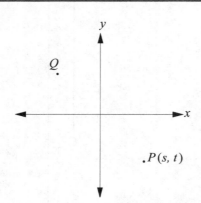

2. In the figure above, point *Q* is the same distance from the origin as point *P* is from the origin. Which of the following could be the coordinates of point *Q* ?

(A) (s, t)
(B) $(s, -t)$
(C) $(-s, t)$
(D) $(-s, -t)$
(E) (t, s)

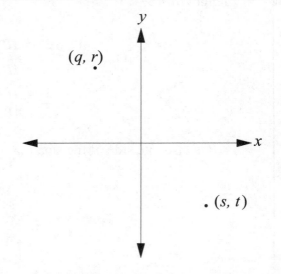

Note: Figure not drawn to scale.

3. Which of the following must be true concerning the figure above?

    I. $t > s$
    II. $q > s$
    III. $r > t$

(A) I only
(B) II only
(C) III only
(D) II and III
(E) I, II, and III

4. The *x*-coordinate is greater than the *y*-coordinate for each point on the graph.

The *x*-coordinate of every point on the graph is positive.

No two points on the graph have the same *x*-coordinates.

Which of the following graphs has the properties stated above?

(A)

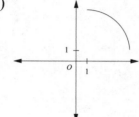

(B)

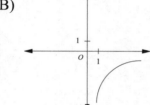

(C)

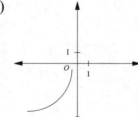

(D)

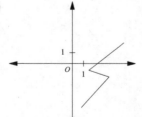

(E)

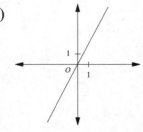

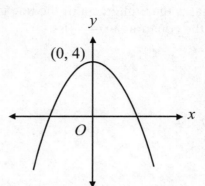

5. Which of the following could be an equation of the parabola pictured above?

(A) $x^2 - 4$

(B) $-x^2 - 4$

(C) $-x^2 + 4$

(D) $-(x + 4)^2$

(E) $-(x^2 + 4)$

6. What is the *x*-intercept of the line given by the equation $3y = -(6x - 12)$?

(A) -4
(B) -2
(C) 0
(D) 2
(E) 4

7. In the *xy*-coordinate plane, lines *r* and *p* are the diagonals of a square. If the points $(0, 3)$ and $(6, 9)$ lie on line *r* and the points $(1, 8)$ and $(7, n)$ lie on line *p*, what is the value of *n* ?

(A) -2
(B) -1
(C) 1
(D) 2
(E) 3

Slope

Slope can best be described as rise over run, or change in *y* over change in *x*. When you have two points on a line, use the formula:

$$\text{Slope} = m = \frac{\text{rise}}{\text{run}} = \frac{\triangle y}{\triangle x} = \frac{y_2 - y_1}{x_2 - x_1}$$

In this equation, *m* is the slope and each *x* and *y* pair represents a point on the line, i.e. (2,1) or (4, −3).

E

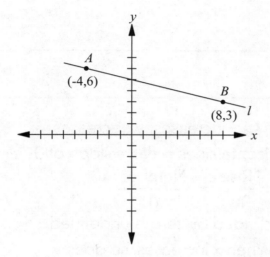

Two points, *A* and *B*, lie on line *l* as shown above. What is the slope of line *l* ?

S We need to work with the slope equation:

$$m = \frac{(y_2 - y_1)}{(x_2 - x_1)}$$

Let's use our 2 points $\overset{(x_1, y_1)}{(-4, 6)}$ and $\overset{(x_2, y_2)}{(8, 3)}$.

$$\frac{(y_2 - y_1)}{(x_2 - x_1)} = \frac{(3 - 6)}{(8 - (-4))} = -\frac{3}{12} = \boxed{-\frac{1}{4}}$$

Slope Identification

Slopes are either positive, negative, zero, or undefined. Label each of the following graphs with one of these slope-types:

A	B	C	D

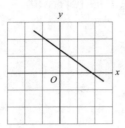 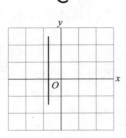 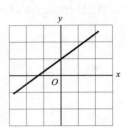

_____   _____   _____   _____

S A: Negative: As x increases, y decreases.

B: Zero: Horizontal lines = flat = slope of 0.

C: Undefined: $\dfrac{\text{Rise}}{\text{Run}} = \dfrac{\text{Number}}{0}$
Anything divided by zero is undefined.

D: Positive: When x increases, so does y.

Parallel Slopes

Two lines that are parallel have the **same** slope.

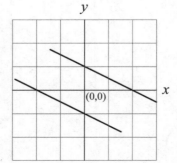 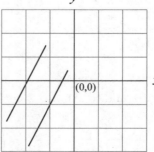 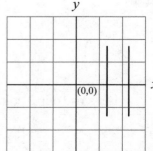

Perpendicular Slopes

Two lines that are perpendicular (meet at a 90° angle) have slopes that are negative reciprocals of each other.

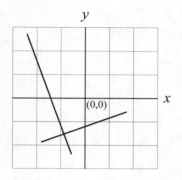 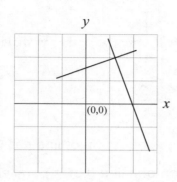 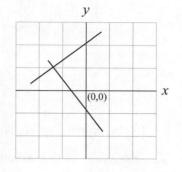

The negative reciprocal of $\frac{3}{4}$ is $-\frac{4}{3}$, and the negative reciprocal of -2 is $\frac{1}{2}$. Simply flip the term and switch the sign to get the negative reciprocal.

Slope-Intercept Form

The SAT frequently presents equations for lines using the **Slope-Intercept Form**. The **Slope-Intercept Form** is:

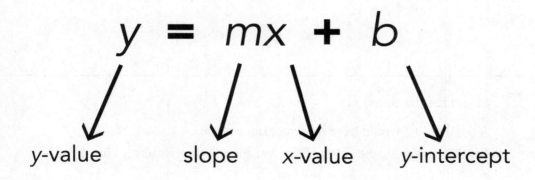

$$y = mx + b$$

y-value   slope   x-value   y-intercept

E

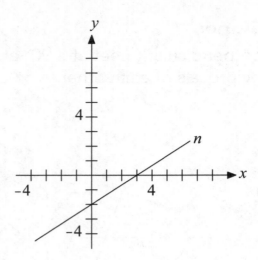

In the *xy*-plane above, the equation of line *n* is $y = \frac{2}{3}x - 2$. Which of the following is the equation of a line that is parallel to line *n*?

(A) $y = 2x + 8$

(B) $y = -\frac{3}{2}x - 2$

(C) $y = -\frac{3}{2}x + 12$

(D) $y = \frac{3}{2}x - 4$

(E) $y = \frac{2}{3}x + 1$

S Line *n* has the equation $y = \frac{2}{3}x - 2$

A parallel line would have the exact same slope.

We can determine the slope of line *n* using the slope-intercept formula.

$$y = mx + b$$
$$y = \frac{2}{3}x - 2$$

The slope of line *n* is $\frac{2}{3}$.

Looking at our answer choices, the line in answer choice **(E)** has the same slope, $\frac{2}{3}$, and it is therefore parallel to line *n*.

E Which of the following is the equation of a line in the *xy*-plane that passes through the point (6, 3) and is perpendicular to the line $y = -3x - 1$?

(A) $y = 3x + 3$

(B) $y = -3x + 6$

(C) $y = \frac{1}{3}x - 1$

(D) $y = \frac{1}{3}x + 1$

(E) $y = -\frac{1}{3}x - 3$

S When you see the word **perpendicular**, you will need to find the slope of the line and then determine the negative reciprocal of that slope.

$$y = -3x - 1$$

We are already in slope-intercept form, so our slope is -3.

The negative reciprocal of $-\frac{3}{1} = +\frac{1}{3}$

The only answer choices that have a slope of $+\frac{1}{3}$ are (C) and (D). One of those must be our answer.

We must determine which of the two lines, either answer choice (C) or (D), passes through the point (6, 3). Let's plug the point (6, 3) into each equation to determine which line passes through it.

(C) $y = \frac{1}{3}x - 1$

$3 = (\frac{1}{3})6 - 1$

$3 = 2 - 1$

$3 \neq 1$ *Nope! (6, 3) is not a point on the line* $y = (\frac{1}{3})x - 1$.

(D) $y = \frac{1}{3}x + 1$

$3 = (\frac{1}{3})(6) + 1$

$3 = 2 + 1$

$3 = ③$ *That's it! (D) is our answer!*

If you plug any point (*x, y*) on a line into the equation of the line, you will get a true result.

Alternatively, if you are more visual, you could always plot the lines, using the *y*-intercepts and the slope, and see which one hits (6, 3).

E

$$6y - rx = 9$$

The equation above is the equation of a line in the xy-plane, and r is a constant. If the slope of the line is 3, what is the value of r?

S First we need to get our equation, $6y - rx = 9$, into slope-intercept form. Let's isolate y.

$$6y = 9 + rx$$
$$y = \frac{9}{6} + (\frac{r}{6})x$$
$$y = (\frac{r}{6})x + \frac{3}{2}$$
$$y = mx + b$$

The slope of our line, $\frac{r}{6}$, equals 3. We can now solve for r.

$$\frac{r}{6} = 3$$
$$r = 3(6)$$
$$r = \boxed{18}$$

E In the xy-plane, the line $4x + 7y = t$ passes through the point $(-9, 4)$. What is the value of t?

S Let's plug the point $(-9, 4)$ into the equation of the line $4x + 7y = t$.

$$4x + 7y = t$$
$$4(-9) + 7(4) = t$$
$$-36 + 28 = t$$
$$\boxed{-8} = t$$

Slope Practice Problems

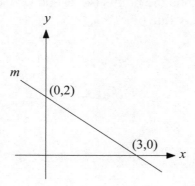

1. In the figure above, what is the slope of line m ?

    (A) $-\dfrac{3}{2}$

    (B) $-\dfrac{2}{3}$

    (C) $\dfrac{2}{3}$

    (D) $\dfrac{3}{4}$

    (E) $\dfrac{3}{2}$

2. In the xy-plane, $y = 3x + 4$ and $y = mx + b$ are perpendicular lines. What is the value of m ?

    (A) $-\dfrac{1}{2}$

    (B) $-\dfrac{1}{3}$

    (C) $-\dfrac{1}{4}$

    (D) $\dfrac{1}{3}$

    (E) 3

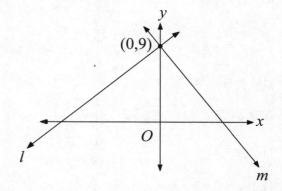

3. The equation of line m in the figure above is $y + 2x = b$. If line l is perpendicular to line m, which of the following could be the equation for line l ?

    (A) $y = 2x + 9$

    (B) $y = -\dfrac{1}{2}x + 9$

    (C) $y = -\dfrac{1}{2}x - 9$

    (D) $y = \dfrac{1}{2}x + 9$

    (E) $y = -x - 9$

4. In the xy-coordinate plane, the graph of the function g is a line. If $g(3) = 5$ and $g(9) = -2$, what is $g(6)$?

    (A) $-3\dfrac{1}{6}$

    (B) $-\dfrac{5}{6}$

    (C) $\dfrac{1}{3}$

    (D) $1\dfrac{1}{2}$

    (E) $3\dfrac{1}{6}$

5. Which of the following is an equation of the line in the xy-plane that passes through the point $(4, 1)$ and is parallel to the line $y = 3x - 4$?

(A) $y = -\frac{1}{3}x$

(B) $y = -3x - 4$

(C) $y = 3x - 11$

(D) $y = 3x + 4$

(E) $y = 3x + 13$

6. In the xy-coordinate plane, lines l and m are perpendicular. Line l contains the point $(0, 0)$ and has a slope of 2. Line m contains the points $(4, 2)$ and $(x, 0)$. What is the value of x ?

(A) -8
(B) -4
(C) 0
(D) 4
(E) 8

Reflections

0.4%

of all math
questions
on the SAT

When we are dealing with graphs, at times we will need to reflect or flip graphs about an axis.

Reflection across the *y*-axis
When you reflect a graph across/about the *y*-axis, it does this:

When you reflect a line across/ about the *y*-axis, the *y*-intercept remains constant. For every point on the line, the *y*-values remain the same, but the *x*-values change sign. So if the point (–3, 2) is on our original line, the point (3, 2) would be on the reflected line.

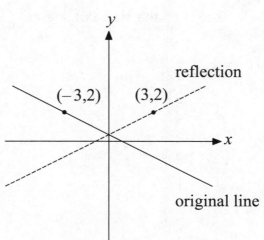

Reflection across the *x*-axis

When you reflect a graph across/about the *x*-axis, it does this:

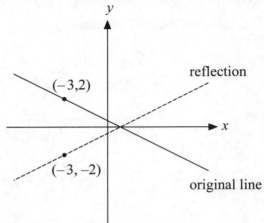

When you reflect a line across/about the *x*-axis, the *x*-intercept remains constant. For every point on the line, the *x*-values remain the same, but the *y*-values change sign. So if the point (–3, 2) is on our original line, the point (–3, –2) would be on the reflected line.

E In the *xy*-coordinate plane, line *r* is the reflection of line *s* about the *x*-axis. If the slope of line *r* is $\frac{3}{4}$, what is the slope of line *s* ?

(A) $-\frac{4}{3}$

(B) $-\frac{3}{4}$

(C) $\frac{3}{4}$

(D) 1

(E) $\frac{4}{3}$

S Line *r* is the reflection of line *s*. We are reflecting about the *x*-axis. Remember when we are reflecting about the *x*-axis, it looks like this.

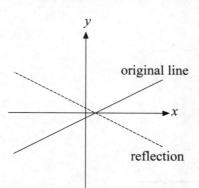

In this case we are looking for the slope of the reflected line. Slope is $\frac{\text{rise}}{\text{run}}$. The *x*-values stay the same, so the "run" does not change and remains 4. The *y*-values, however, switch signs, so the "rise" flips from 3 to -3. This will flip the slope from $\frac{3}{4}$ to $\left(-\frac{3}{4}\right)$.

E

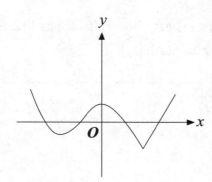

Which of the following graphs is the reflection of the graph above about the *x*-axis?

(A)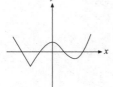

(B)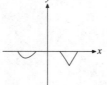

(C)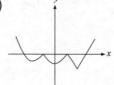

(D)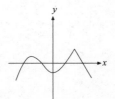

(E)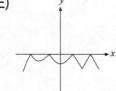

S Remember our horse! Reflecting about the *x*-axis flips the image upside down.

Our graph will flip just like the horse.

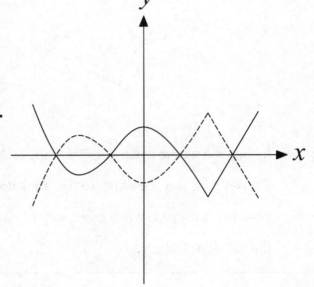

We are looking for the answer choice that looks like the dotted graph. That would be answer choice **(D)**.

Reflections Practice Problems

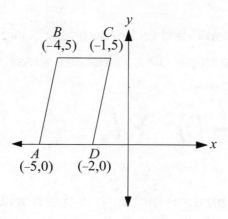

1. If the figure above were reflected about the *x*-axis, on what coordinates would the new point *B* lie?

   (A) (– 4, 5)
   (B) (4, –5)
   (C) (– 4, –5)
   (D) (4, 5)
   (E) (– 1, 5)

2. In the *xy*-coordinate plane, line *r* is the reflection of line *s* about the *x*-axis. If the equation of line *s* is $y = 2x - 3$, which of the following is the equation of line *r* ?

   (A) $y = -0.5x + 3$
   (B) $y = -2x - 3$
   (C) $y = -2x + 3$
   (D) $y = 2x$
   (E) $y = 0.5x + 3$

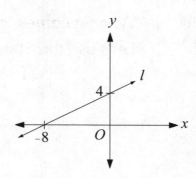

3. Line *l* is shown in the *xy*-plane above. If line *n* (not shown) is the reflection of line *l* about the *x*-axis, what is the equation of line *n* ?

   (A) $y = \frac{1}{2}x - 4$

   (B) $y = \frac{1}{2}x + 4$

   (C) $y = -\frac{1}{2}x - 4$

   (D) $y = -\frac{1}{2}x + 4$

   (E) $y = -\frac{1}{4}x - 4$

Shifting Graphs

1.2%

of all math
questions
on the SAT

When it comes to shifting graphs, you need to know a few basic rules. Let's use the Standard Formula for a parabola to illustrate these rules.

$$y = a(x - h)^2 + k$$

In this equation, **a** is the **stretch** (fat/thin) factor, **h** is the **horizontal** shift, and **k** is the **vertical** shift.

When dealing with the variable inside the parentheses, h, the graph shifting seems counterintuitive. But, remember in the original equation we are subtracting h. This means if you have a + in the parentheses, you are really subtracting a negative (– –). This is why we say h is negative and we move the graph to the left.

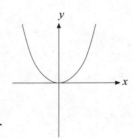

$$f(x) = x^2$$
original equation

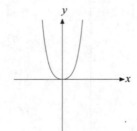

$$f(x) = 3x^2$$
a = integer
graph narrows

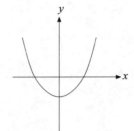

$$f(x) = x^2 - 3$$
k = negative
graph moves down

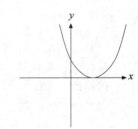

$$f(x) = (x - 3)^2$$
h = positive
graph moves right

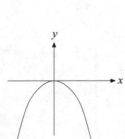

$$f(x) = -x^2$$
a = negative
graph flips down

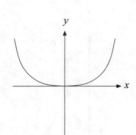

$$f(x) = \frac{1}{3}x^2$$
a = fraction
graph widens

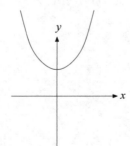

$$f(x) = x^2 + 3$$
k = positive
graph moves up

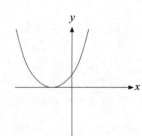

$$f(x) = (x + 3)^2$$
h = negative
graph moves left

Shifting graphs on a calculator

The absolute best strategy to use if you ever forget these rules is to break out your TI and jump to the graphing section. Press the **[y =]** button (bottom left of the screen).

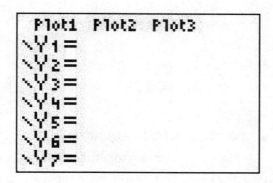

You can refresh all of the shifting graph rules in a matter of seconds using the graphing function. Plug in the following equations, one by one, to refresh the rules:

E (1) $y = x^2$
(2) $y = -x^2$
(3) $y = 2x^2$
(4) $y = x^2 + 2$
(5) $y = (x - 2)^2$

S
(1)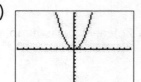
(2)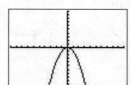
(3)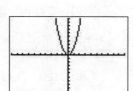

(4)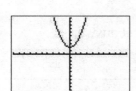
(5)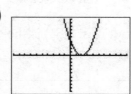

E

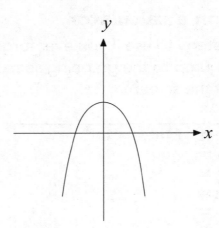

The graph above is a parabola whose equation is $y = -ax^2 + 6$, where a is a constant. If $y = -a(x - 1)^2 + 8$ is graphed on the same axes, which of the following best describes the resulting graph as compared with the graph above?

(A) It will be wider.
(B) It will be moved 1 unit to the right and 2 units upward.
(C) It will be narrower and moved 8 units upward.
(D) It will be moved 2 units upward.
(E) It will be moved 1 unit to the left and 2 units downward.

S Original graph: $y = -ax^2 + 6$

New graph: $y = -a(x - 1)^2 + 8$

When you line them up like we have above, it's clear what is happening:

Our sign +/- is the same. *no flipping*
Our stretch factor, a, is unchanged. *our parabola doesn't get skinny or fat*
Our horizontal shift factor, h, is 1. *we will move 1 to the right*
Our vertical shift factor, k, has increased from 6 to 8. *we move up 2*

Looking through our options, **(B)** is the correct answer.

E

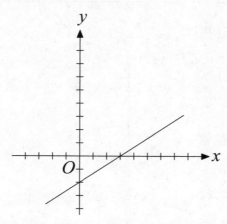

The figure above shows the graph of $y = f(a)$. Which of the following is the graph of $y = |f(a)|$?

(A)

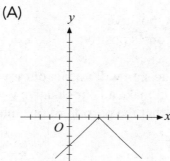

(D)

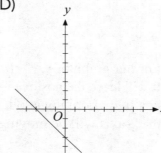

(B)

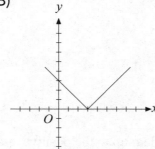

(E)

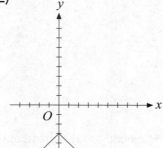

(C)

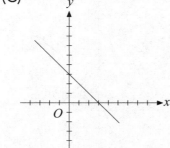

S $y = f(a)$ looks like this:

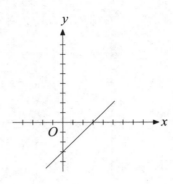

Our new graph will be $y = |f(a)|$

Remember absolute value leaves positive values alone, but it brings everything negative to the positive side.

$$|3| = 3. \text{ Positive stays positive.}$$
$$|-3| = 3. \text{ Negative becomes positive}$$

For our graph of $y = |f(a)|$, the absolute value sign will impact our **y-values**. It will leave the positive y-values alone but will make all our negative y-values positive. Looking at our graph, we can see that the portion of our line under the x-axis will be moving.

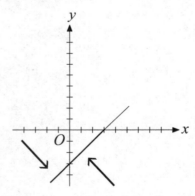

We need to take the negative values and flip them up to the positive, essentially reflecting them over the x-axis. Our positive values will remain unchanged.

Absolute value reflects only the negative portion of the line over the x-axis.

Additionally, using the process of elimination, we can look at all of the answer choices and cross off anything which has negative y values. That would instantly knock off (A), (C), (D), and (E), leaving us with our answer, **(B)**. This matches our graph!

Shifting Graphs Practice Problems

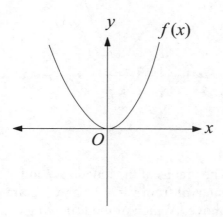

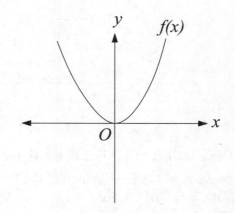

1. The figure above shows the graph of the function $f(x)$. If $g(x) = 2f(x)$ for all values of x, which of the following statements must be true about the graph of g in comparison with the graph of f?

    (A) It is the same width as $f(x)$ and opens downward.

    (B) It is wider than $f(x)$ and opens downward.

    (C) It is narrower than $f(x)$ and opens upward.

    (D) It is wider than $f(x)$ and opens upward.

    (E) It is the same width as $f(x)$ and opens upward.

2. The figure above shows the graph of $y = f(x)$. Which of the following is the graph of $f(x-2) + 1$?

(A)

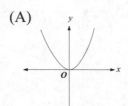

(E)

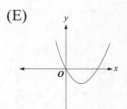

(B)

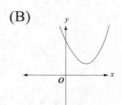

(C)

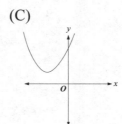

(D)

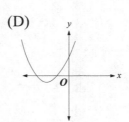

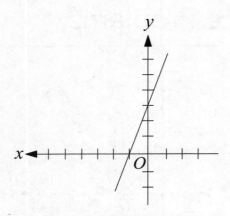

3. The equation of the line in the figure

   above is $y = 3x + 3$. Which of the following
   is the graph of $y = |3x + 3|$?

(A)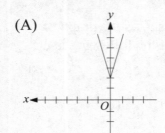

(E)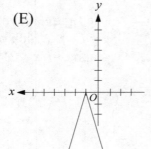

(B)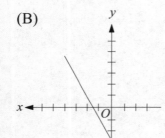

(C)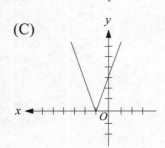

(D)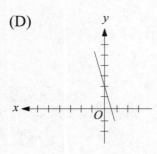

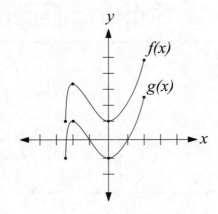

4. The graphs of the functions f and g in the
   interval from $x = -2.5$ to $x = 2$ are shown
   above. Which of the following expresses
   g in terms of f?

   (A) $g(x) = f(x) + 2$
   (B) $g(x) = f(x + 2)$
   (C) $g(x) = f(x) - 2$
   (D) $g(x) = f(x - 2)$
   (E) $g(x) = f(x - 2) + 2$

Advanced Graphing

1.2%

of all math
questions
on the SAT

Sometimes the SAT asks us to do a bit more with graphing. These questions usually involve two shapes on a single coordinate plane. Often the questions require you to use the points where the two shapes intersect. The key to these problems is simple: Take the given points that lie on the curve and plug them back into the equation of the graph. Most of the time, this will take you down the path to the right answer.

E

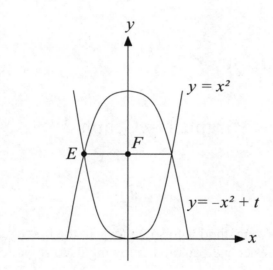

The figure above shows the graphs of $y = x^2$ and $y = -x^2 + t$ for some constant t. If the length of $\overline{EF}$ is 2, what is the value of t?

(A)   4
(B)   8
(C) 10
(D) 12
(E) 14

This rule applies to any intersection of 2 graphs.

S As noted above, this type of Algebra 2 advanced graphing problem involves plugging the given points into the equation.

$\overline{EF} = 2$. This is key. We know that one point of intersection of the 2 parabolas is $(-2, y)$. Because both parabolas, $y = x^2$ and $y = -x^2 + t$, have no horizontal shift and rise evenly to the left and to the right of the y-axis, we know they are symmetrical about the y-axis. This means when the graphs meet again on the other side of the y-axis from point E, the coordinates are $(2, y)$.

For this type of problem, we need to know that at each point of intersection, the equations of the graphs equal each other.

Now we know that at any point where our two graphs intersect, the equation for Graph 1, $y = x^2$, is equal to the equation for Graph 2, $y = -x^2 + t$.

Let's work with a point of intersection we know: $(2, y)$.

Graph 1: $y = 2^2$

Graph 2: $y = -(2)^2 + t$

$$\text{Graph } 1 = \text{Graph } 2$$
$$2^2 = -(2)^2 + t$$
$$4 = -4 + t$$
$$t = \boxed{8}, \textbf{(B)}$$

An alternative method is to solve for y in the first equation, and then plug it back into the second equation, allowing us to solve for t.

$$y = 2^2$$
$$y = \boxed{4}$$

Now plug this into the 2nd equation, $y = -x^2 + t$, and solve for t.

$$y = -(2)^2 + t$$
$$4 = -(2)^2 + t$$
$$4 = -4 + t$$
$$t = \boxed{8}, \textbf{(B)}$$

E

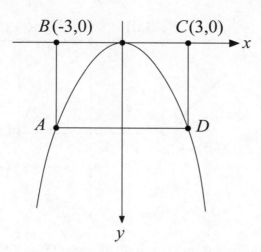

In the figure above, *ABCD* is a rectangle and points *A* and *D* lie on the graph of $y = -ax^2$, where *a* is a constant. If the area of *ABCD* is 24, what is the value of *a* ?

(A) $-\dfrac{9}{4}$

(B) $-\dfrac{4}{9}$

(C) $\dfrac{4}{9}$

(D) 2

(E) $\dfrac{9}{4}$

S First, we need to figure out the dimensions of the rectangle.

Point *B* $(-3, 0)$
Point *C* $(3, 0)$
Our rectangle has a width ($\overline{BC}$) of 6.
We know that the area of *ABCD* is 24.

$$\text{Area} = lw$$
$$24 = 6l$$
$$\boxed{4} = l$$

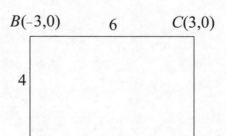

Let's see what that means for the graph.

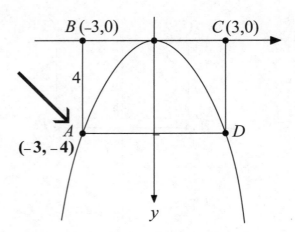

Now we have a point on the curve! Bingo. This is the key to almost every advanced graphing problem. Now we can plug the point into the equation and solve for a.

$$y = -ax^2$$
$$-4 = -a(-3)^2$$
$$-4 = -9a$$
$$\frac{-4}{-9} = a$$
$$\boxed{\frac{4}{9}} = a$$

E

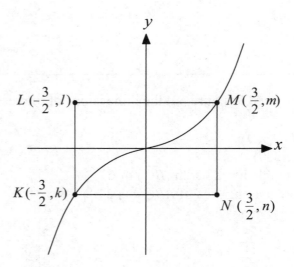

<u>Note</u>: Figure not drawn to scale.

In the figure above, *KLMN* is a rectangle. Points *K* and *M* lie on the graph of $y = dx^3$, where *d* is a constant. If the perimeter of *KLMN* is 24, what is the value of *d* ?

This problem is very similar to the last example. Let's work with the rectangle to find a point we can use later.

Point L $(-\frac{3}{2}, l)$

Point M $(\frac{3}{2}, m)$

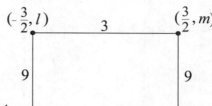

Our rectangle has a length $(\overline{LM})$ of 3.
We know that the perimeter of $KLMN$ is 24.

$$\text{Perimeter} = 2l + 2w$$
$$24 = 2(3) + 2w$$
$$24 = 6 + 2w$$
$$18 = 2w$$
$$\boxed{9} = w$$

Looking at the equation of our curve, $y = dx^3$, we see that there is neither a horizontal nor a vertical shift. So we can divide our 9 cleanly in half. Point M lies 4.5 above the x-axis.

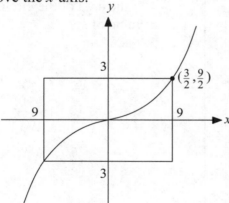

Now we have the coordinates of our Point M, $(\frac{3}{2}, \frac{9}{2})$ that we can plug neatly back into our equation.

$$y = dx^3$$
$$\frac{9}{2} = d(\frac{3}{2})^3$$
$$\frac{9}{2} = \frac{27}{8}(d)$$
$$\frac{9}{2} \times \frac{8}{27} = d$$
$$\frac{36}{27} = d$$
$$\boxed{\frac{4}{3}} = d$$

Advanced Graphing Practice Problems

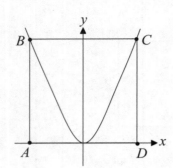

1. In the figure above, points B and C lie on the graph $y = kx^2$. If the area of the square $ABCD$ is 16, what is the value of k?

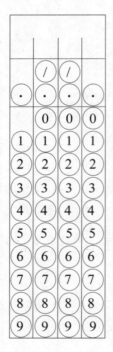

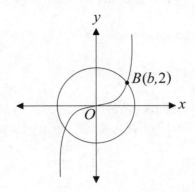

Note: Figure not drawn to scale.

2. In the figure above, point B lies on the graph of $y = kx^3$, where k is a constant. If the area of the circle is 8π, what is the value of k?

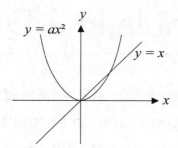

3. The graph above is a parabola whose equation is $y = ax^2$, where a is a constant. If the graph intersects the line $y = x$ where $x = 3$, what is the value of a?

(A) $\dfrac{1}{6}$

(B) $\dfrac{1}{3}$

(C) 1

(D) 3

(E) 6

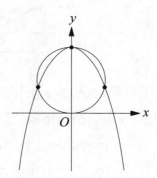

5. The figure above shows the graph of $f(x) = a - x^2$, where a is a constant. If the circle above has area 16π and intersects the graph at the three points shown, what is the value of a?

(A) 4
(B) 8
(C) 12
(D) 16
(E) 32

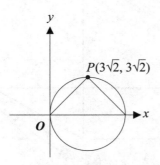

4. In the figure above, an isosceles triangle is inscribed within the circle shown. The circle is tangent to the y-axis at the origin, and point P lies on the circle. What is the area of the circle?

(A) 6π
(B) 9π
(C) 12π
(D) 18π
(E) 36π

Distance Formula in 3-D

0.2%

of all math
questions
on the SAT

The most advanced Geometry problems ask that you find the diagonals of 3-dimensional shapes. The Distance Formula that allows you to find the hypotenuse of a right triangle can also be used in three dimensions to find the diagonal length inside a rectangular box.

$$d = \sqrt{x^2 + y^2 + z^2}$$

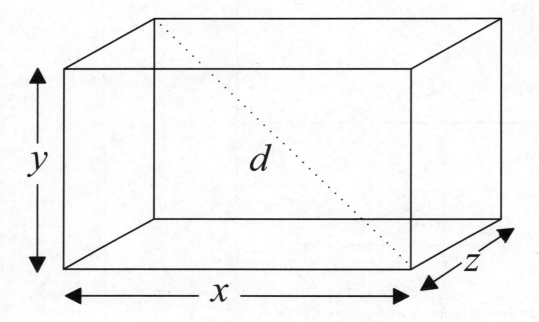

This is a major short-cut. But if you forget this equation on test day, you can still solve these problems using the standard Pythagorean Theorem multiple times. We will walk through both strategies.

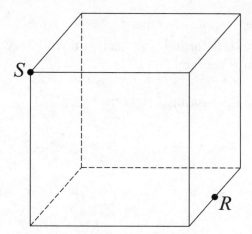

The cube shown above has a volume of 64 cubic inches, and *R* is the midpoint of one of the edges. What is the length of *SR* (not shown) ?

(A) 2
(B) 4
(C) 6
(D) 8
(E) 10

 We have 2 approaches: the super short cut and the multiple triangle solution. Let's use the short cut first.

$$d = \sqrt{x^2 + y^2 + z^2}$$

We need to find our 3 sides. We know that the volume of the cube is 64. Therefore, the length of every side of the cube is

$$\sqrt[3]{64} = 4$$

x and *y* are complete sides of the cube, and therefore $x = y = 4$.
R is the mid-point of our edge, so $z = 2$.
$x = 4$
$y = 4$
$z = 2$
Using our formula:

$d = \sqrt{4^2 + 4^2 + 2^2}$
$d = \sqrt{36}$
$d = \boxed{6}$, **(C)**

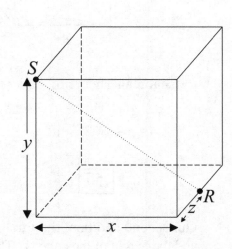

If you forget this formula, you can still work through the problem using the Pythagorean Theorem.

The key here is making 2 right triangles.

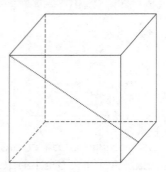

We can get to our diagonal in 2 steps. Knowing that the volume is 64, we find that a full edge is 4 and the half edge is 2. Let's label our shape.

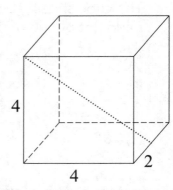

We see our first likely right triangle at the base of the cube using the bottom 4 and the 2.

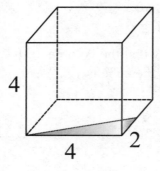
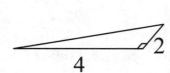

Pythagorean Theorem:

$$a^2 + b^2 = c^2$$
$$4^2 + 2^2 = c^2$$
$$20 = c^2$$
$$\boxed{\sqrt{20}} = c$$

Our second and final right triangle will use our newly found side, $\sqrt{20}$, and the height of the cube, 4. This will allow us to solve for the diagonal.

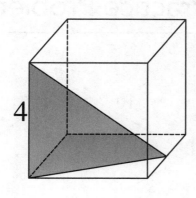 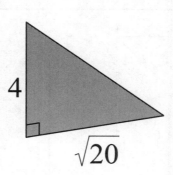

Pythagorean Theorem:

$$a^2 + b^2 = c^2$$
$$4^2 + (\sqrt{20})^2 = c^2$$
$$16 + 20 = c^2$$
$$36 = c^2$$
$$\textbf{6} = c$$

Our answer is still **(C)**.

You have both methods at your disposal. It's a good general rule to know them both. Whenever you are working with Geometry and don't know how to begin, look for a right triangle. Right triangles are the foundation of many advanced geometry problems.

Distance Formula in 3-D Practice Problems

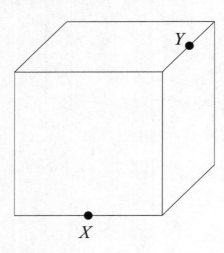

1. The cube shown above has edges of length 4, and X and Y are the midpoints of two of the edges. What is the length of $\overline{XY}$ (not shown?

(A) $\sqrt{5}$

(B) $2\sqrt{2}$

(C) $2\sqrt{6}$

(D) $4\sqrt{3}$

(E) $4\sqrt{5}$

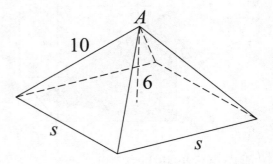

Note: Figure not drawn to scale.

2. The pyramid shown above has altitude of 6 and a square base. The four edges that meet at A, the vertex of the pyramid, each have length 10. What is the value of s ?

(A) 8

(B) $8\sqrt{2}$

(C) $8\sqrt{3}$

(D) 16

(E) $16\sqrt{3}$

Geometry: Review

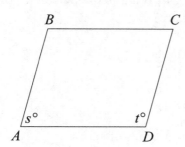

1. If $\overline{AB} \parallel \overline{DC}$ in the figure above, what is the value of $s + t$?

   (A) 45
   (B) 90
   (C) 120
   (D) 180
   (E) 360

2. An equilateral hexagon and a square have equal perimeters. If the hexagon has sides of length 6, what is the length of one side of the square?

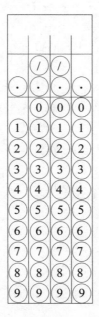

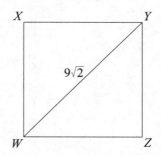

3. What is the perimeter of square *WXYZ* above?

4. In the figure above, point *A* is the center of the larger circle, and point *B* is the center of the smaller circle. If $AB = 8$, what is the sum of the diameters of the two circles?

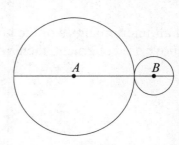

   (A)   8
   (B) 12
   (C) 16
   (D) 24
   (E) 32

5. What is the area of a right triangle whose sides have lengths of 9, 12, and 15?

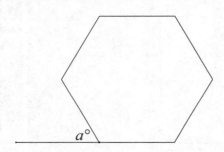

6. If all interior angles of the hexagon above are congruent, then $a =$

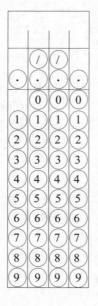

7. In the *xy*-coordinate plane, three vertices of a square are given by the coordinates $(-2, 2)$, $(-2, -2)$, and $(2, 2)$. What is the perimeter of the square?

(A)   8
(B)   12
(C)   16
(D)   18
(E)   24

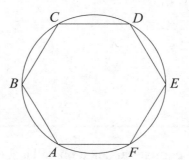

8. In the circle above, hexagon *ABCDEF* is equilateral. If the radius of the circle is 4, what is the length of arc *DEF*?

(A) $\dfrac{\pi}{6}$

(B) 2π

(C) $\dfrac{4\pi}{3}$

(D) $\dfrac{8\pi}{3}$

(E) $\dfrac{16\pi}{3}$

9. A cube with side length 3 has volume a. In terms of a, what is the volume of a cube with side length 6?

(A) $2a$
(B) $4a$
(C) $6a$
(D) $8a$
(E) $10a$

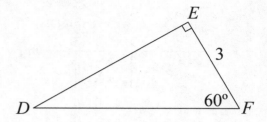

11. In the figure above, what is the area of $\triangle DEF$?

(A) $3\sqrt{3}$

(B) $\dfrac{6\sqrt{3}}{2}$

(C) $\dfrac{9\sqrt{3}}{2}$

(D) $9\sqrt{3}$

(E) 12

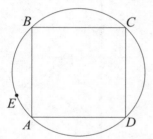

10. In the figure above, square $ABCD$ is inscribed in the circle. If the length of arc AEB is 3π, what is the radius of the circle?

(A) 3
(B) 4
(C) 6
(D) 12
(E) 18

12. If the volume of a cube is $216x^3$, what is the length of one side of the cube?

(A) $64x^2$
(B) $6x^2$
(C) $12x$
(D) $6x$
(E) $3x$

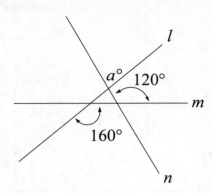

13. In the figure above, $a =$

(A)   45
(B)   60
(C)   80
(D) 100
(E) 120

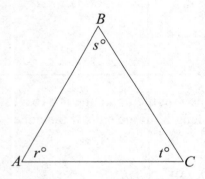

Note: Figure not drawn to scale.

14. In the figure above, $r > s$. Which of the following must be FALSE?

(A) $BC > AC$
(B) $AC > AB$
(C) $BC = AB$
(D) $AC = BC$
(E) $s = t$

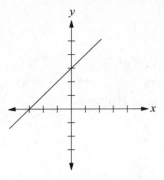

15. The equation of the line in the figure above is $y = x + 3$. Which of the following is the graph of $y = |x + 3|$?

(A)
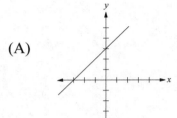

(B)
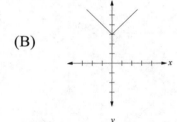

(C)
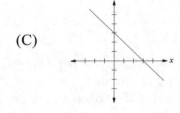

(D)
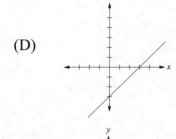

(E)
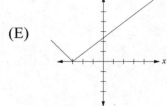

The Geometry Short List

1 There are **180°** on one side of a **line**.

2 The internal angles of a **TRIANGLE** add up to **180°**.

3 The internal angles of a **QUADRILATERAL** add up to **360°**.

4 When you are trying to find the **SUM OF THE INTERNAL ANGLES OF A POLYGON**, you can simply cut it into triangles and quadrilaterals and then add those, but don't cross the lines.

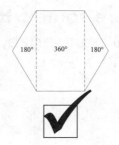 

5 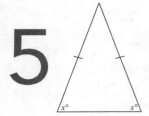 **ISOSCELES** triangles have two equal sides and two equal angles.

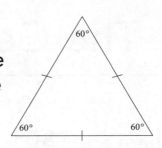

6 EQUILATERAL triangles have three equal sides and three equal angles; the angles are each 60°.

7 When you see a RIGHT TRIANGLE, think PYTHAGOREAN THEOREM.

Pythagorean Theorem

$$a^2 + b^2 = c^2$$

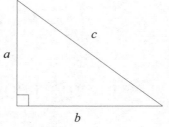

8 There are some SPECIAL RIGHT TRIANGLES you need to memorize.

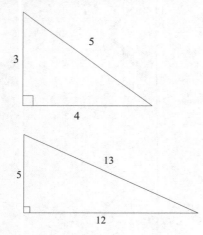

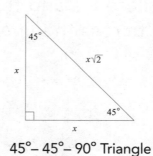

45°– 45°– 90° Triangle

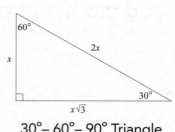

30°– 60°– 90° Triangle

9 The **AREA** of a circle is: $A = \pi r^2$
The **CIRCUMFERENCE** is: $C = \pi d = 2\pi r$

10 $\dfrac{\text{Piece}}{\text{Whole}} = \dfrac{\text{Angle measure}}{360°} = \dfrac{\text{Arc length}}{\text{Circumference}} = \dfrac{\text{Wedge area}}{\text{Circle area}}$

11 A line **TANGENT** to a circle always forms a 90° angle with the radius of the circle.

12 When you are given a shape you don't like (e.g. a trapezoid), **BREAK IT** into shapes you do like (i.e. right triangles and quadrilaterals.

13 When you are asked how many small objects will fit into a larger object or area, just **DIVIDE** the large area or **VOLUME** by the small area or volume.

14 For **PROPORTIONAL SHAPES**, find the **LOCKED RATIO**.

15 Slope $= m = \dfrac{\text{rise}}{\text{run}} = \dfrac{\triangle y}{\triangle x} = \dfrac{y_2 - y_1}{x_2 - x_1}$

16 $y = mx + b$ where x and y represent any point on the line, m is the slope, and b is the y-intercept.

17 When you reflect over the **x-axis**, the y-values change, but the **x-values stay the same**.

18 When you reflect over the **y-axis**, the x-values change, but the **y-values stay the same**.

19 For **ADVANCED GRAPHING** problems, always plug your given points, (**x**, **y**) back into your equation f(**x**) = **y**.

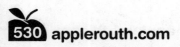

Properties of Numbers

6.0%

of all math
questions
on the SAT

In order to tackle SAT math questions, you must learn some basic number properties and definitions. This section will give you a foundation that will allow you to learn the SAT-specific strategies and tricks in this book.

Definitions and Important Concepts

Positive Integers
Whole numbers greater than zero: 1, 2, 3, 4, 5, ...

Negative Integers
Whole numbers less than zero: $-1, -2, -3, -4, -5, \ldots$

Even
Integers with units digit 0, 2, 4, 6, or 8.

Odd
Integers with units digit 1, 3, 5, 7, or 9.

Zero is an even integer that is neither positive nor negative.

E If n is an odd integer, which of the following must be an odd integer?

(A) $n - 1$
(B) $n + 1$
(C) $2n$
(D) $3n + 1$
(E) $4n + 1$

If the problem says "must be," you can usually pick numbers, and your objective is to DIS-PROVE the four wrong answers in order to find the right one.

S Easy as pie. Just plug in a number! The problem says that *n* must be odd, so let's try **3**.

(A) **3** − 1 = 2   *So, this one is out.*
(B) **3** + 1 = 4   *This one is out, too.*
(C) 2(**3**) = 6   *Not it.*
(D) 3(**3**) + 1 = 10   *Not so much.*
(E) 4(**3**) + 1 = 13   *Now we're talking!*

The Mighty Decimal Point

Make sure you know what the digits *before* and *after* the decimal point are called. This will clear up any possible confusion on the test.

E   Given the number: **5947.382**

List the:

Thousandths digit _____   Hundredths digit _____

Tens digit _____   Hundreds digit _____

Ones/Units digit _____   Thousands digit _____

Tenths digit _____

S   Thousandths digit **2**   Hundredths digit **8**

Tens digit **4**   Hundreds digit **9**

Ones/Units digit **7**   Thousands digit **5**

Tenths digit **3**

E How many three-digit integers have the hundreds digit equal to 2 and the units digit (ones digit) equal to 5?

(A)   9
(B)   10
(C)   20
(D) 190
(E) 200

S The simplest thing to do here is to list the numbers that satisfy the requirements.

2 for the hundreds
5 for the units

2?5

Here's our set:
205, 215, 225, 235, 245, 255, 265, 275, 285, and 295
We have 10 numbers in our set, so our answer is **(B)**.

Prime Numbers

Prime numbers are positive integers greater than **1** and divisible by only **1** and themselves.

1 might be the loneliest number, but it is NOT prime. The lowest prime number is **2**. (2 is also the only even prime number.)

E List the first 10 prime numbers.

S 2, 3, 5, 7, 11, 13, 17, 19, 23, 29

E What is the sum of the smallest prime number greater than 10 and the smallest prime number greater than 30?

(A) 42
(B) 44
(C) 46
(D) 48
(E) 50

S The smallest prime number greater than 10 is 11.
The smallest prime number greater than 30 is 31.
$$11 + 31 = \boxed{42}, (A)$$

Inclusive Problems

Inclusive simply means "count both end points." For inclusive problems, the test makers ask questions like, "How many integers are there from 200 to 300 inclusive?" Most people immediately think "300 − 200 = 100, so there are 100," but actually there are 101 because you have to count both of the end points.

Try it with 10 and 20 to prove it to yourself.
10, 11, 12, 13, 14, 15, 16, 17, 18, 19, 20

Count 'em: not 10 integers, but 11.

To answer inclusive problems, all you have to do is *subtract the end points and add one.*

E How many integers in the set of all integers from 100 to 300, inclusive, are multiples of 10?

(A)   20
(B)   21
(C)   22
(D) 100
(E) 200

S You can write them out and count them, but you can also do the math.

$$300 - 100 \rightarrow \frac{200}{10} \rightarrow 20 + 1 = \boxed{21} \text{ (B)}$$

OR, you can list them:

100, 110, 120, 130..........280, 290, 300
  1   2   3   4............ 19   20 ㉑

Factors and Multiples

Prime factors are prime numbers that divide into a number. A factor tree is an easy way to find prime factors.

E What is the greatest prime factor of 52?

S To create the factor tree, start by dividing the number by the smallest positive integer (greater than 1) that will go evenly into 52. Because 52 is an even number, start with 2. Then, continue to divide by the smallest prime number possible until you have a prime number at the bottom of each branch.

The answer is ⑬.

Least Common Multiple

The *Least Common Multiple* of two integers is the smallest number that both integers will divide into evenly.

E What is the least common multiple of 9 and 15?

S All you have to do with *LCM* problems is find the multiples and see where they match.

	9	15
× 1:	9	15
× 2:	18	30
× 3:	27	(45)
× 4:	36	60
× 5:	(45)	75

Voilà! We have our *LCM*: (45)

Greatest Common Factor

The *Greatest Common Factor* is the largest integer that will divide into a set of numbers.

E What is the greatest common factor of 18 and 12?

S The greatest number that will go into both 18 and 12? We need to make our trees and find the prime factors. Then circle all the prime factors they have in common and multiply them.

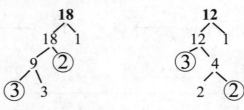

Our *GCF* is 2 × 3 = (6)

The *GCF* is also called the *greatest common divisor*.

Properties of Numbers Practice Problems

16. If the number 4.06 is rounded to the nearest tenth and then tripled, what is the resulting number?

(A) 4.1
(B) 4.2
(C) 8.2
(D) 12.2
(E) 12.3

17. A number was rounded to 23.7. Which of the following could have been the number before it was rounded?

(A) 23.000
(B) 23.604
(C) 23.709
(D) 23.760
(E) 24.000

18. If m and n are positive integers, and $(m + n)(m)$ is even, which of the following must be true?

(A) If m is odd, then n is odd.
(B) If m is odd, then n is even.
(C) If m is even, then n is even.
(D) If m is even, then n is odd.
(E) m must be even.

19. What is the greatest possible 4-digit odd integer whose digits add up to 7?

20. What is the least integer value x such that $(0.3)^x < 0.001$?

21. If a 6 were placed between the tens and units digits of the 3-digit integer ABC, the resulting number would be

   (A) $100A + 10B + C + 6$
   (B) $100A + B + 6 + C$
   (C) $1000A + 100B + 6 + C$
   (D) $1000A + 100B + 60 + C$
   (E) $1000A + 600 + 60B + 10C$

---

22. Set M contains the first 50 positive integers. A new set N is formed by multiplying all the integers in set M by 3 and subtracting 5 from each integer. What is the difference between the greatest number in set N and the greatest number in set M?

   (A)   50
   (B)   65
   (C)   85
   (D)   95
   (E)   145

---

23. If $x, y,$ and z are consecutive integers, and $x < y < z$ which of the following could be the units digit of y if the units digit of the product of x and z is 4?

   (A) 3
   (B) 4
   (C) 5
   (D) 6
   (E) 7

24. For how many integer values of x is $50 > 2x - 7 > 30$ true?

   (A) 8
   (B) 9
   (C) 10
   (D) 11
   (E) 20

---

10. What is the least positive integer that is divisible by the numbers 1 through 6 inclusive?

   (A)   21
   (B)   30
   (C)   40
   (D)   60
   (E)   120

---

11. What is the least positive integer x for which $40x$ is the square of an integer?

12. Which of the following is not a factor of $5^3 - 5^2$?

(A) 2
(B) 3
(C) 4
(D) 5
(E) 10

13. The sum of the prime numbers between 0 and 10 is how much less than the sum of prime numbers between 10 and 15?

(A)   6
(B)   7
(C)   9
(D) 11
(E) 13

14. How many prime numbers are there between 30 and 50 inclusive?

15. Let S be the set of all integers between one and twenty, and let x be a prime number in set S such that $2 \leq x < 10$. Then, x could be equal to how many different integers?

(A) 3
(B) 4
(C) 5
(D) 6
(E) 8

Working Backwards

7%

of all math
questions
on the SAT

There are times when you attempt to solve a problem on the SAT and you get stuck. When you cannot make any progress tackling a problem head-on, a smart approach is to work backwards from the answer choices. This is especially useful when you are in the world of algebra.

E John has x pieces of candy in his pocket. He gives half of the candies to Kerri, and one-third of the remaining candies to Lori. If he is left with 10 candies in his pocket, what is the value of x?

(A) 60
(B) 50
(C) 40
(D) 30
(E) 20

S We could solve this using algebra, but we can also solve this directly using the answer choices. We only have 5 answers to choose from; we know one of these has to be the answer. If we plug each answer choice into the problem, we can determine which one works.

Notice that the answer choices are in order from largest to smallest. It's a good strategy to start from (C) and move out from there.

(C) So If John has 40 pieces and gives half (20) to Kerri, he will be left with 20 pieces. If he then goes and gives $\frac{1}{3}$ of the remaining pieces away $(\frac{1}{3})(20) = 6.667$, he will be left with 13.334 pieces. We need to end with 10 pieces, so our starting number was too high. We need a smaller number.

(D) If John has 30 pieces and gives half (15) to Kerri, he will be left with 15 pieces. If he gives $\frac{1}{3}$ of his 15 pieces (5) to Lori, he will be left with 10. Yeah! That's it, and we solved the problem in only 2 steps. This might even be faster than solving through algebra, and it is considerably easier.

E If $|8 - 3x| \geq 40$, which of the following could equal x ?

   (A) −10
   (B)   −2
   (C)   0
   (D)   9
   (E)   16

S Again — let's start from (C).

(C) $|8 - 3(0)| \geq 40$
     $|8| \geq 40$ *Nope! We need a larger number!*

(D) $|8 - 3(9)| \geq 40$
   $|8 - 27| \geq 40$
    $|-19| \geq 40$ *Nope! Try again.*

(E) $|8 - 3(16)| \geq 40,$
   $|8 - 48| \geq 40$
    $|-40| \geq 40$ *Yes! That's our answer!*

Are you convinced? When you are in a pinch, and you can't go forward, try going backwards.

Working Backwards Practice Problems

1. A kindergarten class wants to buy a $64 aquarium for the classroom. If the teacher and students agree to split the cost such that the teacher pays three times as much as the students, how much, in dollars, should the teacher pay?

   (A) 16
   (B) 32
   (C) 40
   (D) 48
   (E) 56

2. A jar, filled with only red and blue marbles, contains 20 marbles. If John adds one blue and one red marble to the jar, the ratio of red to blue marbles in the jar will increase. What is the greatest number of red marbles that could originally have been in the jar?

   (A)   5
   (B)   9
   (C) 10
   (D) 11
   (E) 19

3. John is 6 years older than Mark. 6 years ago John was twice as old as Mark. How old is John today?

   (A)   6
   (B)   9
   (C) 12
   (D) 18
   (E) 24

4. Arianna bought a camera for $93. This price is 3 dollars less than 80% of the manufacturer's list price. What is the manufacturer's list price?

   (A) $120.00
   (B) $114.00
   (C) $112.50
   (D) $87.50
   (E) $56.00

5. Scott has exactly twice as many trading cards as Todd. Ryan has exactly four times as many trading cards as Scott. If the three of them have fewer than 100 trading cards combined, what is the maximum number of trading cards Todd could have?

(A)   6
(B)   9
(C)   10
(D)   12
(E)   18

6. Two identical 6-inch deep water buckets drain at uniform rates of 1inch per hour. If bucket one begins draining at 12 p.m., and bucket two begins draining at 2 p.m., at what time will bucket two have exactly five times as much water as bucket one?

(A) 4:00 p.m.
(B) 4:30 p.m.
(C) 5:00 p.m.
(D) 5:30 p.m.
(E) 6:00 p.m.

Art of Translation

5.6%

of all math
questions
on the SAT

Wordy Algebra problems are fairly common on the SAT, especially in the beginning of each math section. These problems depend almost entirely on correct translation. If you can correctly turn the words into math, the math is pretty easy.

Here is a quick rundown of common Wordy Algebra terms and their math equivalents:

Word	Math Meaning
What, how much, a number	Some variable (x)
Is, was, equals	=
Sum, increase, more than, greater than	Add (+)
Subtract, less than, exceeds	Subtract (−)
Difference	Subtract (−)
Of, times	Multiply (×)
Product	Multiply (×)
Divisible by, divided by, out of, per	Divide (÷)
Percent (%)	Multiply by $\frac{1}{100}$

With these problems, the best thing to do is mark out the words as you translate them into math.

E The product of two positive integers is 30 and their difference is one. What is the sum of the two numbers?

Don't try to tackle the whole problem at once. Translate it phrase-by-phrase.

S Step 1: Circle what you're solving for.

The product of two positive integers is 30 and their difference is one.

(**What is the sum**) **of the two numbers?**

Step 2: Translate piece-by-piece, marking out as you go.

~~The product of two positive integers~~	~~is 30~~	~~and their difference~~	~~is one~~
$a \times b$	$= 30$	$a - b$	$= 1$

What is (**the sum of**) **the two numbers?**

$$a + b = \, ?$$

There are two rules for a and b :

1) $a \times b = 30$

2) $a - b = 1$

We can approach this problem algebraically or work around the algebra. Let's consider both approaches, starting with the work around. We need to find two factors of 30 ($a \times b = 30$) that are one unit apart $a - b = 1$). Let's find the factors of 30.

30×1

15×2

10×3

6×5

Which factors are one unit apart $(a - b = 1)$?

30×1

15×2

10×3

$\boxed{6 \times 5}$

Now, what was it we were solving for (look at what you circled)? The sum of the two:

$6 + 5 =$ ⑪ *That's our answer!*

If we wanted to tackle the algebra directly, we'd use substitution to solve the problem.

$$a - b = 1$$
$$a = 1 + b$$

We know $a \times b = 30$, and now we can substitue $(1 + b)$ for a. Our new equation is:

$$(1 + b) \times b = 30$$
$$b + b^2 = 30$$
$$b^2 + b - 30 = 0$$
$$(b - 5)(b + 6) = 0$$
$$b = 5, -6$$

Now we know what b is—the problem said it was a *positive* integer—we can solve for a.

$$a = 1 + b$$
$$a = 1 + 5 = 6$$

All we have left is to add our a and b.

$$a + b = 5 + 6 = ⑪$$

We arrive at the same answer at the end, but this clearly takes more time. Working around the algebra seems like a smarter approach!

Always double-check what you circled to make sure that you are solving the correct problem.

E If a given number is divided by x and the result is 6 times the original number, what is the value of x ?

S Step 1: Circle what you're solving for.

If a given number is divided by x and the result is 6 times the original number, (what is the value of x ?)

Step 2: Translate, and mark as you go.

~~A given number is divided by x~~	~~the result is~~	~~6 times the original number~~
$\dfrac{a}{x}$	$=$	$6(a)$

$$\frac{a}{x} = 6a$$

We are solving for x, so we must isolate x.

$$a = 6ax$$

$$\frac{a}{6a} = x$$

$$\boxed{\frac{1}{6}} = x$$

Art of Translation
Practice Problems

---

1. If six is three-fourths of a number, what is the number?

(A) – 6
(B)   4
(C)   2
(D)   8
(E) 10

2. If half of a number is equal to 5 more than twice the number, what is the number?

(A) $-\dfrac{10}{3}$

(B) $-\dfrac{3}{10}$

(C)   0

(D) $\dfrac{3}{10}$

(E) $\dfrac{10}{3}$

3. If 7 more than three times a number is equal to 25, what is half the number?

(A)   2
(B)   3
(C)   4
(D)   6
(E) $3\dfrac{1}{2}$

4. a is the sum of $2b$ and 3 more than b. If $b = 4$, then a is

(A)   8
(B)   9
(C) 15
(D) 18
(E) 19

5. From the set of odd integers between 8 and 18, how many distinct pairs of different numbers have a sum of 26?

(A) 1
(B) 2
(C) 3
(D) 4
(E) 5

6. The sum of s and t is equal to twice u, and t is 39 less than twice the sum of s and u. What is the value of s?

7. If the sum of one-half of a certain number and one-third of the same number is thirty, what is the number?

(A) 20
(B) 25
(C) 30
(D) 36
(E) 40

8. If 6 more than a certain number is tripled, the result is 66. What is the number?

(A) 11
(B) 16
(C) 22
(D) 33
(E) 60

9. If s is t less than four times u, what is t in terms of s and u?

(A) $4u + s$

(B) $4u - s$

(C) $\dfrac{1}{4}u + s$

(D) $\dfrac{1}{4}u - s$

(E) $\dfrac{u + s}{4}$

Picking Numbers

12%

of all math
questions
on the SAT

SAT abstract algebra problems use the phrase **"in terms of,"** and/or have the same variables in all 5 answer choices. If all five answer choices contain the same variables, you've found a **picking numbers** problem.

Strategy 1:

Solve the problem head-on using algebra. This method often takes more time and exposes you to a greater risk of careless errors.

Strategy 2:

Solve the problem by picking numbers. This strategy **gets rid** of the algebra; all you have to do is add, subtract, multiply, and divide. Also, this method is generally faster than the algebraic method.

Let's try strategy 2:

E The sum of two positive consecutive integers is x. In terms of x, what is the value of the smaller of these two integers?

(A) $\dfrac{x}{2} - 1$

(B) $\dfrac{x-1}{2}$

(C) $\dfrac{x}{2}$

(D) $\dfrac{x}{2} + 2$

(E) $\dfrac{x}{2} + 1$

Remember—whenever you see "in terms of" it's time to pick numbers.

S We are adding two consecutive integers which sum to x.

Smaller integer + Larger consecutive integer = x

We need to solve for the smaller of the two integers. Go ahead and circle the term we are solving for to help keep things clear.

(Smaller integer) + Larger consecutive integer = x

Let's keep it simple. Let's make the smaller integer 2. The next consecutive integer is 3.

Smaller integer + Larger consecutive integer = x
2 + 3 = 5

Therefore $\boxed{x = 5}$

Because this is a number that we "picked," it's a good practice to put a box around it so we can keep track of the numbers we have chosen. It is also a good idea to circle what you are solving for. In this case, we are looking for the smaller of the 2 consecutive numbers, which is ②.

Now we need to go through the answer choices and see which answer choice equals 2 when we plug in **5** for x.

(A) $\frac{x}{2} - 1$: $\quad \frac{5}{2} - 1 \rightarrow 2.5 - 1 = 1.5$ *Not 2. This is not our answer*

(B) $\frac{x-1}{2}$: $\quad \frac{5-1}{2} \rightarrow \frac{4}{2} = 2$ *This works. So far so good.*

(C) $\frac{x}{2}$: $\quad \frac{5}{2} = 2.5$ *Nope*

(D) $\frac{x}{2} + 2$: $\quad \frac{5}{2} + 2 = 4.5$ *Nope*

(E) $\frac{x}{2} + 1$: $\quad \frac{5}{2} + 1 = 3.5$ *Nope*

The only answer choice that works and gives us 2 is **(B)**, so that is the correct answer.

Notice that we started with 2, rather than 1 or 0. It's a best practice to start picking with the number 2. Here are some general rules for picking smart numbers.

Put a box around the variables that you have picked.

Circle what you are solving for.

Guidelines for Picking Numbers:

1. **DO NOT** pick 0 or 1. These numbers do strange things to equations and functions that no other numbers do. They can cause confusion, so it's best to steer clear of them when you are picking numbers.

2. If you are solving an equation like $x + y = z$, it's better to pick numbers for the two variables on the same side and SOLVE for the loner. So pick $x = 2$ and $y = 3$, then solve for $z = 5$ and go from there!

3. Pick numbers that follow the rules of the problem. For example: in a problem using the equation $x + y = z$, you couldn't pick 2 for x, 3 for y, and 6 for z : $2 + 3 \neq 6$.

4. If you pick numbers and two answer choices give you the correct answer, you must pick different numbers and repeat the process with the answer choices that worked the first time (this doesn't happen very often).

Let's practice some more problems.

Pick numbers that do NOT appear in the problem. This will minimize confusion.

In two years, Chris will be twice as old as Sally will be. Chris is now n years old. In terms of n, how old is Sally now?

(A) $\dfrac{n}{2}$

(B) $\dfrac{n}{2} - 2$

(C) $\dfrac{n}{2} - 1$

(D) $n - 2$

(E) $2n - 1$

Remember: "in terms of" means PICK NUMBERS!

Always circle what you are solving for.

S This looks confusing, but when you lay it out properly, it becomes clearer.

There are two periods of time, now and 2 years from now. In 2 years, Chris will be twice as old as Sally will be. So let's pick numbers. In 2 years, let's say Chris will be 10, so Sally has to be 5.

	Now	Two years from now
Chris	n	10
Sally		5

Now let's look to our problem. Chris is now n. In 2 years, Chris will be 10, so Chris is currently 8. And $n = 8$.
Let's put a box around it:

$n = 8$

So we've selected a number for our variable. What we are solving for is Sally's current age. Circle it in our table.

	Now	Two years from now
Chris	8	10
Sally	③	5

Sally is currently 3.

We've picked numbers for our variables, and we know what we're solving for. It's time to plug in the numbers that we've picked. Let's plug $n = \mathbf{8}$ into all of the answer choices to see which one gives us 3 (Sally's current age):

(A) $\dfrac{n}{2}$: $\dfrac{\mathbf{8}}{2} = 4$ *nope*

(B) $\dfrac{n}{2} - 2$: $\dfrac{\mathbf{8}}{2} - 2 = 2$ *nope*

(C) $\dfrac{n}{2} - 1$: $\dfrac{\mathbf{8}}{2} - 1 = 3$ *yep!*

(D) $n - 2$: $\mathbf{8} - 2 = 6$ *nope*

(E) $2n - 1$: $2(\mathbf{8}) - 1 = 15$ *not even close*

The only answer that works is ((C)).

E The sum of 5 consecutive even integers is s. In terms of s, what is the largest of these 5 integers?

(A) $\dfrac{s}{5}$

(B) $\dfrac{s-4}{5}$

(C) $\dfrac{s+4}{5}$

(D) $\dfrac{s-20}{5}$

(E) $\dfrac{s+20}{5}$

S Once again we are picking numbers. Are you starting to see a pattern?

Pay close attention to details in the question. We are told the numbers are consecutive and even.

Let's pick an easy even number to begin with: 2.
So our consecutive even numbers are 2, 4, 6, 8, 10 and the sum is $2 + 4 + 6 + 8 + 10 = 30 = s$.

Let's put a box around our variable: $\boxed{s = 30}$
And what are we solving for? The largest number in the set: 2, 4, 6, 8, ⑩
So we are solving for 10.

Now we are ready to plug in.

(A) $\dfrac{s}{5}$: $\qquad \dfrac{30}{5} \neq 10 \quad$ *nope*

(B) $\dfrac{s-4}{5}$: $\qquad \dfrac{30-4}{5} \rightarrow \dfrac{26}{5} \neq 10 \quad$ *nope*

(C) $\dfrac{s+4}{5}$: $\qquad \dfrac{30+4}{5} \rightarrow \dfrac{34}{5} \neq 10 \quad$ *nope*

(D) $\dfrac{s-20}{5}$: $\qquad \dfrac{30-20}{5} \rightarrow \dfrac{10}{5} \neq 10 \quad$ *nope*

(E) $\dfrac{s+20}{5}$: $\qquad \dfrac{30+20}{5} \rightarrow \dfrac{50}{5} = 10 \quad$ *yeah!*

Our answer is **(E)**.

E If r is a number greater than 1, $-r^2$ is how much less than r ?

(A) 2

(B) 6

(C) $r^2 + r$

(D) $2(r + 1)$

(E) $(r^2 + 1)(r - 1)$

Remember that "how much" always translates to x.

S First we need to translate from words into math:

If r is a number greater than 1 $-r^2$ is how much less than r ?

$\qquad\qquad r > 1; \qquad\qquad\qquad\qquad -r^2 = r - x$

To solve, let's start by picking **2** for r.

$\boxed{r = 2}$

Our equation is $-r^2 = r - x$.
Let's plug in our "pick" and solve for x:

$$-(2^2) = 2 - x$$
$$-4 = 2 - x$$
$$-6 = -x$$
$$x = \boxed{6}$$

Time to test the answer choices with our numbers.

(A) 2: $\qquad\qquad\qquad\qquad \neq 6$ *We can eliminate (A).*

(B) 6: $\qquad\qquad\qquad\qquad$ **This works.**

(C) $r^2 + r$: $\qquad\qquad\quad$ $2^2 + 2 \rightarrow 4 + 2 = 6$ *This works, too.*

(D) $2(r + 1)$: $\qquad\qquad$ $(2)(2 + 1) \rightarrow (2)(3) = 6$ *hmm... this also works*

(E) $(r^2 + 1)(r - 1)$: $\quad$ $(2^2 + 1)(2 - 1) \rightarrow (4 + 1)(1) = 5 \neq 6$ *We can eliminate it.*

Remember, if you are picking numbers and multiple answers work, just pick different numbers and try the "correct" answers again.

Let's try with new numbers. Let's pick $\boxed{r = 3.}$
$$-r^2 = r - x$$
$$-(3^2) = 3 - x$$
$$-12 = -x$$
$$x = \boxed{12}$$

We need to see which of the three answers, (B), (C) or (D), will give us ⑫

(B) 6   *not it*

(C) $r^2 + r$ $3^2 + 3 \rightarrow 9 + 3 = \mathbf{12}$ *That is our answer!*

(D) $2(r + 1)$: $(2)(3 + 1) \rightarrow (2)(4) = 8$ *nope*

Ⓒ it is.

Picking Numbers – Special Cases

The SAT tests one special Picking Numbers problem type that requires a slightly different strategy. These problems all use the phrase **"*must be true*."** When you see that phrase, you will need to pick different kinds of numbers. Start with integers, but to get all the way to a single answer choice, you must pick from the complete set of **DINOZ**.

Remember we are trying to pick numbers that will disprove wrong answers.

Decimals
Integers
Negatives
One
Zero

Each one of these number types behaves differently. And each will help us narrow down our answer choices.

E If $x < 2y$, which of the following must also be true?

(A) $x < y$

(B) $x^2 < 4y^2$

(C) $-x < 2y$

(D) $2y < x^2$

(E) $-2y < -x$

Remember, you are trying to find the one that must be true. The easiest way to do that is to *disprove* the other four.

 Step 1: Pick numbers.

$$x < 2y$$

Let's start with easy integers, pick 2 for x and 3 for y.

$$2 < (2)(3). \quad 2 < 6. \quad \text{True. So let's plug in our picks.}$$

$$\boxed{\begin{aligned} x &= 3 \\ y &= 2 \end{aligned}}$$

(A) $x < y$: $\quad\quad\quad\quad$ $(3) < (2)$ $\quad$ *Nope. Scratch A.*

(B) $x^2 < 4y^2$: $\quad\quad\quad$ $(3)^2 < 4(2)^2 \rightarrow 9 < 16$ $\quad$ **True**

(C) $-x < 2y$: $\quad\quad\quad$ $-(3) < 2(2) \rightarrow -3 < 4$ $\quad$ **True**

(D) $2y < x^2$: $\quad\quad\quad$ $2(2) < (3)^2 \rightarrow 4 < 9$ $\quad$ *Also True*

(E) $-2y < -x$: $\quad\quad\quad$ $-2(2) < -(3) \rightarrow -4 < -3$ $\quad$ **True again**

So a positive integer only helped us eliminate 1 answer choice. In order to knock off more answer choices, let's go deeper into **DINOZ** for more options; we need to try different types of numbers. This table can help.

If you try a ...	**Whole Number**	You should also try a ...	**Fraction / Decimal**
If you try a ...	**Positive Number**	You should also try a ...	**Negative Number**
Try the oddballs	**0 (Zero)**	And	**1**

We already tried a positive, so let's try a negative integer to see what happens. Our rule is $x < 2y$. Let's pick

$$\boxed{\begin{aligned} x &= -5 \\ y &= 2 \end{aligned}}$$

$$\begin{aligned} x &< 2y \\ -5 &< (2)(2) \\ -5 &< 4 \quad \text{True} \end{aligned}$$

Plug 'em in.

(A) was already eliminated, so don't worry about it. Let's try the rest with our new numbers.

(B) $x^2 < 4y^2$: $(-5)^2 < 4(2)^2 \rightarrow 25 < 16$ *False. This one is gone.*
(C) $-x < 2y$: $-(-5) < 2(2) \rightarrow 5 < 4$ *False. This one is gone.*
(D) $2y < x^2$: $2(2) < (-5)^2 \rightarrow 4 < 25$ **True**
(E) $-2y < -x$: $-2(2) < -(-5) \rightarrow -4 < 5$ **True**

We're down to (D) and (E); let's pick more strange numbers. Let's try 0 for x and 1 for y.

$$\boxed{\begin{array}{l} x = 0 \\ y = 1 \end{array}}$$

(D) $2y < x^2$: $2(1) < 0 \rightarrow 2 < 0$ *Nope*

(E) $-2y < -x$: $-2 < 0$ **Yes**

There you have it: $(\!(\mathbf{E})\!)$!

For these problems, a good approach is generally to start by picking integers and then dig deeper into **DINOZ** as you go.

Picking Numbers Practice Problems

1. If $x = yz$, which of the following must be equivalent to $\frac{y}{3}$?

   (A) $\frac{3x}{z}$

   (B) $\frac{z}{3x}$

   (C) $3xz$

   (D) $\frac{xz}{3}$

   (E) $\frac{x}{3z}$

3. x, y, and z are integers. Which of the following is equivalent to $2x(y + z)$?

   (A) $xy + xz$
   (B) $2xy + xz$
   (C) $yz + 2x$
   (D) $2xy + 2xz$
   (E) $2(z + y) + x$

2. If a is positive and b is negative, all of the following must be positive EXCEPT

   (A) $a - b$
   (B) $-b + a$
   (C) $(a)(-b)$
   (D) ab
   (E) $(-a)(b)$

4. If a, b, and c are consecutive odd integers and $c < b < a$, what is a in terms of c ?

   (A) $c + 4$
   (B) $c - 4$
   (C) $c + 2$
   (D) $c - 2$
   (E) $\frac{c}{2}$

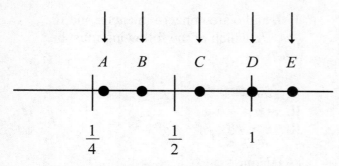

$$\frac{1}{4} \qquad \frac{1}{2} \qquad 1$$

<u>Note</u>: Figure not drawn to scale.

5. On the number line above, which of the following points could indicate the product of C and B?

(A) A
(B) B
(C) C
(D) D
(E) E

6. A gym charges a one-time membership fee of $100 and $12 per hour for use of the facility. In terms of h, which of the following represents the cost, in dollars, to use the gym for h hours?

(A) $10h + 12$
(B) $100h + 12$
(C) $12h + 10$
(D) $12h + 100$
(E) $12h + 1000$

7. Dexter is now $x - 10$ years old. How old will Dexter be 5 years from now in terms of x ?

(A) $x - 20$
(B) $x - 15$
(C) $x - 5$
(D) $x + 5$
(E) $x + 15$

8. A teacher, reading through a student's report, begins at the top of page p and finishes at the bottom of page q. In terms of p and q, how many pages has the teacher read?

(A) $q - p$
(B) $p - q$
(C) $q - p + 1$
(D) $p - q + 1$
(E) $q - p - 1$

9. During a going out of business sale, items are discounted by 20 percent at the end of each week. If an item is originally priced at d dollars, what will the price of the item be at the beginning of the fourth week in terms of d?

(A) $0.008d$
(B) $0.024d$
(C) $0.400d$
(D) $0.409d$
(E) $0.512d$

11. If a and b are nonzero integers, and if $-a > b$, which of the following must be true?

I. $ab < 0$
II. $-a < -b$
III. $a > -b$

(A) None
(B) I only
(C) II only
(D) III only
(E) I and III

10. In the equation $x = \dfrac{a^2c}{b^2}$, if a is doubled, b is divided by 2, and c is quadrupled, by what factor will x change?

12. If x is a positive integer, $3^x + 3^x + 3^x =$

(A) 3^{x+1}
(B) 3^{x+2}
(C) 3^{3x}
(D) 9^x
(E) 9^{3x}

$$
\begin{array}{r}
E \\
+F \\
\hline
G
\end{array}
\qquad
\begin{array}{r}
G \\
+H \\
\hline
IE
\end{array}
$$

13. *E, F, G, H,* and *I* all represent digits in the correctly worked addition problems above. If *E, F, G, H,* and *I* are all greater than zero, then $F + H$ must equal

(A) 2
(B) 4
(C) 6
(D) 8
(E) 10

14. The average (arithmetic mean) of four distinct integers is *n*. If one of the numbers is *m*, what is the average of the remaining 3 numbers in terms of m and *n* ?

(A) n

(B) $\dfrac{2n - m}{3}$

(C) $\dfrac{2n + m}{3}$

(D) $\dfrac{4n - m}{3}$

(E) $\dfrac{4n + m}{3}$

15. A taxi cab company charges a $2.50 pick-up charge, an additional $2.00 per person, and $0.25 for each 1/8 mile driven. Which of the following represents the total fare, in dollars, to take *p* people *m* miles?

(A) $4.5p + 8m$
(B) $4.5p + 2m$
(C) $2.5 + 2\,(p + m)$
(D) $2.5 + 4\,(p + m)$
(E) $2.5 + 8\,(p + m)$

Absolute Value

When you see the absolute value symbol, | x |, you have to take whatever is inside the absolute value lines (in this case x) and make it positive.

For example: $|-3| = 3$ and $|3| = 3$.

That's all there is to it!

Absolute Value Equations

Solving equations with absolute values is only slightly more complicated. Each equation containing an absolute value is actually two equations.

E If | x | = 7, what are the possible values of x ?

This is the key to ALL absolute value problems: You MUST ALWAYS solve **2 equations!**

S There's the obvious solution of $x = \mathbf{7}$, but there's also the less obvious solution of $x = \left(-\, \mathbf{7}\right)$ (after all, $|-7| = \left(\mathbf{7}\right)$, too).

To solve equations of the form $|y| = x$, you have to **solve 2 different equations**:
  1. $y = x$
  2. $-y = x$

E If $y = |7 - 3x|$, what is the value of y when $x = 3$?

S We know that $x = 3$; let's plug it in.

$y = |7 - 3x|$

$y = |7 - 3(3)|$

$y = |7 - 9|$

$y = |-2|$

$y = |-2| = 2$

$y = \textcircled{2}$

Nothin' to it!

E What are all of the solutions for $|5x - 3| = 8$?

S When dealing with absolute values, we have to solve the equation in the positive and negative forms.

First, we have to solve the positive by simply stripping away the absolute value signs.

$|5x - 3| = 8$

$5x - 3 = 8$

$5x = 11$

$x = \dfrac{11}{5}$

To get all the solutions, we also have to solve the negative, where $-(5x - 3) = 8$.

$-(5x - 3) = 8$

$-5x + 3 = 8$

$-5x = 5$

$x = -1$

Our two solutions are $x = \boxed{\dfrac{11}{5}}$ and $x = \boxed{-1}$.

Remember,

$|5x - 3| = |-(5x - 3)|$

Often the SAT will ask about absolute value with inequalities.

E If $| 8 - 4x | > 30$, which of the following could equal x ?

(A) -5
(B) -2
(C) 0
(D) 9
(E) 10

S We could solve the math and generate the 2 equations, but it is usually quicker to simply plug in the answer choices until we find the one that works.

(A) $| 8 - 4(-5) | > 30$
$| 28 | > 30$
$28 > 30$ *So, no.*

(B) $| 8 - 4(-2) | > 30$
$| 16 | > 30$
$16 > 30$ *Nope.*

(C) $| 8 - 4(0) | > 30$
$| 8 | > 30$
$8 > 30$ *Not it.*

(D) $| 8 - 4(9) | > 30$
$| -28 | > 30$
$28 > 30$ *No again.*

(E) $| 8 - 4(10) | > 30$
$| -32 | > 30$
$32 > 30$ *True! This is it!*

But what if this were a grid-in problem? In that case, we have to generate the positive and negative equations.

E If | 12 − 3b | < 27, what is one possible value of b?

S Let's set up our positive and negative equations:
| **12 − 3b** | **< 27**

positive   and   negative
$12 - 3b < 27$ $-(12 - 3b) < 27$

Now let's solve.

Let's start with the easy one, the positive:
$$12 - 3b < 27$$
$$-3b < 15$$
$$\boldsymbol{b > -5}$$

Now the negative:
$$-(12 - 3b) < 27$$
$$-12 + 3b < 27$$
$$3b < 39$$
$$\boldsymbol{b < 13}$$

Putting them together, we get **− 5 < b < 13**, so you could pick any number between − 5 and 13 to satisfy the equation. Be careful with the inequality signs; you CANNOT pick − 5 or 13 because the signs are strictly greater than and less than.

FLIP THE GATOR SIGN!

Always be sure to flip the inequality sign when you multiply or divide by a negative number!

Absolute Value Practice Problems

1. If $x = 11$, then $|7 - x| =$

(A) $- 18$
(B) $- 6$
(C) $- 4$
(D) 4
(E) 18

$$|x + 4| < 7.5$$

2. If x is a positive integer, what is the least possible value of x that satisfies the equation above?

(A) $- 3$
(B) $- 2$
(C) 1
(D) 2
(E) 3

3. If, $7 < |-\dfrac{2}{5}x + 6| < 8$ which of the following could be the value of x ?

(A) $- 3$
(B) $- 2$
(C) 0
(D) 2
(E) 3

4. To pay a discounted admission price at the buffet, a patron's height must be between 75 and 125 centimeters inclusive. Which of the following inequalities can be used to determine whether a person's height (h) meets the regulation for this discount?

(A) $|h - 25| \le 125$
(B) $|h - 75| < 50$
(C) $|h - 75| \le 50$
(D) $|h - 100| < 25$
(E) $|h - 100| \le 25$

5. A machine fills cereal boxes with 64 ounces of cereal. Boxes are rejected if they differ by more than 3 ounces from the desired weight (w) of 64 ounces. Which of the following equations can be used to determine if a box is accepted?

(A) $|w + 64| < 3$
(B) $|64 + w| > 3$
(C) $|64 - w| \le 3$
(D) $|64 + w| < 3$
(E) $|w - 64| = 3$

Inequalities

2%

of all math
questions
on the SAT

First, a basic review of the symbols:

> is the "greater than" sign. Whatever is to the left of this symbol is larger than what is to the right of the symbol.

5   >   3

< is the "less than" sign. Here, whatever is to the left of this symbol is smaller than what is to the right of the symbol.

5   <   7

Remember the old alligator trick from elementary school: The gator always wants to eat the bigger of the two things!

$x < 2$ means "x is less than 2"

$2x \geq 8$ means "$2x$ is greater than or equal to 8"

There are two things to remember about solving inequalities:

1. If the equation is a complex inequality (e.g. $3x - 4 < 6x < 3x + 8$), break the problem up into two different inequalities and solve each piece separately.

   In this case, solve $3x - 4 < 6x$ and $6x < 3x + 8$.

2. When multiplying or dividing inequalities by negative numbers, we have to switch the direction of the sign.

   So, $-3x < 9$ becomes $x > -3$.

$\geq$ means greater than or equal to
$\leq$ means less than or equal to

E For how many integer values of x does $8 < 2x - 4 < 18$?

Remember to flip the sign when dividing by a negative.

S Step 1: Break the problem into two inequalities.
$8 < 2x - 4$ and $2x - 4 < 18$.

Step 2: Solve the first inequality.
$12 < 2x$
$6 < x$

Step 3: Solve the second.
$2x < 22$
$x < 11$

Step 4: Put the answers together.
$6 < x < 11$

There are 4 integers between 6 and 11 (7, 8, 9, 10) so our answer is $\boxed{4}$. That's all there is to it!

E If $0 < 2x < y$, which of the following is the greatest?

(A) 0

(B) y

(C) 2x

(D) $-x$

(E) $\dfrac{y}{2}$

S Step 1: Pick numbers for x and y.

2x must be greater than 0; let's pick $\boxed{x = 3.}$

Likewise, y must be greater than 2x (in this case 6); let's pick $\boxed{y = 7.}$

Step 2: Plug in our chosen numbers to see which option yields the largest number.

(A) 0

(B) $y = 7$

(C) $2x = 2(3) = 6$

(D) $-x = -3$

(E) $\frac{y}{2} = \frac{7}{2} = 3.5$

Our largest option is $\boxed{\text{(B) } 7}$, so that's our answer!

E If $5 < a < 9$ and $-3 < b < 4$, which of the following is the set of all possible values of ab?

(A) $ab = 36$

(B) $-15 < ab < 36$

(C) $-3 < ab < 13$

(D) $-3 < ab < 9$

(E) $-27 < ab < 36$

S Watch out! This one is tricky!

To find the extreme values for *ab*, we have to multiply the extreme values of each variable by *both* of the extreme values of the other variable.

The four boundary possibilities of *ab* are:

1. Smallest *a* (5) × smallest *b* (−3)
$$(5)(-3) = -15$$

2. Smallest *a* (5) × largest *b* (4)
$$(5)(4) = 20$$

3. Largest *a* (9) × smallest *b* (−3)
$$(9)(-3) = -27$$

4. Largest *a* (9) × largest *b* (4)
$$(9)(4) = 36$$

Now simply pick the lowest number as the lower boundary and the highest as the upper.

(E) $-27 < ab < 36$

If you like formulas, check out the standard form for an absolute value: if you plot the solution on a number line, $|x − c| = r$, where *c* is the center and *r* is the radius.

Absolute Value Inequalities

Quite often the SAT likes to combine absolute value problems with inequalities. This will be seen in a form such as:

$$|x + a| > b$$

To solve this kind of problem, just split it into two parts, like so:

$$(x + a) > b \quad \text{and} \quad -(x + a) > b$$

Then solve as you normally would.

E Find the range of *x* values possible for the following equation:

$$|x - 2| < 6$$

Remember to flip the sign when multiplying or dividing by a negative.

S Step 1: Split the equation into two separate problems.

$$(x - 2) < 6 \qquad \text{and} \qquad -(x - 2) < 6$$

Step 2: Solve the problems.

$$(x - 2) < 6 \qquad \text{and} \qquad -(x - 2) < 6$$
$$-x + 2 < 6$$
$$-x < 4$$
$$x < 8 \qquad \text{and} \qquad x > -4$$

Look at it on a number line:

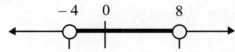

Step 3: Combine into one statement.

$$\boxed{-4 < x < 8}$$

Inequalities Practice Problems

1. If x and y are integers, and $7 < 2x < 9$ and $6 < 3y < 12$, what is the value of $x + y$?

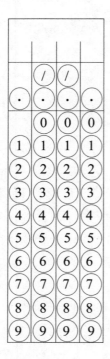

2. If $x > y$, which of the following must be true?

    (A) $x^2 > y^2$
    (B) $y > -x$
    (C) $x > -y$
    (D) $-x < -y$
    (E) $-x > -y$

3. If a, b, and c are positive even integers where $ab = 8$, $bc = 24$, and $ac = 48$, which of the following must be true?

    (A) $a < b < c$
    (B) $a < c < b$
    (C) $b < a < c$
    (D) $b < c < a$
    (E) $c < a < b$

4. If $a + b = 24$ and $b < 12$, then which of the following must be true?

    (A) $a = 13$
    (B) $a < 12$
    (C) $a > 12$
    (D) $b > 13$
    (E) $b = 0$

5. If $1 > 2x - 1 > 0$, what is one possible value of x ?

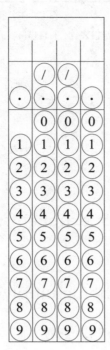

6. If x is a positive even integer and $40 < 4x + 6 < 50$, what is the value of x ?

(A)   9
(B)   10
(C)   11
(D)   45
(E)   44

Exponents

Use your calculator,
please...

Exponents are used to show that a number is multiplied by itself
a certain number of times.

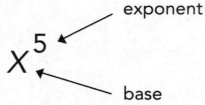

exponent

x^5

base

Let's look at the basic rules of exponents:

1. $x^5 = (x)(x)(x)(x)(x)$

2. $(x^y) \times (x^z) = x^{y+z}$ → When multiplying like bases, add the
exponents.
Example: $(3^4) \times (3^2) = 3^6 = 729$.

3. $\dfrac{x^y}{x^z} = x^{y-z}$ → Multiplication and division have opposite effects.
When you **multiply** like bases you **add** their exponents. When
you **divide** like bases you **subtract** their exponents.

Example: $\dfrac{x^6}{4} = x^{6-4} = x^2$

4. $(x^y) + (x^z) \neq x^{y+z}$ → Nope, can't do it. You cannot add or
subtract like bases with different exponents.
Example: $3^4 + 3^2 = 81 + 9 = 90$, which is NOT $3^6 = 729$.

5. $(x^y)^z = x^{yz}$ → When exponents are raised to a power, you
multiply them. Again, use your calculator.
Example: $(3^3)^4 = 3^{(3 \times 4)} = 3^{12} = 531,441$; You guessed it—
calculator.

6. $x^{-y} = \dfrac{1}{x^y}$ → When you have a negative exponent, simply make that exponent positive and put the whole thing under 1.

Example: $x^{-3} = \dfrac{1}{x^3}$

In the event the negative exponent is already in the denominator, just make the exponent positive and move the base with that exponent to the numerator.

Example: $\dfrac{1}{3^{-2}} = 3^2 = 9$

7. $x^0 = 1$ → Anything raised to the 0 power = 1.
Example: $455^0 = 1;\ 2^0 = 1;\ 1{,}255^0 = 1$

8. $0^y = 0$ → Zero to any power is zero.
Example: $0^1 = 0;\ 0^{10} = 0;\ 0^{468} = 0$

9. $(xy)^z = x^z y^z$ → You can distribute an exponent to items within parentheses if they are multiplied.
Example: $(xy)^2 = (x^2 y^2);\ (3 \times 2)^2 = (3^2)(2^2)$

You <u>cannot</u> distribute an exponent to items within parentheses if they are separated by an addition or subtraction sign. $()^2$ does <u>NOT</u> equal $2 + 2$.

10. $\left(\dfrac{x}{y}\right)^z = \dfrac{x^z}{y^z}$ → You can also distribute an exponent to items within parentheses if they are divided.

Example: $\left(\dfrac{2}{3}\right)^3 = \left(\dfrac{2^3}{3^3}\right) = \left(\dfrac{8}{27}\right)$

11. $x^{\frac{y}{z}} = \left(x^{\frac{1}{z}}\right)^y$
This is nothing more than the power to a power rule (rule 5) in reverse.

Example: $x^{\frac{3}{2}} = \left(x^{\frac{1}{12}}\right)^3$

Notice that when you raise a fraction to an exponent, the fraction gets smaller.

12. $x^{\frac{1}{2}} = \sqrt{x}$
A number to the $\frac{1}{2}$ power is the same as the square root of that number.

Example: $4^{\frac{1}{2}} = \sqrt{4} = 2$

When working with exponents with like bases—focusing only on the exponents saves lots of time.

Working with Like Bases

When you are working with exponents that have like bases, you can create an equation from just the exponents and greatly simplify things.

$$(2^{\textcircled{x}})(2^{\textcircled{3}}) = 2^{\textcircled{5}}$$
$$2^{(x+3)} = 2^5$$
$$x + 3 = 5$$
$$x = 2$$

We don't need the bases at all! The left and right side of the equation are equal. Since the bases on each side are equal, the exponents must also be equal.

E $4^2 \times 4^3 = 4^{15}$, what is the value of ?

   (A) 2.5
   (B) 3
   (C) 5
   (D) 6
   (E) 12

Because answer choices are always in order, a good rule is to start with answer choice (C). If (C) is too big or too small, you have eliminated not only (C), but also the two answer choices above or below it.

S The simplest option involves stripping away the like bases and focusing exclusively on the exponents. Let's try it directly first.

$$4^{\textcircled{2n}} \times 4^{\textcircled{3}} = 4^{\textcircled{15}}$$
$$2n + 3 = 15$$
$$2n = 12$$
$$n = \textcircled{6}, \textbf{choice (D)}$$

Easy as pie! If you forget this rule, it's just as easy to work backwards from the answer choices and plug them in to find one that works. Remember to start with (C)!

(C) 5: $4^{2(5)} \times 4^3 = 4^{10} \times 4^3 = 4^{13} \neq 4^{15}$ *too small*

We need a bigger number, so let's try (D).

(D) 6: $4^{2(6)} \times 4^3 = 4^{12} \times 4^3 = 4^{15} = 4^{15}$ *There it is!*

Just to be safe, check the others.

(A) 2.5: $4^{2(2.5)} \times 4^3 = 4^5 \times 4^3 = 4^8 \neq 4^{15}$ *We're not there yet.*

(B) 3; $4^{2(3)} \times 4^3 = 4^6 \times 4^3 = 4^9 \neq 4^{15}$ *nope*

(E) 12; $4^{2(12)} \times 4^3 = 4^{24} \times 4^3 = 4^{27} \neq 4^{15}$ *way too high*

Remember, when you multiply like bases, you add the exponents.

E If $a = b^2$ for all positive integers b, and $c = a^4 - a$, what is c in terms of b ?

(A) b^6

(B) $b^6 - b^2$

(C) $b^8 - b^2$

(D) $b^2 - b$

(E) $b^2 - b^8$

S We are in the realm of algebra, and the phrase "in terms of" tells us that we can pick numbers. Let's look at both methods: solving it algebraically and then solving it by picking numbers.

The question: What is c in terms of b ?
Notice that all our answer choices are in terms of b. We need to solve for c, converting all the a terms into b terms. This will require substitution. Let's line up our two givens:

$$1) \quad c = a^4 - a$$
$$2) \quad a = b^2$$

Now let's "sub" it out, replacing each a with a b^2

$$c = a^4 - a$$
$$c = (b^2)^4 - b^2$$
$$c = \boxed{b^8 - b^2}$$

To solve for the isolated term, *c*, we must pick for the other terms that are interacting, *a* and *b*.

(C) is the correct answer choice. That was pretty quick if you remember your exponent rules.

Now let's pick numbers and solve it without using the algebra.

Let's pick some numbers for *a*, *b*, and *c*.

1) $c = a^4 - a$

2) $a = b^2$

Let's pick the term that's being manipulated, *b*.

$$\boxed{b = 2}$$

Now let's plug it in to the equation to solve for *a*.

$a = 2^2 = 4;\ \boxed{a = 4}$

Now, let's solve for *c*.

$$c = a^4 - a$$
$$c = 4^4 - 4$$
$$c = 256 - 4$$
$$= 252$$

$$\boxed{c = 252}$$

Time to try our numbers in the answer choices.

(A) b^6: $2^6 = 64 \neq 252$ *nope*

(B) $b^6 - b^2$: $2^6 - 2^2 = 64 - 4 = 60 \neq 252$ *no again*

(C) $b^8 - b^2$: $2^8 - 2^2 = 256 - 4 = 252$ There we go!

(D) $b^2 - b$: $2^2 - 2 = 4 - 2 = 2 \neq 252$ *way off*

(E) $b^2 - b^8$: $2^2 - 2^8 = 4 - 256 = -252 \neq 252$ *The opposite of what we want.*

So you have options: you can tackle the algebra head-on, or you can substitute. For some students, it's a simple matter of preference.

Fractional Exponents

Fractional exponents follow the same rules as regular exponents. For example:

$$x^{\frac{1}{4}} \times x^{\frac{3}{4}} = x^{\frac{1}{4}+\frac{3}{4}} = x^1 \quad \text{and} \quad (x^{\frac{1}{4}})^2 = x^{\frac{1}{4} \times 2} = x^{\frac{2}{4}} = x^{\frac{1}{2}}$$

E If $a^{\frac{3}{4}} = b$, what is a^6 in terms of b?

(A) b

(B) $b^{\frac{2}{3}}$

(C) $b^{\frac{4}{3}}$

(D) b^4

(E) b^8

S This one looks harder. Let's avoid the algebra and just pick numbers.

Let's try $\boxed{a = 3}$

$a^{\frac{3}{4}} = b$

$3^{\frac{3}{4}} = b$

$\boxed{2.2795 = b}$

What is $a^{⑥}$ in terms of b?

$a^6 = 3^6 = \boxed{729}$

And the answers?

(A) b: $2.2795 \neq 729$ *not so much*

(B) $b^{\frac{2}{3}}$: $2.2795^{\frac{2}{3}} = 1.7320 \neq 729$ *no again*

(C) $b^{\frac{4}{3}}$: $2.2795^{\frac{4}{3}} = 3 \neq 729$ *that's a, not a^6*

(D) b^4: $2.2795^4 = 27 \neq 729$ *still not right*

(E) b^8: $2.2795^8 = 729$ *done*

<u>TIME SAVER</u>:

Using logic, if you know that $3^3 = 27$, and we know that b (2.2795) is smaller than 3, then we can be certain that raising b to a fraction (like $\frac{2}{3}$) or to a number smaller than 3 will never give us a number as large as 729. Therefore you can skip over (A), (B) and (C) and look at (D) or (E). This kind of common sense reasoning can save you a lot of time on the SAT.

Use your calculator!

Be sure to use parentheses around the exponent when typing these into your calculator!

Exponents Practice Problems

1. If $4^{r+1} \times 4^3 = 4^8$, what is the value of r?

(A) $\dfrac{1}{2}$

(B) 1

(C) 2

(D) 4

(E) 16

2. If $2^x + 2^x + 2^x + 2^x = 2^7$, then $x =$

3. Which of the following is equivalent to 4.328671×10^4?

(A) 43.28671
(B) 432.8671
(C) 4,328.671
(D) 43,286.71
(E) 432,867.1

4. If $(x^6)^a = x^{18}$ and $x^b x^9 = x^{18}$ what is the value of $a + b$?

(A) 5
(B) 12
(C) 14
(D) 18
(E) 24

5. Which of the following is equal to $(4x^2 y^5)^3$?

(A) $4x^6 (y^3)^5$

(B) $4x^6 y^{15}$

(C) $12x^6 y^{15}$

(D) $64x^5 y^8$

(E) $64x^6 y^{15}$

6. If $\dfrac{x^{10}}{x^a} = x^2$ and $(x^6)^b = x^{18}$ what is the value of $b - a$?

(A) -5
(B) -2
(C) 4
(D) 7
(E) 10

7. If $3^5 = 9^x$, then $x =$

(A) 5

(B) 3

(C) $\dfrac{2}{5}$

(D) $\dfrac{5}{2}$

(E) 2

8. If $16^{15 + x} = 4^{3x}$, then $x = ?$

9. If $x = 2^{2a + 1}$ and $y = 4$, then $\dfrac{x}{y} =$

(A) $2^{2a + 1}$

(B) 2^{2a}

(C) $2^{2a - 1}$

(D) $2^{\left(\frac{a + 1}{2}\right)}$

(E) $\left(\dfrac{1}{2}\right)^{2a + 2}$

10. If $3^x = 9^y = 27^z$, what is the value of $\dfrac{x}{y} + \dfrac{x}{z}$?

12. If $x^{\frac{3}{4}} = y$, what does x^3 equal in terms of y ?

(A) $y^{\frac{4}{3}}$

(B) $y^{\frac{3}{2}}$

(C) y^4

(D) y^6

(E) y^8

11. If $x \neq 0$ and $125x^z$ is equal to x^{z+3}, then $x =$

13. If $r^{-\frac{3}{2}} = m^3$ and $s^{\frac{3}{4}} = n^6$, what is $(rs)^{\frac{1}{2}}$ in terms of m and n ?

(A) 0

(B) $n^4 m$

(C) $\dfrac{n^4}{m}$

(D) $\dfrac{m}{n^4}$

(E) $\dfrac{1}{n^4 m}$

Fractions

3%

of all math
questions
on the SAT

Most SAT questions involving fractions are very basic: you must be able to add and multiply fractions and find a common denominator between them. No big deal. On occasion the SAT will push fraction problems to a much higher level of difficulty, requiring you to manipulate, cross multiply and split fractions into parts.

E If $\dfrac{6}{(r+2)} = \dfrac{8}{(3-2r)}$, what is the value of r?

(A) -4

(B) 0

(C) $\dfrac{1}{10}$

(D) $\dfrac{1}{5}$

(E) $\dfrac{8}{5}$

S We need to somehow isolate r.
Let's set things up:
$$\frac{6}{(r+2)} = \frac{8}{(3-2r)}$$

Whenever you see 2 fractions set equal to each other, you know you will need to cross multiply.

$$\frac{6}{(r+2)} \diagup\!\!\!\!\diagup \frac{8}{(3-2r)}$$

$$6(3-2r) = 8(r+2)$$
$$18 - 12r = 8r + 16$$
$$2 = 20r$$
$$\frac{2}{20} = r$$
$$\boxed{\frac{1}{10}} = r$$

(C) is our answer.

Don't forget to
distribute!

$$\overparen{6(3} - 2r) = \overparen{8(r} + 2)$$

E If $\frac{t}{r} = 6$ and $\frac{r}{s} = 3$, what is the value of $\frac{(t + r + s)}{r}$?

(A) $7\frac{1}{3}$

(B) $7\frac{2}{3}$

(C) $8\frac{1}{6}$

(D) 9

(E) 10

S What are we given?

$$\frac{t}{r} = 6 \quad \text{and} \quad \frac{r}{s} = 3$$

What do we need to find: $\frac{(t + r + s)}{r}$

More than likely, we will need to get everything down to one variable so we can solve.
Let's simplify.

$$\frac{t}{r} = \frac{6}{1}$$

Cross multiplying we find that:

$$t = \boxed{6r}$$

And we also know

$$\frac{r}{s} = \frac{3}{1}$$

Cross multiplying we find that

$$r = \boxed{3s}$$

We need to get everything in terms of 1 variable. It looks like r is the variable for the job. We've already found that $t = 6r$. Let's isolate s. If $r = 3s$, then

$$s = \boxed{\frac{r}{3}}$$

Now we are good to go!

Time to substitute:

$$\frac{(t + r + s)}{r} = \frac{(6r + r + \frac{r}{3})}{r}$$

Now, let's separate this fraction into its component parts:

$$\frac{6r}{r} + \frac{r}{r} + \frac{\frac{r}{3}}{r}$$

The r's cancel in the first two terms, leaving us with $6 + 1 + \dfrac{\frac{r}{3}}{r}$.

The last term is a little trickier.

$$\frac{\frac{r}{3}}{\frac{r}{1}}$$

When you are dividing with fractions, it's the same as multiplying by the reciprocal; just flip the bottom fraction and multiply.

$$\frac{r}{3} \times \frac{1}{r}$$

The r's cancel, and we are left with $\dfrac{1}{3}$ for our last term.

$$6 + 1 + \frac{1}{3} = \boxed{7\frac{1}{3}}$$

(A) is the correct answer.

If the terms in the numerator are separated by addition or subtraction, you can make separate fractions, putting each term, by itself, over the denominator.

Notice that we never solved for any of the variables, but that was not a requirement of the problem. Don't get hung up on solving for things you do not need to solve for! Stick with the problem.

Fractions Practice Problems

1. If $\frac{2}{3}$ of a number is 16, what is $\frac{1}{2}$ of the number?

(A) $\frac{1}{12}$

(B) $\frac{1}{3}$

(C) 8

(D) 12

(E) 24

2. If a movie is 6 hours long, what fraction of the movie is completed 45 minutes after it is begun?

(A) $\frac{1}{16}$

(B) $\frac{1}{12}$

(C) $\frac{1}{8}$

(D) $\frac{1}{6}$

(E) $\frac{1}{3}$

3. If $\frac{4}{(3v+6)} = \frac{4}{(v-2)}$, what is the value of v ?

(A) −4
(B) −2
(C) 0
(D) 2
(E) 4

4. If $\frac{(s-3)}{(s+t)} = \frac{-3}{t}$ and $s = 9$, what is the value of t ?

(A) −3
(B) −2
(C) 0
(D) 1
(E) 3

5. If $\frac{(4a+2b)}{a} = \frac{27}{6}$, what is the value of $\frac{b}{a}$?

Percentages

Generally it's a good idea to convert all percentages or fractions to decimals, which are easier to work with. However, sometimes you must give your answer as a fraction. It is very easy to convert something from a percent to a fraction. Simply treat the % symbol like the number ($\frac{1}{100}$). So if you need to convert 5% to a fraction you'd simply multiply and reduce:

$$5\% = 5 \times \left(\frac{1}{100}\right) = \frac{5}{100} = \frac{1}{20}$$

Percent of a number

With these problems, you are commonly asked to translate words into math:

Twenty percent of a number is

20%	of a number, x	is
$20 \times \left(\frac{1}{100}\right)$	$20 \times \left(\frac{1}{100}\right)(x)$	$20 \times \left(\frac{1}{100}\right)(x) =$

Using the [FRAC] function on your graphing calculator will turn decimals into fractions.

E The price of a dress is reduced by 20%. If the original price of the dress was $70, what is the new price?

S Step 1: Find the amount the dress was discounted.
A 20% price reduction of a $70 dress is:

$$\frac{20}{100}(70) \rightarrow 0.2(\$70) = \$14$$

Step 2: Subtract the reduction from the original price.
$\$70 - \$14 = \boxed{\$56}$

There is a useful shortcut when you are dealing with percent changes like in the problem above.

If a dress is being reduced by 20%, it is quicker to multiply the original amount by (100% – 20%), which is 80%.

So $\$70 \times 0.80 = \boxed{\$56}$.
We arrive at the same answer and save a step!

E What percent of 4 is 5?

(A) 75%
(B) 80%
(C) 125%
(D) 150%
(E) 180%

S Step 1: Translate into an equation.

What percent	of 4	is 5?
$(x)(\frac{1}{100})$	$(x)(\frac{1}{100})(4)$	$(x)(\frac{1}{100})(4) = 5$

Step 2: Solve.

$$x(\frac{1}{100})(4) = 5$$

$$x(\frac{1}{100}) = \frac{5}{4}$$

$$x(\frac{1}{100}) = 1.25$$

$$x = \boxed{125\%}, \textbf{(C)}$$

It is usually easier to work with decimals on your calculator than with fractions. Here we changed $\frac{5}{4}$ to 1.25.

E 65 percent of 90 is the same as 50 percent of what number?

S Translate:

$$0.65 \times 90 = 0.5x$$

$$x = 0.65 \left(\frac{90}{0.5}\right)$$

$$x = 117$$

E A store charges $180 for a TV. The price is 25% more than the amount it costs the store to buy the television. At the close-out sale, store employees can purchase all merchandise at 40% off the store's cost. How much would it cost an employee to purchase the television at this sale?

S Step 1: Set up the equation.

Store charges = 100% (cost of TV) + 25% × (cost of TV)
Store charges = 125% (cost of TV)
Store charges = 1.25 (cost of TV)

Step 2: Solve.

$$\$180 = 1.25 \,(\text{cost of TV})$$

$$\frac{\$180}{1.25} = \text{cost of TV}$$

$$\$144 = \text{cost of TV}$$

Step 3: Find employees' price at sale.

$$\$144 \,(0.60) = \boxed{\$86.40}$$

Remember multiplying by 0.6 (AKA 60%) is the same as taking 40% off.

Remember multiplying by 0.85 (AKA 85%) is the same as taking 15% off.

The most common rookie mistake is to reduce by $1.50 each week, forgetting that there is a new price each week after the discount. That would give you a final price of $7.00, the most common wrong answer.

E A $10 mug is reduced by 15% per week for 2 weeks in a row. What is the final price?

S Step 1: Reduce price for Week 1.
$10 × 0.85 = $8.50

Step 2: Reduce price for Week 2.
After one week, the price is $8.50; then it's reduced again by an additional 15%.

$8.50 × 0.85 = ($7.23) (round to the nearest cent)

Percent Increase/Decrease

Use the same formula for both percent increase and percent decrease problems!

The key to these problems is this simple formula:

$$\frac{(\text{New number} - \text{Old number})}{\text{Old number}} \times 100 \quad \text{or} \quad \frac{\text{Change}}{\text{Original}} \times 100$$

E A certain stock had a price of $7 in May and rose to a price of $11 in June. The stock price in June is what percent greater than the stock price in May?

S $$\frac{\text{Change}}{\text{Original}} \times (100\%) = \frac{11 - 7}{7} \times (100\%)$$
$$= \frac{4}{7} \times (100\%)$$
$$= \boxed{57.1\%}$$

E The price of a $20 purse was first increased by 25%, and then the new price was decreased by 20%. The final price was what percent less than the original price?

S Step 1: 25% increase.
$20 × (125%) =
$20 × (1.25) = $25
Step 2: 20% decrease.
$25 × (100 − 20)%
$25 × 80% =
$25 (0.80) = $20   *so we are back to our original price!*
The answer is (**0**) because the final price was the same as the original!

E Drew has won 40% of the 10 debate tournaments he has entered this year. If Drew is going to compete in a total of 30 tournaments this year, and if he wins 70% of the remaining tournaments, what will be his final winning percentage?

S Step 1: Determine how many tournaments Drew has already won.
(0.40) × 10 = 4

Step 2: Figure out how many he will win for the rest of the season.

With 10 tournaments down, he has 20 left. He will win 70% of those.
(0.70) × 20 = 14

Step 3: Divide total wins by total competitions.

$$\frac{(14 + 4)}{30} = \frac{18}{30}$$

$$= \mathbf{0.6}$$

Step 4: Convert to a percentage.
0.6(100%) = (**60%**)

Percentages Practice Problems

1. 13 is what percent of 65?

(A) 10%
(B) 15%
(C) 20%
(D) 25%
(E) 30%

3. There are 638 students enrolled at Winter Park High School. If 108 of these students are graduating, approximately what percentage of students will **NOT** be graduating?

(A) 17%
(B) 64%
(C) 82%
(D) 83%
(E) 90%

2. Which of the following is equal to 40% of y ?

(A) $\dfrac{4y}{100}$

(B) $\dfrac{2y}{5}$

(C) $4y$

(D) $400y$

(E) $\dfrac{y}{4}$

4. In Sidney's fish tank, 35% of the fish are Angelfish. If there are 28 Angelfish in the tank, how many fish total does Sidney have?

(A) 52
(B) 78
(C) 80
(D) 96
(E) It cannot be determined from the information provided.

5. 30 percent of m is 12. What is m percent of 30?

6. George makes free throws with a 40% accuracy rate. At this rate, how many free throws would George need to shoot in order to make 20 of them?

7. What is the product of 300 percent of 1 and 150 percent of 4?

(A) 2
(B) 3
(C) 9
(D) 12
(E) 18

8. If a coat is on sale for 80% of the original price, by what percent must the sale price be increased to obtain the original price?

(A) 15
(B) 20
(C) 23
(D) 25
(E) 27

9. A class of 50 students is made up of b boys and g girls. In terms of g, what percentage of the class is made up of boys?

(A) $50 - g$

(B) $50 + g$

(C) $100 - 2g$

(D) $100 + 2g$

(E) $\dfrac{g}{50}$

DISTRIBUTION OF GRADES IN
MR. BARRY'S PHYSICS CLASS

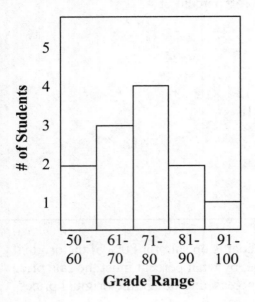

Grade Range

10. The graph above shows the distribution of grades in Mr. Barry's Physics class. If all grades are integers, what percentage of students earned grades between 70 and 91?

(A) 33.33
(B) 40.00
(C) 50.00
(D) 66.66
(E) 91.66

FRANK'S MONTHLY BUDGET

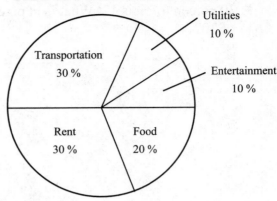

11. The pie graph above shows the allocation of Frank's budget. The amount Frank pays for transportation is only part of the total transportation cost for the car he uses, because Frank carpools with 3 other people. If Frank's total monthly budget is $1000, and the carpoolers split the cost evenly, what is the total transportation cost for each month?

(A) $300
(B) $600
(C) $900
(D) $1200
(E) $1500

12. At a certain university there are 7,500 students. If there are 400 more male students than female students, what percentage of the class is made up of females?

Probability

2%

of all math
questions
on the SAT

Probability represents the likelihood that a particular event will occur. It is expressed as a value from 0 to 1, inclusive.

A probability of **1** tells you it's a sure thing.

A probability of **0** tells you it's just not going to happen.

The formula is simple:

$$\text{Probability} = \frac{\text{\# of outcomes that meet the requirements}}{\text{Total \# of possible outcomes}}$$

E A shelf contains only plastic toys and wooden toys. If 6 out of 15 toys on the shelf are plastic, what is the probability that a toy selected at random will be wooden?

S Let's set things up in mathematical terms.

6 out of our 15 toys are plastic; the remaining 9 toys must be wooden. To find the probability that a toy chosen at random will be wooden, we use this equation:

$$\frac{\text{Wooden Toys}}{\text{Total Toys}} = \left(\frac{9}{15}\right)$$

E There are 90 fish in a pond. 40 are goldfish and 50 are clownfish. If clownfish are added to the pond until the probability of randomly catching a clownfish becomes $\frac{2}{3}$, what will be the total number of clownfish in the pond?

Whenever you have a probability problem and one component is changing while the other is static, or unchanging: ALWAYS focus on the element that is not changing.

S Let's set up our problem.
In the beginning we have:

Goldfish	Clownfish	Total (T)
40	50	90

Currently the probability of randomly catching a goldfish is $\frac{40}{90}$ and the probability of randomly catching a clownfish is $\frac{50}{90}$.

We are going to be adding clownfish, but the number of goldfish will remain constant.

We will add clownfish until we have $\frac{2}{3}$ clownfish and $\frac{1}{3}$ goldfish in the pond. Our original 40 goldfish will now account for $\frac{1}{3}$ of the total fish in the pond.

40 goldfish = $\frac{1}{3}$ of the new total.

$40 = \frac{1}{3} \times T$

$120 = T$

120 Total fish – 40 goldfish leaves **80 clownfish**

E An artist is planning to hold a private art show. Of the pieces he has already completed, 20 are sculptures and 40 are oil paintings. If the artist does not complete any more oil paintings, how many more sculptures must he complete in order to ensure that the probability of seeing a sculpture at the show is $\frac{4}{5}$?

S In the beginning we have:

Sculptures	Paintings	Total (T)
20	40	60

Currently $\frac{20}{60}$ or $\frac{1}{3}$ of the pieces are sculptures and the remaining $\frac{2}{3}$ are paintings. We are going to be adding only sculptures until $\frac{4}{5}$ of the total pieces are sculptures and $\frac{1}{5}$ are paintings. Let's focus on the paintings, as they are the unchanging factor.

When all the works are completed, 40 paintings will comprise $\frac{1}{5}$ of the total pieces in the show.

$$40 = \frac{1}{5} \times T$$
$$200 = T$$

200 Total pieces – 40 paintings = 160 sculptures

But the question asks how many **more** must he create.
Starting from a base of 20, he will need to knock out:

$$160 - 20 = \boxed{\textbf{140 additional sculptures}}$$

E A bag has only pearls and emeralds inside. There are three times as many pearls as emeralds. The pearls are either white or black, and 8 times as many pearls are white as are black. If one jewel is drawn at random from the bag, what is the probability that the jewel drawn will be a black pearl?

S There are multiple ways to approach this problem.

An effective way to handle this kind of probability problem is to draw a probability tree.

You will need to build the tree starting at the top with the most generic detail (Jewels) down to the most specific detail (White or Black). However, when you fill in your information, you must start from the bottom.

Let's fill in our tree from the lowest level and work our way up to the highest level.

Total Jewels

Pearls   Emeralds

White   Black

Step 1: Starting at the lowest level, we have 8 white pearls for each black pearl. This gives us 9 pearls total.

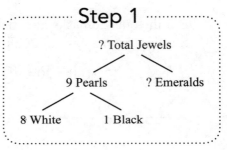

Step 1

? Total Jewels

9 Pearls   ? Emeralds

8 White   1 Black

Step 2: Moving up the tree, we have 3 pearls for every emerald. Since we have 9 pearls, we must have 3 emeralds.

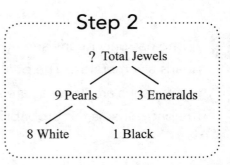

Step 2

? Total Jewels

9 Pearls   3 Emeralds

8 White   1 Black

Step 3: Moving up the tree one more level, we know we have 9 pearls and 3 emeralds. That makes a total of 12 total jewels.

Step 4: What is the probability that the jewel drawn will be a black pearl? For the 12 total jewels, there is only 1 black pearl. So the probability of selecting a black pearl is:

$$\frac{\text{Black Pearl}}{\text{Total Jewels}} = \boxed{\frac{1}{12}}$$

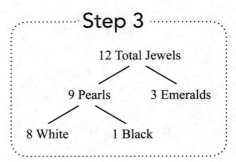

Step 3

12 Total Jewels

9 Pearls   3 Emeralds

8 White   1 Black

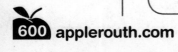

Probability Practice Problems

1. In a certain store, there are 3 blue sweaters, 4 red sweaters, 7 green sweaters, and 4 white sweaters for sale. If these are the only sweaters in the store, what is the probability that a sweater randomly selected from this store is blue?

   (A) $\frac{1}{6}$

   (B) $\frac{1}{3}$

   (C) $\frac{1}{2}$

   (D) $\frac{2}{3}$

   (E) $\frac{11}{18}$

2. Every student in Mr. Smith's class plays exactly one sport. The probability that a student chosen at random from the class plays baseball is $\frac{1}{6}$. If exactly 3 students play baseball, what is the total number of students in the class?

3. A drawer contains only white, black and brown socks. If the probability of randomly selecting a white sock from the drawer is $\frac{1}{5}$, and the probability of selecting a black sock is $\frac{1}{4}$, which of the following could **NOT** be the total number of socks in the drawer?

   (A) 20
   (B) 25
   (C) 40
   (D) 60
   (E) 80

4. The Atlanta Zoo has 3 monkeys that are 10 years old, 6 monkeys that are 6 years old, 2 monkeys that are 4 years old, and 4 monkeys that are 2 years old. What is the probability that a monkey selected at random will be less than 6 years old?

   (A) $\frac{2}{5}$

   (B) $\frac{7}{15}$

   (C) $\frac{3}{5}$

   (D) $\frac{11}{15}$

   (E) $\frac{4}{5}$

Number of Computers per Home in Johnstown

Computers per Home	Number of Homes
0	4
1	16
2	20
3	12
4	8

	Male	Female
Age 0 – 20	35	93
Age 21 – 40	55	49
Age 41 – 60	60	48

5. A survey revealed the data shown in the table above. What is the probability that a home chosen at random from Johnstown will contain exactly 3 computers?

(A) $\frac{1}{5}$

(B) $\frac{1}{4}$

(C) $\frac{1}{3}$

(D) $\frac{1}{2}$

(E) $\frac{2}{3}$

7. The table above shows demographic information for 340 customers at City Mall. What is the probability that a randomly selected person at this mall is a male whose age is 21 or greater?

(A) $\frac{39}{289}$

(B) $\frac{55}{340}$

(C) $\frac{23}{68}$

(D) $\frac{15}{34}$

(E) $\frac{127}{170}$

6. If two of the positive factors of 6 are multiplied together, what is the probability that the result will be a multiple of 2?

(A) $\frac{1}{6}$

(B) $\frac{1}{3}$

(C) $\frac{1}{2}$

(D) $\frac{2}{3}$

(E) $\frac{5}{6}$

8. 64 cubes are joined together to form a single, larger cube. The large cube is then painted green. If the large cube is then broken down into the 64 smaller cubes, what is the probability that a randomly selected cube will have exactly one green face?

Ratios

2%

of all math
questions
on the SAT

When you are working with ratio problems, you must always add the individual parts to find the whole.

E In a certain city the ratio of the number of men to women is 3 to 2. What fraction of the population is female?

(A) $\frac{2}{5}$

(B) $\frac{3}{5}$

(C) $\frac{2}{3}$

(D) $\frac{5}{3}$

(E) $\frac{3}{2}$

S Let's set it up:

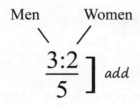

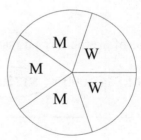

For every 5 people, there are 3 men and 2 women.

Men   Women

Therefore the fraction of the population that is male is $\frac{3}{5}$, and the fraction of the population that is female is $\left(\frac{2}{5}\right)$.

Think of ratios as a pie. Find the total number of pieces in the pie, and you're good to go

E If a $345,000 prize was divided among three game show contestants in the ratio 2 to 7 to 9, what was the largest amount awarded to any one contestant, rounded to the nearest dollar?

(A) $7,041
(B) $38,333
(C) $134,167
(D) $172,500
(E) $345,000

S

Smallest   Largest

$$\frac{2:7:9}{18} \quad] \; add$$

Smallest   Middle   Largest

$$\frac{2:7:9}{18} \qquad \frac{2:7:9}{18} \qquad \frac{2:7:9}{18}$$

Therefore the largest prize awarded is $\frac{9}{18}$ or $\frac{1}{2}$ of the total prize.

$\frac{1}{2}$ of $345,000 = **$172,500**

E If a farmer keeps only cows and pigs in the ratio of 3 to 4, each of the following could be the number of animals on the farm EXCEPT

(A)   7
(B) 10
(C) 28
(D) 42
(E) 84

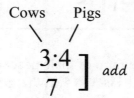

Cows   Pigs

Unless we want to have fractions of animals, we need a multiple of 7 for our grand total. So cold-cuts aside, we need to see totals such as 7, 14, 21, 28.

For example, if we had 28 animals, $\frac{3}{7}$ would be cows and $\frac{4}{7}$ would be pigs. To find the number of cows

$$\frac{3}{7} \times \text{total} = \text{\# of cows}$$

$$\frac{3}{7} \times 28 = 12 \text{ cows.}$$

To find the number of pigs:

$$\frac{4}{7} \times 28 = 16 \text{ pigs.}$$

All whole animals. All good.

So the only odd-ball answer in our current problem is (B). If we have 10 animals, we get animal parts. For cows we are looking at $\frac{3}{7} \times 10 = 4.29$ cows. And for pigs we are looking at $\frac{4}{7} \times 10 = 5.71$ pigs. (B) is our answer.

Ratios Practice Problems

1. A catering order calls for Greek and Caesar salads in the ratio of 4:5. If there are 54 salads in the order, how many are Caesar salads?

 (A)   4
 (B)   5
 (C) 24
 (D) 30
 (E) 54

2. Which of the following is equal to the ratio 3.5 to 14?

 (A)   1 to 2
 (B)   1 to 3
 (C)   8 to 2
 (D)   2 to 8
 (E)   2 to 80

3. In the wild, the ratio of male peacocks to female peacocks is 3 to 5. What percent of peacocks in the wild are female?

 (A) 32.5
 (B) 35.0
 (C) 37.5
 (D) 60.0
 (E) 62.5

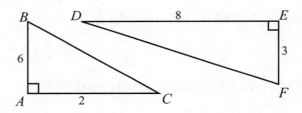

Note: Figure not drawn to scale.

4. In the figure above, what is the ratio of the area of triangle *ABC* to the area of triangle *DEF*?

 (A)   1:2
 (B)   1:3
 (C)   1:4
 (D)   2:3
 (E)   2:5

5. If Kara only owns drama and comedy movies and the ratio of dramas to comedies in her DVD collection is 3:2, which of the following could be the total number of DVDs in her collection?

(A) 15
(B) 16
(C) 17
(D) 18
(E) 19

6. Currently, a certain university has 3,051 students enrolled. Of these students, the ratio of males to females is 7:2. If the university wants to change this ratio to 6:4 by only adding more female students, how many additional females will have to enroll?

7. If 100 cubic meters of compost can fertilize 0.04 square kilometers of soil, how many square kilometers of soil can be fertilized by 10^7 cubic meters of compost?

(A)   400
(B)   4,000
(C)   40,000
(D)   400,000
(E)   4,000,000

8. In preparing for a bake sale, Ryan baked $\frac{1}{3}$ the number of cookies that Olga baked, and Olga baked 4 times the number of cookies that Utibe baked. What was the ratio of the number of cookies that Ryan baked to the number of cookies that Utibe baked?

(A) $\frac{1}{4}$

(B) $\frac{1}{3}$

(C) $\frac{3}{4}$

(D) $\frac{4}{3}$

(E) $\frac{7}{1}$

9. In a parking lot with 168 spaces, there were 48 more filled spaces than empty spaces. What was the ratio of filled spaces to empty spaces?

(A) 5 to 9
(B) 9 to 5
(C) 2 to 1
(D) 5 to 2
(E) 11 to 3

10. All of the following ratios are equivalent EXCEPT ?

(A) 1 : 2.5
(B) 4 :10
(C) 6 :15
(D) 8 :25
(E) 20 : 50

Sequences

4%

of all math
questions
on the SAT

Arithmetic Sequence

In this type of sequence, the difference between any two consecutive terms is the same.

2,   5,   8,   11,   14

+3   +3   +3   +3

Geometric Sequence

In this type of sequence, each term after the first is found by multiplying the previous term by a fixed number.

2,   8,   32,   128,   512

×4   ×4   ×4   ×4

The SAT likes to combine elements of arithmetic and geometric sequences.

 E

2, 4, 10...

In the sequence above, the first term is 2, and each term after the first is 2 less than 3 times the preceding term. What is the 7th term of the sequence?

(A)   − 61
(B)   28
(C)   244
(D)   730
(E) 1458

S In a problem like this, with only 7 terms, it's easiest to simply write them all down, being careful to label each term of the sequence.

		$\times 3 - 2$	$\times 3 - 2$	$\times 3 - 2$	$\times 3 - 2$	$\times 3 - 2$	$\times 3 - 2$
Value	2	4	10	28	82	244	(730)
Term	1	2	3	4	5	6	7

E The first term of a sequence of numbers is -2. If each term after the first is the product of -3 and the preceding term, what is the 5th term of the sequence?

S In a problem like this, with only 5 terms, it's easiest to simply write them all down, being careful to label each term of the sequence.

		$\times (-3)$	$\times (-3)$	$\times (-3)$	$\times (-3)$
Value	-2	6	-18	54	(−162)
Term	1	2	3	4	5

Repeating sequences

Many SAT problems will ask you to find terms of a sequence such as the 192nd term. Good luck writing out 192 terms! The key to problems like these is to find the repeat. You need to physically write/draw out the sequence until you find the repeat, and then you can solve.

E

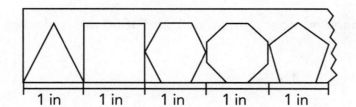

| 1 in | 1 in | 1 in | 1 in | 1 in |

One end of a 128 inch-long piece of fabric is shown above. A student cuts out these 5 shapes from the fabric, over and over, starting with the shape on the left and continuing in order from left to right. If the student uses all of the available fabric and leaves no space between shapes, what will be the number of sides of the last shape the student cuts from the fabric?

(A) Three
(B) Four
(C) Five
(D) Six
(E) Eight

S We are looking for the 128th term. There are 2 approaches. The first approach involves finding a visual pattern.

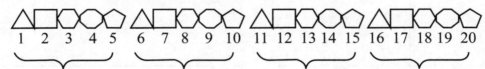

We are looking for a term ending in 8. We can see that the 8th term is a ⬡ as is the 18th term. If you keep repeating, you will see that every term ending in an 8, including 128, will be a ⬡.

The second approach involves remembering a simple rule. Because our pattern repeats every 5 terms, we need to divide the number of the desired term by the repeat.

$$\frac{\text{Desired term}}{\text{Terms repeated}} \quad \frac{128}{5} = 25 \text{ R } \mathbf{3}$$

We are interested in the repeat. We have 25 complete sequences, but what we are really interested in is the remainder. In this case the remainder is 3, so we are looking for the third term of the repeat, △□⬡○⬠

So both approaches indicate that the 128th term is a hexagon and has ⑥ sides, Choice **(D)**.

If you end up with a remainder of 0, the desired term is the last term of the repeat; in this case, that would be a ⬠.

Remember: find the pattern, and you're half way there!

E How many numbers between 1 and 1000 are multiples of either 4, 5, or both?

S Let's write down terms that match our criteria until we see a pattern:

1, 2, 3, ④, ⑤, 6, 7, ⑧, 9, ⑩, 11, ⑫, 13, 14, ⑮, ⑯, 17, 18, 19, ⑳, …

And if we continue, we notice that for every 10 integers, 4 match our criteria:

4, 5, 8, 10,	12,15,16,20	24, 25, 28, 30	32, 35, 36, 40
1 - 10	11 - 20	21 - 30	31 - 40

So for every group of 10, we have 4 that work.

Therefore, if we are looking at a group of 1000, we will have ⑨**400** that work.

Sequences Practice Problems

8, 10, 14, 22 . . .

1. In the sequence above, the first term is 8, and every term after the first is found by doubling the preceding term and then subtracting 6 from the result. What is the seventh term of the sequence?

    (A)   38
    (B)   70
    (C)   134
    (D)   176
    (E)   262

5, 16, 27, 38 . . .

2. The first four numbers in a sequence are shown above. Each term after the first is obtained by adding d to the preceding term. Which term in this sequence is equal to $5 + (17 - 1)d$?

    (A) 5th

    (B) 11th

    (C) 16th

    (D) 17th

    (E) 18th

3. After the first term in a series of positive integers, the ratio of each term to the term immediately preceding it is 1 to 3. What is the ratio of the fourth term to the seventh term in this sequence?

    (A)   3 to 1
    (B)   6 to 1
    (C)   9 to 1
    (D) 18 to 1
    (E) 27 to 1

4. Each term in a certain sequence is greater than the term preceding it, and the difference between any two consecutive terms in the sequence is always the same number. If the second and fifth terms of this sequence are 12 and 30 respectively, what is the tenth term of the sequence?

5. What is the 196th digit after the decimal point of the repeating decimal $0.\overline{49865}$?

(A) 5
(B) 9
(C) 8
(D) 6
(E) 4

$$81, 27, 9, \ldots$$

7. The first term of the sequence above is 81, and each term after the first is one third of the term immediately preceding it. Which of the following expressions represents the nth term of the sequence?

(A) 81^{n-1}

(B) 81^{n}

(C) $81(\frac{1}{3})^{n-1}$

(D) $81(\frac{1}{3})^{n}$

(E) $(\frac{1}{3})81^{n-1}$

6. What is the units digit of 2^{144} ?

(A) 0
(B) 2
(C) 4
(D) 6
(E) 8

Combinations and Permutations | 1.2%

of all math
questions
on the SAT

A combination is a group of elements. When you are asked to create distinct groups of elements from a larger pool, you are working with a combination. For combinations, the order of the group does not matter.

If there are 5 people in a room, how many different groups of 3 can be made?

S A group is a group.

It doesn't matter how we arrange the elements in a group; it doesn't change the group.

To solve this we have 2 options.
1) We can write out every possible combination. This is okay when we are working with a few elements.

Let's name the 5 people in our group

Agamemnon
Bertha
Cassius
Deion
Eustace

And let's lay out all the possible groups **systematically.**

Because we are working with combinations, BCA = ABC. Be careful not to double count.

Start with A and find all the distinct groups:

ABC   ACD   ADE
ABD   ACE
ABE   (6 groups)

Now we move on to B:

BCD   BDE
BCE   (3 groups)

And finally we move on to C:

CDE   (1 group)

In total we have 6 + 3 + 1 = (**10**) distinct groups.

2) If we do not want to write these out by hand, we can use a calculator to save a lot of time. It will also ensure that we will not make a common mistake and forget to include a group. The more advanced calculators, such as the TI-84®, have built-in Combination and Permutation functions.

From the home screen, follow this sequence:

Math → PRB → nCr

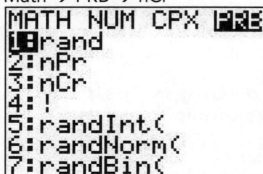
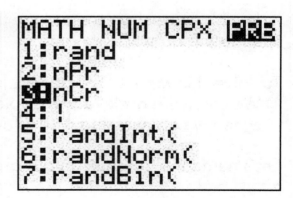

n = the number of total elements you are choosing from
r = the number of elements you are choosing per group
In this case we are choosing from 5 people ($n = 5$), and we are selecting groups of 3 ($r = 3$).

When you follow the steps: Math → PRB → nCr
You will end up with the following screens:

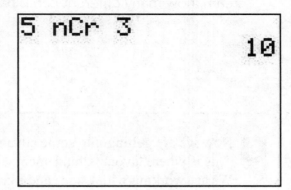

Simply replace the term 'Ans' with our *n* value of 5 and type in '3' at the end of the line.
It will look like this: 5 nCr 3.
Then press enter.
Voila! **10**.

Let's try a few more

E A certain pizza restaurant offers 8 different toppings for its pizzas. How many combinations of 3 different toppings from those offered are possible?

(A) 24
(B) 36
(C) 56
(D) 70
(E) 336

S This is one of the combination problems where you absolutely need your calculator. Writing this out by hand would eat up way too much time. With your trusty TI, this will take seconds.

Let's set it up.
Type in 8 (the number of toppings we have).

Then, type Math → PRB → nCr

Finally, type in 3 (the number of toppings we are choosing).

8 nCr 3 = (**56**)

Piece of cake. Thank you TI!

E A certain ice cream shop offers 31 flavors of ice cream and 3 different types of cones. If each cone comes with two different flavors of ice cream, how many different combinations of flavors and cones are possible?

S Now we are getting into some advanced territory.
This is where layout is fundamental.
We are working with Cones and Flavors.
We have to keep them separated.

First, Ice Cream Flavors: From 31 possible flavors, we are choosing 2.

31 nCr 2 = 465

Next, Cones: From 3 types of cones, we are choosing 1.

3 nCr 1 = 3

So we have 465 ice cream flavor options and 3 cone options.
To find the total number of cone-flavor combinations, we multiply.

465 × 3 = (**1,395**)

Permutations

When we are creating groups and the order of the elements matters, we move from combinations to permutations.

E If 3 people are to be seated in three chairs, how many different seating arrangements are possible?

It's clear that the order matters here; ABC is not the same as CBA when we are considering seating arrangements.

Let's work with our cast of characters:

Archibald
Beyoncé
Coolio

We have several ways to solve this.

Approach 1: The "Slot" method:

Let's draw a line/slot for each of our 3 seats.

$$\underline{\hphantom{XX}} \quad \underline{\hphantom{XX}} \quad \underline{\hphantom{XX}}$$
$$\text{\#1} \qquad \text{\#2} \qquad \text{\#3}$$

How many options do we have for seat #1?
3. Either A, B or C can sit there.

$$\underline{3} \quad \underline{\hphantom{XX}} \quad \underline{\hphantom{XX}}$$
$$\text{\#1} \qquad \text{\#2} \qquad \text{\#3}$$

Once we have filled seat one, how many options remain for seat #2?
2. Someone is already occupying seat #1, so that person cannot simultaneously be in seat 2.

$$\underline{3} \quad \underline{2} \quad \underline{\hphantom{XX}}$$
$$\text{\#1} \qquad \text{\#2} \qquad \text{\#3}$$

How many options remain for seat #3?
1. We have seated two people, so only one person remains to fill the final seat.

$$\underline{3} \quad \underline{2} \quad \underline{1}$$
$$\text{\#1} \qquad \text{\#2} \qquad \text{\#3}$$

Now we multiply: $3 \times 2 \times 1 = \boxed{6}$

We have 6 options.

Approach 2: Write them out:

ABC	BAC	CAB
ACB	BCA	CBA

$= \boxed{6}$

This approach is easy only for groups with few elements.

In this case factorials and permutations give you the same answer, but factorials only work in the rare cases where $n = r$.

Approach 3: Use factorials:

Factorials provide you with a quick way to compute permutations when you have the same number of elements and spaces.
If you have 3 spaces in which to arrange 3 things, you can use 3 factorial, which can be written as "3!"

3! translates to $3 \times 2 \times 1 =$ ⑥

Arranging 3 folks in 3 spots = 3! = $\qquad 3 \times 2 \times 1 = 6$
Arranging 4 folks in 4 spots = 4! = $\qquad 4 \times 3 \times 2 \times 1 = 24$
Arranging 5 folks in 5 spots = 5! = $5 \times 4 \times 3 \times 2 \times 1 = 120$

And your TI can calculate factorials instantly.
To find the factorial function, follow these steps:
Math → PRB → !
Then fill in your number before the '!'.

Approach 4: Use permutations:

Your TI can handle permutations and save you lots of time.
In this case, we are arranging 3 people in 3 spaces, and order matters.
We follow this sequence to arrive at permutations.
Math → PRB → nPr

n = the number of total elements you are choosing from
r = the number of elements you are choosing per arrangement
In this case we are choosing from 3 people ($n = 3$), and we are arranging them in 3 spaces ($r = 3$).

3 nPr 3 = ⑥

Plot 1	Plot 2	Plot 3
Plot 4	Plot 5	Plot 6

Juvencio has a garden with 6 plots, as shown above, and he has 8 types of vegetables.   If he can plant only one type of vegetable in each plot, and if no two plots can contain the same type of vegetable, how many different garden layouts can Juvencio create?

(A)   28
(B)   48
(C)   480
(D)   20,160
(E)   40,320

Factorials cannot help us here, because $n > r$. Remember: you can only use factorials when $n = r$.

S Order matters in this problem, so we are dealing with a permutation.

From 8 possible veggies, he can only plant 6 per configuration.

Let's use our calculator.
$n = 8$
$r = 6$

Math → PRB → nPr

8 nPr 6 = $\boxed{20,160}$

Imagine writing that out by hand!

Combinations and Permutations Practice Problems

1. A certain restaurant serves 4 different entrees with 6 different sides. How many different entree-side combinations are possible at this restaurant?

   (A) 10
   (B) 12
   (C) 16
   (D) 20
   (E) 24

3. Jenny must choose a three-digit number to be the combination for her gym locker. If the first digit is prime, the second digit is odd and the third digit is even (non zero), how many different possibilities are there for her combination?

   (A) 20
   (B) 40
   (C) 60
   (D) 80
   (E) 100

2. At a poker game, each chip is worth 1, 5, or 10 dollars. How many different combinations of these chips are worth 11 dollars?

   (A) two
   (B) three
   (C) four
   (D) five
   (E) six

4. How many 4-digit integers have only odd numbers as digits?

5. How many different 3-digit integers can be formed from the digits of the number 354,678?

6. The web site barbie.com® allows Chandler to make his own Barbies. If he can choose from 3 different skin colors, 2 different eye colors, and 4 different hair colors, how many different Barbies are possible?

7. There are 5 teams in the Monroe County north division. If each team plays every other team exactly once per year, how many games will be played this year in the division?

(A)   5
(B)   10
(C)   15
(D)   20
(E)   25

Square Roots

0.6%

of all math
questions
on the SAT

Roots are the opposite of squares.

Example: $4^2 = 16$; $\sqrt{16} = 4$ and -4

To get rid of a radical (AKA the square root symbol) simply square the term.

Example: $\sqrt{(4)^2} = 4$; $\left(\sqrt{6}\right)^2 = 6$

General Rules

1) You can add and subtract terms when they have the same number under the radical.

    Example: $4\sqrt{2} + 6\sqrt{2} = 10\sqrt{2}$

2) You can multiply or divide terms as long as everything stays under the radical.

    Example: $\sqrt{2} \times \sqrt{8} = \sqrt{16} = 4$

E If $\sqrt{7} = 2s - 12$, what is the value of $(2s - 12)^2$?

(A) $\sqrt{2}$
(B) $\sqrt{7}$
(C) 7
(D) 26
(E) 49

S We know that $\sqrt{7} = 2s - 12$

We are looking to find $\boxed{(2s - 12)^2}$

Simply square both sides.

$\sqrt{7} = 2s - 12$

$(\sqrt{7})^2 = (2s - 12)^2$

Now simplify:

$7 = (2s - 12)^2$

So the answer is $\boxed{(C)\ 7}$

Square Roots Practice Problems

1. What is the value of x for which
$5\sqrt{x} + 15 = 30$?

(A) 3
(B) 9
(C) 15
(D) 27
(E) 81

$$\sqrt{54} = x\sqrt{y}$$

3. If x and y are both positive integers, what is the value of xy ?

(A) 3
(B) 9
(C) 15
(D) 18
(E) 36

2. If $(\sqrt{8})^t = y + 3$, what is the value of $(y+3)^{\frac{2}{t}}$?

0.8%

of all math
questions
on the SAT

Unit Conversions

The SAT will often ask you to convert units. The key here is to be as systematic and organized as possible. You must keep track of any and all conversions you make.

E Angela can type 80 words per minute. At this rate, how many words can she type in 2 hours?

S $$\frac{80 \text{ words}}{1 \text{ minute}} \times \frac{60 \text{ minutes}}{1 \text{ hour}} = \frac{4800 \text{ words}}{1 \text{ hour}} \times 2 \text{ hours} = \boxed{9600 \text{ words}}$$

Just be careful to keep everything lined up.

E A machine can package 20 candy bars in 30 seconds. At this rate, how many hours will it take the machine to package 3000 candy bars?

(A)   0.56
(B)   1.25
(C)   33.3
(D)   7,200,000
(E) 16,200,000

S Step 1: Find your *RATE* in the appropriate units.

This is our rate!

$$\frac{20 \text{ bars}}{30 \text{ seconds}} \times \frac{60 \text{ seconds}}{1 \text{ minute}} \times \frac{60 \text{ minutes}}{1 \text{ hour}} = \frac{2400 \text{ bars}}{1 \text{ hour}}$$

Step 2: Set up your equation, Total = Rate × Time

$$\text{Total} = \text{Rate} \times \text{Time}$$

$$3000 \text{ bars} = \frac{2400 \text{ bars}}{1 \text{ hour}} \times \text{Time}$$

$$\frac{1 \text{ hour}}{2400 \text{ bars}} \times 3000 \text{ bars} = \boxed{\textbf{1.25 hours}}$$

Our answer is (**B**)!

We needed to solve for Time, so we divided by (AKA multiplied by the reciprocal of) the rate.

Unit Conversions Practice Problems

1. A certain computer printer can print 40 pages in 2 minutes. At this rate, how many pages can it print in 5 minutes?

   (A) 45
   (B) 50
   (C) 80
   (D) 100
   (E) 200

2. Arnold can read 5 pages of a certain book in 4 minutes. If each chapter of the book consists of 15 pages, how many chapters can Arnold read in 48 minutes?

   (A) 2
   (B) 3
   (C) 4
   (D) 12
   (E) 60

3. A machine produces x bottle caps every y minutes. At this rate, how many bottle caps will the machine produce in z seconds?

   (A) $60zy$

   (B) $60zx$

   (C) $\dfrac{60y}{zx}$

   (D) $\dfrac{zx}{60y}$

   (E) zx

4. The price of nails is d dollars for 500 nails. In terms of d, how many nails can be purchased for c cents?

   (A) $5c$

   (B) $\dfrac{5c}{d}$

   (C) $\dfrac{5d}{c}$

   (D) $\dfrac{50c}{d}$

   (E) $50c$

Remainders after Division

0.6%

of all math questions on the SAT

First, some quick definitions:

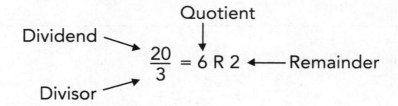

$$\frac{20}{3} = 6 \text{ R } 2$$

Dividend → $\frac{20}{3}$ ← Divisor

Quotient ↓

Remainder ←

The SAT will generally stick a variable in the dividend place and ask you to solve for it. The most basic remainder problem looks like this:

When *n* is divided by 7, the remainder is 3. What is one possible value for *n* ?

$$\frac{n}{7} = ? \text{ R } 3$$

To find a possible value for *n*, just add the remainder (3) to the divisor (7).

$$\frac{n}{7} = ? \text{ R } 3$$

$$+$$

$$3 + 7 = 10$$

That was easy enough, *n* = 10.

More advanced problems have additional requirements, but you begin solving them in the same way.

IGNORE THE QUOTIENT! For SAT remainder problems, the only thing you need to know about the quotient is that it is an integer.

E The number n is a positive integer. When n is divided by 7, the remainder is 3. What is the least possible value for n if $n > 30$?

S This looks familiar:

$$\frac{n}{7} = \underline{\quad} \; R \, 3$$

$$+$$

$$3 + 7 = 10$$

We know that one possible value for n is 10. But to satisfy the "greater than 30" requirement, we need to find other values for n. To find additional values of n, simply add the divisor (7) to our initial value of n (10) as many times as necessary to satisfy the requirements of the problem. 10, 17, 24, 31, 38, 45... all of these are possible values for n. Let's see how this works:

$$\frac{10}{7} = 1 \, R \, 3$$

$$\frac{17}{7} = 2 \, R \, 3$$

$$\frac{24}{7} = 3 \, R \, 3$$

$$\frac{31}{7} = 4 \, R \, 3$$

$$\frac{38}{7} = 5 \, R \, 3$$

See the pattern?

If we keep adding 7 to our dividend we will continue to get the same remainder.

Possible values of n that are greater than 30 include 31 and 38; the smallest is $n = \boxed{31}$.

Often the SAT will throw in an additional step. Remember to solve one step at a time.

E When the positive integer k is divided by 12, the remainder is 4. What is the remainder when $3k + 6$ is divided by 12?

S Step 1: Set up the first part of the problem.

$$\frac{k}{12} = ? \, R \, 4$$

Step 2: Solve for k.

$$4 + 12 = 16 = k$$

Step 3: Set up the second part of the problem.

$$\frac{3k + 6}{12} = ? \, R \, ?$$

Plug in the value for k.

$$\frac{3(16) + 6}{12} = ? \, R \, ?$$

$$\frac{54}{12} = 4 \, R \, 6$$

There is our answer, ⑥.

Remember to use your calculator. Don't do the division in your head.

E When x is divided by 9, the remainder is 5. What is the remainder when $2x + 3$ is divided by 9?

S Step 1: Set up the first part of the problem.

$$\frac{x}{9} = ? \text{ R } 5$$

Step 2: Solve for x.

$$9 + 5 = x$$
$$x = 14$$

Step 3: Set up the 2ⁿᵈ part of the problem.

$$\frac{2x + 3}{9} = ? \text{ R } ?$$

Step 4: Plug in x and solve.

$$\frac{2(14) + 3}{9} = ? \text{ R } ?$$

$$\frac{31}{9} = 3 \text{ R } 4$$

Our answer is ④.

Remainders after Division
Practice Problems

---

1. When a positive integer f is divided by 9, the remainder is 2. What is the remainder when $f + 3$ is divided by 9?

   (A) 1
   (B) 2
   (C) 3
   (D) 4
   (E) 5

2. When a positive integer d is divided by 8, the remainder is 4. Which of the following has a remainder of 1 when it is divided by 8?

   (A) $d - 5$
   (B) $d - 4$
   (C) $d - 3$
   (D) $d + 1$
   (E) $d + 2$

3. A company's machine is periodically scheduled for maintenance. If the machine is repaired on a Saturday, and the next scheduled repair is exactly 260 days later, on which day will the next repair fall?

   (A) Sunday
   (B) Monday
   (C) Tuesday
   (D) Wednesday
   (E) Thursday

4. The number s has three digits, and the digit in the hundreds place is 2. If 5 is the remainder when s is divided by 13, and 10 is the remainder when s is divided by 12, what is the value of s ?

5. When an integer x is divided by 6, the remainder is 3. If the sum of x and 8 was multiplied by 3 and then divided by 6, what would the remainder be?

(A) 1
(B) 2
(C) 3
(D) 4
(E) 5

6. A positive integer m has a remainder of 4 when it is divided by 7 and a remainder of 2 when it is divided by 6. If $0 < m < 100$, what is one possible value of m?

7. Two is the remainder when 20 is divided by a positive integer f. How many possible values are there for f?

(A) one
(B) two
(C) three
(D) four
(E) five

Arithmetic Review

$$|a - 5| = 10$$
$$|b - 3| = 12$$

1. In the equations above, $a > 0$ and $b < 0$. What is the value of $a + b$?

(A) −14
(B) −9
(C)   6
(D)   9
(E) 15

3. If $\frac{5}{8}$ of a number is 25, what is $\frac{1}{8}$ of the number?

(A)   2
(B)   5
(C) 10
(D) 15
(E) 20

2. What is the product of 2.135 rounded to the nearest whole number and 2.135 rounded to the nearest tenth?

4. The ratio of red to blue to green marbles in a jar is 1 to 3 to 4, respectively. What fraction of the marbles in the jar is blue?

(A) $\frac{1}{8}$

(B) $\frac{1}{4}$

(C) $\frac{3}{8}$

(D) $\frac{1}{2}$

(E) $\frac{5}{8}$

5. When the positive integer n is divided by 5, the remainder is 4. What is the remainder when $n + 3$ is divided by 5?

(A) 0
(B) 1
(C) 2
(D) 3
(E) 4

6. A certain cafeteria offers 5 different sides to go with each dinner. How many combinations of 2 different sides are possible with each dinner?

(A) 5
(B) 10
(C) 15
(D) 20
(E) 30

7. On a certain map, 1.2 inches represents 20 miles. If a line on the map representing a certain road is 19.8 inches long, what is the length, in miles, of the actual road?

(A) 23.76
(B) 320
(C) 330
(D) 396
(E) 475.20

8. Which of the following is NOT a factor of 60?

(A) 30
(B) 20
(C) 10
(D)   8
(E)   3

$$-4 < 4x \leq 4$$

9. Which of the following graphs represents all of the values of x that satisfy the inequality above?

(A)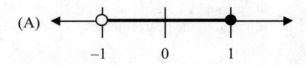

(B)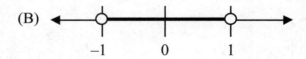

(C)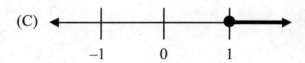

(D)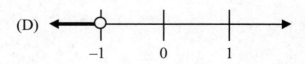

(E)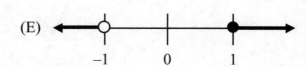

10. The ratio of 10 to .01 is equal to the ratio of 100,000 to:

(A)   0.001
(B)   0.01
(C)   10
(D)   100
(E)   1,000

11. For a certain custom sports car, buyers can choose one of five exterior paint colors and one of three interior colors. How many combinations of exterior and interior colors are there?

(A)   8
(B)   9
(C)   10
(D)   12
(E)   15

$$-2, 2, 10, \ldots$$

12. The first term of the sequence above is -2, and each term after the first is 6 more than 2 times the preceding term. What is the 8th term of the sequence?

(A) -506
(B) -250
(C)   250
(D)   506
(E)   1018

13. A certain plumbing company accepts a pipe from a supplier only if the diameter of the pipe is between $2\frac{9}{10}$ and $3\frac{1}{10}$ inches. If the company accepts a pipe with a diameter of d inches, which of the following describes all possible values of d?

(A) $|d + 3| < \frac{1}{10}$
(B) $|3 + d| > \frac{1}{10}$
(C) $|3 - d| < \frac{1}{10}$
(D) $|3 + d| < \frac{1}{10}$
(E) $|d - 3| = \frac{1}{10}$

14. Jesse is preparing her breakfast. Of the containers of yogurt in the refrigerator, 4 are vanilla. She will reach into the refrigerator and randomly pick one of the containers for her breakfast. If the probability is ¼ that the container she picks will be vanilla, how many containers of yogurt are in her refrigerator?

(A)   4
(B)   8
(C)   10
(D)   12
(E)   16

15. If r is a positive integer satisfying $r^8 = s$ and $r^6 = t^2$, which of the following must be equal to r^{12}?

(A) $s^2 - t^2$

(B) $\dfrac{s^3}{t^4}$

(C) t^3

(D) s^3

(E) $s^4 - \dfrac{s}{t^4}$

The Arithmetic Short List

1 **PRIME NUMBERS** are positive integers greater than 1 and divisible by only 1 and themselves. 2 is the smallest prime number; it is also the only even prime number.

2 Each equation containing an **ABSOLUTE VALUE** is actually two equations.

3 With **REMAINDERS AFTER DIVISION** problems, just add the remainder to the divisor to find a possible solution.

4 SAT **PICKING NUMBERS** problems use the phrase **IN TERMS OF**, and/or have the same variables in all 5 answer choices.

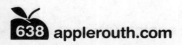

5 **PICKING NUMBERS:** DO NOT pick 0 or 1. These numbers do strange things to equations and functions. Also, try to avoid numbers already used in the problem.

6 **PICKING NUMBERS:** If you are solving an equation like $x + y = z$, it's better to pick numbers for the two variables on the same side and SOLVE for the loner. So pick $x = 2$ and $y = 3$, then solve for $z = 5$ and go from there!

7 **PICKING NUMBERS:** If you pick numbers and 2 answer choices give you the correct answer, you must pick different numbers and repeat the process with the answer choices that worked the first time (this doesn't happen very often).

PICKING NUMBERS: SPECIAL CASES

8

If you try a ...	**Whole Number**	You should also try a ...	**Fraction / Decimal**
If you try a ...	**Positive Number**	You should also try a ...	**Negative Number**
Try the oddballs	**0 (Zero)**	And	**1**

9 There are times when you attempt to solve a problem on the SAT and you get stuck. When you cannot make any progress tackling a problem head on, a smart approach is to **WORK BACKWARDS** from the answer choices, plugging them in until you find the one that works.

ART OF TRANSLATION

Word	Math Meaning
What, how much, a number	Some variable (x)
Is, was, equals	=
Sum, increase, more than, greater than	Add (+)
Subtract, less than, exceeds	Subtract (−)
Difference	Subtract (−)
Of, times	Multiply (×)
Product	Multiply (×)
Divisible by, divided by, out of, per	Divide (÷)
Percent (%)	Multiply by $\frac{1}{100}$

10

11 You can add or subtract the **EXPONENTS** when you multiply or divide like bases. Try to get all of your terms to have the same base.

12 **USE YOUR CALCULATOR** if you forget your exponent rules: plug 2 in for your base. $(x^2)^3$ becomes $(\mathbf{2}^2)^3$ in your calculator

13 For **INEQUALITIES**, flip the sign when you divide or multiply by a negative number.

14 **% CHANGE** $= \dfrac{\text{(New number – Old number)}}{\text{Old number}} \times 100$

15 **Probability** $= \dfrac{\text{\# of outcomes that meet the requirements}}{\text{Total \# of possible outcomes}}$

16 When working on **RATIO** problems, always find the **TOTAL NUMBER** of parts.

17 In **SEQUENCE** problems, always find how many numbers are in the **REPEATING PATTERN**.

18 In **ARITHMETIC SEQUENCES**, the difference between any two consecutive terms is the same.

19 In **GEOMETRIC SEQUENCES**, each term after the first is found by multiplying the previous term by a fixed number.

20 For **COMBINATIONS**, order does **NOT** matter.

Graphing Calulator:
Math → PRB → nCr
n =number you are choosing from
r = number you are choosing at a time

21 For **PERMUTATIONS**, order **DOES** matter.

Graphing Calulator:
Math → PRB → nPr
n =number you are choosing from
r = number you are choosing at a time

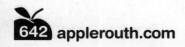

Multiple Equations

4%

of all math
questions
on the SAT

There are three types of Multiple Equation problems.

The first type you can solve by isolating the variable. This allows you to solve the other equations, one at a time.

E If $2x + 2y = 10$, $x + z = 13$, and $3z = 9$ what is the value of y?

S Step 1: We can solve the last equation.

$$3z = 9$$
$$\boxed{z = 3}$$

Step 2: Now we can tackle the other equations, one at a time.

$$x + z = 13$$
$$x + 3 = 13$$
$$\boxed{x = 10}$$

Step 3: Keep solving...

$$2x + 2y = 10$$
$$2(10) + 2y = 10$$
$$20 + 2y = 10$$
$$2y = -10$$
$$y = \boxed{-5}$$

The second type of Multiple Equation problem looks intimidating, but the SAT sets you up to solve these quickly if you know how to handle them. You can skip a whole lot of steps and solve the problem just by *seeing it differently.*

The key to these is recognizing the **relationship between the equations,** which makes solving the problem MUCH easier.

E If $x^2y = 5$ and $x + y = 4$, then $x^3y + x^2y^2 = ?$

(A)   5
(B)   16
(C)   20
(D)   32
(E)   40

Whenever you see multiple equations with exponents, you are dealing with a multiplication $A \times B = C$ relationship.

S The key here is recognizing the relatedness of the 3 equations.

Let's look more closely:

A. $x^2y = 5$

B. $x + y = 4$

C. $x^3y + x^2y^2 = ?$

The SAT sets you up for success if you realize that these 3 equations are intimately connected. There are several types of relationships.

Addition

Sometimes you see $A + B = C$ or $A - B = C$,

or some variation such as $2A + B = C$.

Multiplication

More frequently, the equations are multiples as in the case of $A \times B = C$,

or a variation such as $3A \times B = C$.

Step 1: Let's look for the relationship in this problem.

A. $x^2y = 5$

B. $x + y = 4$

C. $x^3y + x^2y^2 = ?$

Notice that we have multiple exponents. More than likely we have an $A \times B = C$ relationship.

Let's check it out.

$$A \quad \times \quad B \quad = \quad C$$
$$(x^2y) \quad \times \quad (x + y) =$$

Do you see it? If we multiply $A \times B$, do we get C?

$$A \quad \times \quad B \quad = \quad C$$
$$(x^2y) \quad \times \quad (x + y) = x^3y + x^2y^2. \quad \text{Score!}$$

Now we can substitute.

$A = 5$

$B = 4$

$A \times B = 5 \times 4 = \boxed{20}, \textbf{(C)}$

Exponents in Multiple Equations problems are dead giveaways. Most of the time when you see them, you are looking at an $A \times B = C$ relationship!

Stacking Equations

The third type of Multiple Equation problem is a simple stacking problem. The SAT will give you two equations with three variables each, pre-stacked. These problems sometimes appear tricky because they require you to solve for an expression like $y + z$ instead of a single variable like x. To solve these, you still only need addition and subtraction.

$$4x + y + 3z = 26$$
$$3x + y + 2z = 17$$

In the system of equations above, which of the following is the value of $x + z$?

(A) – 9
(B) – 7
(C)   0
(D)   7
(E)   9

S This is nothing but an overgrown subtraction problem. To solve it, all we have to do is subtract the bottom equation from the top equation:

$$4x + y + 3z = 26$$
$$\underline{- (3x + y + 2z = 17)}$$
$$x + 0 + z = \ 9$$

So, conveniently, what we're left with is what we need: $x + z = \textcircled{9}$, **(E)**

The SAT is always changing, so it could easily switch things up with a problem like the example below.

$$x + 2y - 3z = 12$$
$$3x - y + 3z = 9$$

If the equations above are true, what is the value of $4x + y$?

S The objective here is the same; we need to add or subtract to cancel everything on the left side except for $4x + y$. In this case, addition will do that for us.

$$x + 2y - 3z = 12$$
$$+\ 3x - y + 3z = \ 9$$
$$\overline{4x + y + 0 = 21}$$

Let's take a closer
look at that math.

$$\begin{array}{cccc} x & 2y & -3z & 12 \\ +3x & +(-y) & +3z & +9 \\ \hline 4x & y & 0 & \mathbf{21} \end{array}$$

Everything looks right. We're left with:
$$4x + y = \boxed{21}$$

E
$$2x + y + 2z = 21$$
$$4x + y + 2z = 15$$

In the system of equations above, which of the following is the value of $y + 2z$?

(A) – 27
(B)   6
(C)   27
(D)   36
(E)   57

The key is to get rid of all the variables that are not part of our solution. In this case, we need to get rid of the x.

S With this system of equations, if we subtract, we cancel out the y's and z's. If we add the two equations, we don't cancel any of the variables, leaving us no better off than when we started. To get rid of the x's, we need to multiply first.

$$2(2x + y + 2z = 21) \longrightarrow 4x + 2y + 4z = 42$$
$$4x + y + 2z = 15 \longrightarrow \quad 4x + y + 2z = 15$$

Now we can treat it just like a simple subtraction problem.

$$4x + 2y + 4z = 42$$
$$-\ \ 4x + y + 2z = 15$$
$$\overline{0\ + y + 2z = 27}$$

That's it; $y + 2z = \boxed{27}$, **(C)**

Quadratics

There are certain equations that occur frequently on the SAT. You must memorize these or at least be able to instantly recognize them, as they appear so often.

Here are the most common quadratic forms:

- $x^2 + 2xy + y^2 = (x + y)^2$
- $x^2 - 2xy + y^2 = (x - y)^2$
- $x^2 - y^2 = (x + y)(x - y)$

E If $x + y = 12$, and $x^2 - y^2 = 48$, what is the value of $x - y$?

S Do you see the relationship? You know we have multiple equations and exponents: we must be dealing with multiplication! Could we possibly be in an $A \times B = C$ situation? And more than this—we see $(x + y)$ and $(x - y)$; this has to be a difference of squares problem!

Let's check it out:

DIFFERENCE OF SQUARES:

I DISAGREE!

A. $x + y = 12$

B. $x - y = ?$

C. $x^2 - y^2 = 48$

Hmmmm.... we have an $(x + y)$ and an $(x - y)$. This looks a lot like an example we just saw up above.

There it is! $A \times B = C$. Works like a charm. If you know to look for these relationships, you will spot them almost instantly and save a lot of time on the SAT.

So: $A \times B = C$

         $12 \times B = 48$

             $B = 4$

      $x - y = \boxed{4}$

Frequently the SAT will mix it up a little and ask you for $2x - 2y$, a multiple of $x - y$. Watch for this.

E If $x^2 + y^2 = 85$, and $xy = 42$ then $(x + y)^2 =$

(A) 85
(B) 121
(C) 127
(D) 169
(E) 254

S Let's look for one of our relationships.

Because we have exponents again, more than likely this is multiplication.

A. $\quad x^2 + y^2 = 85$

B. $\quad xy = 42$

C. $\quad (x + y)^2 = ?$

I don't see it just yet. My first thought is to solve the quadratic equation in C and see what we are working with.

$$(x + y)^2 = x^2 + 2xy + y^2$$

Let's look more closely at our given equations and see how A, B and C are related.

A. $\quad x^2 + y^2 = 85$

B. $\quad xy = 42$

C. $\quad x^2 + 2xy + y^2 = ?$

Now do you see it? Surprisingly, this is not multiplication, but addition.

A. $\quad \boxed{x^2} + \boxed{y^2} = 85$

B. $\quad \widehat{xy} = 42$

C. $\boxed{x^2} + 2\,\widehat{xy} + \boxed{y^2} = ?$

So the relationship we are working with is as follows:

$$A + 2B = C$$
$$85 + 2\,(42) = \boxed{169}$$

This only happens with this particular quadratic form $(x + y)^2$ or $(x - y)^2$.

Multiple Equations Practice Problems

1. If $r - s = 6$, $r = 4t$, and $2t = 6$, what is the value of s ?

(A)   2
(B)   3
(C)   4
(D)   6
(E)   12

2. If $x + y = 18$, $\dfrac{y}{z} = 5$, and $2y = 40$, what is the value of $x + z$?

3. If $a + 3b = 3c$, and $a + 3b + c = 108$, then $c =$

(A)   9
(B)   18
(C)   27
(D)   36
(E)   It cannot be determined from the information provided.

4. If $10x + 4y = 32$ and $9x + 2y = 24$, what is the value of $x + 2y + 3$?

5. If $11c - 7d = 9$ and $2c - d = 3$, which of the following is the value of $3c - 2d$?

(A) 12
(B) 6
(C) 2
(D) 0
(E) -6

6. If $a^2b = 4$ and $a + b = 8$, then $a^3b + a^2b^2 =$

(A) 6
(B) 12
(C) 18
(D) 24
(E) 32

7. If $a + b = 6$ and $a - b = 4$, what is the value of $a^2 - b^2$?

(A) 2
(B) 10
(C) 20
(D) 24
(E) 36

8. If $x^2 + y^2 = 90$, and $xy = 45$ then $(x + y)^2 =$

(A) 90
(B) 135
(C) 150
(D) 180
(E) 270

9. If $a^2 - b^2 = 9x^3$, $a - b = 9x$, and $x \neq 0$ what is $a + b$ in terms of x ?

(A) x
(B) x^2
(C) $3x^2$
(D) $3x^3$
(E) $9x^2$

Function Notation

Important! $f(x) =$ is not the same thing as $f \times x$.

The term Function Notation simply describes an equation that has been written in the form $f(x) = y$. You plug something in for x, and you get something out on the other side.

So, given the function $f(x) = x^2 + 2$, we know:

$f(\mathbf{3}) = \mathbf{3}^2 + 2 = 9 + 2 = 11$
$f(\mathbf{-5}) = (\mathbf{-5})^2 + 2 = 25 + 2 = 27$
$f(\mathbf{2a}) = (\mathbf{2a})^2 + 2 = 4a^2 + 2$
$f(\mathbf{a+1}) = (\mathbf{a+1})^2 + 2 = a^2 + 2a + 1 + 2 = a^2 + 2a + 3$

Remember, just plug what is inside the parentheses into your equation.

E A group of students painted houses to raise money. The profit R, in dollars, raised by painting m houses is given by the function $R(m) = 90m - 75$. If the students painted a total of 6 houses, what was their profit?

(A) $75
(B) $150
(C) $450
(D) $465
(E) $540

S Let's translate all of these words into math we can use.

R = profit

m = number of houses

$R(m) = 90m - 75$

In this case, $m = 6$

S Let's plug it into our profit function, R

$$R(m) = 90m - 75$$
$$R(6) = 90 \times 6 - 75$$
$$R(6) = 540 - 75$$
$$R(6) = \boxed{\$465}$$

E Let the function f be defined by $f(x) = 3(5 + x^3)$. When $f(x) = -66$, which of the following could be the value of $2x - 1$?

(A) -21
(B) -7
(C) -3
(D) 3
(E) 7

This is simply the transitive property; when $A = B$ and $B = C$, $A = C$.

S To begin, let's solve for x.

$$f(x) = 3(5 + x^3)$$
$$f(x) = -66$$
$$3(5 + x^3) = f(x) = -66$$

We can cut out the middle man, $f(x)$, and that will leave us with

$$3(5 + x^3) = -66$$
$$15 + 3x^3 = -66$$
$$3x^3 = -81$$
$$x^3 = -27$$
$$\sqrt[3]{x^3} = \sqrt[3]{-27}$$
$$x = -3$$

Now that we've solved for x, we need to find $2x - 1$. Let's plug in our x.

$$2(-3) - 1 = \boxed{-7}$$

Don't be fooled and choose (C)! The SAT is waiting for you to fall into that trap.

E Let the function h be defined by $h(t) = 3t - c$, where c is a constant. If $h(8) + h(4) = 12$, what is the value of c?

(A) 3
(B) 4
(C) 6
(D) 12
(E) 18

S

$$h(t) = 3t - c$$
$$h(8) - h(4) = 12$$

What is the value of c?

We need to solve this systematically, one piece at a time, top to bottom, left to right. We need to solve for $h(\mathbf{8})$; let's plug our first t value, **8**, into the h function.

$$h(\mathbf{t}) = 3t - c$$
$$h(\mathbf{8}) = 3(\mathbf{8}) - c$$
$$h(\mathbf{8}) = 24 - c$$

Now let's plug our second t value, 4, into the h function.

$$h(\mathbf{4}) = 3(\mathbf{4}) - c$$
$$h(\mathbf{4}) = 12 - c$$

Now let's use these to solve for c.

$$h(8) + h(4) = 12$$
$$(24 - c) + (12 - c) = 12$$
$$36 - 2c = 12$$
$$24 = 2c$$
$$\boxed{12} = c$$

E The function g is defined by $g(x) = x^2 - bx + 8$, where b is a constant. In the xy-plane, the graph of $y = g(x)$ crosses the x-axis where $x = 4$. What is the value of b ?

(A) -6
(B) -2
(C) 0
(D) 4
(E) 6

Remember
$f(x) = y$, or in this case $g(x) = y$. This is our most basic rule for advanced algebra.

S In math terms:

$$g(x) = x^2 - bx + 8$$
$$g(x) = y = x^2 - bx + 8$$

The graph of $g(x)$ crosses the x-axis where $x = 4$.
Aha! Now we have a point to work with. If our function crosses the x-axis at $x = 4$, then we know that the point $(4,0)$ lies on the graph of $g(x)$.

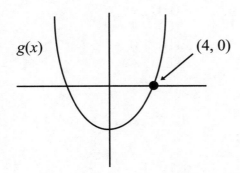

As with most advanced algebra problems, now we need to plug our point $(4,0)$ back into the function. This will allow us to solve for b.

$$y = x^2 - bx + 8$$
$$0 = 4^2 - 4b + 8$$
$$0 = 16 + 8 - 4b$$
$$0 = 24 - 4b$$
$$4b = 24$$
$$b = \boxed{6}$$

Function Notation Practice Problems

1. If $f(x) = x - 3$, then $f(2) =$

(A) −1
(B) 0
(C) 1
(D) 2
(E) 5

$f(x)$	x
0	15
1	a
a	c

2. The table above defines a linear function.

If $f(x) = \dfrac{1}{3}x - 5$, what is the value of c?

(A) − 6.55
(B) 18
(C) 24
(D) 49
(E) 69

3. If the function f is defined by $f(x) = 2x - 5$, then $3f(x) - 5 =$

(A) $2x - 10$
(B) $2x - 15$
(C) $6x - 10$
(D) $6x - 15$
(E) $6x - 20$

4. Let the function f be defined by $f(x) = x - 2$. What is the value of $f(3w) - 3f(w)$?

(A) − 8
(B) − 6
(C) − 4
(D) 0
(E) 4

5. Let the function h be defined by $h(x) = 2x^2 + r$, where r is a constant. If $h(6) + h(4) = 140$, what is the value of r?

(A) 6
(B) 9
(C) 18
(D) 41
(E) 81

6. If $f(x) = 3x - 9$, what is $f(7) - f(5)$?

(A) $f(2)$
(B) $f(3)$
(C) $f(5)$
(D) $f(12)$
(E) $f(18)$

8. If $f(x + 2) = x^2 + 4x + 4$, then $f(x) =$

(A) x^2
(B) $x^2 + 2$
(C) $x + 8x + 16$
(D) $x + 4x + 2$
(E) $x^2 + 4x + 6$

7. If $f(n) = \dfrac{n + 5}{4 - n}$ for all numbers n except $n = 4$. When $f(n) = \dfrac{3}{2}$, what is the value of $2n + 1$?

0.6% | Composite Function Notation

of all math
questions
on the SAT

If you can solve a normal function problem, then you can solve a composite function problem.

E If $f(x) = x^2 + 6$ and $g(x) = 2x^2 - 3$, then $f(3) + g(4) =$

(A) 15
(B) 37
(C) 44
(D) 47
(E) 76

S Let's work this systematically, one piece at a time, from left to right, top to bottom.

$$f(x) = x^2 + 6$$
$$f(3) = (3)^2 + 6 = 15$$
$$f(3) = 9 + 6 = 15$$

$$g(x) = 2x^2 - 3$$
$$g(4) = 2(4)^2 - 3$$
$$g(4) = 32 - 3 = 29$$

$$f(3) + g(4) = 15 + 29 = \boxed{44}, \textbf{(C)}$$

E

x	$g(x)$
-2	10
-1	7
0	6
1	10
2	15
3	22
4	31

Several values of the function g are shown above. The function h is defined by $h(x) = g(4x - 10)$. What is the value of $h(3)$?

(A) 6
(B) 10
(C) 15
(D) 22
(E) 31

S

$$h(x) = g(4x - 10)$$
$$h(3) = ?$$

Here, $x = 3$; let's plug it into our function.

$$h(x) = g(4x - 10)$$
$$h(3) = g(4(3) - 10)$$
$$h(3) = g(12 - 10)$$
$$h(3) = g(2)$$

Now we can reference our table and find the solution for $g(2)$:

x	$g(x)$
-2	10
-1	7
0	6
1	10
2	(15)
3	22
4	31

According to the table, when our x value is 2, $g(2) = $ **15** , **(C)**

The most advanced composite functions that the SAT can throw at you are the "function in a function" problems. These are advanced Algebra 2 problems, and may make their way into future SATs.

E If $f(x) = 2x - 15$ and $g(x) = 3x^2 - x + 3$, what is $f(g(2))$?

S The key to the "function in a function" problems is to begin inside the parentheses and work your way out.

$$f(x) = 2x - 15$$

$$g(x) = 3x^2 - x + 3$$

$$f(g(2)) = ?$$

Let's begin with the inside function: $g(2)$.

$$g(x) = 3x^2 - x + 3$$

$$g(2) = (3)(2)^2 - 2 + 3$$

$$g(2) = 12 - 2 + 3$$

$$g(2) = 13$$

Now we go to the second step:
Because $g(2) = 13$, we can substitute.

$$f(g(2)) = f(13)$$

$$f(x) = 2x - 15$$

$$f(13) = (2)(13) - 15$$

$$f(13) = 26 - 15 = \boxed{11}$$

Composite Function Notation Practice Problems

1. Let the function f be defined by $f(x) = x^2 + 2$ and the function g be defined by $g(x) = f(4x + 2)$. What is the value of $g(3)$?

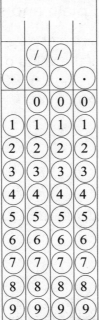

2. $f(x) = 6x - 3$ and $g(x) = 2x + 10$, what is the value of $f(g(5))$?

(A) 43
(B) 67
(C) 89
(D) 117
(E) 215

3. If $f(x) = x^2 - 2$ and $g(x) = \dfrac{x}{2} - 1$, then $g(f(10)) = ?$

(A) 47
(B) 48
(C) 49
(D) 50
(E) 98

Wacked-Out Functions

2%

of all math
questions
on the SAT

The SAT presents you with functions that exist exclusively on the SAT. These functions have no meaning whatsoever outside of the world of SAT math. Don't worry about the funky symbols; the key to these problems is substitution, plain and simple.

E If $\boxed{x \mid y} = x^y - y(x - y)$, then what is the value of $\boxed{4 \mid 2}$?

(A) 8
(B) 12
(C) 16
(D) 24
(E) 28

This is not a typical math function; this is an SAT-only function.

S
$$\boxed{x \mid y} = x^y - y(x - y)$$

The SAT has created a new function!

The double box function $\boxed{x \mid y}$ is defined by this equation: $x^y - y(x - y)$

We are asked to substitute actual numbers $(4, 2)$ for the variables (x, y) just like in a regular function.

Everywhere you see an x, you will sub in 4.
Everywhere you see a y, you will sub in 2.

$\boxed{x \mid y} = x^y - y(x - y)$ becomes
$\boxed{4 \mid 2} = 4^2 - 2(4 - 2)$

And we know how to solve from here:

$4^2 - 2(4 - 2)$
$16 - 2(2)$
$16 - 4 = \boxed{12}, \textbf{(B)}$

E If t, x, and h are integers, let $(t, x) \ominus h$ be defined to be true only if $x > t > h$. If $(t, 1) \ominus -6$ is true, which of the following could be a possible value of t?

   I.   2
  II.   0
 III. -6

(A) I only
(B) II only
(C) III only
(D) II and III
(E) I, II, and III

S This is a lot to handle. We need to break the problem into parts.

t, x, and h are integers: *got it*

$(t, x) \ominus h$ is true only if $x > t > h$

So this function works (is true) only when $x > t > h$

If $(t, 1) \ominus -6$ is true…okay, so we are simply substituting 1 for x and -6 for h.

$(t, x) \ominus h$ is true only if $x > t > h$: therefore
$(t, 1) \ominus -6$ is true only if $1 > t > -6$

Which of the following could be a possible value of t? 2, 0, -6

Our rule is $1 > t > -6$, so the only choice that fits is 0. **(B)** is our answer.

E For all numbers a and b, let $a \times b$ be defined as $a \times b = a - 2b + b^a$. What is the value of $2 \times (3 \times 2)$?

(A) 8
(B) 16
(C) 37
(D) 61
(E) 116

S

$a \mathbf{X} b = a - 2b + b^a$: this is our rule
$2 \mathbf{X} (3\mathbf{X}2)$ So we have a 2-step problem!

This is essentially a composite function.
First we need to work out the function inside the parentheses.

$$a \mathbf{X} b = a - 2b + b^a$$
$$3 \mathbf{X} 2 = 3 - 2 \times 2 + 2^3$$
$$3 \mathbf{X} 2 = 3 - 4 + 8 = 7$$
$$3 \mathbf{X} 2 = \boxed{7}$$

We have solved for the function inside the parentheses, $3 \mathbf{X} 2 = 7$
Time to substitute:

$$2 \mathbf{X} (3\mathbf{X}2) = 2 \mathbf{X} 7$$
$$a \mathbf{X} b = a - 2b + b^a$$
$$2 \mathbf{X} 7 = 2 - 2 \times 7 + 7^2$$
$$2 \mathbf{X} 7 = 2 - 14 + 49 = \boxed{37}, \textbf{(C)}$$

E For all positive integers s, let $\textcircled{s}$ be defined to be $s^2 - 2s + 4$. Which of the following is equal to $\textcircled{3} + \textcircled{2}$?

(A) $\textcircled{4} - \textcircled{3}$
(B) $\textcircled{5} - \textcircled{3}$
(C) $\textcircled{5} - \textcircled{4}$
(D) $\textcircled{7} - \textcircled{5}$
(E) $\textcircled{7} - \textcircled{6}$

S Let's start from the top:

$$\textcircled{s} = s^2 - 2s + 4$$

$$\textcircled{3} = 3^2 - 2 \times 3 + 4$$

$$\textcircled{3} = 9 - 6 + 4 = 7$$

$$\textcircled{2} = 2^2 - 2 \times 2 + 4$$

$$\textcircled{2} = 4 - 4 + 4 = 4$$

$$\textcircled{3} + \textcircled{2} = 7 + 4 = 11$$

Now we need to go back to our answer choices and find which is equal to 11. Let's quickly solve for all the possible function values

$$\textcircled{2} = 2^2 - 2 \times 2 + 4 = 4$$

$$\textcircled{3} = 3^2 - 2 \times 3 + 4 = 7$$

$$\textcircled{4} = 4^2 - 2 \times 4 + 4 = 12$$

$$\textcircled{5} = 5^2 - 2 \times 5 + 4 = 19$$

$$\textcircled{6} = 6^2 - 2 \times 6 + 4 = 28$$

$$\textcircled{7} = 7^2 - 2 \times 7 + 4 = 39$$

We need to subtract one value from another to end up with 11.

That would be $39 - 28 = 11$: $\textcircled{7} - \textcircled{6} = \mathbf{11}$. $\textbf{(E)}$ is our answer!

Wacked-Out Functions Practice Problems

1. For all positive integers a and b, let $a \mathbin{♀} b$ be defined as $a^2 - b^2$. What is the value of $6 \mathbin{♀} 3$?

(A) -27
(B) -25
(C) $\quad 9$
(D) $\quad 25$
(E) $\quad 27$

2. For all real numbers x and y, let $x \mathbin{Ø} y$ be defined as $\dfrac{x-y}{x+y}$. What is the value of $8 \mathbin{Ø} 3$?

3. For all integers m and n, let $m \mathbin{☼} n$ be defined as $m \mathbin{☼} n = m^2 n$. What is the value of $4 \mathbin{☼} 2$?

(A) $\quad 4$
(B) $\quad 8$
(C) $\quad 16$
(D) $\quad 32$
(E) $\quad 48$

4. For all numbers a and b, let $a \mathbin{◊} b$ be defined as $a \mathbin{◊} b = a^2 - 2ab + b^2$. What is the value of $(2 \mathbin{◊} 3) \mathbin{◊} 1$?

(A) -17
(B) $\quad -1$
(C) $\quad 0$
(D) $\quad 1$
(E) $\quad 25$

5. For all positive numbers x and y where $x \neq y$, let $x \, \Theta \, y$ be defined as $x \, \Theta \, y = \dfrac{xy}{x^2 y^2}$. For all positive numbers r and s, which of the following must be true?

I. $\quad r \, \Theta \, s = \dfrac{r}{r^2} - \dfrac{s}{s^2}$

II. $\quad r \, \Theta \, s = \dfrac{r}{r+s} \times \dfrac{s}{r-s}$

III. $\quad r \, \Theta \, s = s \, \Theta \, r$

(A) I only
(B) II only
(C) III only
(D) II and III only
(E) I, II, and III

6. For all positive values of x and y such that $x \neq y$, let $x \, \blacksquare \, y = \dfrac{x^2 - xy}{x^2 - y^2}$. If $a + b = 20$ and $a \, \blacksquare \, b = \dfrac{1}{4}$, what is the value of b?

4%

of all math
questions
on the SAT

Mean, Median and Mode

Mean (Average) = $\dfrac{\textbf{Sum}}{\textbf{Number of Items}}$

Finding the Sum is THE KEY to solving SAT Average problems!!!

MEDIAN

Median: When a set of terms is arranged in ascending or descending order, the median (like the median of a highway) is the middle term. In the event that you have 2 middle terms (for any set with an even number of terms) you must average these 2 terms to find the median.

Mode: The most commonly occurring term (think fashion, in the mode—it's everywhere).

I AM THE MOST COMMONLY OCCURING!

E For the numbers 1, 4, 7, 12, 34, 34, and 83, find the <u>mean</u>, <u>median</u>, and <u>mode</u>.

S Mean (Average) $= \dfrac{1+4+7+12+34+34+83}{7} = \dfrac{175}{7} = \boxed{25}$

Median $= \boxed{12}$

Mode $= \boxed{34}$

General Rule

In dealing with Averages, **always, always** find the grand total and the number of items. The total is the critical factor and from there, things simplify easily.

A nice tool to help with averages is the average box.

Sum		
Average	×	# of terms

To use this tool, you simply need to cover the term you are looking for (sum, average or number of terms) and then solve.

If I know the average of 6 terms is 14, and I want to find the sum, I fill in my average box:

Sum	
14 ×	6

And I do the math: average × number of terms = 14 × 6 = ⟨84⟩

E Greta, Adelaide, and Pooky own a total of 174 purses. If Adelaide owns 112 of them, what is the average (arithmetic mean) number of purses owned by Greta and Pooky?

(A) 31
(B) 56
(C) 57
(D) 58
(E) 62

S We are looking for the *average* of Greta and Pooky's purses, which means we must first find their sum.

$$Adelaide = 112$$
$$G + A + P = 174$$
$$G + 112 + P = 174$$
$$G + P = 62$$

Now we can fill in our average box and solve.

Sum of G and P				62	
Avg of G and P	×	# of terms		Avg of G and P ×	2

The average of G and $P = \dfrac{62}{2} = $ ⟨**31**⟩, **(A)**

E If the average (arithmetic mean) of 5, *c*, and *d* is 4, what is the value of *c* + *d* ?

(A) 1
(B) 2
(C) 4
(D) 6
(E) 7

We could solve for either *c* or *d*, but it's not important. All we NEED to find is *c* + *d*, and then we'll be done!

S When you see the word *average*, you know you will need to find the sum of the terms.

Sum		
Average	×	# of terms

→

$5 + c + d$		
4	×	3

$5 + c + d = 4 \times 3$
$5 + c + d = 12$
$c + d = ⑦$

E   14, 23, 8, *y*, 16, 19, 28, 22, 14, 25, 16

For the set of numbers above, the median is 16. Each of the following could be the value of *y* EXCEPT:

(A) 3
(B) 8
(C) 10
(D) 11
(E) 17

S Because we are working with median, we need to set everything up in ascending order:

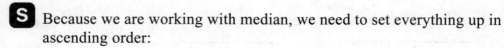

8, 14, 14, 16, (16,) 19, 22, 23, 25, 28, and then we have *y*

Term: 1 2 3 4   5   6 7 8 9 10

          4 terms   5 terms

To make 16 the true middle term, we need another term on the left side. Therefore, any number ≤ 16 will work just fine.

$$y,\ 8,\ 14,\ 14,\ 16,\ \boxed{16}\ 19,\ 22,\ 23,\ 25,\ 28$$

Term: $\quad$ 1 2 3 4 5 $\quad$ 6 $\quad$ 7 8 9 10 11

$$\underbrace{}_{5\text{ terms}} \qquad \underbrace{}_{5\text{ terms}}$$

The only answer choice larger than 16 is $\boxed{17}$, **(E)**.

If the average (arithmetic mean) of a and b is $2r$, which of the following is the average of a, b, and c?

(A) $\dfrac{2r + c}{3}$

(B) $\dfrac{2(r + c)}{2}$

(C) $\dfrac{4r + c}{3}$

(D) $\dfrac{4(r + c)}{3}$

(E) $\dfrac{r + 2c}{2}$

When you see the word *average*, you know you need to find the sum of terms.

Sum		
Average	$\times$	# of terms

$\Rightarrow$

$a + b$		
$2r$	$\times$	2

$$a + b = 2r \times 2$$
$$= 4r$$

The sum of $a + b = 4r$. If we add in c, our new average will be:

$4r + c$		
Avg	$\times$	3

Cover up what we are looking for (Avg), and we are left with:

$\boxed{\dfrac{4r + c}{3}}$, **(C)** is our answer.

Mean, Median and Mode Practice Problems

1. If the average (arithmetic mean) of $3z$, $4z$, and 9 is 10, which of the following is the value of z ?

   (A) 1
   (B) 2
   (C) 3
   (D) 4
   (E) 5

3. Dori and her three siblings used a total of 6,780 minutes of their family's shared cell phone minutes last month. If Dori used 2,310 of the minutes, what is the average (arithmetic mean) number of minutes used by each of her three siblings last month?

   (A) 1,480
   (B) 1,490
   (C) 1,695
   (D) 2,260
   (E) 3,030

Pollen Levels in Sweet Home, OR

Day	Pollen Levels
Monday	7.8
Tuesday	8.5
Wednesday	9.5
Thursday	9.5
Friday	9.4
Saturday	9.4
Sunday	8.2

2. As shown in the table above, the pollen level in Sweet Home, Oregon was recorded each day for a one-week period. What was the average (arithmetic mean) pollen level for the period?

   (A) 7.8
   (B) 7.9
   (C) 8.9
   (D) 9.4
   (E) 9.5

4. The average (arithmetic mean) of 12 consecutive even numbers is 67. If each of these 12 numbers is multiplied by 3, what is the average of the new set?

   (A) 33.5
   (B) 67
   (C) 168
   (D) 201
   (E) 402

$$2, 3, 4, 5, 6, 16$$

5. The number n, if added to the set above, would make the mean of the set equal to the mode of the set. What is the value of n?

(A) -8
(B) -1
(C) 4
(D) 5
(E) 6

6. For which of the following sets is the average (arithmetic mean) of the set equal to the median of the set?

I. $\{1, 2, 3, 3, 3, 7\}$
II. $\{1, 2, 3, 5, 6, 7\}$
III. $\{2, 4, 6, 8, 10\}$

(A) I only
(B) III only
(C) I and II only
(D) II and III only
(E) I, II, and III

7. The average (arithmetic mean) of a, b, and c is 20. If $a = 12$, what is the value of $b + c$?

(A) 12
(B) 18
(C) 24
(D) 48
(E) 60

8. The average (arithmetic mean) of a, b, c, d, e, and f is 40. The average of a, b, c, d, and e is 46. What is the value of f?

9. If the sum of *a, b, c,* and *d* is *e*, what is the average (arithmetic mean) of *a, b, c,* and *d* in terms of *e*?

(A) $\dfrac{a+b+c+d}{e}$

(B) $\dfrac{e}{a+b+c+d}$

(C) $\dfrac{a+b+c+d+e}{5}$

(D) $\dfrac{e}{4}$

(E) $\dfrac{e}{2}$

10. On Ned's pig farm, the average age of his 35 pigs is 12. If 15 new pigs are added to the farm, the new average age for the pigs becomes 10.8. What was the average age of the 15 new pigs?

(A) 7
(B) 8
(C) 9
(D) 11
(E) 13

11. If the average of 8 numbers is *x*, and the average of 6 of the numbers is $x - 4$, what is the average of the remaining 2 numbers?

(A) $x - 12$
(B) $x - 2$
(C) $x + 2$
(D) $x + 4$
(E) $x + 12$

Max and Min

1.2%

of all math
questions
on the SAT

The SAT sometimes asks questions that require you to find the least possible value or the greatest possible value given a certain situation.

- If you are asked for the greatest possible value of one term, minimize all of the other terms.

- If you are asked for the least possible value of one term, maximize all of the other terms.

These are usually level 4 or 5 questions (the hardest questions on the test), and they do not occur on every SAT.

E From a drawer containing 60 pairs of socks, of which 35 are argyle and 25 are striped, Morgan takes 2 argyle and 3 striped pairs. She takes an additional 11 pairs from the drawer. What is the least number of these additional pairs that must be argyle in order for Morgan to have more argyle than striped socks among all the pairs of socks she has taken?

S Take a breath. Let's go piece by piece, translating this monster.

Drawer with $60P$: $35A$ $25S$
Morgan takes 5 pairs: $2A$ $3S$
Morgan takes 11 more pairs.
Morgan's total is $11 + 5 = 16$ pairs.

She needs to end up with more argyle than striped.
Easy. If our total is 16, and we need to have a majority of argyle socks, we need to have at least 9 argyle pairs.

Currently we have 2 argyle pairs, so we need $\boxed{7}$ more.

E

Cheetah Population at the Canseco Nature Reserve

Year	Number of Cheetahs
1983	88
1984	x
1985	84
1986	81
1987	82

The table above shows the number of cheetahs living in captivity in the Canseco nature reserve from 1983 through 1987. If the median cheetah population for the five years was 82, and no two years had the same population, what is the greatest possible value for x?

S To begin, because we are working with median, we need to line up our terms in order from least to greatest:

median

81 （82） 84 88

For 82 to be the median, it must be the middle term, so we will need a term on the left to push it to the center. People who are not careful might pick 81, but the problem specifies that every year has a different population, so it needs to be the largest term less than 81. And don't pick 80.4 either. Have you ever seen 0.4 cheetah? I didn't think so. That's one sorry excuse for a cheetah.

We need （80） whole cheetahs.

E A teacher distributes a note card to each of her four students. She asks each student to write a positive integer less than 100 on his or her card. If the average (arithmetic mean) of these integers is 23, what is the greatest possible integer that any one of the students could have written?

S Step 1: We have an average, so let's use the Average Box, filling in what we know.

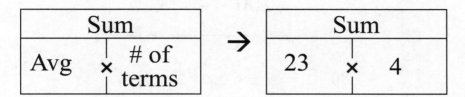

We don't know the sum, so let's find that.

$$23 \times 4 = 92$$

Now, set up the problem:

$$\underline{\hspace{1cm}} + \underline{\hspace{1cm}} + \underline{\hspace{1cm}} + \underline{\hspace{1cm}} = 92$$

Step 2: To max out one of these numbers, minimize the other three. So let's put all three at 1.

The terms sum to 92.
$$1 + 1 + 1 + x = 92$$
$$3 + x = 92$$
$$x = \textbf{89}$$

Pay attention to whether or not the numbers have to be different. If the problem doesn't say that the numbers must be "distinct" or "different," use the same number.

E The average (arithmetic mean) of five positive integers is 200. Two of the integers are 20 and 60, and each of the other integers is greater than 60. If all five integers are different, what is the greatest possible value for any one of the five integers?

S

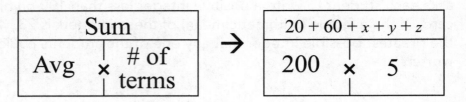

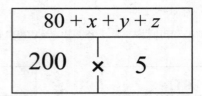

$$80 + x + y + z = 200 \times 5 = 1000$$
$$x + y + z = 920$$

Now we have our sum.

We are trying to maximize one term, so we must minimize the other two.

$$x + y + z = 920$$

$$\left(\underline{x}\right) + \underline{y} + \underline{z} = 920$$

We must minimize two terms. They must each be distinct integers bigger than 60.

So $y = 61$ and $z = 62$.

$$\left(\underline{x}\right) + \underline{61} + \underline{62} = 920$$

Plug in and solve.

$$x + 123 = 920$$
$$x = \boxed{797}$$

Max and Min Practice Problems

1. An actor has 30 pages to memorize over 5 days. On the first and second day, he memorized 3 and 10 pages, respectively. If he memorizes at least one page for each of the remaining days, what is the greatest number of pages he could have left to memorize on the last day?

   (A)   8
   (B)   11
   (C)   15
   (D)   18
   (E) 135

2. The average of four positive integers is 160. If one of the integers is 240, and all the integers are different, what is the maximum value for any one of the other three integers?

3. On a basketball team, there are 8 sophomores, 12 juniors and 10 seniors. What is the minimum number of sophomores that must be added to make the team at least 50% sophomores?

   (A)   10
   (B)   12
   (C)   14
   (D)   18
   (E)   22

8%

of all math
questions
on the SAT

Charts, Tables and Graphs

On the SAT you must be able to read graphs and see trends and changes over time.

 Slug Movement (In Inches) Over Time

Time	11:00	12:00	1:00	2:00	3:00	4:00	5:00
Total Distance Traveled	0	18	36	54	72	90	108

The chart above shows the progress of a racing slug. If the slug began a race at 11:00 and moved at a constant rate until it finished the race at 5:00, which of the graphs below best describes the given data?

(A)
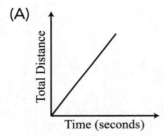

(D)
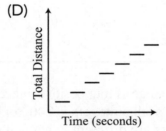

(B)
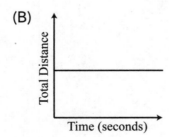

(E)
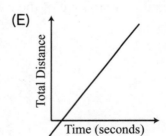

(C)
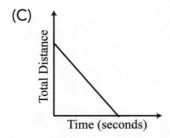

S There are several key words that inform our answer choice. One of them is "constant." If the slug is racing along at a constant speed, we need a straight line.

So we can eliminate (D).

Next we can see from the chart of the slug's progress that he only moves forward from the starting line. It's a race. No looking back, slug. We need a line with a positive slope:

So we can eliminate (B) and (C).

Finally, from the chart, we see that the slug's starting position at 11:00 is 0 inches. So our graph needs to begin where distance = 0, at the base of the Y axis. (E) puts the slug at a negative starting point. It's just not right to handicap the slug. (A) is the only graph that puts the starting point at the origin.

(A) is our answer.

E

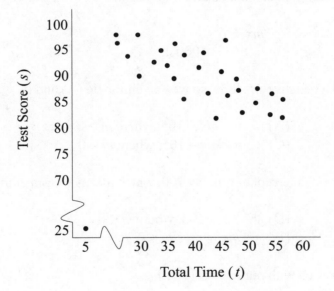

Total Time (t)

Twenty-two students took a test. The scatter plot above shows the total time spent on the test and the score for each of the students. Which of the following could be the equation of the line of best fit?

(A) $y = mx + 105$, where $m > 0$
(B) $y = mx + 105$, where $m < 0$
(C) $y = mx - 105$, where $m > 0$
(D) $y = mx - 105$, where $m < 0$
(E) $y = mx$, where $m < 0$

S When working with a scatter-plot, the line of best fit is the line drawn to balance the number of points above and below itself. Let's draw that line:

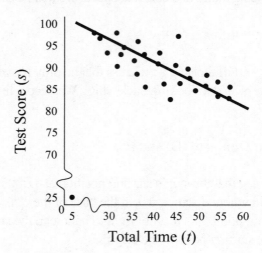

Total Time (*t*)

We can see that the line has a negative slope. And we can see that if we extend the line to the axes, it will hit the *y*-axis close to 100. That's our *Y*-intercept. Now we can populate the equation of our line.

$$Y = mx + b$$
$$Y = (-m)x + 100\text{-ish}$$

We need a negative *M* slope, so we can eliminate (A) and (C)

(A) $y = mx + 105$, where $m > 0$
(C) $y = mx - 105$, where $m > 0$

We need + *Y*-intercept of roughly 100, which means we can eliminate (D) and (E).

(D) $y = mx - 105$, where $m < 0$
(E) $y = mx$, where $m < 0$

That leaves us with our answer, **(B)**.

(B) $y = mx + 105$, where $m < 0$

Rainfall (in inches) for Four Towns

	1989	1990
Mary's Igloo, AK	50.2	51.5
Monkey's Eyebrow, AZ	52.8	53.0
Hygiene, CO	60.8	62.1
Frostproof, FL	49.2	51.2

The table above lists the rainfall for 4 towns in 2 consecutive years. What was the average (arithmetic mean) increase in rainfall, in inches, for these four towns from 1989 to 1990 ?

(A) 0.6
(B) 1.2
(C) 1.6
(D) 2.4
(E) 4.8

S First we need to calculate the difference between the years and create a third column:

	1989	1990	Change
Mary's Igloo, AK	50.2	51.5	1.3
Monkey's Eyebrow, AZ	52.8	53.0	0.2
Hygiene, CO	60.8	62.1	1.3
Frostproof, FL	49.2	51.2	2.0

Our final step is to find the average increase.

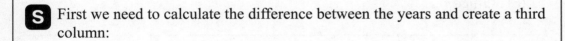

$$\text{Average} = \frac{4.8}{4} = \boxed{1.2}, \textbf{(B)}$$

E

Number of Architects and Engineers by Office

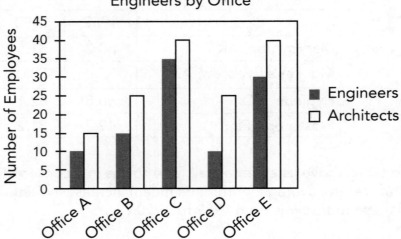

According to the graph above, in which office is the difference between the number of engineers and the number of architects the greatest?

(A) Office A
(B) Office B
(C) Office C
(D) Office D
(E) Office E

S In this instance it's very helpful to label each bar with its numeric value.

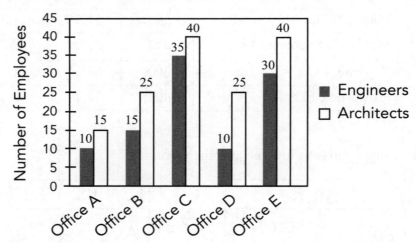

Now we need to calculate the differences for each office:

(A) $15 - 10 = 5$
(B) $25 - 15 = 10$
(C) $40 - 35 = 5$
(D) $25 - 10 = $ ⑮
(E) $40 - 30 = 10$

E

Internet Usage

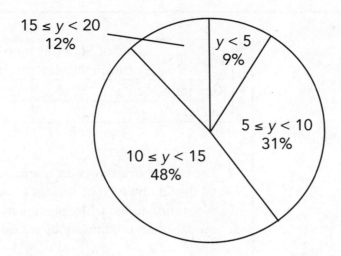

The chart above shows the results when 600 people were asked, "How many hours per week do you spend on the Internet?" The response they gave is represented by y. How many people said that they spend at least 5 hours per week on the Internet?

(A)   54
(B)   72
(C)   288
(D)   474
(E)   546

S We need to find all the people who responded with a value of 5 hours or greater. Of the 4 groups, only one group had members who reported a y value less than 5. That group accounted for 9% of the sample. The remaining 91% of the sample reported spending 5 hours or more on the net.

$$91\% \times 600 \text{ people} = \boxed{546}, \textbf{(E)}$$

Charts, Tables and Graphs Practice Problems

1. A certain community drains its swimming pool by 2 percent of its volume at the end of each month and refills the pool when the water volume reaches 90 percent of the original volume. Which of the following graphs could properly represent the volume of water over a seven-month period?

(A)
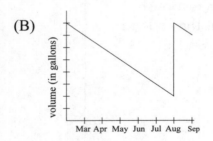

(B)
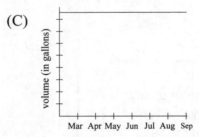

(C)
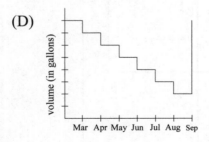

(D)
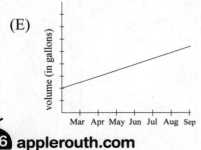

(E)

Type of Shoe	# of Shoes in each Display	# of Displays in Store
Running Shoe	19	2
Sandal	23	3

2. The table above shows the number of shoes on display by type of shoe in a certain store. According to the table, how many more sandals than running shoes are on display?

(A)   1
(B)   4
(C)   31
(D)   69
(E) 107

n	p
4	13
6	19
8	25
10	31

3. The table above defines a line. Which of the following is an equation of the line?

(A) $p = 3n - 1$
(B) $p = 5n + 5$
(C) $p = 3n + 1$
(D) $p = 4n - 9$
(E) $p = 2n - 3$

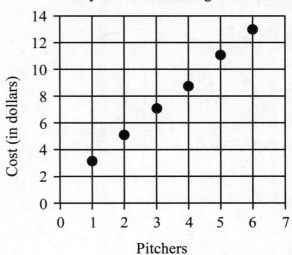

Emily's Cost of Making Lemondae

4. Emily runs a lemonade stand. Her cost of production of lemonade is shown on the graph above for 1-pitcher intervals. If c represents the cost in dollars and p represents the number of pitchers, which of the following equations best describes the data shown?

(A) $c = p + 3$
(B) $c = 2p + 1$
(C) $c = 3p - 2$
(D) $c = 5p + 3$
(E) $c = p^2 - 1$

CD Sales

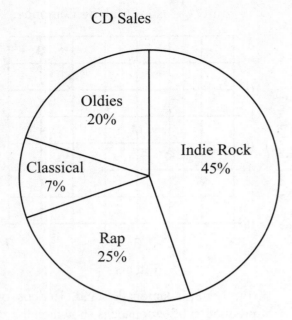

Oldies
20%

Indie Rock
45%

Classical
7%

Rap
25%

5. The graph above shows the distribution of the number of CDs sold last month at Dan's Disks, a local music store. If Dan sold 70 rap CDs last month, how many indie rock CDs did he sell?

(A)   56
(B)   70
(C)   126
(D)   280
(E)   560

Survey Results for Favorite Brand of Cracker

Brand of Cracker	Number of People
Animal Crackers	93
Limp Biscuits	68
Wolf Krisps	19
Slug Squares	45
Exploited Elf Stix	a
Waifer Thins	b

6. The table above shows the results of a survey of 300 people at a grocery store who were asked to choose which brand of cracker they preferred. If each person chose exactly one brand of cracker as his or her favorite, and if each brand was chosen by at least one person, what is the greatest possible value of b ?

(A)   37
(B)   38
(C)   64
(D)   74
(E)   75

Students With a Failing Chemistry Grade

	Year 2002	Year 2003
Month	**2002**	**2003**
January	20	24
February	15	37
March	52	50
April	33	39

Exam Grades and Times

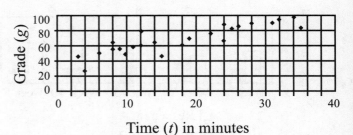

Time (t) in minutes

7. The table above lists the number of students with a failing grade in chemistry at a certain university. What was the percent increase in the number of students receiving a failing grade in chemistry from 2002 to 2003?

(A) 15%
(B) 20%
(C) 25%
(D) 30%
(E) 35%

8. The graph above shows the class results for all students who took Mrs. Twitt's last math exam. If t represents the amount of time each student spent on the exam and g represents the grade each student received, which of the following equations best describes the data shown by the graph?

(A) $g(t) = t$

(B) $g(t) = \dfrac{40 + 5t}{3}$

(C) $g(t) = \dfrac{40 - 5t}{3}$

(D) $g(t) = \dfrac{4t}{3}$

(E) $g(t) = 40t$

Restaurant Patronage

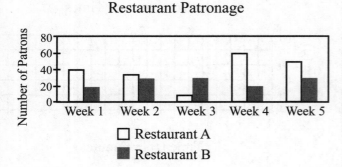

Tide Level

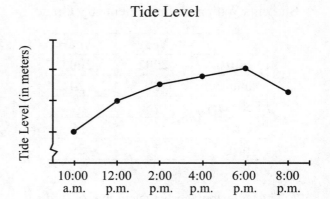

9. According to the graph above, in which week was the number of patrons in Restaurant A triple the number of patrons in Restaurant B?

(A) Week 1
(B) Week 2
(C) Week 3
(D) Week 4
(E) Week 5

10. On a certain day, the tide level was measured along a pier at one-hour intervals, and the results are indicated along the line graph above. Each unit on the vertical axis represents 1 meter. If the tide level increased by 25% between 12:00 p.m. and 6:00 p.m., what was the tide level at 6:00 p.m.?

(A) 2.5 meters
(B) 4.0 meters
(C) 4.5 meters
(D) 5.0 meters
(E) 6.0 meters

Complex Word Problems

5%

The most important skill in handling word problems is the ability to translate words into math. Many students feel overwhelmed when they see so much text in a math problem. The key is to break the problem down, line by line, translating each sentence into the relevant math as you go along.

E Jenny and eight of her friends picked up pieces of trash for two days. Each individual kept track of how many pieces she picked up each day and in total for the two days. The totals for the nine friends were 184, 201, 192, 176, 154, 168, 180, 161, and Jenny's total, which was the average (arithmetic mean) of the nine totals. If Jenny picked up 91 pieces on the first day, how many pieces of trash did she pick up on the second day?

S Yowsers! Lots of text. Let's translate.

Jenny + 8 friends.
Totals for 2 day collections:
184, 201, 192, 176, 154, 168, 180, 161 + Jenny (the average)

Let's find Jenny's total:

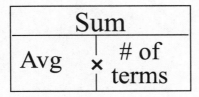

Sum		
Avg	×	# of terms

$184 + 201 + 192 + 176 + 154 + 168 + 180 + 161 + J$		
J (avg)	×	9

$$\begin{array}{c|c} \multicolumn{2}{c}{1416 + J} \\ \hline J\,(\text{avg}) \quad \times & 9 \end{array}$$

$$\frac{1416 + J}{9} = J$$
$$1416 + J = 9J$$
$$1416 = 8J$$
$$\frac{1416}{8} = J$$
$$177 = J$$

We know that Jenny picked up 91 pieces on day 1 and 177 total.

On day 2, Jenny picked up $177 - 91 = \boxed{86}$ pieces!

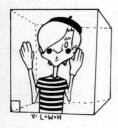

We are not done yet! Remember what you are solving for: day 2 for Jenny!

E 192 riders started the Tour de France in 1990. At the end of the seventh stage of the 21-stage race, only 144 riders remained. If the number of riders decreased by the same percentage every seven stages, what fraction of the starting number of riders remained at the end of the race?

(A) $\dfrac{1}{4}$

(B) $\dfrac{81}{256}$

(C) $\dfrac{27}{64}$

(D) $\dfrac{83}{191}$

(E) $\dfrac{1}{2}$

There are originally 192 riders. After stage 7, 144 riders remain.
Net loss in riders: $192 - 144 = 48$.

What is the percentage decrease in riders?

Percent decrease is $\dfrac{\text{Change}}{\text{Original}} = \dfrac{48}{192} = 0.25$.

So we lose 25% of our riders every 7 stages.

Stage 7: 144 Riders
Stage 14: $144 \times 0.75 = 108$ riders
Stage 21: $108 \times 0.75 = 81$ riders

At the end of the race 81 of 192 riders remain: $\dfrac{81}{192} = 0.421875$.

Let's find that fraction among our answer choices, using our calculator.
The **Math Frac** function is helpful here.
We have our value 0.421875 entered on our calculator.
Next we press the following sequence of buttons:

Math$\rightarrow$ Frac$\rightarrow$ Enter$\rightarrow$ Enter

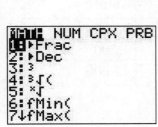 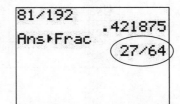

And the answer $\left(\dfrac{27}{64}\right)$ appears on our calculator, **(C)**.

Remember that we are decreasing by the same percentage each interval, not by the same number of riders. If you fall into that trap, you will lose 48×3 riders and end up with answer A, which is wrong.

E A car dealership has 12,000 vehicles on its lot, and the ratio of used vehicles to new vehicles on the lot is 3 to 5. All of the vehicles are either cars or trucks. If 7,500 of the vehicles are cars and 4,000 of the cars are new, how many of the vehicles on the lot are used trucks?

There are 12,000 vehicles.

$$\frac{\text{Used Vehicles}}{\text{New Vehicles}} = \frac{3}{5}$$

When we see the word ratio, we know to find the sum of parts: $3 + 5 = 8$.

$$\text{Used} = \frac{3}{8} \times 12{,}000 = 4{,}500$$

$$\text{New} = \frac{5}{8} \times 12{,}000 = 7{,}500$$

Now we enter the Matrix. This problem is much easier if we set up the structure of the matrix and input our given values.

	Cars	Trucks	Total
Used	?	?	4,500
New	4,000	?	7,500
Total	7,500	?	12,000

Now we need to do the simple math (addition and subtraction) and fill in the values.

	Cars	Trucks	Total
Used	3,500	1,000	4,500
New	4,000	3,500	7,500
	7,500	4,500	12,000

Used trucks→ Find the row and column: ⟨**1,000**⟩

Don't forget that you can sometimes solve these problems by picking numbers and working backwards!

Complex Word Problem Practice Problems

1. A car salesman works Wednesday through Saturday, spending 1 hour on the phone, 5 hours selling on the lot, 1 hour at lunch, and 1 hour doing paperwork each day. What fraction of the total number of hours in these four days does he spend on the phone or doing paperwork?

   (A) $\dfrac{1}{8}$

   (B) $\dfrac{1}{7}$

   (C) $\dfrac{1}{4}$

   (D) $\dfrac{1}{3}$

   (E) $\dfrac{1}{2}$

2. For expected patronage between 100 and 150 customers, the amount, in dollars, a shop owner expects to make is modeled by the equation $c \times (18 - 0.04c)$, where c is the number of customers for that day. The numbers of customers expected on Saturday and Sunday are 120 and 140 respectively. According to this model, how much more is the shop owner expected to make on Sunday than on Saturday?

   (A) $125
   (B) $152
   (C) $1,584
   (D) $1,736
   (E) $3,320

3. The members of a marching band arrange themselves on a field such that the number of columns they form is the same as the number of band members in each column. Which of the following could be the total number of band members on the field?

   (A) 15
   (B) 24
   (C) 38
   (D) 49
   (E) 54

4. Philip's starting salary is $30,000 per year; he is given a 10 percent raise at the end of each year. His salary n years from his start date is given by the function $S(n) = 30{,}000 \left(\dfrac{11}{10} \right)^n$. How many years from his start date will Philip first make more than $40,000 per year?

5. An archer shoots an arrow into the air at a certain speed. The height of the arrow, in meters, is given by the formula $h(t) = 50t - 12t^2$ where $h(t)$ represents the height of the arrow t seconds after it is released for $0 \leq t \leq 4.17$. What will be the height of the arrow two seconds after it is released?

(A) 12 meters
(B) 19 meters
(C) 48 meters
(D) 52 meters
(E) 76 meters

6. Romulus and Remus are both cab drivers. Romulus earns $560 per month plus $0.35 for each mile he drives. Remus earns $720 per month plus $0.15 for each mile he drives. If they both drove the same number of miles and earned the same amount of money last month, how many miles did Romulus drive his cab last month?

Venn Diagrams

1.2%

of all math
questions
on the SAT

Most students have encountered the intersecting circles below and lovingly refer to them as Venn diagrams. What many students do not know is that knowledge of this simple tool can yield great rewards when it comes to the SAT.

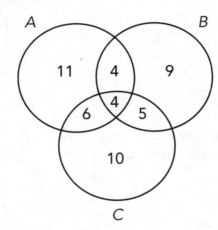

In the Venn diagram above, the number in each region indicates how many elements are in that region. How many elements are in the union of sets A and C?

(A) 8
(B) 10
(C) 16
(D) 40
(E) 50

 We are looking for the overlap for sets A and C:

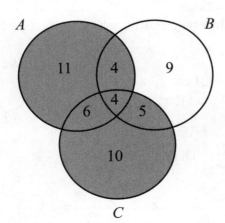

Alternate strategy: Shade all of the regions contained in or and add them one time. No need to worry about double counting issues.

We need to account for each distinct piece, being careful not to double count any piece.

In our diagram: *A* is a circle consisting of 4 pieces with the following values.

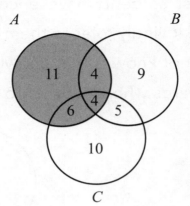

$$\begin{array}{r} 11 + \\ 4 + \\ 4 + \\ 6 \\ \hline 25 \end{array}$$

In our diagram: *C* is a circle consisting of 4 pieces with the following values.

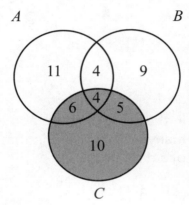

$$\begin{array}{r} 6 + \\ 4 + \\ 5 + \\ 10 \\ \hline 25 \end{array}$$

If we are looking for the union, we need all the pieces contained by both *A* and *C*. But we must be very careful not to double count.

We cannot simply add all the units of *A* (25) and all the units of *C* (25) and come up with a union of 50 units. That would double count the shared units (4) and (6).

When you are finding the union, remember to subtract the intersection, so as to avoid double counting.

This shape, the overlap, is also called the **intersection**.

To find the union of *A* and *C* we can add *A* + *C* and subtract the intersection (4 + 6)

$25 + 25 - 10 = \boxed{40}$. That is the union!

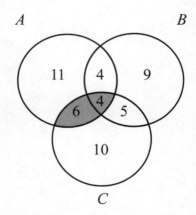

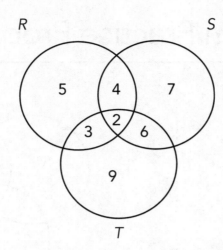

The figure above is a Venn diagram that represents sets *R*, *S*, and *T*. The number in each region indicates how many elements are in that region. How many elements are common to sets *R* and *S* ?

(A) 4
(B) 6
(C) 12
(D) 16
(E) 27

"Elements common to" is another way to say **intersection**.
So we need to find the intersection of *R* and *S*. Let's look at our diagram.

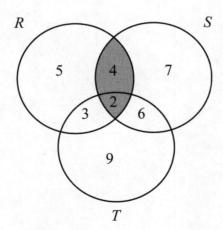

The intersection of *R* and *S* is $4 + 2 = \boxed{6}$, **(B)**

Venn Diagram Practice Problems

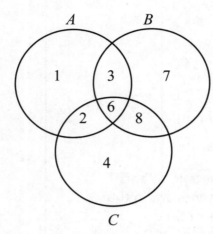

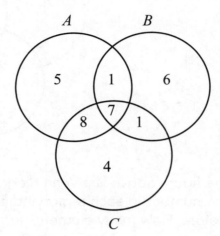

1. In the Venn diagram above, the number in each section indicates how many objects are in that section. How many objects are common to sets A and B?

(A) 3
(B) 6
(C) 8
(D) 9
(E) 27

2. In the Venn diagram above, the number in each region indicates how many objects are in that region. How many objects are in the intersection of sets A and C?

(A) 5
(B) 8
(C) 9
(D) 15
(E) 27

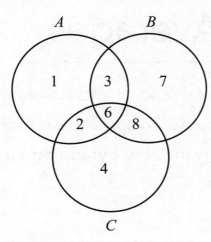

3. In the Venn diagram above, the number in each section indicates how many objects are in that section. How many objects are in the union of sets *A* and *B* ?

(A)   3
(B)   6
(C)   9
(D)   18
(E)   27

4. There are 56 drivers in a fleet. Each driver can drive cars only, trucks only, or both trucks and cars. If 28 drivers drive cars and 31 drivers drive trucks, how many drive both cars and trucks?

(A) 3
(B) 12
(C) 15
(D) 28
(E) 31

0.8%

of all math
questions
on the SAT

Weighted Averages

These problems are usually given in table form and are almost always level 4 or 5 in terms of difficulty. To solve these problems you will need to supplement the given table by adding an extra column that you will have to populate.

Payroll for Tim's Drug Store
Week Ending January 14

Employee	Hours	Hourly Wage
Carolyn	11	$10.00
Sinbad	10	$11.50
Rufus	16	$10.75
Hildegard	14	$9.50

The table above shows the hourly wage and the number of hours worked for each of the 4 employees at Tim's Drug Store for the week ending January 14th. What was the average weekly pay for an employee at Tim's Drug Store that week?

(A) $41.75
(B) $112.50
(C) $132.50
(D) $135.50
(E) $141.00

S To solve, we will need to add a 4th column and multiply the hours by the hourly wage to find the total weekly pay.

Employee	Hours	Hourly Wage	Weekly Pay
Carolyn	11	$10.00	$110
Sinbad	10	$11.50	$115
Rufus	16	$10.75	$172
Hildegard	14	$9.50	$133

To find the average weekly pay, let's use our average box.

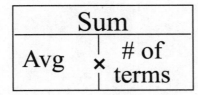

Sum	
Avg ×	# of terms

110 + 115 + 172 + 133	
Avg ×	4

530	
Avg ×	4

Average = $\boxed{132.50}$, (C)

E Number of Hammers Per Carpenter in a Team of Carpenters

Number of Hammers	Number of Carpenters
1	3
2	1
3	1
4	4
5	1

The table above shows how many carpenters in a team of 10 owned 1, 2, 3, 4, or 5 hammers. Later a new carpenter joined the team, and the average (arithmetic mean) number of hammers per carpenter became 1 less than the median number of hammers per carpenter. How many hammers did the new carpenter own?

(A) 1
(B) 2
(C) 3
(D) 4
(E) 5

S To solve this problem, we will need to create a new column for total hammers.

Number of Hammers	Number of Carpenters	Total Hammers
1	3	3
2	1	2
3	1	3
4	4	16
5	1	5

Total: 29

To find the average number of hammers with our team of 10 carpenters we can use our average box.

Sum	
Avg	× # of terms

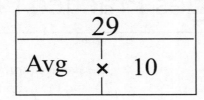

The current average is 2.9.
And the current median is

3.5

Value   1 1 1 2 ③ ④ 4 4 4 5

Term   1 2 3 4 5 6 7 8 9 10

We are adding an additional carpenter such that the new average will be one less than the new median.

The simplest way to solve this is to work backwards from our answer choices. Let's start with (C).

(C) 3. So if the new carpenter has 3 hammers, our new sum is 32 and the new average ($\frac{32}{11}$) will be 2.91. However, the new median will be 3. *So this is too low. Let's try a larger number.*

(D) 4. If the new carpenter has 4 hammers, our new sum is 33 and the new average ($\frac{33}{11}$) will be 3. The new median will be ④ *This is our answer!*

This is another complicated problem made simple by working backwards from the answer choices.

Weighted Averages Practice Problems

1. A restaurant serves 26 tables per day for five consecutive days and n tables per day for the next two days. If the average (arithmetic mean) number of tables served per day for the 7 day period is 30, what is the value of n ?

(A) 28
(B) 30
(C) 34
(D) 38
(E) 40

2. The average (arithmetic mean) grade for two students on an algebra test was 78. The other three students who took the test scored 92, 94, and 96. What was the average test grade for all five students?

(A) 82.4
(B) 84.4
(C) 86.0
(D) 87.6
(E) 90.4

3. The average (arithmetic mean) of a and b is 20, and the average of c, d, and e is 30. What is the average of a, b, c, d, and e ?

(A) 22
(B) 25
(C) 26
(D) 27
(E) 30

4. If 6 sacks of concrete with an average (arithmetic mean) weight of 20 pounds are put into a wheelbarrow with 4 sacks of concrete weighing 30 pounds each, what is the average weight, in pounds, of all 10 sacks in the wheelbarrow?

Directly/Inversely Proportional

of all math
questions
on the SAT

Directly and Inversely Proportional

When two variables, x and y, are proportional to one another, they are locked into a fixed relationship.

If x and y are DIRECTLY PROPORTIONAL, then

$$y = (k)(x)$$

A constant specific to each problem

If x and y are INVERSELY PROPORTIONAL, then

$$y = \frac{k}{x}$$

A constant specific to each problem

How does this work?
If x and y are directly proportional, they move in the same direction:
When x increases, y also increases.
When x decreases, y also decreases.

If $x = 3$ when $y = 6$, what will y be when $x = 9$?
Let's set it up.

$$y = (k)(x)$$
$$6 = (k)(3)$$
$$2 = k$$

So every x will be doubled to give us our y.
Therefore when x is 9, y will be 18.

You could also set this up in terms of proportions where $\frac{3}{6} = \frac{9}{y}$.

There are many ways to solve a problem!

E If x is inversely proportional to y and $x = 5$ when $y = 21$, what is the value of y when $x = 15$?

Remember we are looking for an inverse proportion.

S Let's set it up.

$$y = \frac{k}{x}$$

$$21 = \frac{k}{5}$$

$$(21)(5) = k$$
$$105 = k$$

When $x = 15$:

$$y = \frac{105}{15}$$

$$y = \boxed{7}$$

E

x	$\frac{1}{3}$	$\frac{1}{2}$	?	3	5
y	90	60	40	10	6

In the table above, x and y are inversely proportional. What is the value of x when y is 40?

(A) $\frac{3}{4}$

(B) 1

(C) $\frac{4}{3}$

(D) 2

(E) 18

We can choose any *x, y* pair from the table to begin solving. Let's pick an easy relationship:

$y = 10$

$x = 3$

Now, we need to solve for our constant, *k*.

$$y = \frac{k}{x}$$

$$10 = \frac{k}{3}$$

$$(10)(3) = k$$
$$30 = k$$

When $y = 40$:

$$40 = \frac{30}{x}$$

$$(40)(x) = 30$$

$$x = \frac{30}{40}$$

$$= \boxed{\frac{3}{4}}$$

Directly/Inversely Proportional
Practice Problems

1. If x is inversely proportional to y and $x = 6$ when $y = 20$, what is the value of x when $y = 3$?

2. On a certain map, 1 inch represents 50 miles. How many miles are represented by 4.3 inches?

    (A)   150
    (B)   200
    (C)   215
    (D)   225
    (E)   250

3. If $r \neq 0$ and r is directly proportional to t, which of the following is inversely proportional to $\dfrac{1}{r^4}$?

    (A) $\dfrac{1}{t^4}$

    (B) $-\dfrac{1}{t^4}$

    (C) $\dfrac{1}{t}$

    (D) t

    (E) t^4

$$y = Cx$$

$$F = kD$$

4. In the equation above y is directly proportional to x and C is a constant. If y is 20 when x is 5, what is x when $y = 100$?

(A) 9
(B) 12
(C) 15
(D) 18
(E) 25

5. The force required to stretch a spring past its natural length is determined by the equation above where F is force, D is the distance stretched (in inches), and k is a constant. If a force of 10 pounds stretches the spring 6 inches, what is the force (in pounds) required to stretch the same spring 2 feet?

(A) 3.33
(B) 6.66
(C) 14.4
(D) 24.0
(E) 40.0

0.4%

of all math
questions
on the SAT

Distance, Rate and Time

One of the few formulas that you must memorize is:

Distance = Rate × Time

Just think it through in terms of driving.

If you travel at a speed of 30 miles per hour for two hours, you'll travel a total distance of:

30 miles/hour × 2 hours = 60 miles

Rate × Time = Distance

E Driving at a constant speed, Tareeq traveled 270 miles in 6 hours. At this rate, how many miles did Tareeq travel in 5 hours?

S Step 1: Figure out Tareeq's rate (R):

$$D = R \times T$$
$$270 = R \times 6$$
$$R = \frac{270}{6}$$

Step 2: We have our rate. Let's plug it back into our equation:

$$D = R \times T$$
$$D = (270 \text{ miles}/6 \text{ hours}) \times 5 \text{ hours}$$
$$D = 270 \times \frac{5}{6}$$
$$D = \boxed{225}$$

E

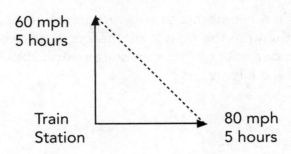

60 mph
5 hours

Train
Station

80 mph
5 hours

Two trains leave a station at the same time and travel for 5 hours. The first train travels due north at an average rate of 60 mph. The second train travels due east at an average rate of 80 mph. What is the straight line distance between them, in miles, at the end of the 5 hours?

S This is a combo $D = RT$ / Pythagorean Theorem Question.
We need to find both sides of our triangle and then solve for the hypotenuse, which is the distance between the 2 trains.

Distance for Train 1:

$$D = R \times T$$
$$D = 60 \times 5$$
$$D = 300 \text{ miles}$$

Distance for Train 2:

$$D = R \times T$$
$$D = 80 \times 5$$
$$D = 400 \text{ miles}$$

Let's find our hypotenuse:

$$A^2 + B^2 = C^2$$
$$300^2 + 400^2 = C^2$$
$$90,000 + 160,000 = 250,000$$
$$\sqrt{250,000} = \boxed{500}$$

E Jennifer ran 4 kilometers at an average speed of 20 kilometers per hour and then ran the next 2 kilometers at an average speed of 15 kilometers per hour. What was her average speed, in kilometers per hour for the 6 kilometers?

(A) 6
(B) 12
(C) 17.5
(D) 18
(E) 24

S Jennifer is booking it! What is her average speed?

$$D_1 = R_1 \times T_1$$

$$4 \text{ km} = 20 \text{ km/hr} \times T_1$$

$$\frac{4 \text{ km}}{20 \text{ km/hr}} = T_1$$

$$\frac{1}{5} \text{ hr} = T_1$$

$$D_2 = R_2 \times T_2$$

$$2 \text{ km} = 15 \text{ km/hr} \times T_2$$

$$\frac{2 \text{ km}}{15 \text{ km/hr}} = T_2$$

$$\frac{2}{15} \text{ hr} = T_2$$

$$\text{Average Speed (Rate)} = \frac{\text{Total Distance}}{\text{Total Time}} = \frac{4 \text{ km} + 2 \text{ km}}{\frac{2}{15} \text{ hr} + \frac{1}{5} \text{ hr}}$$

$$\frac{6 \text{ km}}{\frac{2}{15} \text{ hr} + \frac{3}{15} \text{ hr}} = \frac{6 \text{ km}}{\frac{5}{15} \text{ hr}} = \frac{6 \text{ km} \times 15}{5 \text{ hr}} = \frac{6 \times 3 \text{ km}}{1 \text{ hr}} = \boxed{\frac{18 \text{ km}}{\text{hr}}}$$

Distance, Rate and Time Practice Problems

1. If a cyclist travels at a constant rate of 18 miles per hour, what distance (in miles) will she travel in 40 minutes?

   (A) 10
   (B) 12
   (C) 14
   (D) 18
   (E) 24

2. Gina can run 10 kilometers in one hour. At this rate, how many kilometers can she run in 15 minutes?

   (A) 2
   (B) 2.5
   (C) 3
   (D) 3.5
   (E) 5

3. Car *A* traveled 100 miles in two hours. Car *B* traveled half as far in four hours. What was Car *B*'s average speed in miles per hour?

4. Yoder, Kansas is 200 miles from Speed, Kansas. If a car travels from Yoder to Speed at an average rate of 60 miles per hour and returns at an average rate of 40 miles per hour without stopping, what will be the car's average rate, in miles per hour, for the entire trip?

   (A) 58
   (B) 50
   (C) 48
   (D) 36
   (E) 24

5. It took Linda a total of 6 hours to paddle from one end of a lake to the other and back again along the same path. If she averaged 3 miles per hour for the first leg and 2 miles per hour coming back, how many miles was it from one end of the lake to the other?

(A)   2.4
(B)   3.6
(C)   6.0
(D)   7.2
(E)   8.6

6. On a 1,000 mile trip from New York City to Peoria, Illinois, Samantha drove 5 hours each day for the first two days. If she drove at an average rate of 75 mph the first day and 65 mph the second day, at what rate, in miles per hour, must she drive the third day to finish her trip in exactly 5 hours?

(A) 45
(B) 50
(C) 55
(D) 60
(E) 65

Algebra Review

1. If $(x - 5)^2 = 25$, then x could be

(A) 0
(B) 5
(C) 7
(D) 9
(E) 11

2. A plane flying at a constant speed traveled 2,020 miles in 5 hours. At this rate, how many miles did the plane travel in 4 hours?

(A)   101
(B)   404
(C)   808
(D) 1,212
(E) 1,616

3. If $4x + 18y = 2r$, then $2x + 9y =$

(A) $\dfrac{1}{4} r$

(B) $\dfrac{1}{2} r$

(C) r

(D) $2r$

(E) $4r$

4. A machine can produce screws at the rate of one screw every 5 seconds. If it does this for 8 hours each day, how many days will it take the machine to produce 28,800 screws?

5. In a certain class, 15 students own cell phones, 8 own laptops, and 12 own cars. If 7 students own exactly 2 of the 3 items and all of the rest of the students own exactly 1 item, how many students are in the class?

(A)   25
(B)   28
(C)   31
(D)   32
(E)   35

6. If $x^2 + y^2 = 74$ and $xy = 35$, what is the value of $x + y$, if both x and y are greater than zero?

(A)   4
(B)   12
(C)   70
(D)   109
(E)   144

7. If the function f is defined by $f(x) = 5x - 3$, then $3f(x) - 3 =$

(A) $8x - 9$
(B) $8x - 12$
(C) $15x - 9$
(D) $15x - 12$
(E) $15x + 9$

8. John and Sam each worked for 8 hours on Saturday. If John earned $10.00 per hour, and Sam earned 50% more per hour than John, what was the sum of their wages, in dollars, for the entire day?

(A)   80
(B)   100
(C)   120
(D)   160
(E)   200

9. The cost of gas for a trip is g dollars, and this cost is to be shared equally by a group of students. In terms of g, how many more dollars will each person contribute if there are 4 people in the group instead of 5?

(A) $\dfrac{g}{20}$

(B) $\dfrac{g}{10}$

(C) $\dfrac{g}{8}$

(D) $\dfrac{g}{5}$

(E) $\dfrac{g}{4}$

10. 8 students took an algebra test. The average (arithmetic mean) grade of 5 of the students was 82. The other 3 each scored 74. What was the average test grade for all 8 students?

(A) 76
(B) 77
(C) 78
(D) 79
(E) 80

11. If x, y, and z are positive integers, and $x = y + z$, then the average of x, y, and z is how much more than the average of y and z, in terms of x?

(A) $\dfrac{x}{9}$

(B) $\dfrac{x}{8}$

(C) $\dfrac{x}{6}$

(D) $\dfrac{x}{3}$

(E) $\dfrac{x}{2}$

12. If $(a + b)^2 = 144$, and $ab = 20$, what is the value of $(a - b)^2$?

(A) 40
(B) 64
(C) 84
(D) 104
(E) 184

13. For all numbers x and y, let $x \varnothing y$ be defined as $x \varnothing y = x^2 + 2xy$. What is the value of $2 \varnothing (2 \varnothing 3)$?

14. How many different integer values of n satisfy the inequality $\frac{1}{15} < \frac{3}{n} < \frac{1}{12}$?

15. If the sum of the consecutive even integers from -30 to n, inclusive, is 66, what is the value of n?

The Algebra Short List

1 **DISTANCE = RATE × TIME**
This applies to any rate; bolts per hour, beats per minute, images per second. Just replace "Distance" with "bolts" or "beats" or "images," and make sure your time units line up.

2 **D=RT**, set the distances equal to each other so $R_1T_1 = R_2T_2$

3 Whenever you see **MULTIPLE EQUATIONS WITH EXPONENTS,** you are dealing with a multiplication relationship. ($A \times B = C$)

4 On the SAT, multiple equations are often related; you can generally **STACK THEM** and solve.

5 **COMMON QUADRATICS**
- $x^2 + 2xy + y^2 = (x + y)^2$
- $x^2 - 2xy + y^2 = (x - y)^2$

6 **DIFFERENCE OF 2 SQUARES**
$x^2 - y^2 = (x + y)(x - y)$

7 **Function Notation:** $f(x) = y$
You plug something in for x, and you get something out on the other side.

8 The key to the "function in a function" problems (composite functions) is to **BEGIN INSIDE** the parentheses and work your way out. (Inside-out)

9 MEAN (AVERAGE) = $\dfrac{\textbf{SUM}}{\textbf{\# TERMS}}$

10 When a set of terms is arranged in ascending or descending order, the **MEDIAN** (like the median of a highway) is the **MIDDLE** term.

11 When working with **AVERAGES**, always, always, find the **SUM**.

Sum	
Avg	× # of terms

12 If you are asked for the **GREATEST POSSIBLE VALUE** of one term, minimize all of the other terms. If you are asked for the LEAST POSSIBLE VALUE of one term, maximize all of the other terms.

13 VENN DIAGRAMS:
Don't double-count!

14 When working with **WEIGHTED AVERAGES**, add a column to the table.

15 When you come across **WACKED-OUT FUNCTIONS**, remember, the test is just assigning a math meaning to a random symbol. Substitution is the key!

Math Mantras

Below is a series of Mantras or sayings that will help you remember the key strategies you have learned in this section. Mantras are meant to be repeated over and over in a soothing rhythm that will calm you and help trigger your memory. Repeat these to yourself when you are stuck in traffic, on your way to study hall or in the shower. Know them; love them; use them.

- Read and translate the problem **ONE LINE AT A TIME**.

- CIRCLE ANYTHING IN BOLD: **EXCEPT, NOT**. Students often miss these words and miss the problem.

- **Circle what you are solving** for.

- WHEN IN DOUBT, **WRITE IT ALL OUT**! Label figures; fill in charts and tables.

- Structure your work. Work left to right, top to bottom.

- When in doubt—MAKE A TABLE. Tables are phenomenal for structuring your work.

- **DO NOT DO MATH IN YOUR HEAD**. Work everything out on the paper or on the calculator.

- **Use your Calculator**.

- If you can solve a problem by graphing, GRAPH IT on your calculator.

- If a figure is drawn to scale, you can MEASURE IT to find the answer.

- If you can't work forwards, **WORK BACKWARDS**.

- If you see "in terms of," **PICK NUMBERS**.

Answers

Angles (5%)

1. B (E)
2. B (E)
3. D (M)
4. C (M)
5. D (M)

6. E (M)
7. C (M)
8. 45 (M)
9. C (H5)

Triangles (7%)

1. D (E)
2. B (M)
3. E (M)
4. B (M)
5. D (H)
6. E (M)
7. C (E)
8. 4 (H)
9. A (H)
10. D (H)
11. B (M)
12. D (M)
13. A (H)
14. D (H)

Circles (6%)

1. D (E)
2. B (M)
3. C (M)
4. B (E)
5. B (M)
6. E (M)
7. D (M)
8. D (M)
9. C (M)
10. D (M)
11. 30 (M)
12. 30 (M)
13. E (M)
14. C (M)
15. B (H)

Perimeter, Area and Volume (10%)

1. C (M)
2. C (M)
3. D (M)
4. E (M)
5. 28 (M)

6. D (M)
7. E (M)
8. E (M)
9. A (M)
10. C (M)
11. 448 (M)
12. E (H5)
13. 27 (H)
14. D (H5)

Proportional Shapes (0.6%)

1. E (M)
2. 17.5 or 35/2 (M)
3. B (M)
4. E (M)

Number Lines (3%)

1. A (H)
2. 77.9 (M)
3. C (M)
4. D (H5)

Coordinate Systems 5%)

1. A (M)
2. D (M)
3. C (M)
4. B (M)
5. C (M)
6. D (M)
7. D (H)

Slope (4%)

1. B (E)
2. B (M)
3. D (M)
4. D (H)
5. C (M)
6. E (H5)

Reflections (0.4%)

1. C (M)
2. C (M)
3. C (M)

Shifting Graphs (1.2%)

1. C (M)
2. B (M)
3. C (M)
4. C (H)

Advanced Graphing (1.2%)

1. 1 (H)
2. 0.25 or 1/4 (H5)
3. B (H)
4. D (H5)
5. B (H5)

Distance Formula in 3-D (0.2%)

1. C (H5)
2. B (H5)

Geometry Review

1. D (M)
2. 9 (M)
3. 36 (M)
4. C (M)
5. 54 (M)
6. 60 (M)
7. C (M)
8. D (H)
9. D (M)
10. C (H)
11. C (H)
12. D (M)
13. D (H)
14. D (H)
15. E (M)

Properties of Numbers (6%)

1. E (E)
2. C (E)

Properties of Numbers (6%)

3. A (H)
4. 6001 (M)
5. 6 (M)
6. D (M)
7. D (M)
8. C (M)
9. C (M)
10. D (M)
11. 10 (M)
12. B (M)
13. B (M)
14. 5 (M)
15. B (M)

Working Backward (7%)

1. D (E)
2. B (M)
3. D (M)
4. A (M)
5. B (M)
6. D (H)

Art of Translation (6%)

1. D (E)
2. A (E)
3. B (E)
4. C (M)
5. B (M)
6. 13 (M)
7. D (M)
8. B (M)
9. B (M)

Picking Numbers (12%)

1. E (E)
2. D (M)
3. D (M)
4. A (M)
5. A (M)
6. D (E)
7. C (M)
8. C (M)
9. E (M)
10. 64 (M)

Picking Numbers (12%)

11. A (H5)
12. A (M)
13. E (H)
14. D (H5)
15. C (H)

Absolute Value (2%)

1. D (E)
2. C (M)
3. A (M)
4. E (H)
5. C (H)

Inequalities (2%)

1. 7 (M)
2. D (M)
3. C (M)
4. C (H)
5. $1 > x > 1/2$ ((M)
6. B (M)

Exponents (4%)

1. D (M)
2. 5 (M)
3. D (E)
4. B (M)
5. E (M)
6. A (M)
7. D (M)
8. 30 (M)
9. C (H)
10. 5 (H)
11. 5 (H)
12. C (H)
13. C (H5)

Fractions (3%)

1. D (E)
2. C (M)
3. A (M)
4. A (M)
5. 1/4 or 0.25 (H)

Percentages (4%)

1. C (E)
2. B (E)
3. D (M)
4. C (M)
5. 12 (M)
6. 50 (M)
7. E (M)
8. D (M)
9. C (M)
10. C (M)
11. D (H5)
12. 47.3 (H5)

Probability (2%)

1. A (E)
2. 18 (E)
3. B (M)
4. A (M)
5. A (M)
6. E (M)
7. C (M)
8. 0.375 or 3/8 (H5)

Ratios (2%)

1. D (M)
2. D (M)
3. E (M)
4. A (M)
5. A (M)
6. 904 (H)
7. B (M)
8. D(M)
9. B (M)
10. D (M)

Sequences (4%)

1. C (E)
2. D (M)
3. E (H)
4. 60 (H)
5. E (M)
6. D (M)
7. C (H)

Combinations and Permutations (1.2%)

1. *E (M)*
2. *C (H)*
3. *D (H)*
4. *625 (H)*
5. *120 (M)*
6. *24 (M)*
7. *B (H)*

Square Roots (0.6%)

1. *B (E)*
2. *8 (H)*
3. *D (M)*

Unit Conversions (0.8%)

1. *D (E)*
2. *C (M)*
3. *D (M)*
4. *B (M)*

Remainders After Division (0.6%)

1. *E (M)*
2. *C (M)*
3. *A (M)*
4. *226 (H)*
5. *C (H)*
6. *32 or 74 (H)*
7. *D (H)*

Arithmetic Review

1. *C (E)*
2. *4.2 (E)*
3. *B (M)*
4. *C (M)*
5. *C (M)*

Arithmetic Review

6. *B (M)*
7. *C (M)*
8. *D (E)*
9. *A (M)*
10. *D (M)*
11. *E (M)*
12. *D (M)*
13. *C (H)*

Arithmetic Review

14. *E (M)*
15. *B (H)*

Multiple Equations (4%)

1. *D (E)*
2. *2 (E)*
3. *C (M)*
4. *11 (M)*
5. *C (M)*
6. *E (H)*
7. *D (M)*
8. *D (M)*
9. *B (H)*

Function Notation (4%)

1. *A (E)*
2. *E (M)*
3. *E (M)*
4. *E (M)*
5. *C (H)*
6. *C (H)*
7. *1.8 or 9/5 (H)*
8. *A (H5)*

Composite Functions (0.6%)

1. *198 (H)*
2. *D (H)*
3. *B (H)*

Wacked-Out Functions (2%)

1. *E (E)*
2. *5/11 or .455 (E)*
3. *D (M)*
4. *C (H)*
5. *C (H5)*
6. *15 (H)*

Mean, Median and Mode (4%)

1. *C (E)*
2. *C (E)*
3. *B (E)*
4. *D (E)*
5. *E (M)*

Mean, Median and Mode (4%)

6. D (M)
7. D (M)
8. 10 (M)
9. D (H)
10. B (H5)
11. E (H5)

Max and Min (1.2%)

1. C (M)
2. 397 (H)
3. C (M)

Charts, Tables and Graphs (8%)

1. D (M)
2. C (M)
3. C (M)
4. B (M)
5. C (M)
6. D (M)
7. C (M)
8. B (M)
9. D (E)
10. D (H5)

Complex Word Problems (5%)

1. C (M)
2. B (M)
3. D (H)
4. 4 (M)
5. D (H)
6. 800 (H5)

Venn Diagrams (1.2%)

1. D (M)
2. D (M)
3. E (M)
4. A (M)

Weighted Averages (0.8%)

1. E (M)
2. D (M)
3. C (M)
4. 24 (M)

Directly/Inversely Proportional (1.2%)

1. 40 (M)
2. C (M)
3. E (M)
4. E (M)
5. E (M)

Distance, Rate and Time (0.4%)

1. B (E)
2. B (E)
3. 12.5 or 25/2 (E)
4. C (H5)
5. D (H5)
6. D (H5)

Algebra Review

1. A (E)
2. E (E)
3. C (M)
4. 5 (M)
5. B (M)
6. B (M)
7. D (M)
8. E (M)
9. A (M)
10. D (M)
11. C (M)
12. B (M)
13. 68 (H)
14. 8 (H)
15. 34 (H)

The total of all the percentages does not add up to exactly 100% because many math problems fall into more than one category.

Graphing Calculator Guide

Thanks to your dedication and hard work, you are now a SAT Math Master! Before you go conquering standardized tests everywhere, we are going to show you how to get the most out of your Graphing Calculator. We have provided you with this short, simple and straightforward tutorial on how to solve tricky SAT problems with the punch of a few buttons. This tutorial will mainly deal with the TI-84, but it is applicable to most graphing calculators. While it is fun to impress all your friends in the lunchroom with your amazing mental math skills, please do not rely too heavily on them on the SAT. Sure, you're brilliant. But the added pressure and time constraints of standardized testing can cause you to make careless errors that you normally would not make. Why take the chance? The College Board lets you use a graphing calculator. You might as well take them up on this rare, benevolent offer.

Graphing Basic Equations

First, let's get acquainted with your graphing screen. Hit the **[Y=]** button, which should be in the top row of your buttons. The screen you should see is shown below.

On each **Y=** line, you can enter any equation you want to see graphically. To include a variable, simply use the **[X,T,θ,n]** button.

E   Input the equation $y = 5x^3 - 4x^2 + 2x - 5$.

Isolate your *y*-variable on one side of your equation before you enter it into the calculator.

S

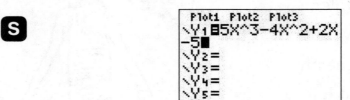

*To graph this equation, hit the **[GRAPH]** button in the top right corner. You should see the graph below.*

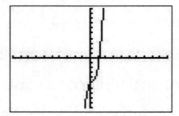

*The graph above doesn't show much detail. To see more information about the function (equation), you will need to shrink your window size. Hit the **[WINDOW]** button found on the top row of your calculator. This shows you the default window settings.*

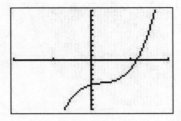

```
WINDOW
 Xmin=-10
 Xmax=10
 Xscl=1
 Ymin=-10
 Ymax=10
 Yscl=1
 Xres=1■
```

Xmin *is the left-most point shown on the window.* **Xmax** *is the right-most point.* **Xscl** *is the scale for the x-axis—how often you will see the hatch-marks on the x-axis. Similarly, the bottom and top of the screen are controlled by the* **Ymin** *and* **Ymax** *values. Change your x values to* **Xmin = -2** *and* **Xmax = 2**. *Your graph will look as follows.*

To return your window to the default setting, hit [ZOOM] and then [6].

Graphing Inequalities

Not only can we graph functions in the *y* = or *f(x)* = format, but we can also graph inequalities and shade the corresponding values.

E Input the equation $y > 5x^3 - 4x^2 + 2x - 5$.

S *Return to the* **Y=** *screen. Use your* **[←]** *button to move your cursor to the left of* **Y=**.

```
Plot1 Plot2 Plot3
\Y1■5X^3-4X^2+2X
-5■
\Y2=
\Y3=
\Y4=
\Y5=
\Y6=
```

Hit **[ENTER]** twice. The ↘ will change to the symbol below, which signifies **Greater Than**.

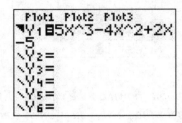

Hit the **[GRAPH]** button to see the figure below. The shaded portion indicates all the values of x which make the equation $y > 5x^3 - 4x^2 + 2x - 5$ true.

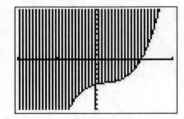

To graph $y < 5x^3 - 4x^2 + 2x - 5$, you will need to change the ↘ to the left of the Y= again. Hit the **[ENTER]** button three times to see the figure below.

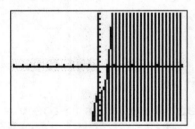

Combining Inequalities

You can combine many different inequalities to show a total correct area. For example, let's use two different equations: $y < 3x + 2$ and $y > 6x - 2$ with a standard window setting (**[ZOOM] [6]**).

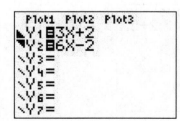

Max and Min

Often on the SAT, you will be able to solve complex problems by using your knowledge of graphing. Some problems will require you to graph two different equations and determine where they intersect. Others will ask what different *y*-values are for an equation given an *x*-value. You will even be asked to find the maximum or minimum of a function. All these can be found using algebra, but sometimes your graphing calculator is quicker.

E Bob and Carol both work for Bikez R Us. Bob makes $250 per week salary with $5 commission per bike sold while Carol makes $100 per week with a $20 commission per bike sold. In a certain week, Bob and Carol made the same amount of money. How many bikes did they sell?

S *This problem can easily be solved graphically! First, we need to determine what equations model Bob and Carol's earnings. Bob's salary is modeled by the equation $y = 5x + 250$ and Carol's salary is modeled by the equation $y = 20x + 100$.*

*To solve algebraically, we would set these equations equal to each other. Instead, let's enter them into the **Y=** screen. Set your **Window** so X is from 0 to 20 and Y is from 250 to 400. See below.*

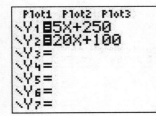 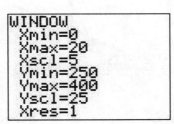 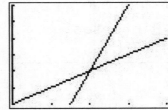

*Now that we have graphed our equations, how can we tell which line is which? Return to the **Y=** screen. Again use your arrow buttons so your cursor is all the way on the left hand side of **Y=**. Every time you hit enter, you cycle through different ways your equations can be depicted. So, let's make Bob's income a bold line, and Carol's a dotted line.*

```
Plot1 Plot2 Plot3
\Y1∎5X+250
\Y2⊟20X+100
\Y3=
\Y4=
\Y5=
\Y6=
\Y7=
```

Now when you hit **[GRAPH]** *you will see 2 distinctly different lines.*

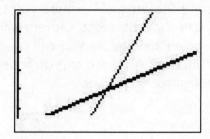

Since the problem states that both Bob and Carol have the same income, their lines must intersect. To find this intersection, hit the **[2ⁿᵈ]** *button and then* **[TRACE]** *(it will have yellow letters that say* **CALC** *above it). This will bring you to the Calculate screen for the graphs (Screen A). Hit* **[5]**. *You will be brought to the second screen (Screen B), where it will ask you to identify the first curve—line—of the two you want to compare. Hit* **[ENTER]**, *and choose a second curve (Screen C). Hit* **[ENTER]** *again, and move your cursor (the small circle with a blinking X over it) close to the intersection point (Screen D). Hit* **[ENTER]** *again and you will see the intersection is X=10 and Y=300 (Screen E). The intersection tells you that they each made $300 and sold 10 bikes.*

Screen A   Screen B   Screen C

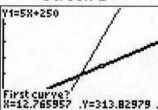

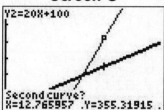

Screen D   Screen E

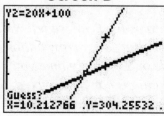

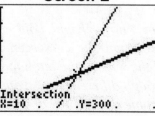

What if they had asked how much more Carol would make if they both sold 12 bikes? Well, return to the **Calculate** *screen (* **[2nd] [TRACE]** *), and hit* **[ENTER]** *(Screen A). The calculator will then prompt you for an x-value (Screen B). Put in 12 and hit* **[ENTER]** *(Screen C). By pressing the* **[↑] [↓]** *buttons you can move between the two lines and see the different values for the two equations at x = 12 (Screens D and E).*

Screen A	**Screen B**	**Screen C**
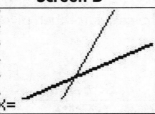		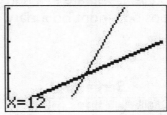

Screen D	**Screen E**
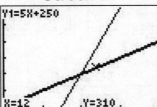	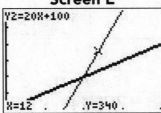

So we can see that if they both sell 12 bikes, Carol will make $340 while Bob will make $310.

Minimum Value of a Parabola or Cubic Function

Go to the **Y=** screen and input the function $0.6x^3 + 3x^2 + x + 1$ with a standard window (**[ZOOM] [6]**).

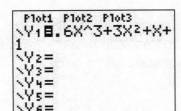
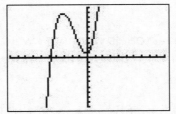

As you can see, this function has both a maximum and a minimum. To find these, we hit **[2ⁿᵈ] [TRACE]** to bring us back to the **Calculate** screen (Screen A). To find the minimum hit **[3]**; to find the maximum hit **[4]**. The rest of the process is the same, so we're going to just walk through how to find the minimum. Once you choose the minimum option, the calculator prompts you to mark a point to the left of the minimum (Screen B). Hit **[ENTER]** and then mark a point to the right of the minimum (Screen C) and hit **[ENTER]**. After choosing the boundaries, the calculator asks you for a guess (Screen D). It isn't very important how close you are. If you are in a hurry, you can go ahead and just hit **[ENTER]** again after choosing a right boundary. The calculator then gives you the minimum (Screen E).

Screen A
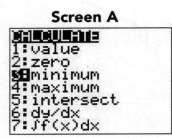

Screen B
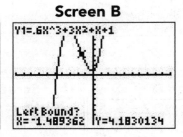

Screen C
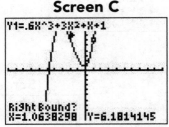

Screen D
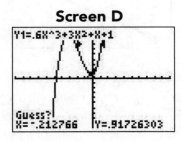

Screen E
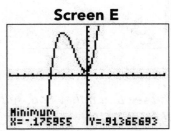

Now, that is pretty much everything you need to be able to use for the graphing portion of the SAT. There are tons of other things that you can do with your calculator in terms of graphing, so just play around with it. Now, let's move on to some other topics.

Factorials

You would use factorials when you want to know how many ways there are to arrange x number of things in x number of spots all at once.

We don't have a set order nor do we have a set number of spaces, which means we can use factorials.

E We have 5 paintings we want to hang in 5 places on the wall. How many ways could we make this happen?

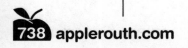

S *We would input* **[5]** *(Screen A). Then hit* **[MATH]**. *Use your* **[→]** *button to highlight* **PRB** *(Screen B). Hit* **[4]** *for* **!** *(the exclamation mark represents factorial). This will return you to your home screen. Hit* **[ENTER]** *to see how many ways we could arrange our 5 paintings in 5 places (Screen C).*

Screen A	Screen B	Screen C
5	MATH NUM CPX **PRB** 1:rand 2:nPr 3:nCr **4**:! 5:randInt(6:randNorm(7:randBin(	5! 120

Combinations

A combination problem is arranging *x* number of items into *y* number of spaces. Here, order doesn't matter.

E There are 12 students in a school. How many ways can these students be arranged into 4 classes if each class has the same number of students?

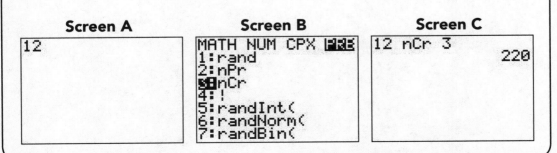

S *Here order doesn't matter, so we need to use combinations. First, input* **[12]** *because we have 12 students (Screen A). Hit* **[MATH]** *and highlight* **PRB** *again. This time we choose option* **[3]** *for* **nCr** *(Screen B). Since we are choosing sets of 3, we would input the number* **[3]** *after nCr on the home screen and hit* **[ENTER]** *to see how many combinations of 3 students we can make out of our total 12 (Screen C).*

Screen A	Screen B	Screen C
12	MATH NUM CPX **PRB** 1:rand 2:nPr **3**:nCr 4:! 5:randInt(6:randNorm(7:randBin(	12 nCr 3 220

The second number is always less than or equal to the first number!

Permutations

In permutations, **order matters**!

E There are 12 runners in the Georgia Marathon. How many different sets of Top 3 runners can there be?

S *Before we use the calculator, we need to plan out how we're going to input the data. First, we have to enter the number we are choosing from (in this case, we would choose 12 since there are 12 runners). Input the number* **[12]** *(Screen A). Then, hit* **[MATH]** *and highlight* **PRB** *again. Hit the number* **[2]** *for* **nPr** *(Screen B). Then on the home screen, input the number we are choosing—in this case* **[3]**, *since we are making groups of 3 (Screen C). Hit* **[ENTER]**. *There are 1320 ways to assemble a Top 3 (Screen D).*

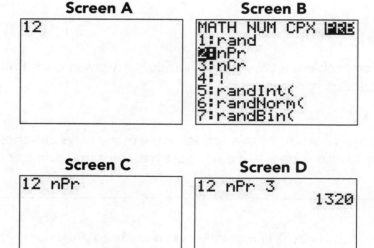

Screen A	Screen B

Screen C	Screen D

College Board Approved Calculators

Straight from the pens (or keyboards) of the rule-makers themselves is a list of the calculators you can and cannot use on the SAT.

Calculators permitted during testing are:

* Graphing calculators
* Scientific calculators
* Four-function calculators (not recommended)

You are not required to clear the memory on your calculator.

Calculating devices NOT permitted during testing:

* Laptop or a portable/handheld computer
* Calculator that has QWERTY (typewriter-like) keypad, uses an electrical outlet, makes noise, or has a paper tape
* Electronic writing pad or pen-input/stylus-driven device
* Pocket organizer
* Cell phone calculator

Visit www.collegeboard.com for more information.

Calculator Tips

Always check your batteries the night before the SAT.

Always bring extra batteries to the testing center.

Do NOT let the calculator be a subsitute for showing your work.

Do NOT use a fancy calculator on test day that you have never seen before. This is not the time to learn new skills.

Math Glossary

Absolute Value	the distance that an equation or number is from zero; always a positive number.
Adjacent	in geometry, an angle that is directly next to and shares a common side with your reference angle (the one you are working with).
Angle	a figure formed by two lines that meet at one point.
Arc	a distance on the circumference of a circle from one point to another; different from a chord because it travels along the circumference, not through the interior of the circle.
Area	the amount of space within a given boundary, given in square units.
Average (Arithmetic Mean)	the sum of a set of numbers divided by the number of terms in the set.
Binomial	an algebraic expression with two terms, one of which must be a variable, connected by a + or − sign; e.g. $(2x + 3)$.
Chord	a straight line that connects two points on the circumference of a circle and travels through the interior of the circle.
Circle	a geometrical figure where all points are equidistant from a central point.
Circumference	the perimeter of a circle; measured using 1-dimensional units (e.g. cm).
Consecutive	numbers or terms that are the next step in a pattern: *Three consecutive even integers are 2,4,6.*
Constant	a quantity that is unchanging: *In the slope-intercept formula $y = mx + b$, m and b are both constants.*
Coordinate	one of a set of numbers used to show the position of a point on a line or graph.

Cube	a 3-dimensional figure where length = width = height.
Denominator	the bottom number in a fraction; what you are dividing the top number (the numerator) by.
Diagonal	a straight line that connects two vertices of a polygon that are not next to each other.
Diameter	a chord that passes through the center of the circle; it is the largest possible chord.
Directly Proportional	This term indicates that two or more values have a constant product so that $y = xk$, where k is a constant. If x is **directly proportional** to y, when x triples, y will triple. Note that this only uses the operations of **division** and **multiplication**. If you add 3 to x, you do NOT just add 3 to y.
Distinct	numbers or symbols or values that are different in some way.
Domain	the x-values over which a function, or a part of a function, is defined.
Equilateral Triangle	a triangle that has three equal angles, each measuring 60°, and three equal sides.
Exterior Angle	the outside angle formed when a side of a polygon is extended.
Factor	a factor of n is a number which divides evenly into n without a remainder.
FOIL	method used to multiply binomials (First, Outer, Inner, Last).
Function	a defined relationship between a set of x-values and a set of y-values: *In a **function** each x-value can ONLY correspond to a single y-value.*
Greatest Common Factor	the largest factor that two numbers have in common.
Hexagon	a 6-sided polygon.

Hypotenuse	the side opposite of the right angle in a right triangle; also the longest side of a right triangle; only right triangles have hypotenuses.
Inclusive	This term indicates that the endpoints of a set of numbers are included in the evaluation. This is represented on a number line by filled in circles at the endpoints of a line or can be expressed algebraically using the greater than or equal to sign ($\geq$) or the less than or equal to sign ($\leq$).
Indirectly Proportional	This term indicates that two or more values have a constant ratio so that $y = \dfrac{x}{k}$, where k is a constant. If x is **indirectly proportional** to y, when x triples, y will be a third of its original value. Note that this only uses the operations of **division** and **multiplication**. If you add 3 to x, you do NOT just subtract 3 from y.
Inscribed	This term indicates that a geometric figure has been produced within another figure so that the points of intersection are maximized without any part of the inscribed figure lying outside the other figure.
Integer	any whole number, whether positive, negative, or zero.
Interior Angle	the angle on the inside of a polygon.
Isosceles Triangle	a triangle with two equal sides and two equal angles; the angles opposite the equal sides are equal.
Least Common Multiple	the smallest number (not zero) that is a multiple of two numbers.
Line	a graphical representation of the equation $y = mx + b$, where m is the **slope**, which is always constant, and b is the **y-intercept.**
Linear Function	an algebraic representation of a line that conforms to the equation $y = mx + b$.
Median	When a set of terms is arranged in ascending or descending order, the **median** (like the median of a highway) is the middle term.

Midpoint	a point that lies exactly half-way (in all components) between two other points.
Mode	the value that occurs most frequently in a set of numbers.
Multiple	the product of any quantity by an integer.
Numerator	the top number in a fraction; the number being divided.
Octagon	an 8-sided polygon.
Ordered Pair	a point in the xy-coordinate plane, whose the first value is the x-coordinate and the second value is the y-coordinate.
Origin	the point $(0,0)$ in the xy-plane.
Parabola	an equation with the general form of $y = Ax^2 + Bx + C$ where A, B, and C are constants; another form of the parabola equation used for graphing is $y = a(x - h)^2 + k$, where (h, k) is the vertex of the parabola and a is a stretch factor.
Parallel	lines that have the same **slope** and never intersect.
Parallelogram	a quadrilateral where sides opposite each other are **parallel.**
PEMDAS	order of operations: Parentheses, Exponents, Multiplication and/or Division, Addition and/or Subtraction.
Pentagon	a 5-sided polygon.
Percent Increase/ Percent Decrease	$\dfrac{\text{(New number} - \text{Old number)}}{\text{Old number}} \times 100$
Perimeter	a 1-dimensional measurement of the outer edge of a figure.
Perpendicular Bisector	a straight line that intersects another line at its midpoint at a right angle.

Perpendicular Lines — two lines that intersect at a right angle and have slopes that are negative reciprocals (e.g. if line 1's slope = m, then line 2's slope = $-\dfrac{1}{m}$).

Prime Number — a number greater than 1 that is divisible only by 2 distinct numbers, 1 and itself; 2 is the lowest and only even prime number.

Probability — $\dfrac{\text{\# of outcomes that meet the requirements}}{\text{Total \# of possible outcomes}}$

Product — a quantity obtained by multiplying two or more terms together.

Proportion — a fancy term for **ratio.**

Pythagorean Theorem — an equation that relates the lengths of the legs of a right triangle to the length of its hypotenuse: $a^2 + b^2 = c^2$.

Radical — the sign that indicates a square root ($\sqrt{}$).

Radius of a Circle — the distance from the center of a circle to the circumference.

Range — the y-values of a function over a specified domain.

Ratio — a comparison of two numbers using division; usually represented by a fraction or with the word "to."

Real Numbers — any number, whether rational or irrational, that is not imaginary and, therefore, does not contain the term i.

Remainder — the whole number left after division.

Right Triangle — a triangle that contains a 90° angle.

Sector — a piece of the area of a circle.

Semicircle — one half of a circle.

Similar Triangles	2 or more triangles where the ratio of the three sides is equal; also, the corresponding angles are congruent: *Two triangles that have sides 3, 4, 5 and 6, 8, 10 are* **similar** *since they both have side ratios of 3:4:5.*
Slope	rise over run; also known as change in y divided by the change in x; constant in a line.
Slope-Intercept Form	$y = mx + b$, where m is the slope and b is the y-intercept.
Square	a 2-dimensional figure where all four sides are equal and all four angles are 90°.
Square Root	the **square root** of a number is a number which multiplied by itself, gives you the original number; e.g. $\sqrt{9}$ is 3 or -3 because $3 \times 3 = 9$ and $-3 \times -3 = 9$.
Sum	a quantity obtained by adding two or more terms together.
Surface Area	the area of all the polygons that are on the surface of a 3-dimensional figure; all measurements should be in square units.
Tangent (to)	touching at a single point in relation to a curve or surface. *Note: two lines do not lie tangent to each other.*
Variable	a value that can change; typically variables are indicated by the letters x, y or z.
Vertex	A point of intersection for any 2 sides of any polygon or 3-dimensional figure.
Volume	a 3-dimensional measurement of space occupied by an object; measured in cubed units (e.g. cm^3).
Whole Number	any number that is not a fraction or a decimal; also known as an **integer.**
X-Intercept	the point where a function crosses the x-axis; where the y-coordinate of the point is 0.
Y-Intercept	the point where a function crosses the y-axis; where the x-coordinate of the point is 0.

BEYOND THE CONTENT

Beyond the Content:
The Mental Component of the SAT

To fully prepare for the SAT, you need to accomplish three goals:

1 Understand the structure and format of the SAT

2 Master the content assessed on all sections of the test

3 Master the test-taking skills needed to thrive in a 5-hour, pressured testing environment

The final component is generally the most neglected aspect of test preparation, and for many students, it is the most important.

Are you a good test-taker or a bad test-taker?

Most of you could answer this question in a heartbeat. Like most students, you've likely already made up your mind about your ability to succeed on tests and, specifically, on the SAT. If you are reading this book you must believe, at some level, that you have the potential to do well on the SAT.

Though some of you believe that you are innately good test-takers, others may not be so confident. Whatever you believe, know that your self-appraisal of your ability is a better predictor of how you will do on the SAT than your actual level of ability! It doesn't matter how good you are in reality; if you repeatedly tell your-self that you are not going to do well on this test, you can override your actual abilities and sabotage your performance. And conversely, **if you believe you will succeed on the SAT, this belief will improve your performance!** Thoughts are powerful things!

Natural Test Takers

Some of you may fall under the category of natural test takers. You don't mind standardized tests. You actually kind of like them and have found a way to treat them like a game. You set challenging goals for yourself and work hard to achieve them. And more than likely, you are actively engaging in a lot of behaviors, both consciously and subcon-sciously, which are helping you to succeed!

Everybody Else

The majority of people have a different relationship with standardized tests than do the natural test takers. Most students don't love the SAT, though they eventually learn how to work with it and succeed on it. Some students get nervous or a little stressed when they have to sit for an SAT. Other students feel eternally cursed when it comes to the SAT or any standardized test. They believe that no matter how much they prepare, they will never do well. Does bad testing karma really exist? Is there no hope for these students?

Negative Beliefs about Testing

If you feel karmically challenged by the SAT, it's important that you examine the origins of your negative beliefs. When did you start to believe that you were "bad at testing"?

Are you focusing on a few isolated instances of poor performance and **ignoring instances of strong performance**?

Are you really **always** bad at testing in **every** possible context?

Have you ever had a **single** instance where you did well on a test?

If you can locate a **single** success in your testing past, you can work with it and begin to build from it.

Watch your words: your mind is listening

When it comes to making global statements about your testing abilities, be careful not to sell yourself short. Rather than saying, "I am miserable at testing," shift and rephrase the statement. "In the past, I have not been successful at testing." Or better yet, "I used to struggle with testing, but now I'm open to the **possibility** of doing better." Your mind likes to be consistent, and it tends to back up your words with actions. Don't limit your options, reinforce negative patterns or close the door on your potential. Stay in the realm of possibility.

Dealing with Test Anxiety

If you are like most students, you will experience some degree of anxiety around the SAT; this is only natural. A low level of anxiety is actually useful because it fuels motivation. A low level of anxiety will drive you to prepare for and stay focused during the SAT. If you didn't care about the outcome and were not concerned with your performance, why would you put in the effort necessary to succeed?

Though some anxiety is useful, too much anxiety can have a negative impact on your performance. There is a tipping point where things shift from good to bad:

Healthy level of anxiety:

"I really need to study to make sure I am prepared."

Unhealthy level of anxiety:

"What if I fail? What if I don't get into college and have to live in my parents' basement for the rest of my life? Oh no!!"

Can you notice the *subtle* difference between these levels of anxiety?

What is anxiety, where does it come from, and why does it matter?

Anxiety, at its core, is simply mental energy. Anxiety on a test stems from a potentially useful thought: "Hey, this test counts, and I need to do well." When this thought becomes invested with too much energy, however, it morphs into something else and ceases to be useful. If you are taking the SAT and are simultaneously dealing with a lot of anxiety, your performance will suffer.

There's a simple graph that illustrates the continuum of anxiety and its impact on performance. As this graph illustrates, some anxiety is good; too much is harmful. We want to reach the optimal point so we have the right amount of anxiety (AKA stress)—where we can completely focus our energies, get into the zone and achieve our strongest possible results.

Some stress is helpful.
Too much is harmful.

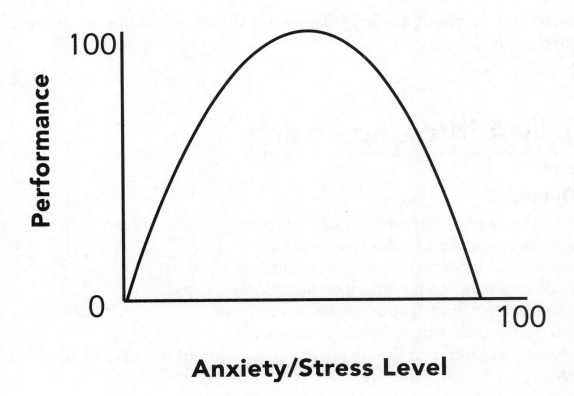

How does anxiety affect you?

The body and mind are intricately connected. Physical changes trigger thought patterns, and thought patterns trigger physical changes. To illustrate, clench your firsts and change your expression into an angry grimace. Hold that pose for 10 seconds. Do you suddenly feel angrier or more aggressive than you did a moment ago? Take a few breaths and shake off that emotion. Now, close your eyes and focus your mental energy on a positive memory involving someone you love. Hold the image in your mind for 10 seconds. Do you notice any changes in your body? The mind and body are intimately bound in a reciprocal relationship.

When you experience a deep level of anxiety about a test or some other task, you will notice physical changes taking place in your body. When you enter a state of elevated anxiety, your muscles begin to tense, your heart rate and respiratory rate change, and your breathing may become increasingly shallow. The body's stress hormones will begin to work their magic and take you into a low-grade "fight-or-flight" response. With less oxygen going to your brain and your body, you invariably lose a bit of your focus. Distracted, you no longer think or process information as clearly, and your working memory becomes impaired. This is not the ideal state to be in during a mentally rigorous test!

So what can you do about anxiety? There are several strategies to address heightened anxiety.

Mentally Addressing Anxiety

Inner Dialogue

Humans continuously engage in inner-dialogue. We each have a number of voices inside of our heads (some of us have more voices than others) that provide a running commentary on life. Some of these voices are negative, but others are positive  and encouraging. Learning to manage your own inner-dialogue and focus on the positive voices is one of the keys to succeeding on the SAT.

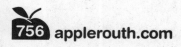

Listening to Your Inner Coach

When it comes to inner dialogue, most good test-takers have a major resource on their side: their inner coach. For most students, their inner coach is actually a composite figure, created from pieces of their favorite coaches, teachers or mentors who are rooting for them to succeed. Other students simply borrow an outside coach or mentor like Vince Lombardi or Yoda and recruit them for this purpose. Both would make excellent inner coaches!

Your inner coach can help you relax or get focused before the test by sending you supportive messages.

"You're ready for this. Go in there relaxed. You can knock this out." You can look to your inner coach to stand on the sidelines and provide ongoing support during the test: *"You're doing great." "It's only one question, don't worry about it. Let it go." "Re-lax...you can do this." "Pace yourself: just two more sections left!"*

It's not difficult to imagine how receiving these kinds of positive messages could help you remain focused and centered during the SAT.

Finding Your Inner Anxiety Monster

For other students who have not yet tapped into their inner coach, another creature may appear instead: the anxiety monster. The monster feeds on fear and is continually scanning the environment for potential catastrophes. He frequently appears behind statements such as these:

- "YOU NEVER DO WELL ON THESE TESTS."
- "YOU ALWAYS FIND A WAY TO MESS THESE UP."
- "WHAT IF YOU DON'T GET THAT SCHOLARSHIP?"
- "WHAT IF YOU DON'T EVEN GET INTO COLLEGE?"
- "WHAT WILL EVERYONE THINK?"
- "EVERYONE WILL BE SO DISAPPOINTED!"
- "IT WILL BE JUST AWFUL!"

If you don't deal with the monster directly and confront these negative statements, you run the risk of being influenced by them. If you allow yourself to focus your energy on thoughts of failure, your mind may subconsciously begin to turn these thoughts into reality. Do not let the monster run rampant in your inner dialogue!

Naming and Taming the Monster

If you can give your monster a name, you can deal with him more easily and address him directly. Though you will know the right name for your monster, for now, we'll call him Rupert. It's important to remember that Rupert actually works for you (though he's not the world's best employee), and he is taking up space in your head. If you stop feeding Rupert energy and attention, he will cease to exist.

If you are about to take the SAT and Rupert is stoking the fire of anxiety, address him directly. "Listen, buddy. I've had enough. I've worked hard and I'm ready for this test. I know this stuff. And I'm going to rock this test. So I'm done listening to you." At this point you may banish Rupert to a deserted island and let him entertain himself while you go in there and rock out the SAT.

If dialogue is not working, you could always call on your coach to bring the SMACKDOWN on Rupert. You've got some options here. Use whatever works and adjust this technique as necessary to make it more effective for you.

Make a short audio-recording to reinforce your positive messages

Some students have been helped by recording short, 5-10 minute audio tracks filled with positive messaging. In their own words, these students have recorded messages of support and encouragement: "You're ready for this. You're going to do great. You've worked so hard. You're the most prepared you've ever been, and you are going to rock this test." Once you've made the recording, saving the file as an mp3 track, upload it to your mp3 player or smart phone. When you drive to the test center, playing this track will help put you in the right frame of mind to do your best on the SAT.

Physically Addressing Anxiety

Just as you can address anxiety by shifting your thoughts and your inner dialogue, you can also address anxiety by making subtle physical adjustments. Below are a few simple physical exercises you can do to regulate your anxiety.

Focus on your breath

The quickest way to shift from anxiety to relaxation is to manipulate your breathing. It is physically impossible to breathe in a deep and relaxed manner and simultaneously feel a heightened sense of anxiety.

Take deep breaths

Deep breaths are rooted in your diaphragm rather than in your upper chest cavity. When you breathe deeply, your stomach should go out (think of the Buddha). If your shoulders rise while you are inhaling, you are breathing from your chest rather than your diaphragm. Remember: Think Buddha.

Slow things down

Count to 3 during the inhalation, pause at the peak of the breath and then count to 3 during the exhalation: this will begin to automatically relax your entire body.

Practice breathing while counting backwards

Count backwards from 10 to 1, silently in your head, breathing slowly and deeply from your diaphragm with each count. 10....9....8....7.... With each breath, imagine yourself becoming more and more relaxed.

Sigh deeply or make yourself yawn

Yawning is like pressing a reset button in your brain. Yawning has many beneficial effects and can actually help you increase your level of focus and energy.

Using a physical trigger to create relaxation

Another relaxation strategy involves a deeper level of self-conditioning. You can use a physical cue or trigger to bring yourself to a more relaxed state. This approach creates a mental link between a simple physical movement and a heightened state of mental relaxation. You are, in effect, conditioning yourself to relax when you perform a certain action or movement.

1 Choose a physical trigger

Find one that works for you or simply make up your own. Here are a few examples:
- squeezing three fingers together three times
- tapping your knee slowly three times
- putting one hand on top of the other

2 Bring yourself into a state of relaxation

- Take 3 deep breaths.
- Feel your body become more relaxed.
- Tense all of your muscles, hold the tension for a full breath, and then relax completely.
- Close your eyes.
- Take 3 more deep breaths using the 3 count: Breathe In. Hold. Breathe Out.

3 Form a mental association

Perform your chosen trigger in this relaxed state, and create a mental association between the physical motion and a state of deep relaxation. You will need to do this a few times to create a stronger association.

4 Perform your physical trigger during the test

During the test, whenever you feel anxiety coming on, perform your physical trigger, and recall your relaxed state. Take several deep breaths and consciously begin to relax.

Using key test phrases to help you relax

Some people begin to tense when they hear certain phrases during the testing process:

> "Open your test booklets to page __."
>
> "Ready? Begin."
>
> "You have 5 minutes remaining."

The 5-minute warning can be really stressful for some people. Some students do brilliantly for the first 20 minutes of a section, but after they hear the "5 minute warning," they get nervous, discard all of their strategies and begin second guessing themselves in their race to finish.

You can work to create a positive, relaxing association with the otherwise anxiety-stimulating phrases. Imagine a proctor saying, "You have 25 minutes; begin..." Then, take a deep breath and visualize yourself relaxing. With reinforcement and repetition, you can turn this phrase into a relaxation-inducing phrase.

During the SAT, when you hear any of the above phrases, put your pencil down for a moment, pause, take a few deep breaths, re-center yourself and then return to the test. The little time you give up in re-centering yourself, you will more than make up for through your increased clarity and peace of mind.

Creative Visualization:
Accessing the Power of Your Imagination

Your imagination can be your greatest ally or your greatest obstacle when you are confronted with a high-stakes test such as the SAT. If you are not actively engaging your imagination, you are missing out on a tremendous opportunity. You can passively allow your imagination to stir up anxiety-inducing scenarios, or you can actively harness the power of your imagination to help you achieve your SAT goals.

Mental Rehearsal

If you want to learn about the power of imagination, you need look no further than to the world's greatest athletes. These individuals must face high stress situations again and again, and to prepare themselves, they tap into the power of creative visualization. Just ask Michael Jordan, Michael Phelps or Mia Hamm. These and many other of the world's greatest athletes practice and rehearse mentally, visualizing their desired outcomes long before they walk onto their respective fields of play.

Why is mental rehearsal helpful? Why do the top performers on the planet spend hours and hours imagining desired outcomes rather than spending more time practicing on the playing field? They do so because the brain has a hard time distinguishing between imagined reality and actual reality. Whether you are imagining an action or performing that action, the same parts of your brain are being activated. When you imagine lifting your hand the same parts of the brain are triggered as when you actually lift your hand. Vividly imagine taking a test or actually take the test, and your brain will respond identically.

Rewiring your brain

The brain is easily fooled and often cannot distinguish between imagined and actual events: the field of false memory is one of the hottest research areas in cognitive science. Cognitive researchers have discovered that when you want to confuse the mind and make an imagined event seem real, feed it more sensory data. The more senses you can engage—the more sights, sounds, smells and textures you can imagine—the more real the memory will seem to your brain. Beyond sensory data, the more emotion you can add to the memory and the more often you repeat the memory, the more real it will become to the brain. So if you can vividly imagine an event, engage your senses, engage your emotions and reinforce this imagined event through repetition, your brain will begin to treat the event like it is real rather than imagined.

THIS IS HUGE!

Normally, when you walk into a testing situation, your brain will scan the environment for familiar cues. "Have I been here before?" "What's my pattern when I encounter this kind of environment?" Your brain will search your long-term memory to try to relate the current situation to past experiences and determine how to respond. If you've only known failure in prior testing situations, you will likely settle in to that familiar "script" of failure: old signals will come up, echoes from your past will arise, and before you blink, you'll be repeating your past behaviors, taking that well-laid path toward a less than stellar performance.

But with guided imagery and visualization, you actually have the power to create a new "script" for your brain to follow when you confront new testing situations. Even if you have no positive memories of past testing events to inform your brain, you can create new "memories" through guided imagery and repetition. Your imagination can help rewire your brain and create a new neural pathway for your brain to follow! Imagine the possibilities!

Creating a new script

Let's take some time and help you create a brand new script for taking the SAT. We'll need to fill this "memory" with as much detail as possible so your brain will believe it. We'll walk through an abbreviated version of the 20-minute script that we have used with students for the last decade. First read the script. Then, once you feel familiar with the content, close your eyes and imagine the whole scenario as if you were watching a movie playing inside of your head. Remember that **you** are the star of this film.

Imagine yourself waking up the morning of the SAT. You turn off your alarm and get out of bed. You do your morning routine—breakfast, shower, brush teeth. (Imagine all the specific details of your personal routine in the order you would do them.) You begin to feel more and more awake and alert. You feel good, relaxed and ready for the task ahead of you. You grab your backpack with your admission ticket, ID, pencils, calculator, water and snacks. As you drive to the test center, you begin to mentally prepare yourself. "I'm ready for this test; I'm going to go in there and knock this out." (Use whatever message feels right for you, in language you would use.) You arrive at the test center and park the car.

Before you open the car door, you pause for a moment and take a deep breath as you look in the rearview mirror: "I've worked hard, and I'm ready for this," you tell yourself. And you believe it. You walk into the school and get in the registration line. You show your ID and admission ticket and make your way to your testing room. You see the people in the room. Some are fidgety; others are relaxed; some are totally zoned out. Hear the sound of people rustling around in their seats. Now find your seat. After you put away your things and get settled in, visualize yourself feeling ready, and relaxed. The proctor asks you to clear your desk and begins

to pass out materials. See yourself bubbling-in all the preliminary info: name, date of birth, testing site, etc. Imagine the feel of the pencil in your hand, the motion of marking the bubbles on the Scantron sheet.

The proctor announces the beginning of the first section. "Open your test booklets to Page 1. You have 25 minutes. Begin." Everyone else in the room quickly opens their booklets to begin. You pause for a moment. You take a deep breath. You are feeling ready, so you pick up your pencil and turn to the first page of the test.

You write your essay, remembering the rules you have practiced so many times before. You use good structure, good vocabulary and lots of detailed examples. The proctor calls time. Pencils down. You feel confident that you wrote a strong essay. "Now we are going to open our test booklets to section 2. You will have 25 minutes to complete this section. You cannot turn to any other section of the test. Ready. And begin."

You turn the page and approach the first problem. It's easy, as you knew it would be. You've practiced this so many times before and you know what to do. You feel relaxed. You choose your answer and move on to the next one. One by one, you work your way through all the problems on the first section. You arrive at the harder problems; you solve them when you can, or omit them if you need to move on. You feel confident and know that you are tracking for your best score ever on this test. You move on through the sections and the breaks. You are doing the best you've ever done on this test. Watch yourself move seamlessly through the sections. You are feeling good and know this is the best test you've ever taken.

Now take a few moments and visualize the score you want

to achieve on the SAT. Imagine the number very clearly and hold it in your head. Now move forward in time. Imagine yourself going online or going to the mailbox to find the letter that contains your official score. You see the College Board's official results sheet. See your score report, and visualize the goal you set for yourself directly next to your name. Really see it. You've accomplished your goal. All your hard work paid off! Feel the emotions that come with that. Think of all the new opportunities you'll have now. Know that you worked hard and achieved your ultimate goal.

Once you have created this vision and filled it with details that work for you, repeat it every few days. With repetition, you are creating and strengthening a new neural pathway for your brain to follow, setting up a new emotional and behavioral script. Once this new script becomes more powerful and invested with energy than your older scripts, it will essentially replace the older ones. The next time you walk into a testing situation and come across the familiar stimuli that you have so frequently imagined, you will begin to follow the new neural pathway. By following this new pathway, you will take your first steps towards the best testing performance of your life. Students who have used this technique and tapped into the power of their imaginations have picked up hundreds of points. Try this out for yourself and see how it works for you.

Practical Tips:
Final Preparation for the SAT

The final week before the SAT

In the last week before the SAT, continue to review your materials; do practice problems and vocabulary drills. You cannot cram for the SAT, but you want to keep the momentum going in the final days leading up to the test.

Two days before the SAT

The Thursday night before the SAT is a very important night. A good night's sleep Thursday will have an enormous impact on your level of energy and ability to focus on Saturday. The effects of a poor night's sleep generally hit you the hardest two days later: i.e., if you sleep poorly Thursday, you'll feel it Saturday morning. So get to bed early Thursday and give yourself a full 7-8 hours of sleep.

The day before the SAT

- If you want to do a short review, walk through a practice test you've completed and go over your notes. Look over your SAT vocabulary. Cramming for the SAT is ineffective, but a short review can be useful for some students.

- Mentally walk through the SAT. Rehearse every step of the process and reinforce the pathway you want to activate in the morning.

- Keep your thoughts positive. You're ready. You've worked hard. Tomorrow you are going to do your absolute best.

- Be sure you get 7-8 hours of sleep.

- Set your alarm clock! Use the alarm on your cell phone as a backup.

The day before the SAT (cont.)

- Pack the following materials in a bag that you can grab in the morning before you go to the test:

    o   Your SAT Admission Ticket

    o   An acceptable photo ID

    o   Printed directions to the test center

    o   3-4 sharpened No. 2 pencils (pens and mechanical pencils are not allowed)

    o   A graphing calculator with fresh batteries (make sure you check, and bring spare batteries if you have them)

    o   A watch with a stopwatch feature. In some testing centers, the clock will be behind you, or the room will not have a clock. Your proctor may or may not give you 5-minute warnings. You need a watch to manage your own timing.

    o   Bottle of water

    o   Snacks: fruit and snack bars are great for the short breaks

The morning of the test

- Wake up early.

- Eat a healthy breakfast.

- Dress in comfortable clothes and in layers.
  Test rooms may be cold or hot; layers give you options.

- Leave early for the testing site. Give yourself plenty of time for traffic or other potential delays, especially if you've never been to the testing location before.

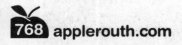

During the test administration

- Don't be thrown off by the energy of others. Stay in your zone. You've worked hard; you're prepared. Keep your energy centered on your optimal performance.

- Bubble-in your Scantron sheet one test-page at a time rather than question-by-question. This will save a few minutes, eliminating much of the time spent going back and forth between the test booklet and the answer sheet. More importantly, this minimizes the likelihood of getting off track with your numbering.

- Pace yourself. Use your watch to regulate your timing.

- Use your breaks. During the three 5-minute breaks, eat a snack or drink water. You will need fluids and some extra fuel to keep you going between 8:00 am and 1:00 pm. Also, take a few moments to refocus: "You're doing great...only a few more sections left."

- Be your own cheerleader. Be your own coach. Use self-talk to keep yourself engaged and focused. It's a long test. It helps to have some encouragement.

After the test

Congratulations! Now go out and play! You deserve it!

Find what works for you

Take a risk and try out some of these techniques: change your self-talk, try a few breathing exercises, walk through a full SAT in your mind and imagine your best performance. See if any of these techniques help you stay more focused and centered. Remember that none of these techniques is a replacement for good old fashioned hard work and practice, but they are supplements. These strategies have helped many students achieve a greater degree of success on the SAT.

Whatever you do, put in the time you need to mentally prepare yourself for success on this test.

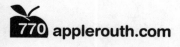

General Test-taking Mantras

Below is a series of Mantras or sayings that will help you remember our most important test-taking strategies. Repeat these to yourself when you are stuck in traffic, on your way to study hall or in the shower. Know them; love them; use them.

■ Write **EVERYTHING** down.

■ The **clock is your ally**: use the clock to pace yourself.

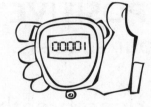

■ A point is a point: don't get stuck on any one problem.

■ GUESS AND OMIT STRATEGICALLY.

■ Save the hardest problems for the end, if you have time.

■ Know the **LEVEL OF DIFFICULTY** of the problem you are working on.

■ **THINK FOR YOURSELF**
before looking at the answer choices.

■ Transfer your answers to the Scantron sheet one page at a time.

■ Stay **POSITIVE** and **FOCUSED** on your success.

■ Take deep breaths when you need to recenter yourself.

■ **BE YOUR OWN COACH:**
keep yourself in the game

Final Words

We hope you have enjoyed using this book in your preparation for the SAT, and we hope you learned a good deal in the process. By now you've been exposed to our methods, our strategies, our subtle attempts at SAT humor and our thoughts on testing. Our goal was to help you raise your score and empower you to continue learning on your own, long after you've completed this book.

If you have completed all the exercises in this book, find new materials to help you move forward with your preparation. Keep learning new vocabulary wherever you come across it. Do more practice tests. Continue to visualize your success. Your intention matters; your effort matters; your commitment to this process matters. With time, hard work and practice, you can achieve the kind of score that will open up many doors for you when it's time to apply to college.

Always stay focused on your goals.
Support yourself along the way.
And best of luck!

Jed Applerouth

The End

Acknowledgements

Passage, page 92:   Williams, Caroline. "10 Mysteries of you: Blushing." <u>New Scientist</u>
05 Aug. 2009. 09 Sept. 2009 < http://www.newscientist.com/article/
mg20327200.700-10-mysteries-of-you-blushing.html> Printed with permission
of newscientist.com.

Passage, page 99:   Young, Emma. "10 Mysteries of you: Superstition." <u>New Scientist</u>
05 Aug. 2009. 09 Sept. 2009 < http://www.newscientist.com/article/
mg20327201.400-10-mysteries-of-you-superstition.html> Printed with permission
of newscientist.com.

Passage, page 109:   Callaway, Ewen. "Orang-utans fashion only known animal instrument."
<u>New Scientist</u> 05 Aug. 2009. 09 Sept. 2009 < http://www.newscientist.com/
article/dn17557-orangutans-fashion-only-known-animal-instrument.html>
Printed with permission of newscientist.com.

Passage, page 139:   van Vugt, Mark. "Triumph of the commons: Helping the world to share." <u>New
Scientist</u>. 25 Aug. 2009. 09 Sept. 2009 <http://www.newscientist.com/article/
mg20327225.700-triumph-of-the-commons-helping-the-world-to-share.html>
Printed with permission of newscientist.com.

Passage, page 145:   Douglas, Kate. "10 Mysteries of you: Altruism." <u>New Scientist</u>. 05 Aug. 2009.
09 Sept. 2009. <http://www.newscientist.com/article/mg20327201.200-10-
mysteries-of-you-altruism.html> Printed with permission of newscientist.com.

Passage, page 145:   Fisher, Richard. "Why altruism paid off for our ancestors." <u>New Scientist.</u>
07 Dec. 2006. 09 Sept. 2009. <http://www.newscientist.com/article/dn10750-why-
altruism-paid-off-for-our-ancestors.html> Printed with permission of newscientist.com.

Passage, page 152:.   Twain, Mark. *A Dog's Tale*. New York: Harper & Brothers, 1904. 1-6.

Passage, page 165:   Bell, Clive. *Art*. London: Chatto and Windus. 1914.

Passage, page 165-166: Reynolds, Sir Joshua. "Discourse I." *Seven Discourse on Art*. 1769.

Passage, page 185:   Marchant, Jo. "World's first computer may be even older than thought." <u>New
Scientist</u>. 29 July 2009. 09 Sept. 2009. < http://www.newscientist.com/blogs/
shortsharpscience/technology/2009/07/> Printed with permission of
newscientist.com.

Acknowledgements

Passage, page 185:   "Cosy social networks 'are stifling innovation'." New Scientist. 05 Aug. 2009.
09 Sept. 2009 <http://www.newscientist.com/article/mg20327195.600-cosy-
social-networks-are-stifling-innovation.html> Printed with permission of new
scientist.com.

Passage, page 186:   Middleton, Lucy. " The last place on earth to make contact with civilisation" New
Scientist. 16 June 2007. 09 Sept. 2009 <http://www.newscientist.com/article/\
mg19426081.500-the-last-place-on-earth-to-make-contact-with-civilisation.html>
Printed with permission of newscientist.com.

Passage, page 186:   "The Kuna People." Applerouth Tutoring Services, LLC. 2009.

Passage, page 187:   "The Crossing." Applerouth Tutoring Services, LLC. 2009.

Passage, page 189:   "Henry David Thoreau and Civil Disobedience." Applerouth Tutoring Services,
LLC. 2009.

Passage, page 191:   Howard, Wendell Stanton. "'A Northeaster,' by Winslow Homer." Harper's
Magazine. March 1910.

Passage, page 191:   "Art At Home and Abroad; Examples of Winslow Homer's Work in the Light of
Fulfilling a Notable Ideal." The New York Times. 12 Feb. 1911. SM15

Passage, page 194:   Fitzgerald, F. Scott. *This Side of Paradise*. New York: Charles Scribner's Sons,
1920. 3-5.

About the Author

Jed Applerouth knows the SAT. He has scored a 2400 in a single administration of the SAT and has achieved perfect 800s on both the Writing and Critical Reading sections during five consecutive SAT administrations.

Jed has been teaching the SAT to students since 2001 and has guided hundreds of families and students through the collegiate testing and admissions process. Many of his students have achieved gains of 400 and 500 points on the SAT. He has travelled as far as Provence, France to teach groups of SAT students.

Jed was raised in Atlanta, Georgia, and graduated Valedictorian of Pace Academy's 1994 class. In 1998 he graduated with honors from the University of Pennsylvania's Huntsman Program for International Studies and Business with a B.S. in Economics from the Wharton School and a B.A. in International Studies from the College of Arts and Sciences. Jed volunteered with the AmeriCorps program and worked as an analyst for McKinsey and Company.

Jed returned to school in 2003 to pursue a Masters Degree in Professional Counseling from Georgia State University. In 2007 Jed received an M.S. in Professional Counseling and became a Nationally Certified Counselor. Jed is currently enrolled in the PhD program in Educational Psychology at Georgia State University. Through his studies and research, Jed hopes to gain further insight into academic motivation, test-anxiety, memory and other educational domains in order to better serve his students.

Jed is the CEO and founder of Applerouth Tutoring Services, LLC, one of the nation's premier SAT tutoring operations. ATS operates out of Atlanta and serves satellite markets in New York and Washington, DC. Through its cutting-edge online tutoring system, ATS tutors work with students across the country and around the globe. ATS is dedicated to innovation and continually develops new materials and methods to better serve its students and all students preparing for standardized tests.

Beyond education, Jed is passionate about photography and landscape painting; he has travelled extensively to find inspiration for his work. He exhibits his artwork in Atlanta galleries and online.

Homework & Notes

Homework & Notes

Homework & Notes

Homework & Notes

Homework & Notes

Homework & Notes

Homework & Notes

Homework & Notes